Time before History

Time before History

The Archaeology of North Carolina

H. Trawick Ward

R. P. Stephen Davis Jr.

The University of North Carolina Press
CHAPEL HILL

© 1999 The University of North Carolina Press
All rights reserved

Designed by Heidi Perov
Set in Caslon and Caslon Antique
by Keystone Typesetting, Inc.

Library of Congress Cataloging-in-Publication Data
Ward, H. Trawick, 1944–
Time before history: the archaeology of North Carolina /
H. Trawick Ward and R. P. Stephen Davis, Jr.
p.   cm.
Includes bibliographical references and index.

ISBN 978-0-8078-4780-0 (pbk.)
ISBN 978-1-4696-4777-7 (ebook)

1. Paleo-Indians—North Carolina.   2. Indians of North America—
North Carolina—Antiquities.   3. Indians of North America—North
Carolina—History.   4. Excavations (Archaeology)—North Carolina—
History.   5. North Carolina—Antiquities.   I. Davis, R. P.
Stephen.   II. Title.
E78.N74W37   1999
975.6′01—dc21   99-13683
                                                                 CIP

for DOUGLAS L. RIGHTS,

whose scholarship and early interest in our state's native heritage laid the foundation for modern archaeology in North Carolina

Contents

Preface xi
Acknowledgments xiii

1. Introduction 1

   Cultural-Historical Overview 1
   Paleo-Indian Period (before 8000 B.C.) 2
   Archaic Period (8000–1000 B.C.) 2
   Woodland Period (1000 B.C.–A.D. 1600) 3
   Historic Period (after A.D. 1540) 5

   A Brief History of North Carolina Archaeology 6
   Exploring Indian Mounds 6
   A New Focus on North Carolina Archaeology 8
   Following in the Footsteps of Lederer and Lawson 9
   The Keyauwee Excavation 11
   Federal Archaeology Begins at Peachtree 12
   Stalking the Piedmont Siouans 12
   Building Cultural Chronologies 15
   The Cherokee Project 17
   North Carolina Archaeology Expands 18
   Recent Research Programs across North Carolina 20
   Notes on Organization 23

2. The Paleo-Indian: An Elusive Quarry 27

   Paleo-Indian Chronology in the Southeast 29
   Early Paleo-Indian Subperiod (about 9500–9000 B.C.) 29
   Middle Paleo-Indian Subperiod (9000–8500 B.C.) 31
   Late Paleo-Indian Subperiod (8500–7900 B.C.) 31

   Paleo-Indian Settlement and Subsistence 32

   The Paleo-Indian Period in North Carolina 35
   The Coastal Plain 36
   The Piedmont 36
   The Mountains 46

3. The Archaic Period: A Time of Regionalization and Specialization 47

   The Archaic Period in the Piedmont 49
      Early Archaic Period (8000–6000 B.C.) 51
      Middle Archaic Period (6000–3000 B.C.) 58
      Late Archaic Period (3000–1000 B.C.) 64

   The Archaic Period in the Mountains 67
      Early Archaic Period (8000–6000 B.C.) 69
      Middle Archaic Period (6000–3000 B.C.) 70
      Late Archaic Period (3000–1000 B.C.) 70

   The Archaic Period on the Coast and Coastal Plain 72

   Summary 75

4. The Woodland Period in the Piedmont 76

   The Piedmont Village Tradition 78

   The Early Woodland and Middle Woodland Periods (1000 B.C.–A.D. 800) 80
      The Badin Phase 80
      The Yadkin Phase 83
      Recent Research and the Early-Middle Woodland Chronology 85
      Early Excavations in the Northeast Piedmont 87
      The Whites Creek Survey and the Forbush Creek Excavations 95
      Summary 97

   The Late Woodland Period (A.D. 800–1600) 98
      The Uwharrie Phase (A.D. 800–1200) 100
      The Haw River Phase (A.D. 1000–1400) 103
      The Dan River Phase (A.D. 1000–1450) 105
      The Donnaha Phase (A.D. 1000–1450) 109
      The Hillsboro Phase (A.D. 1400–1600) 112
      The Early Saratown Phase (A.D. 1450–1600) 117

   The Southern Piedmont 119
      A Brief History of Early Excavations 119
      The Pee Dee Culture 123
      The Caraway Phase (A.D. 1500–1700) 134

5. The Woodland and Mississippian Periods in the Appalachian Summit Region: The Search for Cherokee Roots 138

   The Woodland Period 139
      The Early Woodland Period (1000–300 B.C.) 140

The Middle Woodland Period (300 B.C.–A.D. 800) 146
The Late Woodland Period (A.D. 800–1100) 157

The South Appalachian Mississippian Tradition 158
The Pisgah Phase (A.D. 1000–1450) 160
Mound Structure and Political Complexity 175
Lamar Culture and the Qualla Phase (after A.D. 1350) 178
The Eastern Fringe of the Appalachian Summit 190

Summary 192

6. The Woodland Period on the Coast and Coastal Plain 194

A Brief History of Coastal Plain Archaeology 195

The Early Woodland Period (1000–300 B.C.) 199
The Deep Creek and New River Phases 200
Hamp's Landing 202

The Middle Woodland Period (300 B.C.–A.D. 800) 203
The Mount Pleasant Phase 203
The Cape Fear Phase 204
Sand Burial Mounds 206

The Late Woodland Period (A.D. 800–1650) 210
The Colington Phase 211
The White Oak Phase 216
The Cashie Phase 223

Summary 226

7. The Contact Period: Tribes, Traders, and Turmoil 229

The Contact Period in the Central Piedmont (A.D. 1600–1710) 233
The Mitchum Phase (A.D. 1600–1670) 235
The Jenrette Phase (A.D. 1600–1680) 237
The Fredricks Phase (A.D. 1680–1710) 242

The North Central Piedmont during the Contact Period 247
The Middle Saratown Phase (A.D. 1620–1670) 247
The Late Saratown Phase (A.D. 1670–1710) 248

Contact, Interaction, and Cultural Change in the Piedmont 254
Trade 254
European Plants and Livestock 256
Intertribal Relations 256
Disease 257

The Contact Period in the Appalachian Summit 260
  The Late Qualla Phase (A.D. 1700–1838) 267
The Contact Period along the North Carolina Coast 272
Summary 275

References Cited 277
Index 299

Preface

This book grew out of a strong sense of public responsibility and a desire to open the windows of North Carolina's past to an audience beyond the small clique of professional archaeologists. The first work of this kind, *The American Indian in North Carolina*, was written by Douglas L. Rights and published in 1947. Rights's book was primarily a summary of various historic accounts of Indian tribes across the state. Only two brief chapters were devoted to the archaeological past. In 1959, Stanley South authored a pamphlet entitled *Indians in North Carolina*, which was published by the North Carolina Division of Archives and History. Written primarily for schoolchildren, this little book blended historical information with the archaeological data that were current at the time. South's very readable and entertaining account has sold over 70,000 copies and was reprinted seven times between 1959 and 1976. In 1985, the Division of Archives and History published another pamphlet entitled *Native Carolinians, the Indians of North Carolina*. Written by Theda Perdue, this pamphlet was designed to update South's book.

The first statewide synthesis dealing primarily with the archaeological past was published in 1983. Titled *The Prehistory of North Carolina: An Archaeological Symposium*, this study synthesized the then current archaeological knowledge of each region of the state with an eye toward developing a statewide preservation plan. By and large, its target audience was the professional archaeological community.

Since 1983, the deep roots of North Carolina archaeology have spread throughout the state to nourish a canopy of new knowledge. From the coast to the mountains, there has been a virtual explosion of research projects, fueled by academic and preservation interests. Much of the new information pouring out of these projects can only be found in obscure technical reports or in professional monographs. We feel the time is ripe for a new synthesis and a fresh look at what is known about North Carolina's unwritten past.

Although we hope a wide audience will read this book, we also recognize an obligation to the professional archaeological community. By bringing together a broad range of new and old data, we have attempted to do more than simply summarize the standard interpretations. Wherever possible and warranted, we offer new ideas and hypotheses. The nonprofessional reader is encouraged to keep in mind that what follows is in no way presented as the final word. Even as this book goes to press, the rich fields of North Carolina archaeology are undoubtedly turning up new information that may gainsay conclusions presented here.

We hope to inspire students of all ages and persuasions, whether in grade school or graduate school, to learn more about the past. We also recognize that our professional colleagues will have their own interpretations and ideas that may not always agree with those presented in the following chapters. In this regard, our goal is to serve as a forum for open exchange and debate in the continuing quest to understand the archaeology of North Carolina.

Acknowledgments

The idea for this book took shape over several years, and many people have influenced its final form, both directly and indirectly. Some individuals we wish to acknowledge will never read what we have to say; their help came to us from the past rather than the present. Others have supported our efforts on a daily basis.

It is no exaggeration to say that without the patient guidance of Vin Steponaitis, this book never would have been written. As director of the Research Laboratories of Archaeology, Vin generously gave us free reign to pursue the necessary research and put it in a readable form. But most of all, he shared his vast knowledge and quiet wisdom, saying just the right thing or nudging in just the right direction when progress seemed to be logjammed.

We owe a special debt of gratitude to Bennie Keel. Bennie was an archaeologist with the Research Labs long before either of us arrived there. During his tenure, he directed many of the excavations that provided the raw data that are digested in the chapters that follow. More than an excavator, Bennie was also a teacher. We were fortunate to work with him in the field and in the lab during the few years that our paths crossed in Chapel Hill. Bennie also freely provided information and insights that only he could during the preparation of this book.

We also benefited greatly from the research of David Phelps and Stanley South. David and Stanley began their archaeological careers as students at the University of North Carolina. Often we pored over their detailed drawings and careful notes when trying to understand some of the early excavations at sites like Gaston, Hardaway, and Town Creek. We were always impressed with the level of archaeological expertise that these two "students" displayed. David and Stanley also read various drafts of this manuscript and provided helpful comments from their unique perspectives.

We also have relied heavily on the knowledge and expertise of Randy Daniel. As this book began, Randy's UNC graduate student days were ending. Though caught up in the firestorm of writing and defending a dissertation, Randy never hesitated to read chapter drafts and share his considerable knowledge of Paleo-Indian and Archaic research. While at UNC, Randy patiently nursed us to an appreciation of the subtleties of stone tool analysis.

Mark Mathis helped considerably in making current the chapter on coastal archaeology. Mark freely shared his research and knowledge, and was always available to discuss the latest archaeological developments along the coast. We also learned from Mark that currency on the coast is as fleeting as the last wave.

Much of the information we present here comes from obscure, unpublished reports of cultural resource–management projects. Without the always friendly help of Dolores Hall, finding and combing through these reports would have been drudgery. Dolores's thorough knowledge and incredible memory made trips to the Office of State Archaeology library productive and pleasurable.

We would also like to thank Susan Myers for proofreading and indexing the manuscript. Her keen eye, conscientious attention to detail, and general knowledge of North Carolina archaeology made her the ideal person for this tedious but necessary task.

Finally we would like to acknowledge the pioneers of North Carolina archaeology. It is difficult to imagine a book like this without the hard work and dedication of individuals like James Bullitt, Harry Davis, Herbert Doerschuk, Guy Johnson, and Douglas Rights. In particular, Joffre Coe must be singled out for his long-term and unique role in starting and maintaining the archaeology program at the University of North Carolina at Chapel Hill. Much of the information presented in the chapters that follow comes from studying files, notes, and artifacts that were carefully excavated and meticulously curated under Coe's direction and are housed at the Research Laboratories of Archaeology.

1. Introduction

Most people react with awe and surprise when they first learn that North Carolina was settled more than 10,000 years ago. And this reaction is understandable given the brief and usually superficial treatment the unwritten past is given in elementary and high school curricula. For most people, history begins in North Carolina with the voyages of Sir Walter Raleigh and the ill-fated English settlement on Roanoke Island in 1585. Few realize that this "history" only scratches the surface of the real but unwritten history of our state. How these early North Carolinians lived and how they changed through the centuries cannot be discovered from lost documents and the written word. Instead, this history has to be painstakingly reconstructed from the fragmentary and fragile record these early settlers left buried beneath our feet. The shovel and trowel of the archaeologist must be used to recover and decipher our unwritten past.

Cultural-Historical Overview

Most archaeologists working in North Carolina recognize five major cultural traditions. From earliest to latest, these are Paleo-Indian, Archaic, Woodland, Mississippian, and Historic. These traditions reflect general cultural patterns and changes through time. Sometimes they are defined by precise chronological brackets, other times they are not. In some regions of the state, a tradition may begin at one point in time, while in another region, the same tradition may start later or earlier. As the reader will soon come to realize, most things archaeological are shaped by fuzzy, unfocused boundaries rather than by sharp, clearly defined lines.

Paleo-Indian Period (before 8000 B.C.)

The Paleo-Indian period represents the initial stage of human presence in the Western Hemisphere. The first immigrants to North America came from northeast Asia across a land bridge that spanned the Bering Strait. Exactly when the initial wave of settlers arrived is a subject of considerable debate among archaeologists, but there is firm evidence that they occupied most of the continent by around 10,000 B.C. Evidence of these first people, or Paleo-Indians, was first discovered at "kill sites" such as Clovis and Folsom in the southwestern United States. There, distinctive, fluted spear points were found in direct association with now-extinct Ice Age mammals. In North Carolina, and throughout most of the eastern United States, we know of the Paleo-Indians' presence primarily from scattered, usually isolated, surface finds of Clovis- and Folsom-like spear points (Perkinson 1971, 1973).

The oldest site that has been excavated in North Carolina is the Hardaway site, which, based on the kinds of artifacts that occur there, can be dated to the close of the Paleo-Indian period. However, because no radiocarbon dates were obtained from the site, there is some disagreement regarding the precise age of its earliest use and whether the early Hardaway complex should be placed within the Paleo-Indian period or subsequent Archaic period.

Archaic Period (8000–1000 B.C.)

The Archaic period is much better known than the Paleo-Indian period. While most Paleo-Indians hunted animals that lived during the last stages of the Ice Age, the Archaic period heralds the final retreat of the glaciers and a moderating of climatic conditions. It is believed that Archaic peoples settled into an environment similar to what exists today and lived by: (1) hunting mostly animals that can still be found, like the white-tailed deer, black bear, and wild turkey; (2) fishing and collecting both freshwater and saltwater shellfish; and (3) gathering a variety of plant foods such as acorns, hickory nuts, walnuts, seeds, greens, and berries. Because these food resources did not always occur at the same time or place, it was necessary for Archaic peoples to move among several different campsites during the course of a year. Given this mobile way of life, they probably lived in small bands composed of extended families or groups of families.

Archaic peoples used a variety of tools that permitted them to survive successfully and efficiently within their environment. Although many tools were made from perishable materials such as plant fibers, wood, bone, and animal skins, in most instances only their stone tools and the waste flakes from making these tools have survived the ravages of time. Archaic hunters did not possess the bow and arrow but instead used a highly efficient weapon called the atlatl, or spear-thrower. The distinctive notched and stemmed points that tipped their spears commonly occur at Archaic campsites. Because of their relative abundance and the fact that their shapes, or styles, evolved over time, these spear points have been used successfully by archaeologists in North Carolina and elsewhere to develop a chronological sequence of Archaic cultures.

Woodland Period (1000 B.C.–A.D. 1600)

In general, the Woodland period is viewed as a time when peoples throughout the eastern United States began the gradual shift toward agriculturally based economies and their settlements correspondingly became larger and more permanent. It is also seen as a period during which societies became more internally complex, developed elaborate mortuary rituals, sometimes constructed earthen burial mounds and house platforms, and engaged in far-reaching trade and exchange of exotic items. However, the degree to which North Carolina's Woodland peoples engaged in these activities varied greatly from the mountains to the coast.

From a practical standpoint, North Carolina archaeologists usually define the onset of the Woodland period by the appearance of pottery-making, and they use the various styles of the potters to chronologically order artifact assemblages and to study relationships among Woodland period cultures. Potsherds found on early Woodland sites that date prior to about A.D. 200 mostly represent conoidal cooking pots that were stamped with cord-wrapped or fabric-wrapped wooden paddles before they were fired, whereas those from later Woodland sites often reflect a greater range of vessel forms, functions, surface treatments, and decorations. Despite the technological innovation that pottery-making represented, the remaining stone artifacts from early Woodland sites indicate the continuation of an Archaic way of life heavily based upon hunting and gathering.

Because of the dramatic cultural changes that occurred during the course of the Woodland period, it is necessary to summarize it by subperiods. In addition to the introduction of pottery, the Early Woodland period (1000 B.C.–A.D. 200) was also marked in some areas by the incipient development of small villages in localities considered favorable for crop production. Although there is no direct evidence of gardening in North Carolina during the Early Woodland, there is ample evidence from surrounding states that by this time some tropical and indigenous southeastern plants were being cultivated. Squash, maygrass, sunflower, chenopod, and sumpweed were all being planted in small garden plots around Early Woodland houses (Yarnell and Black 1985:99).

During the Middle Woodland period (A.D. 200–800), gardening continued to grow in importance and influences from vigorous cultural developments taking place elsewhere in the East began to affect some local Woodland groups. This influence was perhaps greatest in the mountains where Middle Woodland peoples were engaged in trade with Hopewell societies in the Ohio Valley and Swift Creek cultures in central Georgia. Elsewhere in North Carolina, equally distinctive cultural traditions emerged as groups in each region responded in their own way to increasing population density, greater economic sophistication, and their own increasingly unique history and network of external relationships. By the end of the Middle Woodland period, each of the major physiographic regions within the state had developed into a culturally distinct area.

One of the hallmarks of the Late Woodland period (A.D. 800–1600) was a broadening of agricultural pursuits. Corn became a staple for the first time, and around A.D. 1200 beans were added to the inventory of cultivated plants. Throughout most of the state, this was a time of growth. Population size increased, and villages became larger and more complex. The intensification of agricultural practices also caused broad fertile bottoms to become prized locales for the establishment of villages.

Along with this growth came conflict. Stockades were constructed around villages to ward off attacks by outsiders. Perhaps these hostilities resulted from conflicts over favored agricultural lands, or maybe they came as a consequence of villages containing stores of surplus produce that could be looted by less industrious neighbors. Sources of conflict may even have been rooted in social or ideological differences that must have accompanied the emergence of regionally distinct cultural traditions earlier in the Woodland period. For whatever reasons, large- and small-scale tribal conflicts were probably commonplace during much of the Late Woodland period.

During the latter half of the Late Woodland period, several elaborate and complex cultures developed throughout the heart of the Southeast. These Mississippian cultures were typified by massive ceremonial mound centers, villages containing several hundred inhabitants, and a highly stratified society with political, religious, and craft specialists. These developments only touched the western fringe of North Carolina in what has been described as the South Appalachian Mississippian complex (Ferguson 1971). Although mounds were constructed and villages grew in size and complexity from Marion to Murphy, Mississippian culture in North Carolina never reached the heights it obtained in the neighboring states of Tennessee and Georgia. The only area outside the Appalachian Summit that exhibits evidence of Mississippian influence is the Piedmont Sandhills, where the Pee Dee culture developed around the ceremonial center at Town Creek State Historic Site.

Historic Period (after A.D. 1540)

Following the voyages of Christopher Columbus, Spanish exploration of the Western Hemisphere began in earnest during the sixteenth century. After establishing a foothold in the Caribbean, the Spanish, in their search for wealth and power, quickly turned their attention to Mexico, the Peruvian Andes, and the southeastern United States. During the first few decades of the century, the Spanish explorers restricted their activities to the Atlantic and Gulf coasts of Spanish Florida, never venturing very far inland. However, when they failed to find riches comparable to what had been found by Hernán Cortés in Mexico and Francisco Pizarro in Peru, they began to mount expeditions into the interior Southeast.

The first of these, led by Hernando de Soto from 1539 until his death in 1541, passed through southwestern North Carolina. A quarter century later, Juan Pardo retraced the portion of de Soto's route that took him into the state. While there is much debate concerning the exact routes taken by these intrepid Spanish explorers and how they impacted the native populations, there is little evidence to suggest that their presence had any lasting effects on the native tribes. They did not introduce the scourge of diseases that apparently followed their trail in other areas of the Southeast, nor did they attempt to establish permanent forts and missions like they did along the coasts of Florida, Georgia, and South Carolina.

The story of English exploration in North Carolina is quite a different tale. Unlike the Spanish, the English were not looking for gold and treasure. They were looking for land to settle and new markets for their goods. Although Jamestown was established in 1607, it was half a century later before the English adventurers began to explore the Carolina backcountry in search of new trading partners. During the brief era that followed, native peoples from the coast to the mountains were ravaged by a host of Old World diseases that accompanied the English traders. Shortly thereafter, most native villages east of the mountains were vacated. The remaining native population either left or dispersed, and the land was laid open for the waves of settlers that poured down the Shenandoah Valley into the Carolina heartland.

Unlike the Piedmont and coastal tribes, the Cherokees, ensconced in the southern Appalachian mountains, not only managed to survive, but they also retained at least part of their ancestral lands. Even after many were killed and others forcibly removed in the 1830s, some of the Cherokees still managed to avoid capture. Today, their descendants continue to live in their mountain homeland west of Asheville.

A Brief History of North Carolina Archaeology

Exploring Indian Mounds

The beginning of archaeology in North Carolina dates back to the last century and was closely tied to the scientific debate that was raging in academic institutions and museums over who built the numerous earthen mounds that dotted the landscapes of eastern North America. Many believed that the mounds and other earthworks were constructed by an ancient civilization of "Mound Builders" unrelated and superior to the American Indians. Only a minority of scientists were convinced that the ancient earthworks were built by Native Americans. The only way to find out for sure was to dig into the mounds and see what clues their builders had left behind.

Not all of the early interest in mound exploration was fueled by scientific curiosity. Mounds were easily recognized by the trained as well as the untrained eye, and many were dug into by relic collectors interested only in the exotic artifacts they contained. During the latter half of the nineteenth century, these specimens began to line the shelves of museums.

Except for J. Mason Spainhour's excavation into a small mound in Burke County (Spainhour 1873:404–6), most of the early archaeological activity in North Carolina was conducted by individuals from outside the state. Many of these early excavations were inspired by a Virginian, Mann S. Valentine, and his sons. During the 1880s, the Valentines and their North Carolina agent, A. J. Osborne of Haywood County, dug into several mounds located in the western part of the state, including the Peachtree Mound in Cherokee County, the Garden Creek mounds in Haywood County, the Cullowhee Mound in Jackson County, and the Kituwah, Nununyi, and Birdtown Mounds in Swain County (Valentine 1883).

The Valentines were searching for artifacts that would later be exhibited in the Valentine Museum in Richmond, but they were also caught up in the question of who built the mounds. By examining the pottery dug from the mounds and comparing it with the clay pots that were being made by Cherokee women on the Qualla Reservation at the time, the Valentines quickly recognized similarities between the two. These similarities led Mann Valentine to surmise that the mounds were made by a race of people ancestral to the Historic Cherokees.

FIGURE 1.1. *Fake artifacts from western North Carolina. These carved steatite sculptures of a bear eating a man (left) and an angel (right) are two of the many fake Indian artifacts that were purchased by Mann Valentine in the North Carolina mountains. (Courtesy of the Research Laboratories of Archaeology)*

This was a remarkable revelation for the time, especially considering that Valentine was an art collector and not a scientist or student of ancient history.

Unfortunately, Mann Valentine became the victim of an elaborate hoax that tainted his otherwise sound archaeological interpretations. Realizing that Valentine would pay top dollar for Indian artifacts, some North Carolinians began to create their own versions of relics they thought would be most appealing to the wealthy Virginian. Using the soft soapstone readily available throughout the western mountains and their fertile imaginations, these local artisans produced an abundance of elaborately carved figurines representing everything from angels to camels (fig. 1.1).

The Valentines were completely duped and concluded that these artifacts were products of an ancient race distinct from the Cherokee and their ancestors. When the fraud was finally exposed, an embarrassed Mann Valentine decided to get out of archaeology altogether and afterward devoted his museum to displaying the fine arts of Richmond (see Coe 1983:162–64).

At about the same time the Valentines were making the folks of Haywood County rich by buying their fake artifacts, Cyrus Thomas of the Smithsonian Institution sent John W. Emmert and John P. Rogan into the mountains and western Piedmont of North Carolina to explore mounds there (Thomas 1887:61–75; 1894:333–50). Thomas was motivated by a desire to debunk the

Mound Builder myth. His efforts in North Carolina were minor compared to other expeditions he directed throughout the eastern United States as the head of the Smithsonian's Division of Mound Exploration (Thomas 1887, 1894).

Probably the most significant sites examined were the Nelson Mound and Nelson Triangle in Caldwell County. These were excavated by Rogan with the aid of J. M. Spainhour. Although Rogan's interpretation of the archaeological record revealed at these nearby sites must be viewed with a healthy dose of skepticism, he did make one notable observation. One of the many human burials uncovered by Rogan and Spainhour contained three chisel-like objects made of iron (Thomas 1887:65–66).

Cyrus Thomas used this evidence to bolster his argument that the mounds were built by the recent ancestors of living Indians who had been in contact with early European explorers. After reviewing the ethnohistoric record, Thomas further concluded (1887:87–95) that the North Carolina mounds were built by the Cherokees.

The pots and potsherds collected by Rogan in Caldwell County and at sites in nearby Wilkes County were later studied by William H. Holmes of the Smithsonian Institution. In his important substantive work on aboriginal pottery in the eastern United States, Holmes (1903) interpreted these artifacts as representing the northeastern limit of his South Appalachian ceramic group. This classificatory group formed the basis for what archaeologists today call South Appalachian Mississippian, a Late Prehistoric cultural complex that extended from coastal Georgia to eastern Tennessee and encompassed the western Piedmont and mountains of North Carolina.

After the Smithsonian Institution left western North Carolina, the Museum of the American Indian–Heye Foundation stepped in. In 1915, George G. Heye, following in the footsteps of the Valentines, revisited the Garden Creek mounds. The excavation of a small mound at the site also sparked Heye's interest in the ancient Cherokees. After leaving Haywood County, Heye and his colleagues continued their Cherokee research, excavating sites in eastern Tennessee and northern Georgia (Heye 1919; Heye, Hodge, and Pepper 1918; Harrington 1922).

A New Focus on North Carolina Archaeology

After a hiatus of some twenty years, interest in North Carolina archaeology surfaced again. This time, it was inspired by a Moravian minister, the Reverend Douglas Rights, who published the first book on the history and prehistory of North Carolina Indians. Rights's book was aptly titled *The American Indian in North Carolina*, and, although published in 1947, it had been "assembled bit by bit at odd moments over a score of years" (vii). Most of Rights's book focused on the Historic tribes encountered by the early Spanish and English explorers; however, two concluding chapters were devoted to archaeology and Indian antiquities.

Rights's terse treatment of archaeology in no way reflected his lack of interest in the subject. He was an avid artifact collector, and he was one of the first to recognize and appreciate the archaeological potential of the state. When the initial organizational meeting of the Archaeological Society of North Carolina was held in 1933, Rights was elected the Society's first president and he presented a paper entitled "North Carolina as an Archaeological Field" (1934). In this paper, he assessed the state's archaeological potential from the mountains to the coast, and he concluded that although many sites had been looted and destroyed by floods, "the field . . . still offers abundant opportunity for exploration that should yield much important material for the archaeologist" (7).

This opportunity was seized shortly thereafter by a young, teenage upstart named Joffre Coe, who also attended the first meeting of the new archaeological society. The following year, Coe presented a paper to the group outlining a statewide survey program (1934:11). The editor of the Society's bulletin at that time was Guy Johnson, a sociologist and anthropologist at the University of North Carolina. In a parenthetical editor's note preceding Coe's paper, Johnson made the following prophetic statement: "The author of this paper is a young man from Greensboro who has shown a deep interest in the Society and has devoted most of his spare time to reading, thinking, and exploring during the past year." Coe went on to lay out a strategy for surveying the state, and he even presented the Society with an archaeological survey form to ensure the consistent recording of site data across the state. From this point until his retirement from the University of North Carolina at Chapel Hill in 1982, the enthusiastic young man from Greensboro dominated the state's archaeological endeavors (fig. 1.2). Following in Rights's footsteps, Coe opened the ground where Rights had surveyed its surface.

Another influential force during the early days of the Archaeological Society of North Carolina was Dr. James Bullitt, a professor of pathology at UNC from 1913 until his retirement in 1947. He and Johnson gave the Society academic respectability, and Bullitt was also an active fund-raiser for the Society's early excavations.

Following in the Footsteps of Lederer and Lawson

Rights and Coe were both interested in using historic documents to locate Indian villages described by early European explorers. One of the earliest of

FIGURE 1.2. *Joffre L. Coe operating a bulldozer in 1966 at the Coweeta Creek site. Coe was the dominant figure in North Carolina archaeology from the late 1930s until his retirement in 1982 from the University of North Carolina at Chapel Hill. (Courtesy of the Research Laboratories of Archaeology)*

these intrepid adventurers was John Lederer, a German physician who left the Virginia settlement at the falls of the James River (near present-day Richmond) on May 20, 1670, with a contingent of Indians and a militiaman named Major Harris. Less than a month later, all of Lederer's faint-hearted companions abandoned him except for a Susquehannock Indian named Jackzetavon. Undaunted, the German and his guide continued their trip southward into the uncharted wilds of the Virginia and North Carolina Piedmont. Here, they visited the Saponis, Occaneechis, Enos, Shakoris, and other interior tribes. Lederer sketched an intriguing picture of the native people, their likes and dislikes, and how best for foreigners to approach them (Cumming 1958).

John Lederer's descriptions whetted the appetites of subsequent English explorers such as John Lawson, who turned out to be not only literate but also blessed with the eyes of an ethnographer. Being a bit more ambitious than Lederer, Lawson undertook what he claimed to be a 1,000-mile journey that carried him and his party northwestward from Charleston, South Carolina, through the North Carolina Piedmont, and then eastward to the English settlements along Pamlico Sound. He began his adventure on December 28, 1700, and arrived at the plantation of Richard Smith on Pamlico River on February 23, 1701. Lawson's journey, which was actually closer to 500 miles, took him through numerous Indian towns and villages scattered along well-established native paths and trails. Many of the Indians Lawson met had been visited earlier by Lederer as well as by other less literate traders.

Lederer's account, translated from Latin into English and published in 1672, and Lawson's 1709 work titled *A New Voyage to Carolina* provide fascinating clues to the locations of the many Indian villages they visited. Using these clues to find the archaeological remains of Lederer's and Lawson's native hosts, Rights and Coe began the modern study of North Carolina archaeology. It was at one of these village sites that the young Joffre Coe and the Archaeological Society of North Carolina introduced the scientific method of archaeological excavation to the Piedmont.

The Keyauwee Excavation

In 1936, the Society uncovered a small portion of what was thought to be the Keyauwee village visited by Lawson (see Lefler 1967:56–59). Apparently the Society's interest in the site was aroused by earlier "test pits" excavated by some of its members in 1935. The 1935 digging had uncovered a human skeleton accompanied by numerous grave goods. According to the April 1936 *Bulletin of the Archaeological Society of North Carolina*, the individuals to be in charge of the 1936 Keyauwee excavation were Dr. James B. Bullitt (director), Rev. Douglas L. Rights (assistant), Mr. Joffre L. Coe (assistant), and Mr. Harry Davis (assistant). The stated purpose of the project was "not so much to find Indian material as it is to increase the interest of the members and other citizens of the state in the problems of archaeology. In too many cases collectors, 'amateur archaeologists,' and professional archaeologists place too much emphasis on the finding of 'relics,' and in doing so lose sight of the real problems which they are digging to solve." Sanford Winston, the bulletin's editor, went on to stress a theme as current today as it was in 1936 and one that forms the heart and soul of modern anthropological archaeology: "The finding of a handful of potsherds, broken implements, charcoal, and broken or burned bones in a carefully excavated refuse pit will tell more about the life of the people than a dozen perfect pots or axes obtained from careless digging" (Winston 1936a:14).

Apparently the Keyauwee excavation was a smashing success, at least in terms of the stated goals of the project, and interest in North Carolina archaeology increased.

Federal Archaeology Begins at Peachtree

Modern archaeology was born in the eastern United States during the height of the Great Depression. And while these were not good times for research and scientific pursuits in general, they were boom times for archaeology. Throughout the Southeast, massive excavation programs were implemented beginning in 1933 as part of the relief program of the Civilian Works Administration (CWA). Archaeological field research was particularly amenable to these federal programs because large numbers of unskilled workers could be employed for long periods with minimal supervision. The first of these projects in North Carolina preceded the Keyauwee excavations by almost three years.

In December 1933, excavations began on the Peachtree Mound, a Late Prehistoric and Historic site located near the town of Murphy in Cherokee County. The Peachtree Mound had been explored earlier by the Valentines. The federally sponsored work was carried out under the auspices of the Smithsonian Institution and was directed by Jesse D. Jennings, a graduate student at the University of Chicago.

Jennings's excavation crew consisted of 104 unemployed local men provided by the CWA. The large size of the crew forced him to modify the formal excavation procedures he had learned at the University of Chicago's archaeological field school. Instead of approaching the mound with a single trench, Jennings advanced his troops simultaneously from three sides. By April 1, 1934, less than four months after the project began, the Peachtree Mound, 200 feet in diameter and 10 feet high, had been leveled (Lyon 1996:36–37). These excavations are noteworthy because they provided North Carolina with its first modern, professional, archaeological publication (Setzler and Jennings 1941), which was based in part on Jennings's master's thesis.

Stalking the Piedmont Siouans

In 1937, the federal archaeology program moved into the Piedmont when excavations began at the Frutchey Mound (better known today as the Town Creek Indian Mound) on Little River in Montgomery County. This Works Progress Administration (WPA) project initiated research that would span half a century, train some of the Southeast's finest archaeologists, and create North Carolina's only state historic site dedicated to its native peoples (fig. 1.3).

When the investigations at Town Creek began, Joffre Coe was ready to take the supervisory reins. Although still an undergraduate student at the University of North Carolina, he had attended the University of Chicago's field school under the direction of Thorne Deuel in 1935, and the following summer he

FIGURE I.3. *Members of the Frutchey Mound (Town Creek Indian Mound) Excavation Committee in 1937.* Left to right: *Professor James B. Bullitt, UNC; Professor Wallace E. Caldwell, UNC; Joffre L. Coe, UNC; Herbert M. Doerschuk, Archaeological Society of North Carolina; Harry T. Davis, N.C. State Museum; and Rev. Douglas L. Rights, Archaeological Society of North Carolina. (Photo by Coe, 1937; from Coe 1995:15)*

worked with Will McKern on excavations sponsored by the University of Wisconsin and the Milwaukee Public Museum (Griffin 1985:291–92). Coe would remain in charge of excavations at the Town Creek site until his retirement in 1982 (Coe 1995).

The same year the Town Creek project began, Glenn Black, an archaeologist at Indiana University, wrote Coe suggesting that he (Black) might be able to raise some money for research on historically documented Siouan sites in North Carolina. Black was interested in using archaeological data from North Carolina to establish cultural patterns that might help to identify the presence of early Siouan-speaking groups in Indiana. Black was able to convince Eli Lilly, the pharmaceutical magnate, to finance Coe's Siouan research through the Indiana Historical Society.

In May 1938, on his way back to Chapel Hill from the Society for American Archaeology meetings in Milwaukee, Coe stopped by Indianapolis and picked up a check for $1,200. This money was turned over to the University of North Carolina and designated as the Fund for Southeastern Archaeology. Mr. Lilly's gift has the distinction of being the first grant received by the University of

North Carolina to sponsor archaeological research. The only condition attached to Mr. Lilly's generosity was that a report be prepared at the end of the field season (letter from Johnson to Black, May 1938, on file, Research Laboratories of Archaeology [hereafter RLA]).

In the summer of 1938, Coe began his Siouan project at the Wall site located near Hillsborough in Orange County. This site was believed to represent the remains of the Occaneechi village visited by Lawson in 1701 (Lefler 1967:61). After a brief excavation there, Coe moved to the Tutelo and Saponi Islands located near Clarksville, Virginia, just downstream from the confluence of the Dan and Staunton Rivers, where he sought to identify the Historic villages of these two Siouan tribes. Excavations were also conducted at a site on a large island below Saponi Island and on the mainland south of Tutelo Island.

The summer of 1938 was extremely wet, and Coe was not pleased with the results of his work. The Wall site excavations uncovered rich cultural deposits, but the only evidence that it represented a Historic village consisted of a single glass bead. A well-preserved human burial was found on Tutelo Island, but almost nothing turned up on Saponi Island. On the island just below Saponi Island, a rich site was located, but no burials or European trade artifacts were found. The mainland site was also rich, but the material did not "tie in with what we have been finding and apparently is not what we are looking for" (letter from Coe to Black, August 31, 1938, on file, RLA).

Coe requested an additional $400 to continue the Siouan project with excavations at the Lower Saratown site on the Dan River in Rockingham County and at the Trading Ford site on the Yadkin River in Davidson County. Mr. Lilly sent the check, and Coe returned to the field. He began his work at Lower Saratown and ended it at the Trading Ford site in the fall of 1938. He continued to be disappointed with the results that, to him, seemed "entirely too skimpy" (letter from Coe to Black, November 15, 1938, on file, RLA).

The winter and spring of 1939 seem to have been seasons of despair for Joffre Coe. Guy Johnson, his chief supporter at the university, was on leave, and he was left to try to put together an application for a statewide WPA archaeological project. At the same time, Coe was taking courses at UNC and struggling to survive with very little support from the Archaeological Society or the university. This frustration is evident in a letter Coe wrote to Glenn Black on April 28, 1939: "I need to get away from this place a little while. I have been having a terrible time this year, and I have sunk so low in a rut that I can hardly see out. We could probably secure funds enough to do another season's work at the Frutchey Mound this summer, but I would much rather get away for a while and be with someone who knows some archaeology than to work by myself for another year. It is hard to realize how depressing it is to be working by yourself with very meager funds and not seeing more than two people a year who have any interest in your field" (on file, RLA).

Less than a year after writing this letter to Black, Coe would finally have an archaeological colleague with whom to talk at UNC. The statewide WPA project was finally approved in 1940, and the university hired Robert Wauchope, who had just completed a similar project in northern Georgia, to head the program. Shortly after his arrival, Wauchope resumed excavations at the Wall site while Coe focused his energies on Town Creek and began organizing the statewide archaeological survey.

Building Cultural Chronologies

The onset of World War II in late 1941 brought archaeology programs throughout the country to a screeching halt. Archaeological research in North Carolina did not resume until 1948, when Coe returned from a tour of duty in the Army Air Force (1942–46) and had subsequently received his M.A. in anthropology at the University of Michigan (Griffin 1985:298–99). After the war, the research emphasis in North Carolina and other areas of the East shifted from identifying historically documented Indian villages to isolating early stratified cultural sequences.

The development of the atomic bomb during World War II not only revolutionized modern warfare and global politics; it also had a dramatic effect on modern archaeology. One of the technological spin-offs from research on the bomb was radiocarbon dating. This new dating technique was of particular importance to archaeologists working in the eastern United States. While their colleagues in the West had been able to demonstrate the considerable antiquity of tools found at sites like Folsom in New Mexico and Dent in Colorado by their association with extinct animals, no such associations had been found in the East. Archaeologists working on Southwestern Pueblo sites also were able to date their finds by comparing, correlating, and counting sequences of annular tree rings. This technique, called dendrochronology, was possible because of the excellent conditions of preservation offered by the arid southwestern environment. Archaeologists working in eastern North America did not have the benefit of such preservation. Before World War II, archaeological dates in the East were, for the most part, sheer guesses.

This situation changed with the advent of radiocarbon dating. All that was required to determine something's age was a handful of associated charcoal—or any suitable organic material. However, eastern archaeologists were not completely out of the woods. Finding buried, intact cultural horizons where tools and charcoal could be reliably assumed to be contemporary was not an easy task.

Because of erosion, plowing, and other ground-disturbing activities, the archaeological remains left at many ancient habitation sites, which often were occupied repeatedly for several thousand years, have been mixed and homogenized on a single surface rather than stacked or stratified in discrete soil layers.

Coe was one of the first to recognize this problem. Early in his professional career, Coe spent many hours attempting to define distinct archaeological cultures based on spear point and other artifact types that consistently had been found together on surface sites in the North Carolina Piedmont. In 1952, he published descriptions of two such cultures—the Badin focus and the Guilford focus—based on those surface associations of artifacts. Recognizing the folly in this exercise, he later wrote that the artifacts included in each of those complexes represented anything but coherent and contemporary cultural assemblages (1964:8).

To correct the muddled chronologies that were being developed throughout the East, Coe began to search for buried sites along the alluvial terraces flanking the lower Yadkin River, focusing upon unique topographic niches that were characterized by geological forces of deposition rather than erosion. This search led to test excavations at the Lowder's Ferry and Doerschuk sites in 1948. These preliminary tests proved promising, and full-scale excavations were carried out the following year. Coe wrote later that "the work at these sites demonstrated two important facts: first, that stratified sites of depth and antiquity do exist in the alluvial floodplains of the Piedmont; and second, that when an occupation zone can be found that represents a relatively short period of time the usual hodgepodge of projectile points are not found—only variations of one specific theme" (1964:9). These observations had a resounding impact on the archaeology of the eastern United States, and they inspired others to search for similar settings, with similar results (e.g., Broyles 1966; Chapman 1975; Claggett and Cable 1982).

After his success at the Doerschuk and Lowder's Ferry sites, Coe investigated the Hardaway site located just upstream from Doerschuk. This important site produced the earliest stratified evidence of human occupation in North Carolina, and, when coupled with the work at Doerschuk and at sites in the Roanoke Rapids Reservoir, Coe was able to link together an unbroken chain of occupations dating from about 10,000 to 2,500 years ago, or roughly 8000 B.C. to 500 B.C. The cultural sequence that Coe developed formed the basis for his doctoral dissertation at the University of Michigan, which was subsequently published in 1964 by the American Philosophical Society. It remains a standard for the layman's identification of spear points used during the millennia preceding settled village life and the manufacture of pottery.

During this early postwar period, the University of North Carolina began offering a master's degree in the Department of Sociology and Anthropology. In addition to directing the newly established Research Laboratories of Anthropology, Coe began teaching archaeology and anthropology courses in the department. For the first time, he had a small but dedicated cadre of students on whom he could depend for help with the archaeology program.

Lewis Binford, Hester Davis, Ernest Lewis, David Phelps, and Stanley South were the first in a long line of students who would receive their training at UNC under Coe. Binford and South worked in the Roanoke Rapids Reservoir; Phelps worked in the Gaston Reservoir; South and Phelps excavated at the Hardaway site; Lewis reported on Coe's 1938 work at Lower Saratown; and Lewis, South, and Phelps continued excavations at Town Creek.

Working for the North Carolina Division of Archives and History, South conducted excavations at Brunswick Town, near Wilmington, between 1958 and 1968. While there, he also surveyed portions of New Hanover and Brunswick Counties in North Carolina and Horry County in South Carolina. In 1959, South published *Indians in North Carolina*, a pamphlet designed to inform the general public and high school students about North Carolina archaeology.

The Cherokee Project

During the 1960s, work continued at Town Creek, and, by 1964, the reconstruction of the site was complete. Shortly thereafter, the first detailed report on the site, "Pee Dee Pottery from the Mound at Town Creek" (1967), was submitted by Jefferson Reid as his master's thesis at UNC. Although surveys and limited test excavations also were carried out between 1960 and 1962 in the Cowans Ford, Gaston, and Wilkesboro Reservoirs, the most important archaeological project of the 1960s was the Cherokee project. The goals of this project were: (1) to define Cherokee culture at the beginning of the Historic period; (2) to study regional variation among the Cherokee settlements; and (3) to identify the ancient cultures from which the Historic Cherokees emerged (Coe 1965). As a prelude to this project, extensive surveys were conducted in the mountainous western counties of North Carolina and adjacent states during 1963 and 1964, and small excavations were carried out in 1964 at the Tuckasegee and Townson sites (Keel 1976:15).

Supported by the National Science Foundation, major excavations commenced in 1965 with two long-term projects. The first focused on mounds and associated village remains at the Garden Creek sites in Haywood County; the second entailed extensive excavation of the mound and village at the Coweeta

Creek site in Macon County. The Garden Creek excavations were completed in 1967, while the work at Coweeta Creek continued until 1971.

Excavations were also begun on the campus of Warren Wilson College in the winter of 1965 and continued during the following summer (Dickens 1976). This stratified, Late Prehistoric Cherokee village was continuously excavated every summer between 1966 and 1985, except 1977 and 1983. Of all the sites studied during the course of the Cherokee project, more has been written about Warren Wilson than all the others combined. Two books, Keel's *Cherokee Archaeology* (1976) and Dickens's *Cherokee Prehistory* (1976), as well as four Ph.D. dissertations, two master's theses, and numerous journal articles, have dealt directly with various aspects of the Warren Wilson excavations. Today, data collected by research carried out as part of the Cherokee project are still being analyzed (Rodning 1996).

North Carolina Archaeology Expands

The 1960s witnessed tremendous growth in the archaeology program at UNC. Whereas before it had been primarily a one-man show in the person of Coe, two permanent staff positions were added between 1961 and 1964 to create the Research Laboratories of Anthropology in its modern form (renamed the Research Laboratories of Archaeology in 1997). Also, the Department of Anthropology gained its autonomy from the Sociology Department in 1965 and implemented a Ph.D. program. Both changes were responsible for substantially increasing the number of students interested in archaeology as a career. The National Science Foundation's sponsorship of the Cherokee project helped ensure that these students were kept fed and, to some extent, happy. Bennie Keel directed the project in the field and was assisted by several graduate students who would go on to become well-known researchers in their own right. Roy S. Dickens Jr., Brian J. Egloff, Keith T. Egloff, Leland G. Ferguson, and J. Jefferson Reid formed the core of the Cherokee project graduates.

During the 1970s, new programs across the state proliferated as more and more universities added archaeologists to their faculties. David Phelps joined the Department of Sociology and Anthropology at East Carolina University in 1970 and began developing a research program focused on the northeastern coastal area. Ned Woodall of Wake Forest University organized systematic surveys and excavations in the upper Yadkin River valley in 1971. In the mountains, Appalachian State University recruited Harvard Ayers and Burt Purrington to train their students, and John Dorwin became the first of several archaeologists who would staff the Western Carolina University archaeology program during the decade.

It was not by chance that colleges and universities across North Carolina began to hire archaeologists during the early 1970s. Nor was it an isolated phenomenon. Throughout the United States, new archaeology programs blossomed at small colleges, and many of the established programs at the larger universities grew at an unprecedented rate. Archaeologists even began to find jobs in the private sector, working for engineering and environmental-consulting firms. Some enterprising individuals started their own consulting businesses, and others joined various federal and state agencies.

The rapid growth in archaeology programs was primarily the result of federal and state preservation legislation that was passed mostly after 1970. These new laws declared that archaeological sites as "cultural resources" were important components of the environment that must be protected and managed along with natural resources. As a result, almost any ground-disturbing activity financed by public funds or requiring federal authorization had to be reviewed by archaeologists to determine if important or "significant" archaeological sites might be damaged or destroyed.

This government-mandated archaeology, more commonly known as "contract archaeology" or "cultural resource management," precipitated a flurry of archaeological surveys across North Carolina. Because roads, transmission line corridors, and sewer outfalls often traverse eroded knolls, hill flanks, and swamps, archaeologists began to look for sites in environmental and topographic settings that had previously been ignored. They also no longer had the luxury of just walking freshly plowed fields in their search for the surface scatters of artifacts that indicate the presence of "sites." Contract archaeologists were forced to develop techniques to find sites in wooded and overgrown areas with poor to nonexistent surface visibility. Everything from raking the surface bare of vegetation to excavating small "shovel tests" was tried, with varying degrees of success.

One of the largest and most successful cultural resource–management projects carried out in North Carolina was brought about by the proposed flooding of the New Hope River and Haw River valleys to create B. Everett Jordan Lake. Archaeological surveys located over 350 archaeological sites within the impoundment area. In 1979, extensive excavations were carried out at two sites where deeply buried cultural strata dating from the Early Archaic through the Early Woodland periods were discovered. This project, conducted by archaeologists affiliated with Commonwealth Associates Inc. of Jackson, Michigan, was funded by the U.S. Army Corps of Engineers. Today, the Jordan Lake project still stands as the largest salvage archaeology program to be undertaken in North Carolina (Claggett and Cable 1982).

Recent Research Programs across North Carolina

Although contract archaeology dominated the North Carolina scene during the 1970s and 1980s and continues to be important today, archaeologists affiliated with academic institutions and other state agencies also continued more traditional research programs. At the University of North Carolina at Chapel Hill, excavations continued at the Warren Wilson site during the 1970s. In 1972, work began at Upper Saratown, a Historic village of the Sara Indians on the Dan River in Stokes County, and excavations were resumed at the Hardaway site in 1975 (Daniel 1998; Wilson 1983). The Upper Saratown and Hardaway excavations were undertaken in response to extensive looting by relic collectors.

In 1983, a new Siouan project was begun at UNC–Chapel Hill as a multiyear research program to study the impact of European contact on the native peoples of the North Carolina Piedmont. At the time of this writing, the Siouan project is still active. Excavations have been conducted at Late pre-Contact and Historic period sites in the Haw, Eno, and Dan River drainages in the north central Piedmont (Dickens, Ward, and Davis 1987; Ward and Davis 1993).

While recent archaeological research by University of North Carolina archaeologists has focused on the north central Piedmont, Wake Forest University concentrated its efforts in the Great Bend of the upper Yadkin River valley in the northwestern Piedmont. Ned Woodall and his students began their Great Bend Research Project in 1972 with excavations at the Late pre-Contact Donnaha site (Woodall 1984). Surveys in the upper Yadkin River valley located numerous sites, several of which also have been excavated by Wake Forest crews (Marshall 1988). The overriding goal of the Great Bend project was to address changes in subsistence and settlement patterns, particularly during the Late pre-Contact period, and to examine native trading networks (Woodall 1990).

David Phelps of East Carolina University tested and excavated many sites along the northeast coast and Coastal Plain. Phelps's work has refined the Woodland period coastal chronology and provided much-needed linkages between the Late pre-Contact and Historic Algonkian- and Iroquoian-speaking tribes of the region. His most recent research efforts have been directed toward the Historic Tuscarora villages of the Coastal Plain and Historic Algonkian villages on the Outer Banks. Tom Loftfield, at the University of North Carolina at Wilmington, was active in redefining the chronological sequence of the southwest coastal region through numerous excavations and surveys. Recently, Loftfield's interests have shifted to the seventeenth-century site of Charles

Town and the interaction between Native Americans and the English settlers. Mark Mathis, of the North Carolina Office of State Archaeology, has recently completed an extensive salvage excavation of a large coastal Algonkian village, the Broad Reach site, located in Carteret County. The site was occupied for several hundred years and has offered one of the most complete pictures archaeologists have of fishing and shellfishing villages on the North Carolina coast. Billy Oliver, also of the Office of State Archaeology, began a long-term archaeological project in the 1980s to study the Pee Dee culture of the southern Piedmont and Sandhills regions. Oliver's work has resulted in a refinement of the Late Prehistoric Pee Dee chronology and also has provided insights into the lives of the village farmers living around the ceremonial center at Town Creek in Montgomery County (Oliver 1992).

Although the University of North Carolina ceased its research activity in the mountains in 1985, marked by the last season of the Warren Wilson excavations, others have filled the void. In 1982, David Moore, working out of the Asheville branch of the Office of State Archaeology, began an active program of public archaeology. Moore, Kenneth Robinson of Wake Forest University, and Ruth Wetmore, a consulting archaeologist from Brevard, have worked with a cadre of volunteers to refine the cultural sequence of the western part of the state. Moore also has carried out pioneering research in the upper Catawba River valley. Downstream on the Catawba, archaeological research by Alan May and Ann Tippitt of the Schiele Museum and Janet Levy of the University of North Carolina at Charlotte have complemented Moore's work. Levy, May, and Moore also have collaborated in an attempt to verify the locations of sixteenth-century Indian towns visited by Hernando de Soto and Juan Pardo.

The archaeology program at Western Carolina University, under the direction of Anne Rogers, also has focused on finding and verifying evidence of the sixteenth-century Spanish expeditions through the western part of North Carolina. Recently, Rogers and her students have studied European trade artifacts from the Spikebuck Town site in Clay County. Their research is part of an effort to understand the broad network of trade that existed among Cherokee villages during the eighteenth century (Rogers and Brown 1995).

Brett Riggs of the University of Tennessee has conducted archaeological investigations in the Hiwassee Reservoir area and located several Historic period Cherokee homesteads dating between 1780 and the time of the removal of many Cherokees from their homeland in 1838. Riggs's research has documented noticeable social and economic changes in Cherokee society prior to removal (Riggs 1995).

In 1972, archaeologists at Appalachian State University (ASU) began a long-term excavation project at the Ward site in Watauga County. This site was

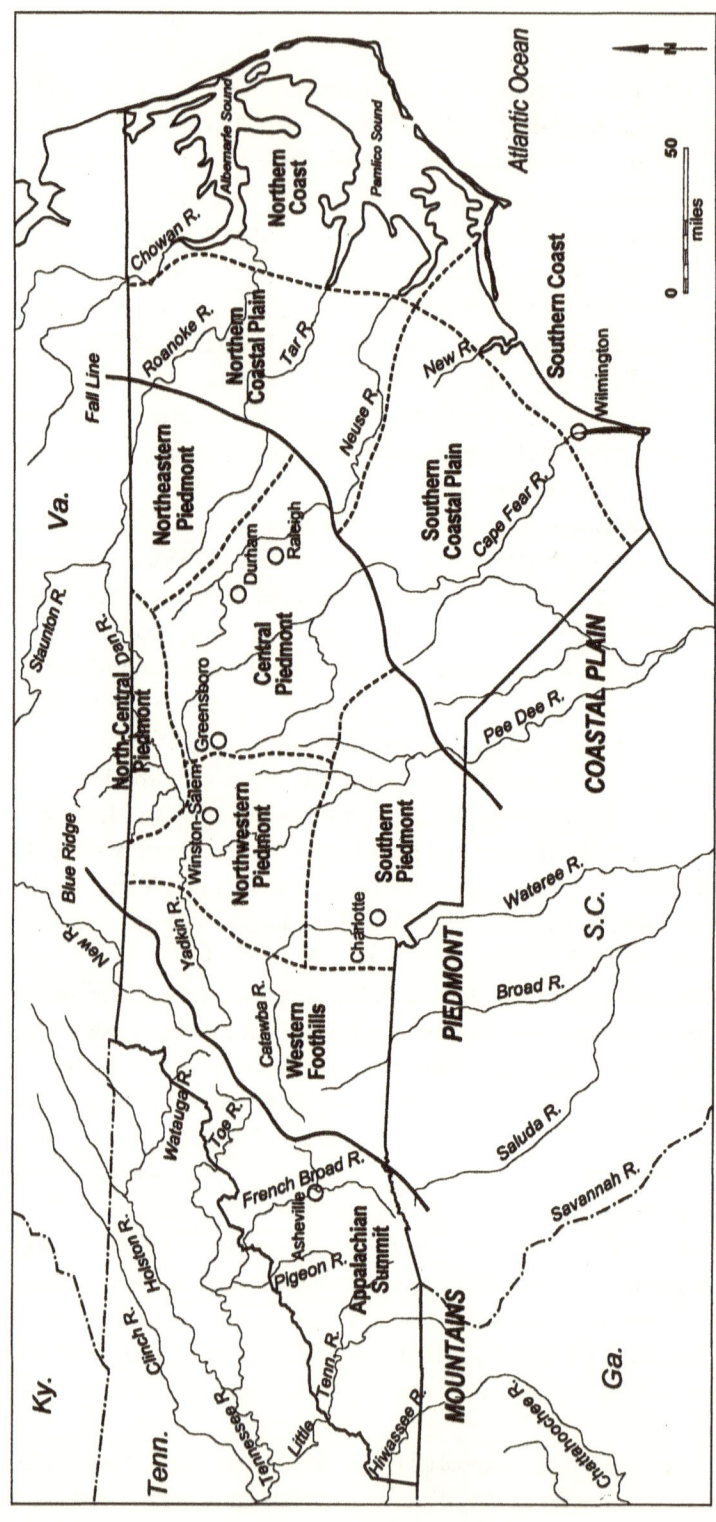

FIGURE 1.4. A map of North Carolina showing physiography, river drainages, and archaeological regions.

discovered by Stanley and Jewel South in 1952 (see RLA files). The Appalachian State research made it the first site in the northwestern mountains of North Carolina to be systematically excavated (Ayers, Loucks, and Purrington 1980). Although the Ward site was occupied sporadically for over a thousand years, the main occupation took place around A.D. 1400, during the Pisgah phase. Since 1972, the Ward site excavations have been complemented by numerous surveys and excavations conducted by ASU archaeologists Harvard Ayers, Jill Loucks, and Burt Purrington (Purrington 1986).

Recently, Larry Kimball, also of ASU, completed a testing project along the Swannanoa River near Asheville. Kimball (1991) was able to show that many sites may be deeply buried in the floodplain and not visible on the surface. These sites can only be detected by systematic subsurface testing.

More projects have been started and others have been expanded while this book was in preparation. We have tried to be as inclusive as possible, but as with any publication, the time lag between preparation and printing forces some research to be left out. However, we have maintained contacts with archaeologists across the state during the preparation process in an effort to keep the following chapters as current as possible.

Notes on Organization

Although native cultural diversity gradually increased over time, the archaeological records of the earliest two periods—Paleo-Indian and Archaic—are similar from the coast to the mountains and indicate similar patterns of economy, technology, and social organization. Consequently, each of these periods is treated as a separate chapter that covers the entire state. With the beginning of the Woodland period, about 3,000 years ago, distinctive cultural traditions began to emerge within each of the state's three major physiographic regions. By the Historic period, when the first European contacts with the native populations occurred, these regional traditions coincided with four distinct linguistic and cultural groups: Algonkian, Tuscarora, Siouan, and Cherokee, which occupied the coast, Coastal Plain, Piedmont, and mountains, respectively. Because of this regional diversity, the Woodland and Historic periods are presented in chapters that focus on the cultural developments that took place within each of the major physiographic regions. Figure 1.4 provides a map of North Carolina showing these physiographic regions and the subregions within them as they are employed within this book. Figure 1.5 provides a chronological chart showing the archaeological sequences within each subregion as they are currently understood.

The purpose of this book is to present an introduction to our native past in a

DATE	CULTURAL PERIOD	MOUNTAINS		PIEDMONT		
		Appalachian Summit	Western Foothills	Southern Piedmont	Central Piedmont	Northwestern Piedmont
	Historic Tribe(s)	Cherokee	Catawba	Keyauwee	Occaneechi Sissipahaw Shakori, Eno	?
	Contact	Late Qualla	?	Caraway	Fredricks	?
AD 1500	Late Woodland / South Appalachian Mississippian	Middle Qualla	Burke		Mitchum/Jenrette	
		"Early Qualla"?		Leak	Hillsboro	
		Pisgah	McDowell	Town Creek	Haw River	Donnaha
AD 1000				Teal		
		Late Connestee	Late Connestee			Uwharrie
AD 500	Middle Woodland	Connestee	Connestee / Yadkin?		Yadkin	
AD 1		Pigeon	Pigeon? / Yadkin?			
1,000 BC	Early Woodland	Swannanoa	Swannanoa / Badin?		Badin	
2,000 BC	Late Archaic	Otarre				
3,000 BC		Savannah River			Savannah River	
4,000 BC	Middle Archaic	Guilford			Halifax Guilford	
5,000 BC		Morrow Mountain			Morrow Mountain	
6,000 BC		Stanly			Stanly	
7,000 BC	Early Archaic	St. Albans / LeCroy / Kanawha Kirk			St. Albans / LeCroy / Kanawha Kirk	
8,000 BC		Palmer			Palmer	
9,000 BC	Late Paleoindian	Hardaway - Dalton			Hardaway	
	Middle Paleoindian	Cumberland - Suwannee - Simpson				
10,000 BC	Early Paleoindian	Clovis				

FIGURE 1.5. *North Carolina chronology chart showing the archaeological sequences recognized in various regions of the state.*

PIEDMONT		COASTAL PLAIN			
North-Central Piedmont	Northeastern Piedmont	Northern Coast	Northern Coastal Plain	Southern Coast	Southern Coastal Plain
Sara	Occaneechi Tutelo Saponi	Carolina Algonkins	Meherrin Tuscarora	Cape Fear Indians Waccamaw	Lumbee
Late Saratown Middle Saratown Early Saratown Dan River	? Gaston	Colington	Cashie	White Oak	?
Yadkin	Clements Vincent	Mount Pleasant		Cape Fear	
Badin		Deep Creek		New River	
Savannah River		Savannah River			
Halifax Guilford		Guilford			
Morrow Mountain		Morrow Mountain			
Stanly		Stanly			
St. Albans / LeCroy / Kanawha Kirk		Kirk			
Palmer		Palmer			
Hardaway		Hardaway			
Cumberland - Suwannee - Simpson					
Clovis					

way that will be informative to the lay person as well as the professional archaeologist. Rather than a final statement on the archaeology of North Carolina, this book is a beginning, a summary of what is currently known. We hope it will see many revisions in the future as more and more light is shed on our past by the shovels and trowels of new generations of North Carolina archaeologists.

2. The Paleo-Indian
An Elusive Quarry

If you ask any amateur archaeologist or collector what he or she most dreams of finding, invariably the quick response will be "a fluted point." This fascination with the oldest and the rarest is to be expected and has led to some of the most worthwhile joint efforts between professional archaeologists and collectors. A statewide survey of Paleo-Indian points has been conducted in almost every state east of the Mississippi River, and often these have been carried out by amateurs (e.g., McCary 1947; Perkinson 1971, 1973). In fact, most of the Paleo-Indian data, at least in the eastern United States, has been gathered by amateur collectors (see Anderson 1990:166–67). In North Carolina, most fluted point finds have been made by amateurs, and it is usually the amateur collector who calls the professional archaeologist to report a possible Paleo-Indian site. This relationship has a long tradition. In 1937, Herbert M. Doerschuk directed Joffre Coe to the Hardaway site, and, more recently, Randy Daniel has solicited and received the help of countless collectors from across the state in his study of Early Archaic and Paleo-Indian settlement patterns (Daniel 1998).

Paleo-Indian research did not begin in the eastern Woodlands but in the Southwest. In 1926, near the little town of Folsom, New Mexico, a group of paleontologists from the Denver Museum of Natural History discovered the now-famous Folsom points unequivocally associated with the bones of extinct bisons. Although this association of man-made tools with a now-extinct Pleistocene animal was clear to the paleontologists, J. D. Figgins, the director of the museum, had trouble convincing archaeologists.

The skepticism that Figgins faced was deep-rooted. During the last half of the nineteenth century, extravagant claims had been made regarding the time when the first settlers arrived in the New World. Some, like Fiorino Ameghino of Argentina, believed humans evolved in his country some 15 million years ago, before spreading over the rest of the world. By the turn of the century, when rigorous scientific studies began in American archaeology, the pendulum was swinging against an early arrival for humans in the New World. This movement was led by two of the most influential scholars of prehistory in the United States, William H. Holmes and Ales Hrdlička. Holmes, although trained as an artist, was an eminent prehistorian with the Smithsonian Institution's Bureau of American Ethnology. Hrdlička was an equally eminent physical anthropologist who arrived at the United States National Museum in 1903. Both men were so successful in refuting all evidence for Paleo-Indians in the New World that the subject became taboo, and still was when Figgins made his finds in 1926 (Willey and Sabloff 1974:57; Wilmsen 1965:179).

Still, Figgins continued his excavations at the Folsom site. In 1927, he found an additional spear point associated with more extinct bison bones. This time Figgins halted the work and sent out telegrams to his skeptical colleagues, inviting them to come and examine his find in situ. A few, including Hrdlička, did visit and were convinced, but many archaeologists still refused to accept the fact that people had been in the New World for such a long time. A third expedition, more in situ points, and more telegrams finally proved sufficient to convince even the most skeptical archaeologists of the time that man did indeed once hunt now-extinct animals in North America (Figgins 1927; Wormington 1957).

Six years after the Folsom find, a discovery of even earlier evidence was made. This find also was not made by archaeologists, or even paleontologists, but by a foreman for the Union Pacific Railroad, Frank Garner, and a Catholic priest, Father Conrad Bilgery. At the Dent site, in Colorado, three relatively large fluted points, named Clovis, were uncovered in association with the bones of a dozen extinct mammoths (Wormington 1957:44). By this time, the archaeological world was prepared to accept the antiquity of humans in the New World, and Paleo-Indian research was off and running. Since 1926, numerous Paleo-Indian sites have been excavated in the United States and Canada. These sites have provided clear evidence for the association of a variety of stone tools and Pleistocene animals.

Although an earlier, pre-Clovis migration of people into the New World has been hypothesized by some archaeologists, currently there is no firm evidence of people anywhere in the continental United States before 10,000 B.C. (Anderson 1990:164; Meltzer 1989:484). However, as Meltzer cautions, there is also no compelling reason to deny the existence of New World inhabitants before Clovis. If these early migrants failed in their attempt to adapt to the new environment, evidence of their presence will be difficult to find and recognize (1989:483).

Recent excavations in Brazil have uncovered a rich, deeply buried midden in a cave near Monte Alegre. In addition to thousands of flakes, numerous tools, including four spear points, were recovered. These artifacts have been dated to between 9300 B.C. and 7880 B.C. The points show no affinities to Clovis or Folsom types but rather look similar to contracting-stemmed points in the Southeast. The Brazilian cave dwellers did not hunt big game but rather foraged a broad spectrum of rain forest and riverine food resources (Roosevelt et al. 1996). The Monte Verde site in Chile has also produced recent evidence that suggests Pleistocene hunters and gatherers occupied the Southern Hemisphere before the big game hunters of the Clovis tradition. Presumably, if people were living in Chile by 10,500 B.C., they would have arrived in North America even earlier (Dillehay 1997; Meltzer et al. 1997). If this evidence stands, it lends support to the idea that Paleo-Indians other than Clovis may have migrated to the New World, and some of these people may have arrived before Clovis.

Paleo-Indian Chronology in the Southeast

Although many more Paleo-Indian spear points have been found in the East than in the West, the eastern specimens have almost all been isolated surface finds. Only rarely have buried sites been discovered, and even rarer are sites with tools in association with Pleistocene animals. Still, archaeologists working in the Southeast recognize marked differences in spear point forms and frequencies during the Paleo-Indian period. And this variability in stylistic attributes—even in the absence of artifacts from clear stratigraphic contexts—has led to the development of several regional chronologies (Anderson 1990; Gardner and Verrey 1979; Williams and Stoltman 1965). By studying the changing frequencies and spatial distribution of the various types of Paleo-Indian spear points, questions regarding settlement and subsistence have been addressed.

The chronology presented below follows closely the sequence proposed by David G. Anderson (1990). Using the current Paleo-Indian database, Anderson divides the Paleo-Indian period into Early, Middle, and Late subperiods.

Early Paleo-Indian Subperiod (about 9500–9000 B.C.)

The time of the earliest, generally accepted arrival of people in the southeastern United States is between 9000 and 10,000 B.C. The projectile points that date to this time are large, fluted lanceolates, very similar to the classic Clovis points of the West (fig. 2.1). Although low numbers of Early Paleo-Indian points are widely distributed throughout the region, many areas appear not to have been

FIGURE 2.1. *Early and Middle Paleo-Indian spear points and point preform (bottom left) from North Carolina. The bottom right specimen was reworked into a knife.*

occupied at all, or only briefly visited. Large sections of the Gulf and Atlantic Coastal Plains, as well as southern Florida, do not appear to have been settled during this subperiod. On the other hand, concentrations of Early Paleo-Indian points have been noted in the Tennessee, Cumberland, and Ohio River valleys as well as portions of western South Carolina, southern Virginia, and the northern Piedmont of North Carolina. Outside the Southeast, similar geographic concentrations have been noted in New Jersey and eastern Pennsylvania. Anderson (1990:164–71) sees these locations as staging areas where the new arrivals settled while acclimating to the changing eastern Woodland environment. What we know about these earliest inhabitants is based almost entirely on surface finds of spear points (McCary 1947, 1948; Perkinson 1971, 1973).

Middle Paleo-Indian Subperiod (9000–8500 B.C.)

Regional variability in spear point form characterizes the Middle Paleo-Indian subperiod in the Southeast. The Cumberland, Suwannee, and Simpson point types are thought to be typical of this subperiod. Some of these large, lanceolate spear points like the Cumberland type are fluted, whereas others like the Suwannee are not. The one thing they all have in common, in addition to their lanceolate form, is a narrowing or "waisting" at the base, which sometimes creates an eared effect (Anderson 1990:6).

The Middle Paleo-Indian subperiod appears to have been a time when the early inhabitants spread out from the aforementioned staging areas and settled into the frontiers of their new environment. The number of Middle Paleo-Indian spear points increases considerably over the number of Early Paleo-Indian points. For example, in Alabama there is an almost fourfold increase, and in Mississippi the number of points doubles from that of the earlier subperiod (Futato 1983:183–84; McGahey 1987:11). The North Carolina data are hard to assess because the only statewide surveys of Paleo-Indian artifacts have dealt solely with fluted points (Perkinson 1971, 1973). However, a cursory examination of Perkinson's illustrated spear points reveals many more specimens that typologically seem to fit better in the Middle Paleo-Indian than in the Early Paleo-Indian subperiod.

Late Paleo-Indian Subperiod (8500–7900 B.C.)

According to Anderson (1990:201), populations continued to increase during the Late Paleo-Indian subperiod. The evidence he cites for this trend is an increased number of sites producing Dalton points, the diagnostic Late Paleo-Indian type. Several varieties of Dalton points have been identified, but all share a lanceolate blade form, a concave base, and grinding along the hafting edges. Often the bases are thinned and display faint ears. In North Carolina, the Hardaway-Dalton point type is representative of the Late Paleo-Indian subperiod. In addition to distinctive spear points, large side scrapers are also part of the Late Paleo-Indian tool kit (Coe 1964). By the end of this subperiod, Holocene climatic conditions prevailed and the basic hunting-and-gathering lifeway that would persist for the next 5,000 years was set.

The sequence of diagnostic tools that define the Early, Middle, and Late Paleo-Indian subperiods have neither been found in a stratigraphic column nor been radiocarbon-dated on any site in the Southeast. However, there are a few sites that have produced buried deposits containing primarily Middle or Late Paleo-Indian materials. Unfortunately, the diagnostic Paleo-Indian tools are usually mixed with later Early Archaic artifacts. This stratigraphic mixing has made it extremely difficult, if not impossible, to separate nondiagnostic tool types that may belong to the Paleo-Indian period from those that were used by Early Archaic peoples. Also confusing the issue is the fact that several Paleo-Indian stone-tool types other than spear points continued to be used during the Early Archaic period. Goodyear, Michie, and Charles (1989:41) note that some of these tools, such as end scrapers, side scrapers, gravers, true blades, and bipolar cores, were made and used for over 3,000 years.

Paleo-Indian Settlement and Subsistence

With a few, rare exceptions, no Paleo-Indian tools have been discovered in clear association with Pleistocene fauna east of the Mississippi River. Part of the reason for this lack of evidence may be poor preservation. Animal bones and other organic subsistence remains of Paleo-Indians simply do not have the same potential for being preserved in the humid East, with its acidic soils, as they do in the more arid and alkaline West. But just as environmental conditions vary between the two sections of the country today, they also exhibited marked differences during the Late Pleistocene when the first inhabitants arrived.

The earliest settlers in the Southeast, arriving around 10,000 B.C., found a rapidly changing landscape—one where stands of oak, hickory, beech, birch, and elm were in the process of replacing forests of spruce and pine. A patchy boreal forest, interspersed with parklands, was giving way to a homogeneous cover of mesic hardwoods. In North Carolina this transition was completed by 7000 B.C. (Delcourt and Delcourt 1983:269). Also, Late Pleistocene megafauna—including the horse, mastodon, and mammoth—were becoming extinct during this time. Current evidence suggests that many of these extinctions were complete by 8500 B.C. (Mead and Meltzer 1984:47).

In addition to these changes, the coastline was in a state of flux. The massive amounts of water trapped in the Late Pleistocene glaciers that covered most of Canada and a large portion of the northern United States caused a drop in sea level of 150 feet or more. This in turn pushed the Atlantic and Gulf shorelines several miles to the east and south of their present positions. However, by 7000 B.C. the warming trend that had drastically changed the forest cover of the Southeast had also melted much of the glaciers to the north, thus causing a rise in sea level and a retreat in the shoreline to near its present-day location (Anderson 1990:3).

While many of the fluted points of the Early Paleo-Indian subperiod in the East are virtually identical to those from the West found in association with now-extinct animals, the environmental differences between the two regions during the Late Pleistocene may have necessitated very different adaptations. Extensive grasslands in the Southwest supported large herds of mammoth and bison, which formed the focus of Paleo-Indian subsistence. It is not clear, however, that eastern Paleo-Indians followed a similar subsistence course.

Although there have been numerous discoveries of extinct elephant and bison remains in the eastern United States, very few have been found in unquestionable association with Paleo-Indian artifacts. To date, the Kimmswick site in eastern Missouri is the only site outside of the Southwest where fluted points and elephants have been found in association (Graham et al. 1981; Meltzer 1988:23).

In the Southeast, Florida's clear-water lakes and bogs have produced numerous finds of extinct Pleistocene fauna, and a few of these may be related to Paleo-Indian hunters. Perhaps the most famous candidate for a Paleo-Indian kill is the Little Salt Springs tortoise. The tortoise was found submerged in the spring, lying on its back on a ledge. A sharpened wooden spear was wedged between the carapace and plastron. Traces of charring on the shell indicated to the investigators that the animal had been cooked by the hungry hunters who didn't bother to remove their spear. The spear yielded a radiocarbon date of 10,030 B.C. (Clausen et al. 1979:609–10). In northern Florida, a *Bison antiquus* skull embedded with the fragment of a stone spear point was found in the Wacissa River. Unfortunately, the point fragment did not possess any diagnostic attributes (Webb et al. 1984). There are also reports from Florida and South Carolina of bone fragments from extinct Pleistocene animals that display possible butchering marks and other modifications reflecting human behavior (Goodyear 1989:26; Webb et al. 1984:390).

If Paleo-Indians over much of the eastern United States were not primarily big-game hunters, what else did they do? Given the lack of direct subsistence evidence, such as preserved food remains in association with stone tools, studies of the eastern Paleo-Indian must rely primarily on inference and indirect evidence. This is particularly true for the Southeast, where buried sites of any kind are extremely rare. In fact, most sites in the East and Southeast consist of isolated finds of spear points, which has led one archaeologist to observe—tongue in cheek—that eastern Paleo-Indians "ate nothing and lived as isolated individuals" (Brose 1978:729).

David Meltzer, an archaeologist at Southern Methodist University, has recently investigated Paleo-Indian subsistence. Meltzer's research has led him to question the assumption that Paleo-Indian groups in the East hunted the same kinds of now-extinct megafauna that their cousins in the West did. He has also questioned whether the preponderance of kill sites in the West reflects a cultural adaptation to these animals or the predilections of the first generation of archaeologists working in the region. Before radiocarbon dating, all the early sites had to be kill sites in order to verify their antiquity. Without the association between stone tools and the bones of extinct animals, there was no way to demonstrate their age. As a consequence, archaeologists overlooked sites without bones and, in doing so, may have inflated the importance of hunting in the overall subsistence practices of Paleo-Indians (Meltzer 1988:3).

In the Southeast, the presumption that big-game hunting dominated the subsistence scene is even more problematic. For years, the argument for big-game hunting was based solely upon the similarities between the fluted points of the West and those found in the East. Today, more and more archaeologists like Meltzer are beginning to question this argument as new paleoenvironmental data become available, and as more studies are done on the ecology of contemporary hunters and gatherers.

Meltzer suggests that the fundamental differences between the southeastern, southwestern, and high plains environments necessitated the deployment of subsistence strategies that also were fundamentally different. Rather than having made a specialized adaptation to one or a few species, he views Southeastern Paleo-Indians as having been more generally adapted to a variety of resources. Meltzer reasons that a specialized adaptation requires an environment with few species but an abundance of the animal species that are present. These low-diversity areas were usually treeless grazing lands supporting large herds of ungulates. Such environmental conditions prevailed during the end of the Pleistocene in the western United States. On the other hand, in the unglaciated Southeast, forests dominated the landscape, and forests are typically species-rich and species-diverse. Lacking expansive natural grazing areas, these areas could not support large herds of ungulates. Under these conditions, a generalized subsistence strategy would have been more productive and not dependent on an abundance of a single or few species (Meltzer 1988:5–6). "Groups who occupied this area likely responded with a generalized foraging strategy exploiting a variety of resources: seeds and nuts, small mammals, and, perhaps, an occasional large mammal" (8).

This subsistence pattern is indicated by the fact that most eastern Paleo-Indian sites consist of isolated finds of spear points. And as one moves from north to south in the East, the number of sites producing more than an isolated projectile point decreases even more. Most of the southeastern Paleo-Indian sites where more than a single point has been found are related to stone-quarrying activities (Meltzer 1988:11–14). This site pattern reflects generalized foraging where groups rarely engaged in subsistence activities that produced recognizable traces in the archaeological record. The fact that quarry sites are the only type of large sites found in the Southeast further indicates that high-quality stone was the only spatially restricted resource. These lithic resource areas were repeatedly exploited and, thus, made highly visible archaeologically (14).

Randy Daniel of East Carolina University recently completed a regional study of the Hardaway complex and reached a similar conclusion: "In brief, present evidence suggests that sources of knappable stone (i.e., Uwharrie rhyolite and Allendale chert) rather than watersheds formed the geographical focus of Early Archaic adaptation; in fact, band ranges cross-cut several drainages. At some point during the early Holocene, hunter-gatherer groups coalesced around the Uwharrie and Allendale sources forming at least two regions. . . . While band mobility was restricted by and included scheduled visits to primary quarry sources, movement was otherwise quite variable across the Piedmont and Coastal Plain" (1998:194).

Whether or not settlement and subsistence reconstructions like Meltzer's and Daniel's are accurate in every detail must await new data from the excavation of buried sites. However, it is highly unlikely that large, now-extinct mammals ever played a dominant role in the subsistence practices of southeastern Paleo-Indians. Rather, the subsistence pattern—certainly by the Middle Paleo-Indian period—was probably very similar to that of the Early Archaic period, when presumably a large variety of seasonally available plants and animals was exploited.

The Paleo-Indian Period in North Carolina

With this background in chronology and subsistence, we can now enter the hazy world of the Paleo-Indian period in North Carolina. This discussion will follow a regional outline beginning with the Coastal Plain and then moving westward across the Piedmont to the Mountains. It will soon become obvious that our level of understanding of the Paleo-Indian period across the state is highly uneven. Some of the reasons for this unevenness are no doubt related to the history of the development of North Carolina archaeology. Other reasons are more direct and are related to environmental and geological factors.

The Coastal Plain

During much of the Paleo-Indian period, the coast of North Carolina was situated several miles to the east of its present location. David Phelps has estimated that the eastern edge of the Coastal Plain at this time was some 230–300 miles from the Piedmont. As a consequence, many Paleo-Indian sites lie submerged today, and those that we do find on the coast represent an adaptation to what was then the central Coastal Plain region (Phelps 1983:22).

Based on palynological data from the inner Coastal Plain of South Carolina, the earliest inhabitants of the region would have found a deciduous forest dominated by beech and hickory but also containing oak, elm, sugar maple, black walnut, sugar maple, and hazelnut trees. Climatic conditions were cooler and wetter than today and may have been very similar to the modern climate of New York (Watts 1980:192–97). The coastal fringe may have been somewhat warmer, given the ameliorative effect of the ocean.

Phil Perkinson (1973:50), in his statewide survey of fluted Paleo-Indian spear points, reported fifteen such artifacts from the coast and Coastal Plain of North Carolina. A third of these came from the small, adjacent, northeastern coastal counties of Camden and Pasquotank. The others were scattered, isolated finds that reveal little in terms of a distributional pattern. In addition to these finds by amateurs, Phelps has documented fluted points from Beaufort, Craven, and Gates Counties. Although the total number of Coastal Plain sites producing Paleo-Indian points is still less than fifty, Phelps has suggested that the dearth of Paleo-Indian sites is more a reflection of the state of research in the region than an indication that Paleo-Indians avoided the area. The Coastal Plain has simply not been surveyed by archaeologists as extensively as other regions of North Carolina (Phelps 1983:18).

The Piedmont

Although most of the pollen studies that have been used to reconstruct the environment that existed during the Paleo-Indian period have relied on data from outside the North Carolina Piedmont, some inferences can be made from reconstructions of neighboring areas. The summary presented below is based on fossil pollen records from Anderson Pond, Tennessee; Hack Pond, Virginia; White Pond, South Carolina; Rockyhock Bay, North Carolina; and other fossil-pollen sites in the eastern United States situated between 32 and 38 degrees north latitude (Delcourt and Delcourt 1983:270).

During the full glacial period (17,000–14,500 B.C.), before Paleo-Indians arrived, jack pine and spruce were the main species comprising a boreal forest. As temperatures warmed and the northern glaciers began to retreat, vegetative conditions began to destabilize as conifers of the boreal forest were gradually replaced by deciduous species such as oak, hickory, walnut, elm, willow, and sugar maple. Although the boreal forest was gone from the Piedmont by 10,500 B.C., a continual warming trend gave rise to new forests comprised of deciduous species such as sweet gum, chestnut, red maple, and tupelo gum. This transition was complete by about 7000 B.C. (Delcourt and Delcourt 1983:268). During the early Holocene interval (10,500–6000 B.C.), when people would have first ventured into the Piedmont, the winters were harsher and the summers cooler than they are today. However, the growing season was probably about the same as it is now (Goodyear, Michie, and Charles 1989:24).

Although the record pertaining to the kinds of animals that were present in the Piedmont during this same period is not nearly as complete as that for the vegetation, some inferences can be made given the types of forest covers that were present and the climatic conditions they reflect. During the full glacial period, mastodons, mammoths, horses, and bison may have roamed the area along with other now-extinct animals. But evidence suggests that by the time the first people arrived, these animals were becoming extinct as a more modern vegetation pattern emerged. As mentioned earlier, many authorities believe that the Pleistocene megafauna had generally died out by 8000 B.C., or even earlier. It has been estimated that only about a 1,000-year span existed when both people and now-extinct Pleistocene animals co-existed in the Southeast (Goodyear, Michie, and Charles 1989:26). It is therefore likely that the Paleo-Indian hunters of the Piedmont, as elsewhere in the Southeast, spent most of their time hunting animals other than mammoths and mastodons.

Following Meltzer's argument (1988:8) for the Southeast as a whole, the early bands that moved into the Piedmont region had, or quickly developed, a generalized foraging subsistence strategy. The broadleaf forests offered a rich variety of resources, both animal and vegetable. Small mammals, seeds, nuts, and fruits probably provided the mainstay of the diet. Perhaps an occasional bison or mastodon was killed, but these animals certainly were not the focus of Paleo-Indian subsistence.

Rather than being determined by the availability of particular food resources,

Paleo-Indian settlements were probably tied instead to the locations of outcrops of stone suitable to make their tools and weapons (Gardner 1974). In the North Carolina Piedmont, this raw material consisted of high-quality metavolcanic rocks found in the Slate Belt. This wide geological structure runs along the eastern edge of the Piedmont from Granville County in the north to Anson County in the south. Most stone tools found in the Piedmont that date to the Paleo-Indian period, as well as later periods, were made from a fine-grained, metamorphosed volcanic rock called rhyolite. Rhyolite outcrops are restricted to the area of the Slate Belt in and around the Uwharrie Mountains of Stanly and Montgomery Counties (Daniel and Butler 1991:66). And it is not by accident that the site of the most important Paleo-Indian and Early Archaic research in North Carolina—the Hardaway site—also is located in the Uwharrie Mountains.

Hardaway is the most recognizable site name in North Carolina. If an amateur collector knows nothing else about the state's archaeology, he knows that the Hardaway site (31St4) contains the earliest cultural remains that have been excavated in North Carolina. Just how early is open to debate, but most archaeologists date the earliest Hardaway levels to at least the Late Paleo-Indian subperiod. Some have argued that, in its earliest form, the Hardaway complex is as early as Clovis (Ward 1983), whereas others prefer to place Hardaway within the Early Archaic period or Late Paleo-Indian–Early Archaic transitional period (Daniel 1994, 1998). We will present these arguments later, but first this important site merits a historical discussion because of its significance in the development of not only North Carolina archaeology but southeastern archaeology in general.

The Hardaway site is located in Stanly County, just outside the small town of Badin. It is situated above the Yadkin River on the flat top of a ridge that forms the west side of a gorge called the Narrows. The site was named for the Hardaway Construction Company of Columbus, Georgia, the company that in 1917 completed the dam that blocks the Yadkin at the Narrows and impounds the waters of Badin Lake. The dam was needed to provide the electrical energy necessary to process aluminum from bauxite ore, which was shipped in by rail. Today, the Aluminum Company of America (ALCOA) continues to produce aluminum in Badin just as the Carolina Aluminum Company did during the 1930s when interest in the Hardaway site was first sparked.

The site had no doubt been a focal point of arrowhead collectors for years, but it was Herbert M. Doerschuk, an electrical engineer for the Carolina Aluminum Company, who first reported it to professional archaeologists. Doerschuk was an avid collector and one of the original members and officers of the Archaeological Society of North Carolina. He first showed the Hardaway site to Joffre Coe in 1937. At that time, Coe was busy trying to get federally sponsored excavations off the ground at the Frutchey Mound, known today as Town Creek Indian Mound, in neighboring Montgomery County. In April of 1938, Coe asked Doerschuk to write up a brief description of the site and some of its artifacts for the first edition of the Society's newsletter. Coe was particularly interested in the engraved slate pieces that are unique to Hardaway. Coe advised Doerschuk, "In dealing with the projectile points it might be worth while to take an *unselected* group of around a hundred specimens, pick out the various shapes, make outline drawings of them and note the distribution or number of times occurring" (letter from Coe to Doerschuk, April 23, 1938, on file, Research Laboratories of Archaeology [hereafter RLA]). Thus we have the beginning of random sampling in North Carolina archaeology. Doerschuk followed Coe's advice. His article, entitled "An Interesting Archaeological Site in Stanley [*sic*] County," was published in the *Archaeological Society of North Carolina News Letter* in May 1938, giving it the distinction of being the first published account of the Hardaway site.

The first formal excavation at the Hardaway site did not occur until after World War II. In 1948, Coe, Paul Strieff, a Michigan graduate student working at Morrow Mountain State Park, and Doerschuk excavated a small 5'×5' unit at the site. Unfortunately, at least from the standpoint of gaining insight into the site's stratigraphy, they encountered a burial at the base of the plowed soil. The excavation of the burial required all the time they had scheduled at Hardaway (Coe 1964:57; notes on file, RLA).

Another isolated 5'×5' unit was excavated in 1951, but it was not until 1955 that work began in earnest (fig. 2.2). All the soil was excavated in arbitrary levels with, as Coe would say later, arbitrary results (1964:60). A great variety of projectile point types was found in all levels with no apparent vertical separation. Finally, during the summer of 1958, this strategy was changed and an effort was made to distinguish natural soil zones. These natural layers were then used to maintain vertical control, rather than the arbitrary 6-inch levels that had been used during the earlier work (Coe 1964).

This approach proved successful, and Coe was able to divide the cultural sequence at Hardaway into three distinct chronological phases based on vertically separated spear point forms. The name "Hardaway" was given to the earliest type, which was followed by "Palmer" and "Kirk" types. The latter two names can be seen today on many of the tombstones in the small Badin cemetery.

The results of the Hardaway excavations were published in Coe's revised doctoral dissertation, aptly titled *The Formative Cultures of the Carolina Piedmont* (1964). The book sold well. Professional archaeologists and amateur col-

FIGURE 2.2. *View of excavations at the Hardaway site in 1956. (Courtesy of the Research Laboratories of Archaeology)*

lectors alike rushed out to buy copies. Unfortunately, the book also fell into the hands of unscrupulous relic collectors or "pot hunters," as they are known to archaeologists. These individuals not only used the book's excellent photographs to identify specimens in their collections, but they also used its maps to locate the important archaeological sites that were described. After all, why be content to just read about Hardaway points when you could go dig up your own from the type site itself? And that's exactly what the pot hunters did. They came from Virginia, Georgia, Alabama, and Tennessee, as well as from every corner of North Carolina.

All of the excavations that had been carried out at the Hardaway site before the publication of Coe's book had been conducted on a small scale with little funding. During the 1950s, Stanley South and David Phelps brought crews working at the nearby Town Creek site over to Hardaway as time permitted. The excavation strategy during this period was to use small crews to open enough trenches to gain an understanding of the stratigraphy. These trenches formed a border around what was considered to be the heart of the site, which was left untouched (see Coe 1964:58; Daniel 1998:14). This block was to be saved until such time as adequate funding could be obtained to do the job properly.

Unfortunately, this is the area of the Hardaway site that was targeted by the

FIGURE 2.3. *View of excavations at the Hardaway site in 1975. (Courtesy of the Research Laboratories of Archaeology)*

hordes of pot hunters that came after 1964. The University of North Carolina held a lease on the property from 1954 until the early 1980s, and staff and graduate students spent many long weekends guarding the site, chasing away pot hunters, and even "going undercover." But it was impossible to stem the tide of destruction. By 1972, when the authors first visited Hardaway to tack up more "keep out" signs, it had the appearance of a heavy artillery impact zone. Massive, craterlike holes covered the entire site, from the original area of excavations to the very tip of Hardaway Point at water's edge. By this time, the site was heavily overgrown and almost impenetrable. Still, the relic hunters came. They braved the rattlesnakes, the briars, and the archaeology "police" from the university. The relic hunters who were caught in the act invariably remarked that Coe had done all he was ever going to do at the site, so why shouldn't they be allowed to dig now that he was finished?

Well, Coe wasn't finished. Excavations resumed in the summer of 1975 (Daniel 1998:14–17) (fig. 2.3). It was hoped that at least portions of the more deeply buried Hardaway and Palmer zones might have escaped the looters, who by now had begun to dig in one another's backfill. This phase of excavation at Hardaway continued every summer through 1980. The large patches of undisturbed Hardaway and Palmer zones were never found, and frustration mounted each summer as it became obvious that the pot hunters had not only been very diligent but also very thorough. Some graduate students who were assigned to work at the site began to feel as though they were being banished to Badin. Work at Hardaway ended in 1980 much like it had begun—with a whimper, not a bang. Only two 5' squares and a few test pits south of the main site area were excavated during two weeks in August of that final year.

Although the stratified deposits at Hardaway were not as well preserved as had been hoped, the excavations between 1975 and 1980 yielded literally tons of stone tools and chipping debris. Since most flakes and other nondiagnostic specimens were discarded in the field during the earlier excavations, these new collections had the potential for answering important questions about Prehistoric stone-tool manufacture and use that had become important to archaeologists during the 1970s and 1980s.

Recently, Randy Daniel has re-examined much of the Hardaway material excavated during the 1950s, as well as many of the artifacts collected during the final phase of excavation (Daniel 1994, 1998). Daniel's research focused on how the Hardaway site articulated with other Late Paleo-Indian and Early Archaic settlements. He also surveyed the Uwharrie area with geologist J. Robert Butler to identify the stone quarry sites that were exploited by people living at Hardaway (Daniel and Butler 1994). By combining these data with an analysis of over 3,000 Late Paleo-Indian and Early Archaic projectile points from sites throughout the North Carolina and South Carolina Piedmont, Daniel has placed Hardaway within a broad regional settlement model. His research has resulted in an important new perspective on Paleo-Indian and Early Archaic adaptations in the Piedmont. In Chapter 3, we review Daniel's study.

Some archaeologists view the Hardaway and Hardaway-Dalton complexes as manifestations of the Early Archaic period. This position is anchored by radiocarbon dates on Dalton points from the Midwest that range from 8500 B.C. to 7900 B.C. Also, Hardaway-Dalton points are more widespread and are made from a greater variety of raw materials than the earlier fluted points. It has been argued that these characteristics are more typical of Early Archaic than Paleo-Indian assemblages (Daniel 1994, 1998; Goodyear, Michie, and Charles 1989:38–39).

While Coe (1964:67) viewed the variety of projectile point forms comprising the Hardaway complex (i.e., Hardaway Blade, Hardaway-Dalton, and Hardaway Side Notched) as reflecting temporal differences, others have regarded them as evidencing stages of tool modification that resulted from use and resharpening, or perhaps geographical differences (Daniel 1998:52; Goodyear 1974:19–33) (fig. 2.4). However, all agree that other stone tools associated with the Hardaway complex are very similar to those used by Paleo-Indians. The

THE PALEO-INDIAN 43

FIGURE 2.4. *Hardaway Blade (top row, left two specimens), Hardaway-Dalton (top row, right two specimens, and second row), and Hardaway Side Notched (bottom two rows) spear points from the Hardaway site.*

FIGURE 2.5. *Chipped-stone tools from Late Paleo-Indian and Early Archaic contexts at the Hardaway site: end scrapers (top row), side scrapers (middle row and bottom row, second from left), oval scrapers (bottom row, right two specimens), and Dalton adz (bottom row, far left).*

unifacial end scrapers and side scrapers especially are identical to those found on Paleo-Indian sites (Coe 1964:120; Goodyear 1982:384) (fig. 2.5).

If Coe is correct, and the variety of Hardaway spear points reflects an evolution of types through time, then the earliest type, the Hardaway Blade, could date as early as Clovis in the East (Coe, personal communication; Ward 1980:63). Unfortunately, the stratigraphic record at Hardaway is unclear on this point. Daniel (1998:63–65) found that more Hardaway-Daltons than Hardaway Blades occurred in the lowest zone at Hardaway. This vertical distribution suggests that Hardaway Blades more likely represent preforms or unfinished Hardaway-Dalton points than a distinct point type.

This argument is a good one. Nonetheless, the 8500–7900 B.C. range suggested by Goodyear (1982) for the Hardaway-Dalton complex does not allow much time for the development of an assemblage as varied as Hardaway. And to add to this variety, Daniel (1998:54–55) has identified another type, the Small Dalton. Small Daltons reflect the transition from Hardaway Side Notched to Early Archaic Palmer Side Notched points. When compared to other stylistic and functional changes in spear point types during the Paleo-Indian and Archaic periods, 600 years does not seem long enough to allow for the evolution of the Hardaway complex.

During the late 1970s, Steve Claggett and John Cable excavated at two sites (31Ch29 and 31Ch8) located approximately one-half mile apart on the east side of the Haw River in Chatham County. Today, both sites lie beneath B. Everett Jordan Lake. Large-scale block excavations uncovered a stratified sequence of artifacts that generally confirmed the chronology and typology that Coe had published in 1964 and that had been refined by researchers in other states, such as Jefferson Chapman (1975, 1976) in Tennessee and Bettye Broyles (1971) in West Virginia. At 31Ch29, Hardaway-Dalton artifacts, including two spear points, were found in the lowest level, but other varieties of Hardaway points were not present in this or other levels. Unfortunately, no organic material was recovered that could be radiocarbon dated (Claggett and Cable 1982).

The only way questions regarding the age of the Hardaway complex will be resolved is with the discovery of other stratified sites containing intact deposits that can be dated using radiometric techniques. And regardless of the age of the Hardaway complex, it still represents the earliest evidence found in stratified context of humans in North Carolina.

Most researchers see the Paleo-Indian period, like the Early Archaic period, as a time of roaming bands of hunters and gatherers. In the Piedmont, they probably enjoyed a wealth of natural resources that were exploited seasonally as they became available. While some scholars have suggested that differences between interriverine and floodplain environments would have necessitated different strategies of resource exploitation (House and Ballenger 1976; Mathis 1979), these perceived differences probably are more imagined than real, and based on how the Piedmont looks today rather than what it was like 10,000 years ago (Ward 1980:68).

The Mountains

Evidence for Paleo-Indians is extremely rare in the North Carolina mountains, and no buried, stratified sites have been found. In terms of the Early and Middle Paleo-Indian subperiods, Phil Perkinson (1973:50) reported eight fluted points from the Appalachian Summit region. These were scattered from Cherokee County in the south to Ashe County in the north. Most of these specimens were made of local material, suggesting that Paleo-Indians did occupy the region and were not just passing through (Purrington 1983:108). Hardaway-Dalton specimens of the Late Paleo-Indian subperiod occur as rarely as the earlier fluted forms.

With this meager evidence, little can be said about upland subsistence and settlement patterns during Paleo-Indian times. The only observation that can be made with certainty is that the climate in the mountains was harsher than it was in the Piedmont. Delcourt and Delcourt (1981:147) suggest that a boreal forest comprised of spruce and fir persisted in the higher elevations of the southern Appalachian Summit throughout Paleo-Indian times. And, if anyone in North Carolina hunted now-extinct Pleistocene animals, they probably hunted them in the mountains where the upland environment could have attracted the large herd animals just prior to their extinction.

3. The Archaic Period
A Time of Regionalization and Specialization

William A. Ritchie, a member of the founding generation of twentieth-century American archaeologists, first used the term "Archaic" to describe the early post-Pleistocene hunting-and-gathering cultures of central New York State (Ritchie 1932; Willey and Phillips 1958:104). Shortly thereafter, the concept of an Archaic culture was adapted by many, but not all, archaeologists working throughout the eastern United States. James Ford and Gordon Willey (1941) defined Archaic as a developmental stage that preceded the origins of horticulture and the widespread use of pottery. This broad-reaching concept meant different things in different geographic regions. However, most archaeologists agreed that Archaic referred to nonagricultural cultures relying on hunting, fishing, and the gathering of wild plant foods. They also agreed that Archaic folks did not live in permanent villages and did not make pottery.

University of Michigan archaeologist James B. Griffin was one of those who initially rejected the idea of an Archaic Stage. He believed that the concept was too widely used and broadly defined to have comparative value. Griffin even tried to do away with the use of the term "Archaic" by archaeologists (Griffin 1946; Willey and Phillips 1958). Unable to convince his colleagues, Griffin (1952) compromised and redefined the Archaic as a "period" of cultural development in the eastern United States, which was divided into two subdivisions, Early and Late. Although pottery-making and horticulture were absent during both periods, the Late Archaic was distinguished from the Early Archaic by the presence of ground- and polished-stone tools, steatite bowls, and decorated bone and shell ornaments (Griffin 1952:355). While refining the Archaic chronology, Griffin also described what Archaic life may have been like. According to him, Archaic social groups were organized in small bands of twenty to thirty individuals that moved frequently within tight, well-defined territories to take advantage of seasonally available food resources. Status was achieved through individual prowess in hunting or by unique talents in curing and magic. Craft specializations were lacking. Rules of exogamy forced members of different bands to intermarry and, by doing so, extended social ties across territories and introduced new people and ideas to local groups (354–55).

Griffin's model of Archaic lifestyle has been greatly elaborated upon and refined as more information has come forth from surveys and excavations. And today archaeologists recognize a Middle Archaic period, as well as the Early and Late periods proposed by Griffin. However, much of what he had to say forty years ago is still valid today.

In 1958, Joseph R. Caldwell, a University of Chicago–trained archaeologist at the University of Georgia, published a revised version of his dissertation entitled *Trend and Tradition in the Prehistory of the Eastern United States*. Caldwell's study was one of the first to go beyond artifact styles and trait lists to understand the prehistory of the eastern United States. Taking an evolutionary, ecological approach, Caldwell outlined what he considered to be major trends in the cultural development of the East: "The history of the Eastern Woodlands can be regarded as a single structure of interrelated parts, connected in large degree as a great interaction sphere from a time as remote as the first (Archaic) period for which we have any considerable information" (vii).

Caldwell saw the beginning of the Archaic as a time dominated by highly nomadic hunters and collectors. As these nomads gradually gained familiarity with their environment, they began to use a wide variety of seasonally available food resources. Over time, the exploitation of natural foods became more productive and culminated in the development of what Caldwell called "primary forest efficiency." Groups located in areas with abundant resources began to settle into more-or-less permanent residences. There, the "seeds" of agriculture, pottery-making, and settled village life were planted (Caldwell 1958:6–13).

Today some of Caldwell's ideas, like Griffin's, have been modified and refined. New data suggest that "primary forest efficiency" existed even during the Early Archaic period when a wide variety of natural foods was harvested (e.g., Chapman 1977; Chapman and Shea 1981). However, Caldwell's work still stands as a major regional synthesis, with a broad theoretical underpinning, that was ahead of its time.

As we begin our discussion of the Archaic period in North Carolina, the reader will quickly recognize two things. First, like the preceding Paleo-Indian period, much more is known about the Piedmont than either the mountains or the coastal areas. Second, in recent years, most significant Archaic research has taken place in states that border North Carolina. As a consequence, any understanding of the Archaic period in North Carolina must rely heavily on research that has been conducted in Georgia, South Carolina, and Tennessee. David Anderson, Albert Goodyear, Glen Hanson, and Kenneth Sassaman have made major contributions working in Georgia and South Carolina, and Jefferson Chapman has conducted extensive Archaic research in southeast Tennessee (fig. 3.1).

The Archaic Period in the Piedmont

While Joseph Caldwell was writing his synthesis of the archaeology of the eastern Woodlands, most Archaic research in the Southeast focused on rockshelter excavations. These sites were chosen for study because alkaline deposits often found in caves and rock shelters helped preserve organic remains like animal bones. At the Stanfield-Worley Bluff Shelter in northern Alabama, David DeJarnette of the University of Alabama and his team excavated over 5,000 fragments of animal bones from an Early Archaic level. Excavators at the nearby Russell Cave site found equally good preservation conditions. Both sites also contributed a rich array of artifacts and features as well as numerous radiocarbon dates for the Archaic period (DeJarnette, Kurjack, and Cambron 1962; Griffin 1974).

Unfortunately, the advantages that rock shelters have because of good preservation conditions are overshadowed by one glaring disadvantage: The cramped living spaces protected by the rock overhangs virtually assured that each group occupying the shelter would severely disturb the living surface of the preceding group. The preparation of storage, cooking, and burial pits further ensured that the remains from previous occupations would be thoroughly churned and mixed. Rodent burrows are also notorious in rock shelters for creating a stratigraphic nightmare for archaeologists (cf. Griffin 1974:9-10). Because of these disturbances, early rock-shelter excavations in the Southeast did not prove to be particularly productive in defining long chronological sequences (cf. Goodyear 1982:387-88).

Recognizing the stratigraphic turmoil found in most rock shelters, archaeologist began to search for deeply buried, stratified sites in alluvial floodplains. In North Carolina, this task was begun by Herbert Doerschuk along the banks of the Yadkin-Pee Dee River in the southern Piedmont. Doerschuk, an avocational archaeologist from Badin, North Carolina, led Joffre Coe to many of the sites that would ultimately become landmarks in North Carolina archaeology. Through controlled excavations at the Doerschuk and Lowder's Ferry sites, and

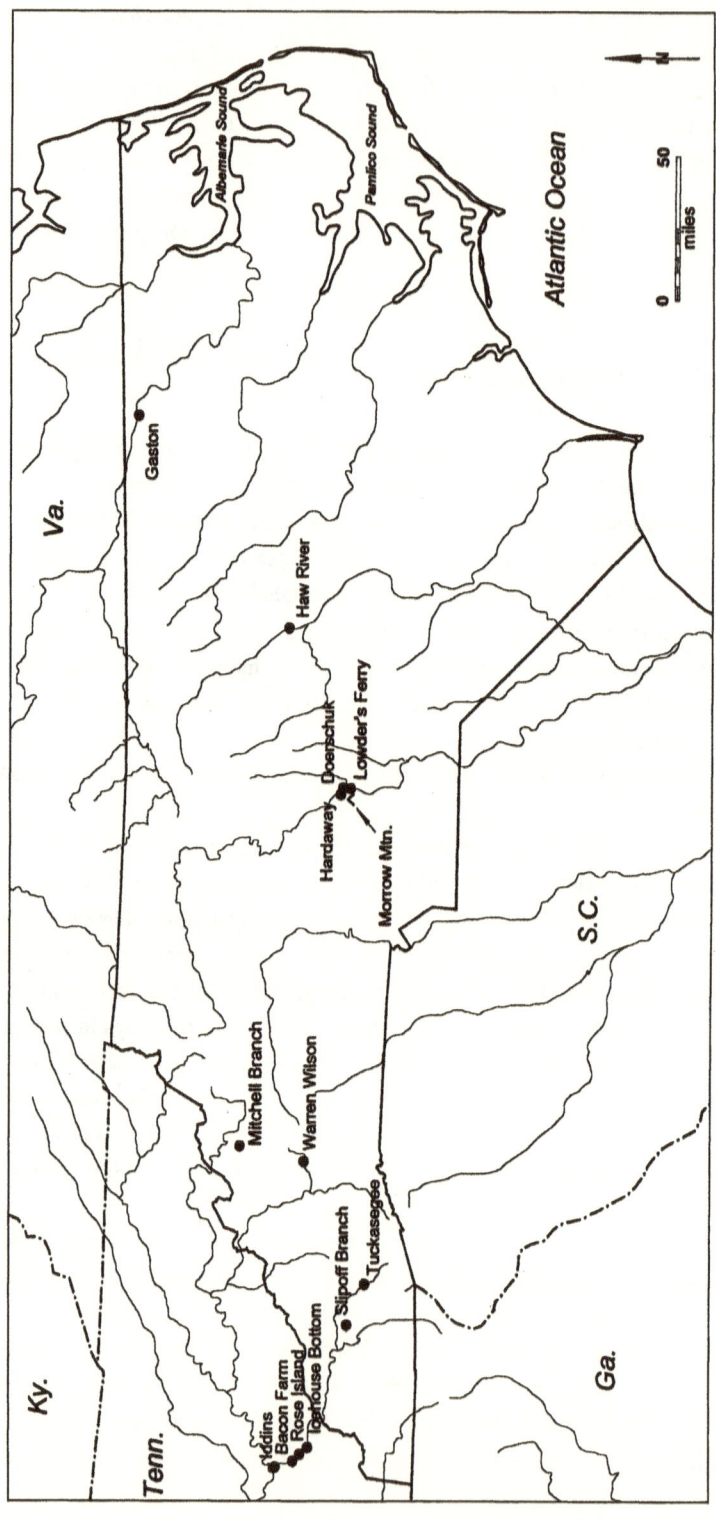

FIGURE 3.1. *Map of North Carolina showing Paleo-Indian and Archaic sites discussed in the text.*

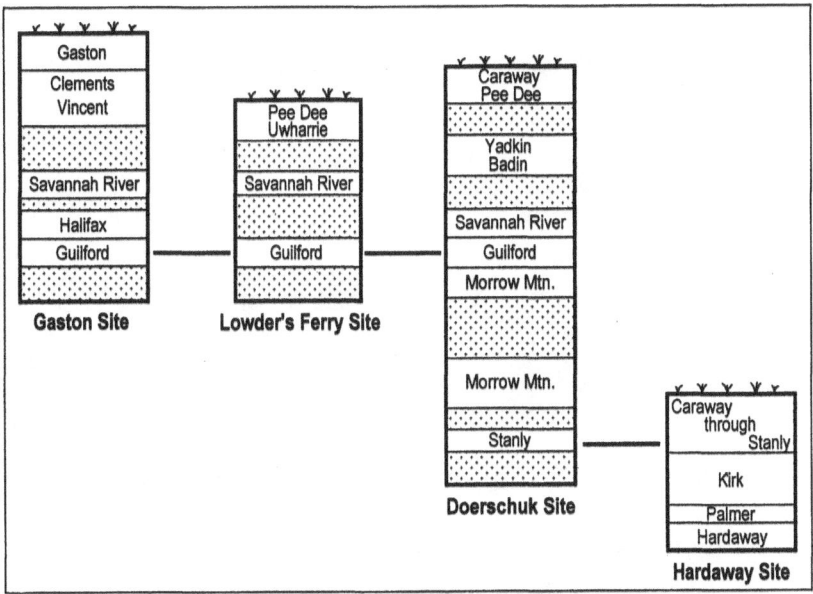

FIGURE 3.2. *Chronological sequence for the Archaic period in Piedmont North Carolina as constructed from stratigraphic excavations at the Gaston, Lowder's Ferry, Doerschuk, and Hardaway sites. (Based on Coe 1964:123)*

at the nearby upland site of Hardaway, Coe (1964) established the cultural sequence that still serves as the chronological backbone of the Archaic period in North Carolina and throughout much of the eastern United States (figs. 3.2 and 3.3).

Early Archaic Period (8000–6000 B.C.)

The Early Archaic is generally viewed as the period when native populations began to adapt to an environment created by Holocene climatic conditions—conditions very similar to those of today and unlike the colder weather of the late Pleistocene. Big game animals had disappeared and groups of hunter-gatherers began to follow more general subsistence pursuits. The available subsistence information, though sparse, suggests that plant food collection focused on hickory nuts and acorns (Chapman and Shea 1981). Although no Early Archaic animal remains have been uncovered in North Carolina, archaeologists presume that the white-tailed deer provided the main source of meat. Subsistence strategies on the Piedmont probably changed little from those of the Late Paleo-Indian subperiod. However, Early Archaic tool kits did change. New

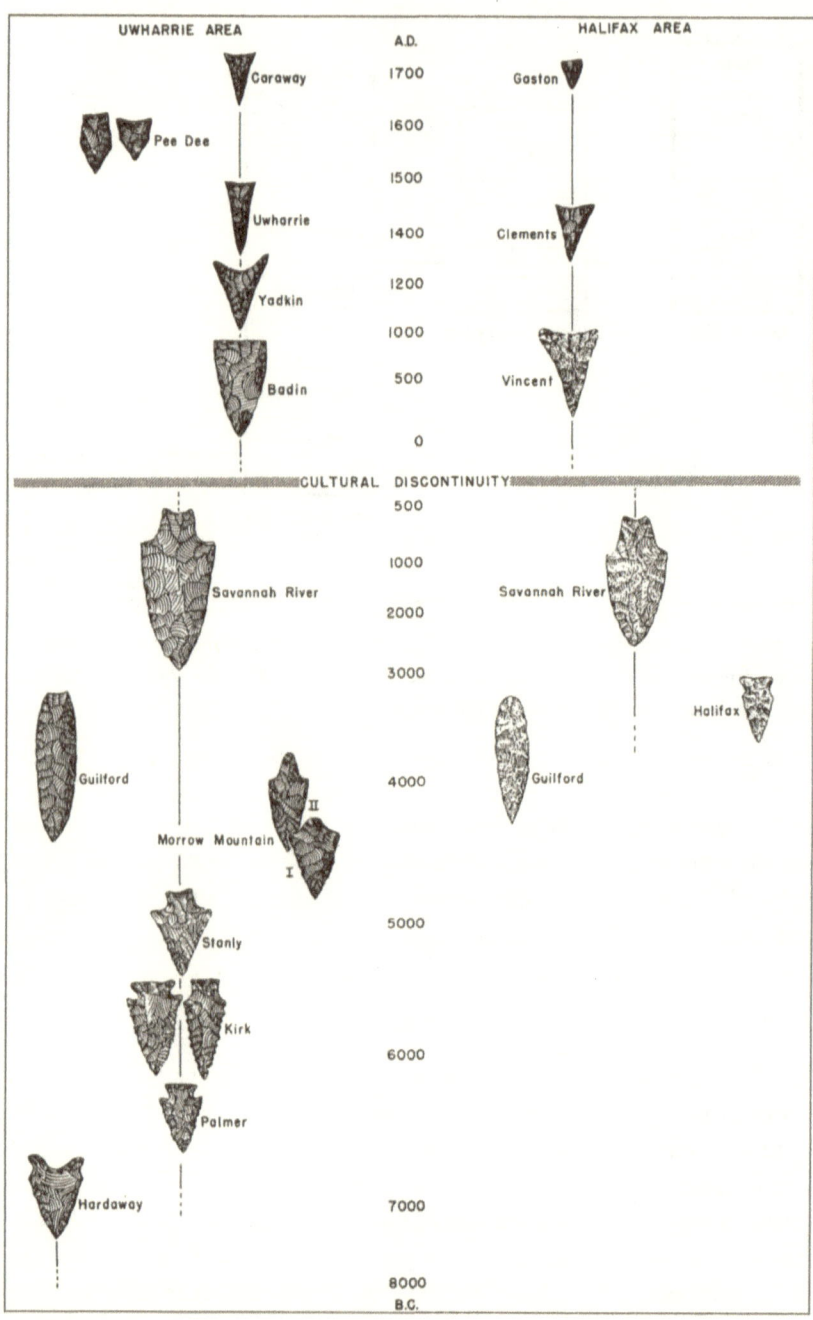

FIGURE 3.3. *Joffre Coe's delineation of the projectile point traditions for the North Carolina Piedmont, based on stratigraphic excavations at the Gaston, Lowder's Ferry, Doerschuk, and Hardaway sites. (From Coe 1964:121)*

ways of attaching spear points to their shafts resulted in marked changes in the way the points were made. Also, the number of Early Archaic sites across the state increased dramatically, suggesting an increase in the overall population.

In the North Carolina Piedmont, the Hardaway site provided the first excavated clues of an Early Archaic occupation. Between 1948 and 1957, several frustrating attempts were made to sort out the Hardaway stratigraphy. Success was finally achieved in 1958 (see Chapter 2) when four natural soil zones were identified in a 20' section of a previously excavated trench. The 1958 excavations proceeded using these zones, rather than arbitrary levels, as the vertical control units. Hardaway-type spear points of the Late Paleo-Indian subperiod were found in the lowest soil zones, whereas Early Archaic points with triangular blades and corner-notched bases were recovered from the upper zones (Coe 1964:61).

Coe (1964:67–70) originally separated Early Archaic corner-notched points into two types—Palmer Corner Notched and Kirk Corner Notched—based upon size and the presence or absence of basal grinding (fig. 3.4). Palmer points are generally smaller and have U-shaped notches. The bases are usually straight and are always smoothed by edge-grinding. Kirk points are similar in form, but they are larger and lack edge-grinding along the base.

While reanalyzing the Hardaway materials, Randy Daniel identified a transitional type of spear point that resembles both Hardaway and Palmer points. This transitional form was recognized by excavators during the 1970s and casually referred to as "Hardapalmers." In his formal description, Daniel labeled these transitional points "Small Daltons" to reflect their similarity to points of the widespread Early Archaic Dalton culture of the Midwest and southeastern United States (1998:54; Goodyear 1974).

Today, researchers recognize that basal grinding is not always helpful in distinguishing between Palmer and Kirk spear points. Bettye Broyles, working at the St. Albans site on the Kanawha River in West Virginia, discovered small Palmer-like points whose bases were not ground (Broyles 1971:63). Jefferson Chapman, excavating at the Icehouse Bottom site in the lower Little Tennessee River valley, also found that basal grinding was not associated exclusively with the earliest corner-notched spear points. In fact, Chapman (1977:53) suggested that the Palmer type probably should be subsumed within a more broadly defined Kirk Corner Notched Cluster. At the Haw River site in Chatham County, North Carolina, researchers found that although Early Archaic corner-notched points seemed to increase in size through time, many of the larger forms still displayed ground bases. Instead of eliminating the Palmer type, as Chapman suggested, John Cable recommended eliminating the Kirk Corner Notched type (Claggett and Cable 1982:381–82).

FIGURE 3.4. *Small Dalton (or "Hardapalmer") (bottom row), Palmer Corner Notched (third row), and Kirk Corner Notched (top row, left two specimens, and second row) spear points and chipped-stone drills (top row, right two specimens) from the Hardaway site.*

Daniel (1998:59) has suggested looking at other criteria for differentiating between Palmer and Kirk points, rather than lumping them together. One thing he observed was that the tangs on Palmer points are less pronounced than those on Kirk points, giving the Palmer specimens a "stubbier" appearance. This attribute can be statistically expressed by comparing the ratios of tang length to tang width. Palmer points have a consistently smaller ratio than Kirk points.

These differences of opinion highlight the considerable variability in the way Early Archaic spear points were made and used. What might be a distinguishing attribute in one region may not be in another. Variations in form and shape may reflect changes through time, differences in the way contemporary specimens were used and resharpened, or even the type or quality of stone used. Even within the Piedmont, considerable variability exists, as evidenced by Claggett and Cable's findings at the Haw River sites in the central Piedmont and Coe's results from the Hardaway site in the southern Piedmont.

In addition to spear points, several kinds of scraping and cutting tools have been recovered from Early Archaic contexts in the Piedmont. During the Palmer phase (about 8000–7000 B.C.), small and well-made end scrapers characteristic of the Late Paleo-Indian subperiod continued to be used. Scrapers of the Kirk phase (about 7000–6000 B.C.) were more crudely made and vary greatly in size and form. These scraping tools were used primarily to prepare animal skins for use as clothing and containers. Adzes, gravers, drills, and perforators were added to the Early Archaic tool kit for working wood, hides, and animal bones into a variety of tools and ornaments. Fist-sized river cobbles were used as hammers and anvils to fashion other stone tools or to crush and grind plant and animal resources into food products. Ground-stone tools have rarely been found in an Early Archaic context (Coe 1964; Daniel 1994, 1998).

Archaeologists agree that Early Archaic inhabitants of the Piedmont were organized into small, mobile bands of hunter-gatherers. But there is debate regarding the extent of the territories exploited by these bands and the reasons they moved around so much. Some researchers believe that Early Archaic bands, consisting of between 50 and 150 people, ranged over entire drainage systems, extending from the Piedmont to the coast (Anderson and Hanson 1988). In North Carolina these territories included the Catawba-Wateree, Yadkin–Pee Dee, Cape Fear, and Neuse River basins (fig. 3.5).

This drainage-based settlement-subsistence model can be summarized as follows: During the winter, when plant and animal food resources were patchy and unpredictable, bands occupied relatively stable base camps in the Coastal Plain or along the fall line. These camps were supplied by small groups who regularly foraged for whatever resources that were immediately available. Dur-

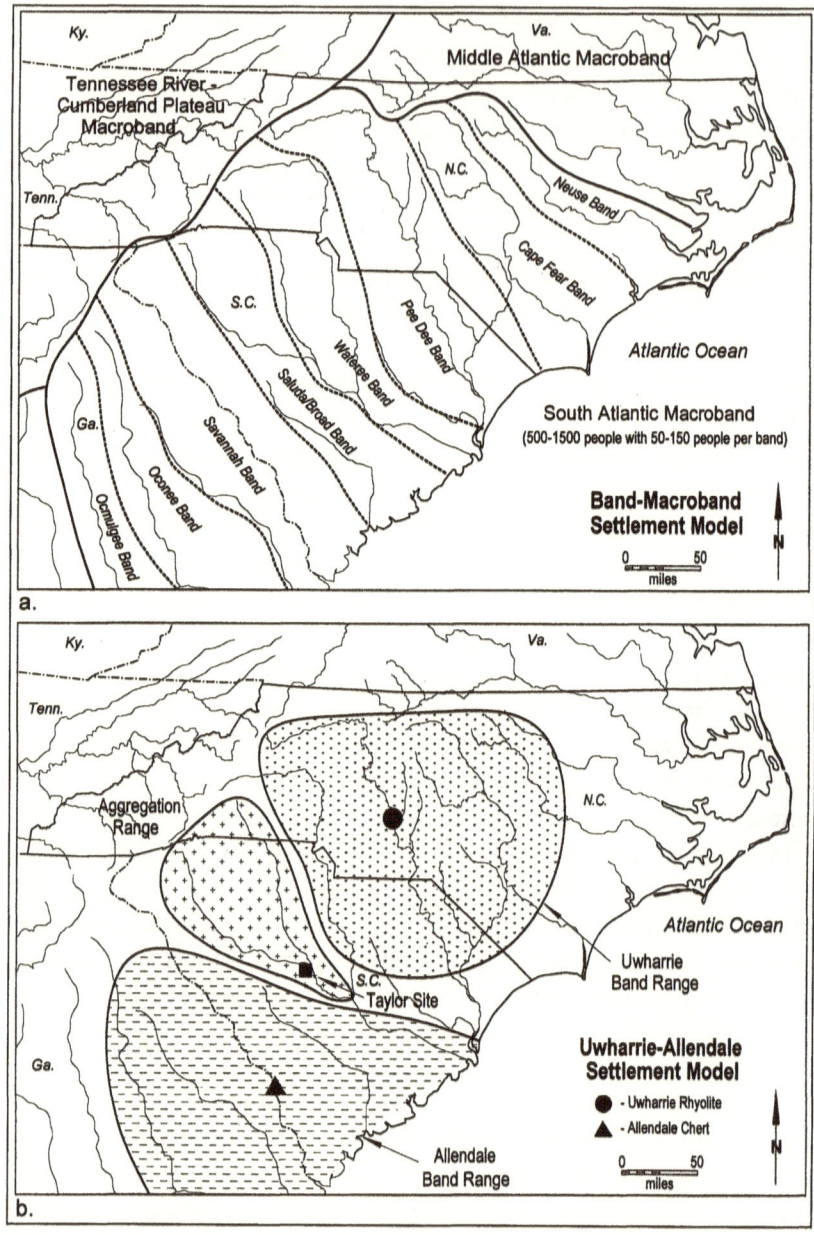

FIGURE 3.5. *Models of Archaic settlement proposed for North Carolina, South Carolina, and Georgia by Anderson and Hanson (1985) (a) and Daniel (1994) (b).*

ing the early spring, the base camps broke up, and the bands moved toward the coast to take advantage of ripening plant foods. By late spring, they moved back into the upper Coastal Plain; by the late summer and fall months, they again moved upstream into the Piedmont. Depending on the kinds and availability of plant and animal food resources, the bands may have moved en masse at times and dispersed into smaller family units at other times. Contacts between bands from different drainages, though not frequent, occurred periodically to facilitate the exchange of information and marriage partners (Anderson and Hanson 1988:267–71).

Randy Daniel has recently questioned the primary role of food resource availability in establishing Early Archaic settlement patterns in the Piedmont. Because food resources were relatively abundant in most areas of the Southeast, and the Piedmont in particular, Daniel believes that the restricted distribution of good-quality stone for making tools was more important in determining band territories and movement. Rather than seasonally determined movements within the major drainage basins, Daniel suggests that bands readily moved between drainages in their quests for stone that could be easily chipped into spear points, scrapers, and other tools. Early Archaic (and later) people found a major source of the raw material they were looking for in the massive rhyolite outcrops of the Uwharrie Mountains in the southern Piedmont. Early Archaic artifacts made from Uwharrie rhyolite have been found throughout the Carolina Piedmont. Daniel believes that small bands with shifting territories were "tethered" to the Uwharrie Mountain rhyolite sources throughout the Early Archaic period (1998:202–4).

Many of the ideas archaeologists have about how Early Archaic people lived are based on studies of contemporary hunter-gatherer groups living in marginal environmental regions with limited resources (Anderson and Hanson 1988; Binford 1980; Claggett and Cable 1982). Some researchers have questioned the applicability of studies using these groups as analogs for explaining Early Archaic settlement patterns in the Piedmont (e.g., Daniel 1994, 1998; Ward 1983). All evidence suggests that the Piedmont provided a varied, and relatively evenly distributed, resource base throughout the Early Archaic period. Extensive stands of oaks, hickories, and chestnuts would have provided a bountiful supply of nuts and mast, while several understory and edge species would have produced a variety of fruits and berries. These forests also provided a rich habitat for an assortment of wildlife, including deer, bear, turkey, and a multitude of small mammals. The numerous streams were filled with fish, turtles, and mollusks, and these species also would have attracted huge flocks of migratory fowl. In short, the North Carolina Piedmont would have offered a cornucopia of plant and animal foods for hungry hunters and gatherers. There is no doubt that these groups were small, probably in the 50–150 range suggested by Anderson and Hanson. But given the abundant resources of the Piedmont, we can question whether or not it was necessary for them to roam over large territories on a tight seasonal schedule in order to survive (Ward 1983:69).

As is the case with Paleo-Indian studies of settlement and subsistence, many of the ideas archaeologists have about Early Archaic adaptations in North Carolina are little more than speculation. Most of the research so far has focused on the development and refinement of chronologies. Studies that have gone beyond temporal issues and looked at how the people lived—the size of their social groups, what they ate, and how they used their environment—have had to rely on a fragmentary and foggy record of indirect evidence to answer these questions. Until better-preserved sites are discovered, we will never know for sure how large, how mobile, or how socially complex these Early Archaic groups were.

Middle Archaic Period (6000–3000 B.C.)

In the North Carolina Piedmont, the Middle Archaic period has been divided into three phases: Stanly, Morrow Mountain, and Guilford. These divisions are based on distinctive styles of spear points originally identified at the Lowder's Ferry site (31St7) in Stanly County and the Doerschuk site (31Mg22) in Montgomery County (Coe 1964).

Although the Lowder's Ferry site never achieved the recognition of Hardaway and Doerschuk, it was the first to be excavated. The site is located on the west bank of the Yadkin River, directly across from the Yadkin's confluence with the Uwharrie River. Today, much of the Lowder's Ferry site is under a parking lot that services a boat ramp in Morrow Mountain State Park.

During the summer of 1948, Paul Strieff, who had been a graduate student at the University of Michigan with Joffre Coe, tested the Lowder's Ferry site and determined that buried Archaic deposits were present. In March 1949, the parking lot area was mechanically graded, exposing the tops of several Late Prehistoric aboriginal pits. Work on the parking lot was halted temporarily while Coe and six University of North Carolina students conducted a two-day salvage excavation (Coe 1949:20).

Because of the richness of the Lowder's Ferry site, construction of the parking lot was delayed further, and archaeological excavations continued in the graded area during the summer of 1949. These excavations focused on the Archaic levels of the site. James Wood, a UNC student, was hired to supervise the work. Before Wood left in August, five trenches had been excavated across the area that had been graded the previous spring.

Barton Wright, a student from the University of Arizona, continued the excavations at Lowder's Ferry in September 1949. Although Wright was hired to supervise excavations at Town Creek, located some twenty miles away, his first assignment was to finish the salvage operation at Lowder's Ferry (Coe 1995:25). Wright continued trenching the site, excavated several small test pits, and opened a large block excavation adjacent to Wood's first trench. By the time the Lowder's Ferry excavations were completed in December, Wright had developed a clear understanding of the stratigraphy and was able to separate a Middle Archaic Guilford level from a Late Archaic Savannah River level. Both components were found primarily within a deeply buried reddish soil zone sandwiched between two layers of almost sterile yellow sand (Drye 1998; notes on file, Research Laboratories of Archaeology).

Herbert Doerschuk discovered the site that would be named after him in 1928. The Doerschuk site is located on the east bank of the Yadkin River near the Falls Dam, two miles upstream from the Lowder's Ferry site. In 1948, Joffre Coe and Paul Strieff, who was working at Lowder's Ferry at the time, excavated a small test pit at Doerschuk. The following year Coe took James Wood and "two high school boys from Albemarle" back to the Doerschuk site to expand the test pit he and Strieff had excavated earlier (Coe 1964) (fig. 3.6).

The Doerschuk site was everything Lowder's Ferry was and more. Again, Late Archaic Savannah River and Middle Archaic Guilford materials were found beneath ceramic-bearing zones. However, more deeply buried archaeological deposits also were present. Beneath the Guilford zone were zones that contained Morrow Mountain– and Stanly-type spear points (fig. 3.7).

The Doerschuk site excavations suggested that the Stanly phase ushered in the beginning of the Middle Archaic period in the North Carolina Piedmont. The most diagnostic Stanly artifact is a stemmed spear point, which is quite different from the corner-notched specimens of the Early Archaic. Stanly Stemmed points are characterized by broad triangular blades with small, basally notched, square stems. They have been described as being shaped like a Christmas tree (Coe 1964:35). Morrow Mountain points, on the other hand, have tapered stems and triangular blades. The Guilford phase is characterized by lanceolate-shaped spear points with long, narrow, thick blades and straight, rounded, or concave bases (37–43) (fig. 3.8).

Excavations by South (1959a) at the Gaston site (31Hx7), located in Halifax County on the Roanoke River, also uncovered a deeply buried Middle Archaic component that underlay a Late Archaic zone. In addition to Guilford Lanceolate points, like those from Doerschuk, the Gaston site produced a new style of Middle Archaic point, called Halifax Side Notched. These points are similar to Guilford points except they are usually shorter and have very shallow side

FIGURE 3.6. *View of the 1949 stratigraphic excavation at the Doerschuk site. (Courtesy of the Research Laboratories of Archaeology)*

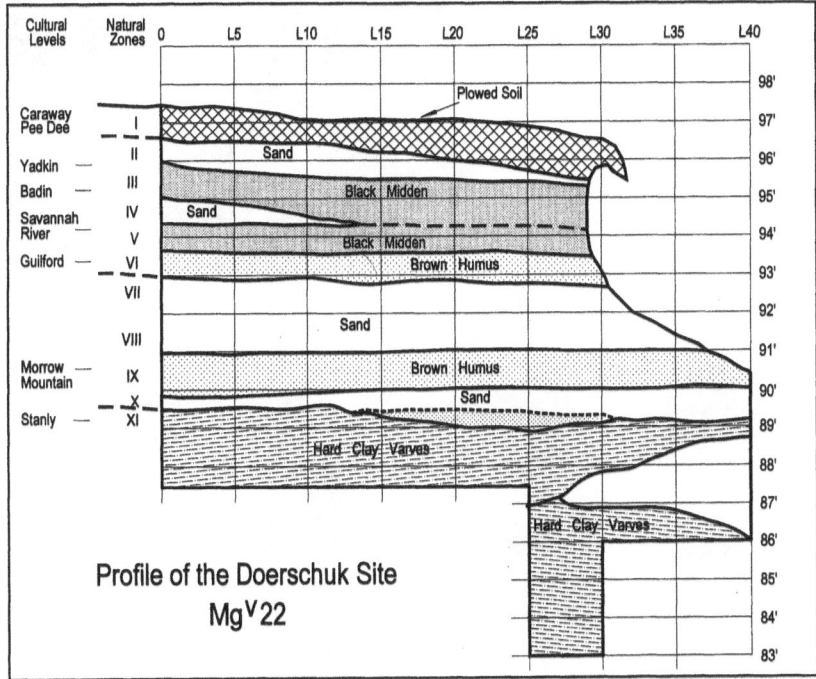

FIGURE 3.7. *Soil profile from the 1949 excavation at the Doerschuk site showing the natural stratigraphy and cultural levels. (Based on Coe 1964:22)*

notches. Although no clear stratigraphic separation was found at the Gaston site, Coe believed that the Halifax specimens, which he had radiocarbon-dated to the mid-fourth millennium B.C., occurred slightly later than the Guilford phase (1964:95–99) (fig. 3.8).

Initially, archaeologists believed that the differences between Stanly spear points and the Morrow Mountain, Guilford, and Halifax types reflected the sequential arrival of groups with different cultural traditions (Coe 1964:54–55). Looking at the same specimens today with a clearer understanding of how these stone tools were made, used, and refurbished, there appear to be more similarities than differences among the Stanly, Morrow Mountain, Guilford, and Halifax projectile point traditions. In particular, a close stylistic relationship seems to exist between Stanly and Morrow Mountain points and between Guilford, Halifax, and Savannah River points. These similarities suggest cultural continuity rather than discontinuity. The results of more recent excavations, such as those of Chapman (1985) and Claggett and Cable (1982), appear to support this interpretation. And even at the Doerschuk site, which contained deeply buried cultural strata, the various Middle Archaic types were found mixed together

FIGURE 3.8. *Stanly Stemmed (bottom row), Morrow Mountain I Stemmed (third row, left two specimens), Morrow Mountain II Stemmed (third row, right two specimens), and Guilford Lanceolate (second row) projectile points from the Doerschuk site and Halifax Side Notched projectile points (top row) from the Gaston site.*

throughout most of the deposits, suggesting some stylistic overlap and a degree of contemporaneity (Coe 1964:34–35).

Evidence for the use of the atlatl, or spear-thrower, is first seen during the Stanly phase. Fragments of stone weights that were attached to their handles were found associated with Stanly points at the Doerschuk site. Atlatl weights have not been found in Morrow Mountain or Guilford phase contexts in the North Carolina Piedmont. However, crude chipped-stone axes with lateral hafting notches have been recovered with Guilford spear points at the Gaston site (Coe 1964:113). Other than these two innovations, there does not appear to be much that stands out about Middle Archaic tool assemblages.

Except for spear points, atlatl weights, and the axes mentioned above, there were few formal tools. Scraping and cutting tasks were accomplished with simple, ad hoc, or "expedient" tools that show little evidence of sharpening or shaping. These usually consist of flakes of stone that were removed from larger fragments, or cores. After being used, the flakes were discarded without further modification (Blanton and Sassaman 1989:64; Claggett and Cable 1982).

The sites on which these discarded Middle Archaic tools occur are numerous and appear to represent mostly temporary encampments. They occur across the landscape without any obvious preference for particular environmental niches. In the South Carolina Piedmont, Blanton and Sassaman (1989:61–62) have noted that Middle Archaic sites are more numerous in interriverine zones, but they are larger and more extensive in floodplain settings. They suggest that these differences in size and frequency of occurrence probably are the result of landform differences and reoccupation. Middle Archaic groups reoccupying the same locales over several years could "spread out" more easily along the flat topography of a floodplain than they could on a more restricted ridge top. Blanton and Sassaman also note that in South Carolina, more Middle Archaic sites are located in the Piedmont than in the Coastal Plain. For whatever reasons, the same appears true in North Carolina.

The simple but ubiquitous tool assemblages associated with the Middle Archaic period are believed to reflect a foraging kind of subsistence. Site distributions suggest that small, kin-related groups moved as a unit from place to place to obtain food and other resources. Some archaeologists believe that this new settlement and subsistence pattern was caused by a change in climatic conditions that occurred at the end of the Early Archaic period. This change is referred to as the Altithermal or Climatic Optimum, a time when the weather became drier and warmer (Wendland and Bryson 1974). The Altithermal began around 6000 B.C. and lasted until around 2000 B.C. These climatic conditions created a patchy, less predictable environment that required flexible and inventive subsistence strategies. By allowing groups to move easily among a variety of resources as they became available, foraging was ideally adapted to the Altithermal environment (Claggett and Cable 1982:671–88).

Late Archaic Period (3000–1000 B.C.)

As climatic conditions improved, population dramatically increased and there was a gradual trend toward more sedentary life. This period is known as the Late Archaic. In the North Carolina Piedmont, it is difficult to walk over any plowed field with a nearby source of water and not find evidence of a Late Archaic campsite. Although Late Archaic sites are numerous in Piedmont North Carolina, the full spectrum of Late Archaic culture is not seen here. One has to travel to the south Atlantic coast, where large shell middens with cooking hearths, sand floors, and human and dog burials occur, to see the evidence of the socially complex, semipermanent settlements of a vigorous culture unlike any before. Or one could travel to Georgia, Alabama, Tennessee, and Kentucky where the broad shoals of the Savannah, Tennessee, and Green Rivers are lined by equally impressive middens of freshwater mollusk remains (Claflin 1931; Webb 1946; Webb and DeJarnette 1942). It is at sites like these that pottery first appeared and native plants were gradually domesticated.

The most characteristic artifact of the Late Archaic period is a large, broadbladed spear point with a square stem, called Savannah River Stemmed (fig. 3.9). This name comes from the Stallings Island site on the Georgia side of the Savannah River, where the broad-bladed spear points were first recognized in a Late Archaic context (Claflin 1931). In reality, these "points" were probably multipurpose tools used for a variety of cutting tasks, as well as tips for spears. In the Carolina Piedmont, these large, stemmed points became smaller through time, culminating in a type called Small Savannah River Stemmed (Oliver 1985:204). Savannah River points are the index fossil for the Late Archaic period from New York to Florida.

In addition to making spear points, Late Archaic peoples used hammerstones to peck and grind hard granitic rocks into axes with grooves for hafting (fig. 3.10). They also made a variety of scrapers, drills, and other chippedstone tools, as well as polished-stone weights for atlatls. Seeds and nuts were ground with stone mortars, and the use of fish nets is attested to by the presence of notched stone pebbles that served as netsinkers (Chapman 1981:48; Davis 1990:225).

Where available, steatite, or soapstone, was a favorite raw material. At first, this soft stone was used primarily for making atlatl weights and as "cooking stones," which were small perforated slabs of soapstone that were first heated and then placed in perishable vessels containing soups and stews. This indirect-

FIGURE 3.9. *Savannah River Stemmed projectile points from the Doerschuk site.*

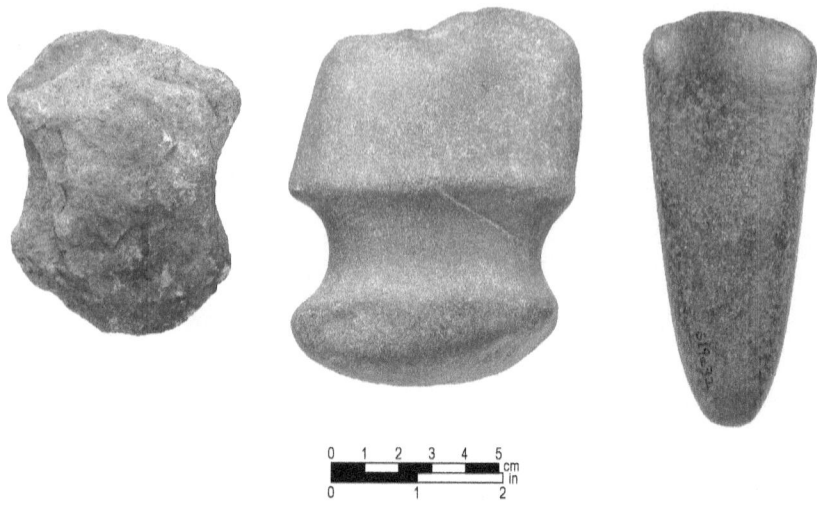

FIGURE 3.10. *Chipped-stone and ground-stone axes from North Carolina: Middle Archaic Guilford axe from Northampton County (left), Late Archaic grooved axe from Nash County (center), and Late Woodland celt from the Gaston site (right).*

cooking technique was used at a time when such containers were made of hides, baskets, wood, and gourds. During the latter half of the Late Archaic period, hemispherical bowls were pecked and carved from soapstone, and cooking directly over a fire replaced the indirect-cooking method (Coe 1964:123; Wood et al. 1986:324) (fig. 3.11). Along the coasts of Florida and South Carolina, the first pottery vessels were invented at the end of the Late Archaic period, and these soon became popular throughout the eastern United States (Stoltman 1974).

Squash and gourds were cultivated as early as the third millennium B.C., and by the end of the Late Archaic period, sunflower, maygrass, and chenopodium were selectively harvested as a precursor to active cultivation (Chapman and Shea 1981; Yarnell and Black 1985).

Many Late Archaic sites in the North Carolina Piedmont represent small, temporary camps, but others suggest more permanent occupations. Although large shell middens, like those found elsewhere, do not occur in the Piedmont, at the Doerschuk, Lowder's Ferry, and Gaston sites, thick, organically stained soil zones reflect an occupation intensity unlike that of the preceding Early Archaic and Middle Archaic periods. Small, circular pit hearths, lined with stones, further suggest a degree of permanence not observed during earlier occupations (Coe 1964:119).

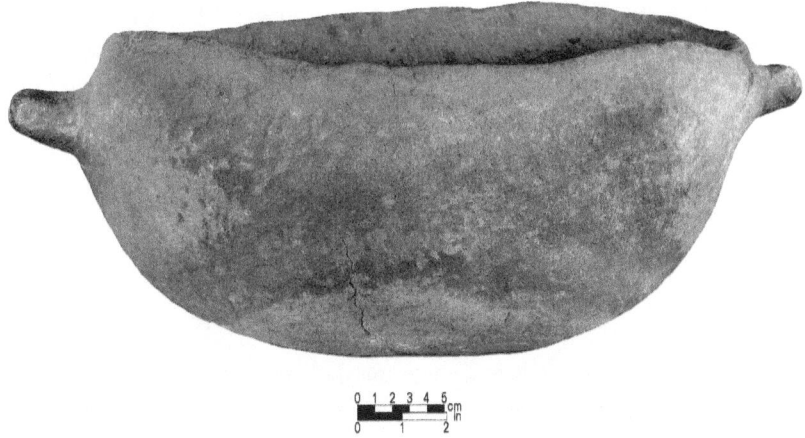

FIGURE 3.11. *A Late Archaic soapstone bowl from Mecklenburg County.*

Although no food remains have been analyzed from a Late Archaic context in the North Carolina Piedmont, indirect evidence points to a varied diet. Base camps represented by sites with thick midden zones, like Doerschuk, Lowder's Ferry, and Gaston, are all located along major streams. This suggests that fish, turtles, and migratory water fowl, if not the freshwater mussels enjoyed by other Late Archaic groups, were important seasonal resources. The small, temporary camps that dot the interriverine uplands point to an equally important reliance on hunting-and-gathering activities. No doubt white-tail deer, bear, and small mammals were regularly hunted, while acorns, hickory nuts, and a variety of wild fruits and berries were seasonally gathered. By Late Archaic times, Caldwell's "primary forest efficiency" (1958) had been realized in the North Carolina Piedmont, and groups living in areas rich in natural resources began to settle into more permanent residences.

The Archaic Period in the Mountains

Very little Archaic period research has been conducted in the Appalachian Summit region. Few sites have been excavated with Archaic components, and even fewer have been reported. The Warren Wilson site (31Bn29), located in Buncombe County, and the Tuckasegee site (31Jk12), located in Jackson County, contained Archaic strata beneath Late Prehistoric and Historic occupations. At both sites, the later components were the main focus of study, although Bennie Keel did analyze several units from the Warren Wilson site that contained

Archaic materials. He also reported on the much smaller Archaic excavation at the Tuckasegee site (1976). While at Appalachian State University, Burt Purrington excavated Slipoff Branch, a Middle Archaic site, in Swain County and the Mitchell Branch site, an Early Archaic site, in Yancey County (Purrington 1980, 1981). These few reports represent most of the published record from excavated Archaic sites in the North Carolina mountains.

In contrast, extensive Archaic period research has been carried out in neighboring southeastern Tennessee. Between 1967 and 1979, Jefferson Chapman and his colleagues from the University of Tennessee at Knoxville conducted surveys and excavations along the lower Little Tennessee River, prior to its inundation by the Tellico Reservoir (Chapman 1977, 1985). At some sites, preservation was remarkably good, and Chapman's research has contributed more to our understanding of the Archaic period in the Southeast than anyone's since Coe's (1964) work in the North Carolina Piedmont. The close proximity of the lower Little Tennessee River to the heart of the North Carolina mountains makes Chapman's research especially important to North Carolina archaeologists.

Although several surveys have been conducted since 1972 as a result of cultural resource–management requirements, only a few of the reports from these surveys have been published, and the information they provide usually consists of descriptive temporal assessments that rely on the Archaic chronology of the Piedmont. An exception to this generalization is the Great Smoky Mountains National Park survey conducted in 1975 by Quentin Bass, then a graduate student at the University of Tennessee, Knoxville. Bass began his study by analyzing materials that had previously been collected in the park between 1936 and 1941 by George McPherson and Hiram Wilburn. McPherson was the park surveyor and Wilburn served as park historian during this period. In all, Bass studied 205 sites, most located on the North Carolina side of the Great Smoky Mountains Park. Bass's research is important because he went beyond the simple chronological ordering of the sites and developed ideas regarding settlement and subsistence changes during the Archaic period (1977).

The Appalachian Summit region presented an environment to Archaic hunters and gatherers that was very different from that of the Piedmont and Coastal Plain. The rugged topography has some of the highest peaks east of the Rocky Mountains. The higher elevations range from 4,000 to 6,000 feet and are characterized by gaps, ridges, knobs, and knolls. Lower elevations consist of steep slopes, often narrow valleys, and floodplains. The Appalachian Summit has been aptly referred to as a "sprawling confusion of mountain ranges" (Dickens 1976:4). Obviously this roller-coaster terrain had a dramatic effect on how the region was used—or not used—by Native Americans during the Archaic period.

Early Archaic Period (8000–6000 B.C.)

No deeply buried, undisturbed Early Archaic components have been excavated in the North Carolina mountains, although Burt Purrington reported a single-component Kirk phase site, the Mitchell Branch site, located in the uplands of Yancey County. This site was shallow and disturbed but contained artifacts similar to those described by Chapman (1977, 1978) from Early Archaic contexts in the lower Little Tennessee River valley. A Kirk Corner Notched spear point was found along with two scrapers, a few flake tools, and a possible mano (Purrington 1980, 1983:110–11).

As mentioned earlier, the Early Archaic materials from southeastern Tennessee differ from those recovered from the Hardaway site in the North Carolina Piedmont. The earliest points from the Icehouse Bottom, Rose Island, and Bacon Farm sites, although corner-notched, were not basally ground like the Palmer type described by Coe (1964). Chapman (1977:52–53) designated this type "Lower Kirk," whereas later corner-notched specimens, sometimes with ground bases, were designated "Upper Kirk." Also, the latter half of the Early Archaic period in eastern Tennessee is marked by a tradition of side-notched and stemmed spear points with bifurcated bases. These have been referred to as St. Albans Side Notched, LeCroy Bifurcated Stemmed, and Kanawha Stemmed (Broyles 1966; Chapman 1975).

Early Archaic Kirk Corner Notched and bifurcated point types also were found by Bass in his survey of the Great Smoky Mountains National Park. Over 90 percent of these specimens were made from nonlocal cherts that are found in outcrops in eastern Tennessee. This pattern suggested to Bass that Early Archaic groups established only temporary camps in the rugged Appalachian Summit region while maintaining more permanent base camps in the Ridge and Valley province of east Tennessee. Most of the Early Archaic sites were located in high, upland areas and produced a wide range of tools reflecting hunting, butchering, hideworking, and woodworking activities (Bass 1977:51, 67). A similar distribution of Early Archaic upland sites has been noted in the upper Watauga valley (Purrington 1983:113).

Bass's ideas regarding Early Archaic settlement patterns is reinforced by Chapman's Tellico Reservoir research. At the Bacon Farm, Icehouse Bottom, and Rose Island sites, located in the Little Tennessee River valley, evidence of relatively large, repeatedly occupied, residential base camps was found. Sites like these probably represent the home bases of bands who periodically split into smaller, more mobile, units to explore and exploit the uplands of the rugged Appalachian Summit.

In addition to butchering and hideworking tools, manos, grinding stones, and other food-processing implements were found at sites interpreted as base camps, indicating a wide range of activities and more permanent residences. Also, large quantities of charred acorn and hickory nut fragments were recovered. More permanent occupations were further suggested by the presence of prepared clay hearths, 2 to 3 feet in diameter and shaped like "pancakes." Impressions of basketry and textiles were present on the surfaces of some of the hearths. These impressions provide the earliest well-dated evidence of weaving in eastern North America (Chapman 1975, 1977, 1978; Chapman and Adovasio 1977:624).

Middle Archaic Period (6000–3000 B.C.)

The Middle Archaic period in the North Carolina mountains is indicated by the occurrence of Stanly Stemmed, Morrow Mountain Stemmed, and Guilford Lanceolate spear points. In contrast to Early Archaic tools, most Middle Archaic specimens were made from locally available rock, either quartzite or vein quartz (Bass 1977:71). Stone atlatl weights provide the first concrete evidence for the use of the atlatl. Stone netsinkers also were first used, suggesting an increasing importance in fishing (Chapman 1985; Davis 1990).

The spatial distribution of Middle Archaic sites also contrasts with that of earlier sites. During the Great Smoky Mountains survey, Bass found that almost half of the Middle Archaic sites were located in upland areas, whereas the others were located in valleys and coves. A similar pattern was found in the Tellico Reservoir. Most Middle Archaic settlements consisted of dispersed camps situated on a variety of valley and upland landforms. Although a few larger sites were found on terraces adjacent to the Little Tennessee River, they were not characteristic (Chapman 1977; Davis 1990). This dispersed settlement pattern is similar to that described for the Haw River valley in the central North Carolina Piedmont, and it may reflect the slightly warmer and drier climatic conditions of the Altithermal (Claggett and Cable 1982; Delcourt and Delcourt 1979).

Late Archaic Period (3000–1000 B.C.)

As in the Piedmont, the Late Archaic period in the mountains was a time of rapid population increase and larger and more numerous sites. Jefferson Chapman describes Late Archaic period sites as "widespread and frequent" (1985:150). Variety could also be added to Chapman's characterization. In the Great Smoky Mountains National Park, most Late Archaic sites were located in the floodplains of large river valleys, in close proximity to outcrops of quartzite. This stone was used exclusively for making Savannah River Stemmed spear points and other tools. Only a few small hunting camps were found in the higher elevations (Bass 1977:77). However, in the upper Watauga valley, Late Archaic sites were more dispersed and occupied a wide range of habitats, similar to Middle Archaic settlements. The people who occupied the upper Watauga valley preferred to camp along the valley margins rather than on floodplains (Purrington 1983:127).

In southeastern Tennessee, the Late Archaic period has been divided into two phases. The earlier phase is marked by the presence of large, Savannah River Stemmed spear points, whereas the later phase is indicated by the presence of a smaller, stemmed point called Iddins Undifferentiated Stemmed. Sites of the Iddins phase also frequently contain steatite bowl fragments and are much larger and more numerous than those of the Savannah River phase. They are usually located adjacent to large streams, which suggest a greater reliance on riverine resources and more tightly bounded territories than Savannah River phase sites. Excavations at the Iddins site on the Little Tennessee River uncovered an almost unbroken string of hearths along the first terrace of the river, adjacent to a series of shoals. These hearths consisted of pits or basins filled with large river cobbles. Many of the stones had been fire-cracked or heat-spalled (Chapman 1981; Davis 1990).

Excavations at the Warren Wilson site on the Swannanoa River in Buncombe County also have uncovered an extensive Late Archaic occupation that was very similar to that of the Iddins site. Savannah River Stemmed points and a smaller type of stemmed point called Otarre Stemmed co-occurred within a dark, organically enriched band of sandy loam found beneath deposits dating to the Early Woodland and Late Prehistoric periods. Also within this zone were fragments of steatite vessels and numerous rock-filled hearths, like those from Iddins (figs. 3.12 and 3.13). Radiocarbon dates were obtained from charcoal found in two of these hearths. One of these also contained a Savannah River Stemmed spear point and was dated to around 3000 B.C. The other hearth did not contain any diagnostic artifacts and dated to 1500 B.C. (Keel 1976:175). Although there was no clear stratigraphic separation between Savannah River Stemmed and Otarre Stemmed points, the Iddins site data suggest that the Warren Wilson site was probably inhabited most intensely during the Otarre phase, or second half of the Late Archaic period (fig. 3.14).

No Late Archaic food remains from Warren Wilson have been analyzed, but, based on the site's location, fish, turtles, and other riverine resources were no doubt important. Large numbers of spear points and other butchering and hideworking tools indicate a reliance on hunting as well. The southeastern

FIGURE 3.12. *View of the 1966 excavation at the Warren Wilson site showing exposed Late Archaic rock hearths. (Photo from Dickens 1976:23)*

Tennessee data show that hunting and fishing was supplemented by harvesting large numbers of acorns and hickory nuts. Also, squash and gourds were cultivated as early as 3000 B.C., and toward the end of the Late Archaic period sunflower, maygrass, and chenopodium were well on their way to being domesticated (Chapman and Shea 1981; Yarnell and Black 1985).

The Archaic Period on the Coast and Coastal Plain

Numerous Archaic sites have been discovered on the North Carolina coast and Coastal Plain. Many of these have come to light as a result of cultural resource–management studies carried out since the early 1970s. Unlike the Piedmont, where excavations have placed the Archaic sequence in a stratified context, the coastal Archaic is known primarily from surface collections.

The diagnostic spear point styles recognized in the Piedmont are duplicated in artifact collections from the coast and Coastal Plain (Phelps 1983:22). The Early Archaic period is represented by the occurrence of Palmer Corner Notched and Kirk Corner Notched types, and the Middle Archaic period is well documented through the occurrence of Stanly Stemmed, Morrow Moun-

FIGURE 3.13. *Roy Dickens plotting Feature 43, a Late Archaic rock hearth at the Warren Wilson site. (Courtesy of the Research Laboratories of Archaeology)*

tain Stemmed, and Guilford Lanceolate points. The Savannah River phase of the Late Archaic period is also well represented in artifact collections from Coastal Plain sites. Because of the rising sea level at the end of the Pleistocene (ca. 14,500 B.C.), many of the earliest sites now lie inundated by the sounds and waters off the shores of the barrier islands (Goodyear, Michie, and Charles 1989:19; Phelps 1983:22–23).

Campsites of the Archaic period are widely scattered and can be found almost anywhere near water. Phelps (1981, 1983) recognizes two types of sites: base camps and small, temporary, procurement sites. Temporary procurement sites outnumber base camps roughly ten to one. Sites interpreted as base camps tend to be found near stream confluences, whereas the smaller sites can be found in a variety of environments, depending upon the seasonal availability of various food resources.

The number of Archaic sites in the Coastal Plain generally increased through time, though there seems to be a slight peak in the number of sites during the Middle Archaic period. An analysis of 3,888 spear points from northern (n = 2,717) and southern (n = 1,171) coastal sites revealed that Middle Archaic specimens occurred a little more frequently than Late Archaic points. This holds true only if the so-called transitional types like Small Savannah River Stemmed

74 ARCHAIC PERIOD

FIGURE 3.14. *Savannah River Stemmed projectile points from the Garden Creek (bottom row, left two specimens) and Warren Wilson (bottom row, right two specimens) sites and Otarre Stemmed points from the Warren Wilson site (top and middle rows).*

and Gypsy Stemmed points are not included in the Late Archaic counts. In the northern and southern portions of the coastal region, Morrow Mountain points far outnumbered other Middle Archaic types. This is particularly true for the northern coastal area (Daniel and Davis 1996; Davis and Daniel 1990).

During the Late Archaic period, there appears to have been a shift in settlement location away from upland tributary streams and toward the mouths of major rivers. Here, fishing and shellfishing led to larger and more sedentary camps where the rudiments of pottery-making and horticulture began.

It is hard to assess the Archaic data from the North Carolina coast. More carefully designed archaeological surveys are needed in regions not dictated by the locations of power lines, roads, and other projects, which trigger cultural resource–management review. Excavated data are also badly needed in order to refine the coastal chronology, collect subsistence data, and answer questions regarding site size and function. Researchers in the South Carolina Coastal Plain have already faced the fact that they can no longer rely solely on the North Carolina Piedmont sequence. In portions of the South Carolina Coastal Plain, Stanly and Guilford points are rare to nonexistent, and no excavated sites anywhere in South Carolina have thus far duplicated the North Carolina Piedmont sequence (Blanton and Sassaman 1989:58).

Summary

From the coast to the mountains, from Manteo to Murphy, the Archaic period began with wandering bands of hunters and gatherers who faced a wide variety of changing environmental conditions. These bands occasionally came together at favored locations along major river valleys, but most of their time was spent in small family groups scattered across the landscape foraging for food and raw materials.

As climatic conditions stabilized, population grew, and, with time, increased knowledge of the environment led to new technologies and a more efficient exploitation of selected resources. Toward the end of the Archaic period, large groups began to settle down and live most, if not all, of the year in areas rich in raw materials and food resources. This settled life spawned the beginnings of plant domestication and the use of pottery, hallmarks of the succeeding Woodland period.

4. The Woodland Period in the Piedmont

Most archaeologists agree that three interrelated innovations marked the end of the Archaic period and the beginning of the Woodland period: pottery-making, semisedentary villages, and horticulture. All of these innovations had their origins at the end of the Archaic period, but during Woodland times they became the norm rather than the exception.

During the Late Archaic period, people living along the south Atlantic coast from Florida to North Carolina, as well as on shell midden sites in the interior Southeast, began to make and use fiber-tempered pottery. The earliest expression of this pottery along the Carolina coast is called Stallings series, after the type site located on an island in the Savannah River (Claflin 1931). Most Stallings series pottery was formed by molding lumps of clay into simple vessel forms. Periwinkle shells, reeds, and sticks were used to create punctated decorations. Incising and finger pinching were also popular techniques used to decorate the surfaces of Stallings series vessels. The fibrous material used as temper is believed to have been Spanish moss that was carbonized when the pots were fired. As a result, this "hole-tempered" pottery is very porous, and some Stallings sherds will almost float in water, like a cork (Simpkins and Allard 1986). Stallings pottery was made as early as 2500 B.C. until about 1000 B.C. (Stoltman 1974; Trinkley 1980, 1989).

In the Carolina coastal region, a pottery type called Thom's Creek began to be made at about the same time as Stallings series pottery but seems to have persisted longer. The methods and styles of decoration on Thom's Creek pottery are nearly identical to those of Stallings. However, more Thom's Creek pottery was made by coiling annular segments of clay, and sand replaced fiber as the tempering agent (Trinkley 1980).

At about the same time fiber-tempered pottery was being made along the southern coast and elsewhere in the Southeast, steatite-tempered vessels were being made in the tidewater area of the Middle Atlantic region. This pottery, called Marcey Creek, contains large amounts of steatite (soapstone) particles that vary in size from a powder to the size of pebbles. The exterior surfaces of these vessels are plain except for basal portions that often show the impressions of a woven mat. In form, Marcey Creek vessels are similar in shape to earlier stone pots made from steatite. They also contain large lug handles around the rim that are identical in form to those found on steatite vessels. Marcey Creek pottery dates between 1200 and 800 B.C. (Egloff 1985; Manson 1948).

In the Virginia Coastal Plain, Marcey Creek pottery is partially contemporary with, and succeeded by, a variety of wares that contain clay and sometimes a mixture of clay and steatite as tempering agents. Around 800 B.C., a ware tempered with sand and crushed quartz, called Accokeek, made its debut in the Potomac region, while south of the James River, a sand-tempered ware called Stony Creek was made. Vessels of both types share a conoidal shape and surfaces that were finished with cord-wrapped, fabric-wrapped, and sometimes net-wrapped paddles (Egloff 1985; Stephenson and Ferguson 1963).

By the beginning of the Woodland period in North Carolina, several different ceramic traditions had been established across the state. From the coast to the mountains, Early Woodland pottery types share many attributes that reflect varying degrees of influence from the cradles of pottery-making to the south and north. Sand was the most popular tempering agent, but crushed quartz was also used. Vessels were formed by coiling annular segments of clay into simple bowls and conical jars with pointed bottoms. These coils usually were welded together by stamping a vessel's exterior surface with a wooden paddle wrapped with cordage or textiles. Sometimes carved paddles also were used.

The widespread appearance of pottery-making throughout the Southeast at this time is usually viewed as going hand in hand with an increasing reliance on wild and domesticated seed crops and more permanent settlements (Smith 1986).

The processes of plant domestication that began at the end of the Late Archaic period intensified and diversified during the Woodland period. Knotweed, sumpweed, squash, bottle gourds, sunflower, maygrass, and goosefoot were planted and harvested in small garden plots as Woodland villages drew closer to floodplain environments to take advantage of the fertile, friable soils they offered. Archaeological evidence of small-grain crop foods, namely charred seeds, increases substantially at Early Woodland and Middle Woodland sites (Yarnell and Black 1985:Table 4; Smith 1992:14). Still, there is no reason to suspect that gardening was of overriding importance in the subsistence cycle.

The relatively large quantities of seeds found in Early and Middle Woodland contexts could have been easily produced in small garden plots. It seems likely that subsistence during this time still depended primarily on the hunting and gathering of wild plant and animal foods (Steponaitis 1986:378).

The primary importance of these early local cultigens probably lies in the fact that the knowledge and skills that led to their domestication also laid the groundwork for the acceptance of new, more productive crops that were originally domesticated in Mexico. Corn, the first of these so-called tropical cultigens, appears to have arrived in the eastern United States around A.D. 200, but it was not widely grown until more than half a millennium later. In North Carolina and many other areas of the Southeast, corn did not become an important food crop until around A.D. 1000. And, it was not until about A.D. 1200, with the introduction of beans, that the eastern agricultural triad of corn, beans, and squash was completed (Smith 1992:203). The combination of these three crops permitted true agricultural systems to develop over much of the East and supported the rise of large, complex societies during the Mississippian period. These societies rivaled their contemporaries in Europe and the rest of the world in political complexity and territorial control.

The Piedmont Village Tradition

The Woodland cultures of the North Carolina Piedmont were only marginally influenced by cultural traditions that evolved elsewhere in the eastern United States. The rich and elaborate Hopewell and Swift Creek cultures that influenced wide areas of the Southeast had little impact on cultural developments in the Piedmont. And the powerful Mississippian chiefdoms that later dominated most of the Southeast were only able to penetrate the southern fringe of the Piedmont.

Although we know comparatively little about their origins during the Early Woodland period, from about A.D. 1000 until the time of first contacts with Europeans, cultures throughout most of the Piedmont steadily evolved along an unbroken continuum with few outside influences. Small villages and scattered hamlets gradually developed into larger, more nucleated settlements as agriculture, particularly corn agriculture, became more important. But even as agriculture increased in importance, hunting and gathering continued to make a significant contribution to the diet. The subsistence base seems to have remained evenly balanced between crop production and wild plant and animal resources.

The dead were buried in simple pits with few belongings, usually within or

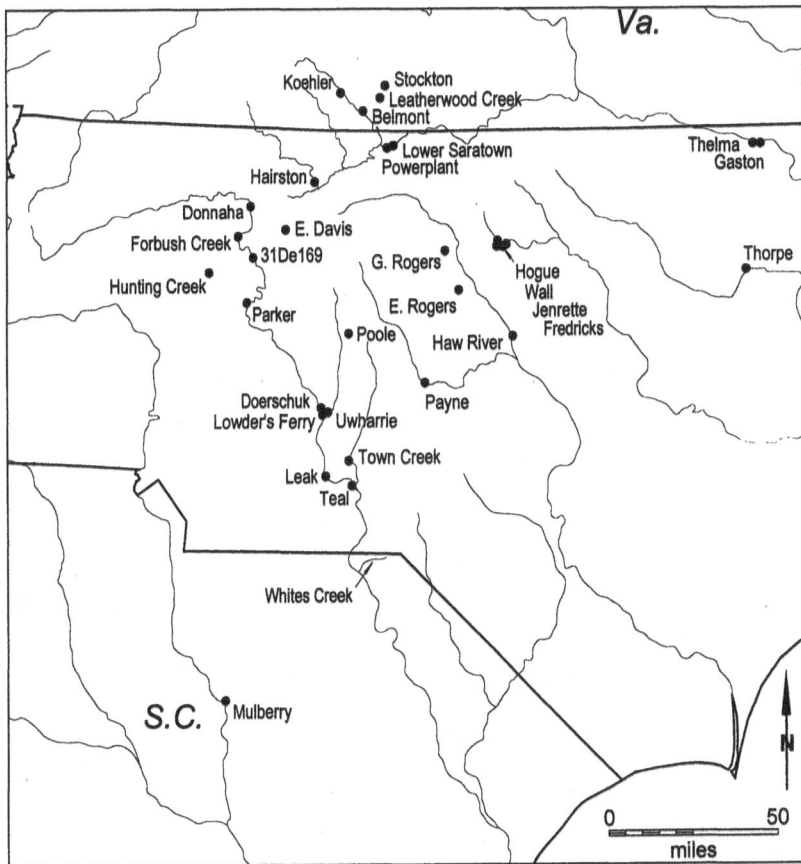

FIGURE 4.1. *Map of the North Carolina Piedmont showing Woodland and South Appalachian Mississippian sites discussed in the text.*

close to houses. Mortuary studies show that social distinctions were based primarily on age and sex. Woodland societies were egalitarian, woven together by a web of kinship where leadership roles were achieved rather than ascribed.

Like other features of Woodland culture, patterns of pottery-making changed gradually. Innovations reflecting ideas derived from outside the Piedmont are seen mainly at the beginning and end of the Woodland period, and even then old styles and techniques persisted alongside the new.

We call this continuum of cultural development the Piedmont Village Tradition. And only in the southern Piedmont is it broken by the spread of the South Appalachian Mississippian tradition into the Yadkin–Pee Dee River valley (fig. 4.1).

The Early Woodland and Middle Woodland Periods (1000 B.C.–A.D. 800)

The Badin Phase

One of the earliest archaeological phases in the Piedmont Village Tradition is called Badin, named for the small Stanly County town of Badin located in the southern Piedmont, near the Doerschuk site. Pottery attributed to the Badin phase was first recognized at Doerschuk, where it occurred within a soil zone overlying the preceramic Savannah River level. This early pottery, defined as the Badin ceramic series (Coe 1964:27–29), was well made and tempered with sand and an occasional pebble. Vessels were formed by building up annular segments of clay that were then welded together using a cord-wrapped or fabric-wrapped paddle. Vessel forms were simple, consisting of straight-sided jars with conical bases (fig. 4.2).

The fact that Badin pottery was so well made led archaeologists to believe that there must be an ancestral ceramic type that was not present at the Doerschuk site. This hypothetical ancestral type was seen as bridging the gap between the Late Archaic Savannah River phase and the beginning of the Early Woodland period (Coe 1964:27).

Joseph Caldwell (1958:23–27) included Badin pottery in what he called the "Middle Eastern" tradition of fabric-impressed ceramics. This tradition extended over much of the deciduous forest region of the eastern United States. Also included in Caldwell's Middle Eastern tradition was the Kellog focus of northern Georgia. Because of the "discontinuity" in artifact styles between the Late Archaic period and the Early Woodland Kellog focus, Caldwell believed that Kellog and Badin ceramics, as well as other similar types, resulted from a migration of people out of eastern Tennessee into the Georgia and Carolina Piedmont regions.

North Carolina archaeologists, like Caldwell, also proposed a "cultural discontinuity" between the Late Archaic Savannah River phase and the Early Woodland Badin phase. In addition to the abrupt introduction of ceramics, an entirely different form of projectile point was thought to be associated with the Badin phase. These crudely flaked, triangular "Badin" points represented quite a departure from the large, stemmed spear points of the Savannah River phase, and were thought to mark the beginning of a tradition of triangular points associated with the arrival of the bow and arrow (Coe 1964:124) (fig. 4.3).

Without the benefit of radiocarbon dates, it was initially believed that the Badin phase dated to around the first century A.D. (Coe 1964:55). Today we know that this estimate is too late. Basing their belief primarily on radiocarbon dates for the succeeding Yadkin phase, archaeologists now say that the Badin phase must date to around 500 B.C. (Blanton, Espenshade, and Brockington 1986:10).

WOODLAND PERIOD: PIEDMONT 81

FIGURE 4.2. *Badin Fabric Marked (bottom row), Badin Cordmarked (third row), Yadkin Fabric Marked (second row), and Yadkin Cordmarked (top row) potsherds from the Doerschuk site.*

FIGURE 4.3. *Badin Crude Triangular (bottom row) and Yadkin Large Triangular (top two rows) projectile points from the Doerschuk site.*

Badin ceramics appear to be related to the Early Woodland Deep Creek wares of the North Carolina coastal region, and it has been observed recently that Badin and Thom's Creek pottery have a similar "feel," although their surfaces were finished in very different ways (Coe 1995:154). Whereas most of the early ceramic wares that evolved from the fiber-tempered pottery along the south Atlantic coast display surfaces stamped with a carved paddle, Badin and Deep Creek wares were usually finished with a cord-wrapped or fabric-wrapped paddle. Although the exact chronological relationships among Early Woodland ceramics in the North Carolina Piedmont and elsewhere in the Southeast are unclear, the use of sand as a tempering agent seems to tie these early wares together.

Other than ceramics, we know very little about aboriginal lifestyles during the Badin phase. Probably little changed from the Late Archaic period except for the gradual incorporation of the bow and arrow and ceramic containers in a technology that was still primarily adapted to a hunting-and-gathering way of life. One thing that is surprising in the North Carolina Piedmont is the small number of Badin and subsequent Yadkin phase sites compared with the relatively large number of Late Archaic Savannah River phase sites. Current data suggest that the Piedmont was not a favorite place to live during the Early Woodland period, and therefore population density was relatively low.

The Yadkin Phase

The Yadkin ceramic series was defined based on additional evidence from the Doerschuk site excavations. Yadkin phase pottery is generally thought to follow Badin (Coe 1964:30–32; 1995:154); however, the stratigraphic evidence at Doerschuk was inconclusive. These two pottery series are very similar, except that Yadkin pottery is tempered with crushed quartz. Vessel forms are the same, and vessel surfaces were still stamped with cord-wrapped and fabric-wrapped paddles (figs. 4.2 and 4.4).

Yadkin pottery also exhibits three new kinds of surface treatments—check stamping, linear check stamping, and simple stamping. These stamp designs were created by using a carved wooden paddle instead of one wrapped with a cord or fabric. A simple-stamped surface treatment is produced by using a paddle with parallel grooves carved on its surface. A check-stamped treatment is achieved by adding another series of grooves perpendicular to the first. The linear effect is created by some of the grooves being more pronounced than others and by differences in groove spacing.

These kinds of surface treatments tie Yadkin phase pottery to the Early Woodland Deptford wares common in Georgia and South Carolina. A few

FIGURE 4.4. *Reconstructed Yadkin Fabric Marked pot from Stanly County.*

Yadkin potsherds also were tempered with particles of clay, similar to Hanover phase ceramics found along the southern North Carolina coast and Coastal Plain (South 1976). Projectile points associated with Yadkin pottery are typically large triangular forms that resemble Badin points but are more finely flaked (Coe 1964:30).

Although typologically separated, Badin and Yadkin ceramics were found in the same soil zone, Zone III, at the Doerschuk site. The upper levels at Doerschuk, where the ceramics occurred, were disturbed to varying degrees by natural processes, and the sandy soils comprising the Badin and Yadkin zone were not conducive to the formation of stable soil horizons. These natural conditions were exacerbated by pit digging and other cultural activities that took place on the site during the last millennium of its occupation. The extent of the mixing and disturbance of the stratigraphy at Doerschuk is illustrated by the fact that the sherds from a single vessel were found scattered throughout five vertical layers and across nine 5' excavation units (Coe 1964:27).

These conditions should be considered when evaluating the stratigraphic basis for typologically separating Badin and Yadkin ceramics, although both occurred in the same soil zone. The rationale for this separation was the fact that a larger percentage of Badin sherds was recovered from the bottom of Zone III, whereas a larger percentage of Yadkin sherds occurred in the upper portion of Zone III and within Zone II. The same was true with the distribution of Badin and Yadkin projectile points. However, in terms of total numbers of potsherds, the counts were relatively small. Only 63 Yadkin specimens and 346 Badin sherds were recovered from all of Zone III. It also should be noted that 90 Late Woodland Dan River phase sherds, dating at least a thousand years later than Badin, were recovered from the bottom of Zone III (Coe 1964:29).

In short, there is no strong stratigraphic evidence at the Doerschuk site to suggest that Badin and Yadkin wares represent two distinct periods of development within the same ceramic tradition. The typological distinctions between the two pottery types may be valid, but today this distinction has become blurred and still lacks stratigraphic verification. Moreover, Badin Crude Triangular points have not been found in a clear stratigraphic context that separates them from Yadkin Large Triangular points. Most researchers today see the Badin type as probably reflecting Yadkin-like points in their early stage of manufacture, a possibility that was recognized earlier but dismissed (Coe 1964:45).

Yadkin phase sites occur more frequently than Badin phase sites, especially in the southern Piedmont and the South Carolina Coastal Plain (Coe 1995; Ward 1978). Still, subsistence remains and other evidence relating to the way Yadkin people lived are rare. Evidence that some Yadkin sites may have been occupied for relatively long periods of time can be seen at the Town Creek site, where a large circle of overlapping Yadkin phase hearths were uncovered. In addition to fire-cracked rocks comprising the hearths, large amounts of pottery and animal bones were found with the hearths. It is believed that these hearths date to the latter part of the Yadkin phase, around A.D. 500 (Coe 1995:90, 154).

Recent Research and the Early-Middle Woodland Chronology

Probably the greatest advance in Woodland period research since the pioneering work of the 1950s and 1960s has been the accumulation of a relatively large number of radiocarbon dates for the early end of the Woodland period. These have pushed back in time considerably the original Piedmont Woodland chronology that rested primarily on intuition.

More recent stratigraphic excavations also have shown that a transitional period existed between the end of the Late Archaic period and the beginning of the Woodland period. Today, archaeologists believe that the use of pottery and other types of artifacts associated with Woodland culture were gradually incorporated into the Archaic lifestyle. There were no cultural "disruptions" caused by migrations of newcomers into the Piedmont, as earlier investigators had proposed (Claggett and Cable 1982:771).

Excavations at 31De169, on the Yadkin River in Davie County, uncovered sherds from a sand- and grit-tempered, cordmarked pot that was believed to be typologically similar to Badin ware. Some of the sherds from the vessel were recovered from a burned tree stump that was radiocarbon dated to 140 ± 70 B.C. (Webb and Leigh 1995:19–21). Given the dates for Yadkin discussed below, this date appears to be too late, if the Badin phase does represent the earliest ceramic-making archaeological complex in the Piedmont.

Radiocarbon dates for Yadkin and Yadkin-like ceramics generally fall between 290 B.C. and A.D. 60 (Blanton, Espenshade, and Brockington 1986:10). At the E. Davis site in Forsyth County, a radiocarbon date of 220 ± 80 B.C. was obtained from charcoal contained in a rock-filled pit. The pit also contained Yadkin pottery and a small, stemmed Gypsy point (Davis 1987; Eastman 1994b:43). At one of the Haw River sites, 31Ch8, a date of 290 ± 95 B.C. was obtained from charcoal in a refuse pit containing two Yadkin series vessels. The stratigraphic level where this pit originated also contained a Badin Cordmarked pot (Claggett and Cable 1982:601). This date is in line with those from Kellog phase sites in South Carolina and Georgia, where pottery types similar to Badin and Yadkin have been found (Blanton, Espenshade, and Brockington 1986:12). Also at 31Ch8, stratigraphic and typological evidence suggest that a "pre-Badin" ceramic complex might exist (Claggett and Cable 1982:769).

These dates, coupled with the lack of strong stratigraphic evidence from Doerschuk and the Haw River sites, make it unclear as to whether Badin ceramics predate Yadkin in all areas of the Piedmont. As Webb and Leigh noted (1995:29), the situation may be that there is no "neatly linear, developmental relationship between Badin and Yadkin ceramics." As Early Woodland research continues across the Piedmont, we will probably see more and more variability in the early ceramic traditions and find that what holds true for one region may not hold true for another. Badin-like ceramics may be earliest in some areas, whereas Yadkin-like pottery may represent the earliest ceramic tradition in other areas. And future excavations may verify the "pre-Badin" ceramic phase suggested by Claggett and Cable.

Early Excavations in the Northeast Piedmont

Excavations at the Doerschuk site consisted of small block units that were designed to recover artifacts in their stratigraphic contexts. Mostly potsherds and projectile points were found. A different strategy was used at sites located in the Roanoke Rapids Reservoir in the northern Piedmont. At the Gaston and Thelma sites extensive site areas were examined, and a broad range of Early-Middle Woodland artifacts were found in association with numerous archaeological features.

The archaeological investigations within the Roanoke Rapids Reservoir were salvage archaeology in the purest sense of the term. The project was initiated by plans of the Virginia Electric and Power Company (VEPCO) to construct a hydroelectric dam that would create Roanoke Rapids Lake on the Roanoke River. The initial survey to locate sites began the very day an agreement to fund the project was worked out between the University of North Carolina at Chapel Hill and VEPCO. Because the project was initiated in April, during the middle of the spring semester at the university, most of the archaeological surveys were undertaken on weekends (Coe 1964:84; South 1959a:4).

During the survey phase, seventy-three sites were recorded and six were tested, including the Gaston and Thelma sites. Most of the excavation effort was devoted to the Gaston site, where Stanley South, Lewis Binford, and Stanley's wife, Jewel, worked from sunrise until sunset every day during June until the site was flooded on June 29, 1955 (Coe 1964:90; South 1959a:4).

The Gaston site was located on the south side of the Roanoke River, across from the upstream end of Vincent Island, in an area of narrow floodplain. Initially, twenty $5' \times 5'$ squares were excavated by hand in order to determine the site's stratigraphy and to provide control for the mechanical stripping that would follow. In addition to the buried Archaic strata found there, discussed in Chapter 3, a rich, ceramic-bearing midden extended across the site. Because time was precious, the decision was made to use a road grader to remove the midden from large areas of the site. This procedure exposed the tops of pit features, which were easily recognized as dark organic stains in the yellow sand beneath the midden (South 1959a:252).

The mechanical stripping exposed 200 features, most of which were described as "garbage pits" or "fire pits" (fig. 4.5). Some of the garbage pits were large, up to 7 feet across and as much as 4.5 feet deep. They contained varying amounts of refuse, including animal bones, potsherds, freshwater mussel shells, stone tools, charcoal, and burned clay daub. A few of the garbage pits also contained human skeletal remains. These consisted of teeth, finger and toe bones, skull fragments, and a mandible. The fire pits were described as pits

88 WOODLAND PERIOD: PIEDMONT

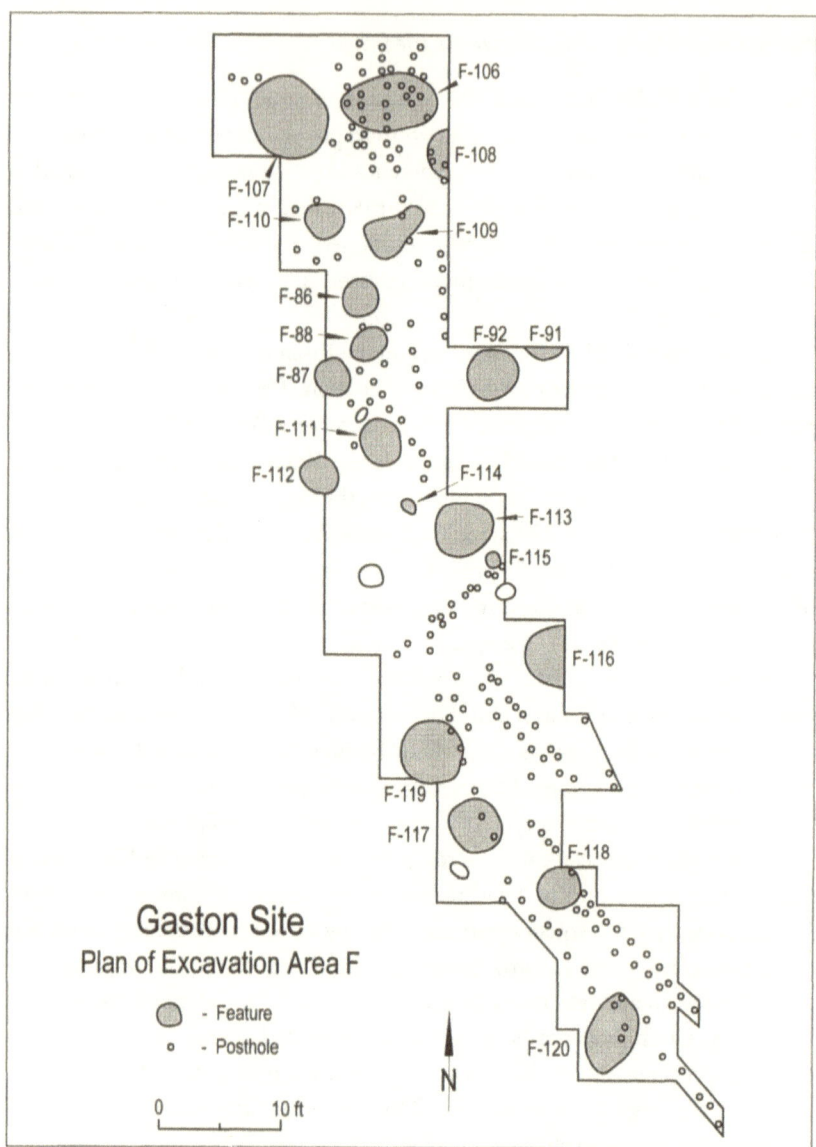

FIGURE 4.5. *Excavation plan of Area F at the Gaston site showing Woodland features and palisade posthole alignments. (Based on South 1959a:269)*

containing either layers of charcoal and ash or, in a few cases, rock-lined bottoms that showed evidence of having been exposed to high temperatures (Coe 1964:92–93; South 1959a:272–75).

Other pits at the Gaston site contained human and dog burials. The human remains, with one exception, were tightly flexed and placed in simple oval pits.

FIGURE 4.6. *Stone pipes found during excavations at the Keyauwee (top) and Gaston (bottom) sites.*

One burial consisted of a bundle of disarticulated bones, indicating that the flesh had been removed prior to interment. Only one burial contained an associated artifact: an engraved stone pipe made from chlorite (fig. 4.6). This burial contained the remains of at least two, and perhaps three, individuals (South 1959a:297). In contrast, most of the articulated dog remains, also placed in simple oval pits, were accompanied by offerings of deer bones (Coe 1964:93; South 1959a:275).

Coe (1964:106) and South (159a:391) identified three primary ceramic traditions while working at the Gaston site—Vincent, Clements, and Gaston (fig. 4.7). Vincent series pottery occurred near the bottom of the midden at the Gaston site, whereas Gaston specimens were concentrated near the top. Clements potsherds were not clearly associated with any particular level; instead, they appeared to be scattered throughout the midden deposit. Vincent

FIGURE 4.7. *Vincent Fabric Marked (bottom left), Clements Cordmarked (bottom right), Clements Fabric Marked (top left), and Gaston Simple Stamped (top right) rim sections from the Gaston site.*

and Clements ceramics were assigned to the Early and Middle Woodland periods, whereas Gaston pottery was thought to have been made as late as A.D. 1700.

The features at the Gaston site usually contained potsherds representing all three ceramic series, although a seriation of the feature pottery indicates that in most of the pits one ceramic series clearly dominated the others (fig. 4.8). These seriation charts also suggest that most of the features contained a larger portion of Vincent series sherds than either Clements or Gaston pottery (Coe 1964:100, Fig. 94; South 1959a:333, Fig. 37). At the time, it was believed that the mixing of

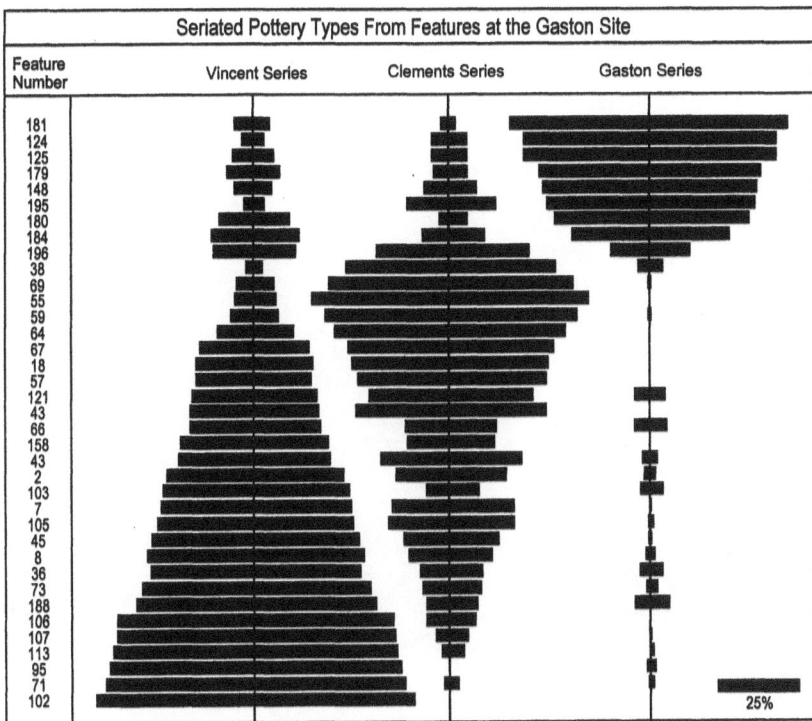

FIGURE 4.8. *A seriation of Vincent, Clements, and Gaston series pottery from excavated features at the Gaston site. (Based on Coe 1964:100)*

earlier and later ceramic series in most of the pits was clear evidence of disturbances created by the later inhabitants of the site (Coe 1964:107).

This "mixing" of pottery also reflects the difficulty the archaeologists had typologically distinguishing many of the potsherds. It was particularly difficult to separate the Vincent and Clements sherds. In fact, Stanley South simply referred to the two series as the Vincent-Clements tradition and did not attempt to separate them in many instances. These typological problems were viewed as a consequence of the fact that both ceramic series represented a single tradition over a long period of time. And during most of the tradition, both were being used (Coe 1964:102; South 1959a:393).

Vincent series pottery has a hard, compact paste that was tempered with sand and an occasional pebble or fragment of crushed quartz. Vessel surfaces were finished by being malleated with a cord-wrapped or fabric-wrapped paddle. Interiors were usually smoothed by hand. Vessel forms consist of bowls and jars with straight to slightly flaring, undecorated rims. Bases are usually pointed, but sometimes are rounded (Coe 1964:101–2; South 1959a:62) (fig. 4.9).

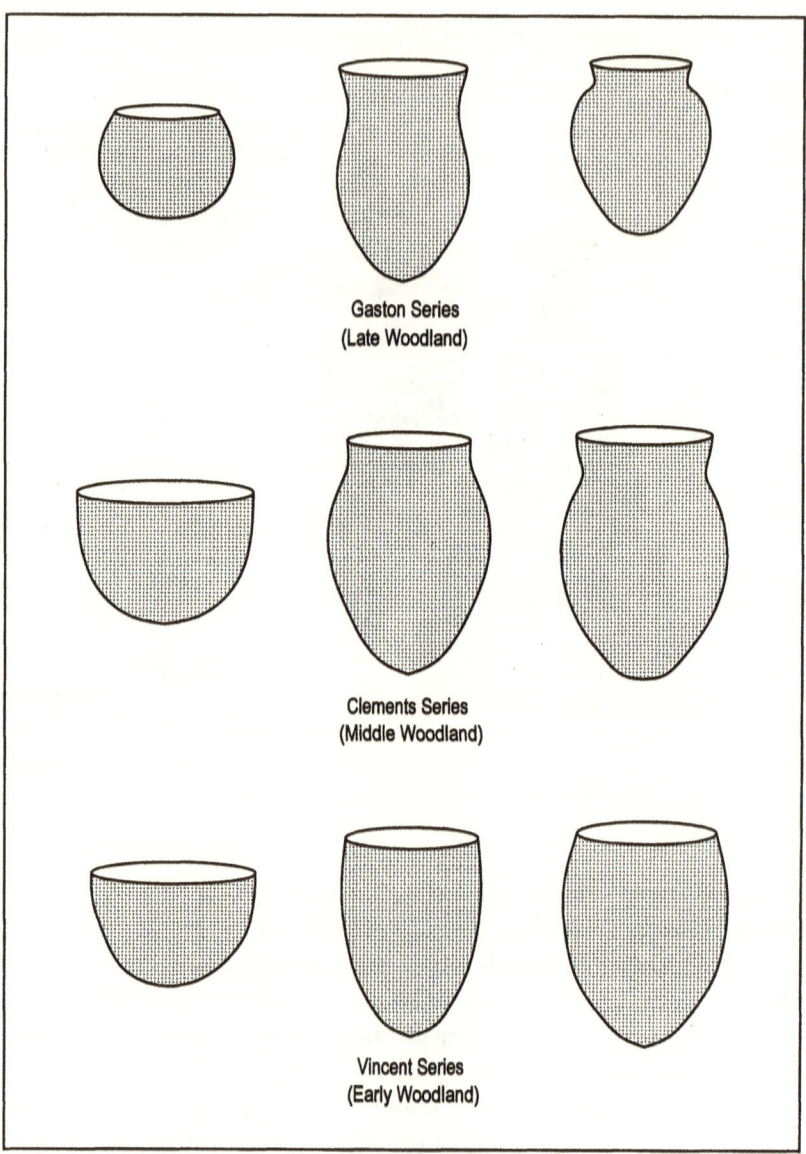

FIGURE 4.9. *Evolution of Woodland pot forms in the lower Roanoke valley. (Based on Coe 1964:107)*

Clements pottery also contains sand temper and crushed quartz. The particle sizes of the tempering materials are variable, ranging from fine to large, angular fragments. Cord-wrapped and fabric-marked paddles were also used to stamp the exterior vessel walls. The interiors of Clements vessels were generally hand-smoothed, but a few sherds were slightly scraped, using tools other than the hands. Bowls and jars were both made with bases varying from conical to rounded. In general, the cord and fabric finishes on Clements pottery are finer than those of the Vincent series, and the vessels' walls are also thinner (Coe 1964:103–4; South 1959a:83–85).

A distinctive type of projectile point was also associated with the Vincent and Clements ceramic series at the Gaston site. These large, triangular points were called Roanoke Large Triangular, and although large and small varieties were recognized, Coe considered them to represent a single type. South, on the other hand, distinguished Roanoke points from a type he called simply Large Triangle, but he did not feel that the data were sufficient to place the two types in their relative chronological positions. Coe, however, believed that the larger varieties of triangular points were earlier and affiliated with the Vincent phase (Coe 1964:111; South 1959a:358).

The chronological relationship between Clements and Vincent was somewhat clarified about a mile upstream at the Thelma site. Here, the main occupation occurred during the Vincent phase, and Clements ceramics were present only in the upper level of the midden (South 1959a:416). At the Thelma site, Vincent ceramics were associated with a small, stemmed point, appropriately named "Thelma." These points, although smaller, represent a continuity of form from the Late Archaic Savannah River styles (409). The Thelma site also contrasted with the Gaston site in other ways. Although some features at the Gaston site contained freshwater mussel shells, there is no indication that the midden was rich in mollusk remains. However, the midden at the Thelma site was described as a "shell midden" (396).

Perhaps the most distinguishing feature of the Thelma site was the presence of a group burial, or ossuary, containing the remains of four individuals. The ossuary was discovered below a flexed, primary burial within a pit that also contained a large piece of a Vincent pot. The ossuary remains had been covered by a layer of clean white sand and probably would not have been discovered, except for the fact that a skull was exposed while the excavation unit was being cleaned after the removal of the primary burial (South 1959a:403).

Several atlatl weights were also found in association with Vincent, but not Clements, ceramics. These weights may represent the last gasp of the atlatl in the northern Piedmont as the use of the bow and arrow became more popular.

This transition is also reflected in the shift from small, stemmed Thelma points to the Roanoke triangular varieties (cf. Oliver 1985:209).

Just how early is the Vincent ceramic complex? At the time of the excavations, archaeologists believed that Badin and Vincent pottery were in use "at about the same time" (Coe 1964:27). At the Gaston site, a single radiocarbon date was obtained from a charcoal sample that combined smaller samples from four different features. When the samples were submitted for dating, the ceramic typology had not been worked out, and it was subsequently determined that two of the samples were from Clements phase, and not Vincent phase, pits. Thus, the date of A.D. 916 ± 200 was considered to be too late and A.D. 500 was thought to be closer to the mark (Coe 1964:118–19; South 1959a:384).

Several years after the Roanoke Rapids excavations, a date of A.D. 685 ± 75 was obtained for Clements pottery found in a pit feature at the Thorpe site (31Ns3). This site is located in Nash County, approximately sixty miles south of the Roanoke Rapids Reservoir (Phelps 1980:71). Obviously, if the Clements phase dates to the end of the Middle Woodland period, Vincent must be earlier and probably overlaps temporally with the first half of the Yadkin phase in the southern Piedmont.

Based on the abundance of shell within the midden at the Thelma site and the lack of evidence for extensive use of mollusks at the Gaston site, significant differences in subsistence and settlement patterns may have existed between the Vincent and Clements phases. However, such differences were not reflected in the other faunal remains from pits at the Gaston site. In the samples of animal bone collected from Vincent, Clements, and Gaston phase features, deer, muskrat, raccoon, beaver, opossum, otter, turkey, and turtle were represented in roughly the same relative frequencies. Dog remains were found only in pits dating to the Vincent and Clements phases, and half of these pits were intentional burials.

Of course, the animal bones reflect only a portion of the total subsistence remains. The charred plant food remains were not collected using fine-grained recovery techniques such as flotation. Nor were they systematically analyzed, except to note that corn was absent and hickory nuts were plentiful. The relative amounts of mussel shells from different features also were not tabulated (Coe 1964:117–18; South 1959a:352–54).

In terms of settlement variability, two patterns were observed by South. First, there were about twice as many Vincent phase sites as there were Clements and Gaston phase sites combined. Secondly, most of the sites containing a preponderance of Vincent pottery were located at the western end of the reservoir (South 1959a:229, 234). While the meaning of these patterns is still unclear, the relatively large number of Early-Middle Woodland sites within the Roanoke

Rapids Reservoir stands in stark contrast to patterns observed to the south and west in the heart of the Piedmont, where such sites occur only infrequently.

The Whites Creek Survey and the Forbush Creek Excavations

Before summarizing our discussion of the Early Woodland and Middle Woodland periods in the Piedmont, two additional studies should be mentioned. The first study was a survey carried out along Whites Creek in Marlboro County, South Carolina, just south of the North Carolina state line, in the Sandhills region (Ward 1978). The second study was of the mostly unreported excavations conducted at the Forbush Creek site (31Yd1) in Yadkin County, North Carolina. This site, located on an alluvial terrace of the Yadkin River, lies in the western section of the Piedmont (Keel 1972; McManus 1985).

The most interesting aspect of the Whites Creek survey was the fact that of the sixty-seven sites recorded, twenty-seven produced Yadkin-like pottery, and several of these sites also contained Savannah River Stemmed spear points. A similar co-occurrence of Savannah River points and Early Woodland ceramics has also been noted in the upper Yadkin River valley (Woodall 1976). Although not all of the Savannah River phase sites in the Whites Creek survey produced ceramics, most were situated in the same topographic setting as ceramic-bearing sites. Several low ridges lie perpendicular to Whites Creek, and the toes of these ridges are normally bounded on three sides by low, poorly drained, swampy land. The last high ground on the ridge toes, closest to the creek, was favored by the Savannah River and Yadkin occupants of the area. Apparently they established their camps there to exploit the rich and varied environment of the surrounding swamp and creek. These campsites were also well situated to take advantage of food resources within the pine-hardwood forests covering the higher, better-drained elevations of the ridges.

The Whites Creek survey data pose several questions. The most obvious and basic questions center on what the co-occurrence of Yadkin phase pottery and Savannah River Stemmed points means. Does it indicate that the Late Archaic points and the Early Woodland pottery were being made at the same time in the Whites Creek area? Or does their occurrence on sites occupying similar environmental niches indicate a persistence in settlement and subsistence strategies from the end of the Archaic period into the Early Woodland period? If Late Archaic settlement-subsistence practices did persist, where are the earlier ceramic-bearing sites coeval with the Badin phase? Or does the Yadkin material represent the earliest pottery in the region? Unfortunately, these and similar questions cannot be adequately addressed using information from only surface artifact distributions. Excavations to retrieve hard subsistence information and radiocarbon dates are sorely needed before we can go any further in sorting out the Whites Creek puzzle and assessing how it fits in the broader regional picture of the Archaic-to-Woodland transition in the Piedmont.

Like the Whites Creek survey, the Forbush Creek site investigations also hold tantalizing clues to our understanding of the Early Woodland and Middle Woodland periods in the Piedmont. However, the Forbush Creek data were derived from archaeological excavations. While most of the artifacts recovered by these excavations have never been analyzed, some of the stone tools from Forbush Creek have been studied (McManus 1985).

The first excavations at the Forbush Creek site, located on the west bank of the Yadkin River just west of Winston-Salem, were carried out in November and December 1957. Stanley South, working for the North Carolina Department of Archives and History, directed the work that salvaged portions of the site that would be destroyed by the construction of U.S. Highway 421.

In 1972, the North Carolina State Highway Commission proposed to construct a second bridge across the river and to widen the highway to four lanes. In order to salvage the portion of the site that lay within the new highway corridor, Bennie Keel of the University of North Carolina led a second salvage project. The excavations lasted from early March until mid-May and uncovered a large area of the site adjacent to South's earlier excavations (Keel 1972).

Based on South's and Keel's excavation notes, and a brief field report by Keel (1972), a few observations can be made that seem relevant to our discussion of the Early and Middle Woodland periods in the Piedmont. The Forbush Creek site appears to have been occupied intermittently throughout most of the first half of the Woodland period. Based on Keel's (1972:13) field observations and a cursory examination of the pottery from Keel's and South's excavations, most of the sherds appear to be associated with the Uwharrie phase (discussed later in this chapter), which dates around A.D. 1000. Some of the ceramics, however, are earlier and represent a Yadkin phase occupation.

There are marked differences between the archaeological features that Keel found in 1972 and those that South encountered in 1957. South uncovered twenty-eight human graves, whereas Keel found none. South also excavated two dog burials. There were none in the area of Keel's excavation. At least two distinct types of burials were encountered, and some of the burials can only be described as unusual. Eighteen of the twenty-eight graves were made in simple pits dug into the subsoil. These pits contained the articulated, flexed skeletons of single individuals. Six of the graves were ossuaries, or group burials, that contained the disarticulated, bundled remains of between three and thirteen individuals each. Of the four remaining features with human remains, two were simple inhumations that were accompanied by a second skull, which may represent a "trophy" taken in combat. One was the fragmented skeleton of an individual placed within the pit fill above an articulated dog skeleton, and the final burial was that of a child placed in the bottom of a refuse-filled pit. Other than the trophy skull, no grave goods were associated with any of the interments. Although the burials were all located within the same area of the site, the ossuaries were generally segregated from the primary pit burials (field notes on file, Research Laboratories of Archaeology [hereafter RLA]).

In addition to the burials, several rich pit features were excavated by South and Keel. Some of these contained human skeletal fragments mixed in with food remains and other refuse. Several of the pits also contained thick, compact deposits of freshwater mollusk shells. While most of the features were described as "refuse" or "storage" pits, a few were identified as "hearths."

The similarities between the Forbush Creek site and the Gaston and Thelma sites are many. Simple pit burials, burials in ossuaries, dog burials, a heavy reliance on freshwater mollusks, and the presence of human remains in refuse pits argue strongly for Early-Middle Woodland connections between the western and northern Piedmont. The Forbush Creek site data also provide a glimpse of the transition between the Yadkin phase and the beginning of the Late Woodland Uwharrie phase.

Summary

The stratigraphic and stylistic relationships among the various ceramic types made during the first half of the Woodland period are still unclear. Badin, Yadkin, Vincent, and Clements series ceramics reflect varying degrees of influence from regions to the north and south, where pottery-making seems to have originated. Although later in time, the sand-tempered Badin ware suggests a relationship with southern coastal types such as Thom's Creek (Coe 1995:154). Yet its cordmarked and fabric-impressed surfaces are more reminiscent of types of the "northern tradition" such as Accokeek and Stony Creek wares of Virginia. Yadkin pottery also points to multiple areas of influence. In addition to the fabric-marked and cordmarked surfaces, the use of crushed quartz temper is a trait common to pottery throughout the Virginia Coastal Plain and appears to have evolved from the earlier use of steatite as a tempering agent. At the Marcey Creek site, crushed steatite gave way to crushed quartz and vessel surfaces changed from plain to cordmarked (Manson 1948:226). Still, the Yadkin check-stamped and simple-stamped types show affinities to the widespread Deptford wares of the Georgia and South Carolina Coastal Plain.

During the Early and Middle Woodland periods, the Piedmont of North Carolina seems to have been an area of merging influences from different regions. A carved-paddle, sand-tempered tradition of pottery-making arrived from the south, whereas a tradition of using crushed stone and fabric- and cord-wrapped paddles arrived from the north. The exact timing of the arrival of these ideas in the Piedmont is still unclear, but we know today that the previous notion of a simple lineal progression from Badin to Yadkin or from Vincent to Clements wares is untenable. Badin pottery may be earlier in some areas, whereas Yadkin pottery may be earlier in others. And both types may occur at roughly the same time in still other parts of the Piedmont. The chronological position of Vincent and Clements wares is even less clear since they can be tied to other Piedmont wares by only a single radiocarbon date for the Clements phase.

The Roanoke Rapids Reservoir sites and the Forbush Creek site suggest that freshwater mollusks and other aquatic resources were important food resources during the first half of the Woodland period. A wide variety of mammals and birds were also eaten. During this period, the bow and arrow completely replaced the atlatl as the weapon of choice.

Evidence from sites in Tennessee and elsewhere in the Southeast indicate that several species of weedy plants, including maygrass, knotweed, goosefoot, and sunflower, were cultivated and that hickory nuts and acorns were seasonally harvested. No direct evidence (such as charred plant food remains) of horticultural practices has been found on the North Carolina Piedmont. However, the floodplain locations of the Doerschuk, Haw River, Gaston, Thelma, and Forbush Creek sites suggest that a similar array of plants may have been grown around these Early-Middle Woodland settlements to begin the Piedmont Village Tradition.

The Late Woodland Period (A.D. 800–1600)

No sharp breaks or glaring innovations distinguish the beginning of the Late Woodland period in Piedmont North Carolina. However, between about A.D. 1100 and 1600, major cultural changes took place across the Piedmont as regional manifestations of the Piedmont Village Tradition began to emerge. This was a time of population consolidation and the beginning of intertribal conflicts. Larger villages were often surrounded by stockades to protect their inhabitants from raids by hostile neighbors. It should be kept in mind, however, that these developments did not take place uniformly across the region. In some areas of the Piedmont, scattered hamletlike settlements, rather than compact villages, were the norm. Sometimes the two settlement types appear to have coexisted in the same region at roughly the same time. Still, when viewed from an overall perspective, a developmental trend toward larger, more permanent villages is evident.

Most archaeologists and anthropologists see this evolutionary trend as the result of an increase in agricultural production and efficiency. Intervillage rivalries and hostilities arose as access to good agricultural lands became increasingly important to the subsistence economy. The increased reliance on crop cultivation also meant that it was possible to produce food surpluses that required storage. Raids were no doubt also carried out to purloin these surpluses from neighbors. This is not to say that game and other wild foods were abandoned in favor of foods produced from domesticated plants. They certainly were not. Hunting, gathering, and collecting continued to play a balanced role in the overall subsistence economy.

It is during the Late Woodland period that archaeologists can begin to identify archaeological complexes left by cultures that may be ancestral to the linguistic and tribal groups described by European explorers during the subsequent Contact period. Siouan-speaking groups occupied the central and northern Piedmont when the first Europeans arrived. The Dan River and Saratown phases of the northern Piedmont probably represent the remains of peoples ancestral to the Sara Indians. In the north central Piedmont, along the Eno River, the Late Woodland Hillsboro phase may be related to the Historic Eno, Shakori, and Occaneechi tribes. A little farther south in the Haw River drainage, the Haw River, Hillsboro, and Mitchum phases define archaeological complexes possibly linked to the Sissipahaw Indians. Although poorly defined, the Gaston phase may represent the ancestral remains of the Occaneechis, Tutelos, and Saponis.

The southern Piedmont saw the arrival of new ideas and innovations from the south. Archaeologically, this infusion is known as the Pee Dee culture, first identified at the Town Creek site in Montgomery County. During their heyday, the Pee Dee were mound builders, and atop their mounds they placed temples and chiefly residences. They organized themselves in a highly stratified and politically complex society that had not been seen before in Piedmont North Carolina. However, by the end of the Late Woodland period, the past glory of the Pee Dee was only hinted at by a few surviving ceramic styles (Coe 1952, 1995; Oliver 1992; Reid 1967).

Pee Dee culture shares more traits with the Pisgah phase of the Appalachian Summit than with the Siouan cultures of the Piedmont. Pee Dee and Pisgah phase people participated in a cultural tradition known as South Appalachian Mississippian (Ferguson 1971; Griffin 1967). This tradition was part of the widespread Mississippian cultural pattern that witnessed the consolidation of large, highly stratified political systems headed by a hereditary elite. Before its decline, the influence of Mississippian culture was felt from Minnesota to Florida, and from Texas to Georgia.

It is important to remember that although these archaeological phases and cultures are distinct from each other, their connections with specific Piedmont tribes of the Contact period are often tenuous. When native cultures were first encountered by Europeans, they were observed to make frequent moves, and we suspect that similar movements, although probably not as frequent, took place prior to the arrival of Europeans. As a consequence, establishing linkages between archaeological complexes and specific tribal groups is often difficult and sometimes impossible. There is, however, a marked increase in the diversity of the archaeological record throughout the Piedmont during the latter half of the Late Woodland period, and much of this diversity no doubt coincides with ethnic and tribal differences that were beginning to take shape at this time.

The Uwharrie Phase (A.D. 800–1200)

The earliest Late Woodland phase defined in the Piedmont was called Uwharrie, after the Uwharrie River in Montgomery and Randolph Counties (Coe 1952). The Uwharrie-type site (31Mg14) is located on a large sandbar at the mouth of the river, where it empties into the Yadkin. This location places the Uwharrie site across the river from the Lowder's Ferry site and less than two miles downstream from the Doerschuk site.

Like Doerschuk, the Uwharrie site was also discovered by Herbert M. Doerschuk. Although excavations have never been conducted at the site, Doerschuk was able to obtain a collection of artifacts, mostly pottery, that washed out during the 1916 flood (notes on file, RLA). The name Uwharrie was assigned to the cultural complex represented by Doerschuk's artifact sample and excavated materials from the Lowder's Ferry (see Chapter 3) and Keyauwee sites (Coe 1952:307–8). Although initially discovered in the southern North Carolina Piedmont, Uwharrie phase sites have a wide distribution, occurring throughout central North Carolina. In fact, it can be said that the Uwharrie phase is the "mother" of all succeeding phases that comprise the Piedmont Village Tradition.

From what we know today, Coe's 1952 description of life during the Uwharrie phase is remarkably accurate, given the limited amount of information that was available to him at that time. Though still relatively small, Uwharrie villages were more sedentary than those of the preceding Woodland periods. Hunting, gathering, and fishing were still the mainstays of Uwharrie subsistence, but garden crops, including corn, became important, particularly toward the end of the Uwharrie phase. This increased reliance on domesticated plant foods is not only reflected in the archaeobotanical record but also in the large subterranean storage facilities found on Uwharrie phase sites. These pits were presumably used to store surpluses produced by growing crops (Coe 1952; Newkirk 1978; Woodall 1990). Woodall (1990:82) has suggested that the typical Uwharrie pottery vessel, a large conical jar, was also ideally suited for storing and preserving seasonally available food resources.

Uwharrie pottery continued to be made in the same basic tradition as the Badin, Yadkin, Vincent, and Clements styles. However, the wickerlike fabric wrapped around paddles to finish earlier vessel surfaces was gradually abandoned in favor of a coarse, netlike material. Large particles of crushed quartz were added to the clay as tempering agents, and vessel interiors were usually finished by scraping with a serrated tool. Uwharrie potters also began to decorate their pots with crudely incised parallel lines that encircled the vessel just below the rim (Coe 1952:308) (fig. 4.10).

Burials were placed in simple oval pits. The bodies were tightly flexed and sometimes were adorned with shell beads and other ornaments. It also appears that some Uwharrie burials were placed in cemeterylike areas located away from the main habitation site. It seems likely that most of the flexed primary burials at the Forbush Creek site date to the Uwharrie phase. Although they cannot be securely dated, dog burials from the Parker (31Dv25) and Donnaha (31Yd9) sites on the Yadkin River in Davidson and Yadkin Counties suggest further continuity between the Yadkin and Uwharrie phases (Newkirk 1978:108).

Surveys along the Great Bend of the upper Yadkin River in Yadkin and Surry Counties found that, although Uwharrie phase sites were spaced widely apart along this section of the river, they still occurred more frequently than Early and Middle Woodland sites. Increased site frequency coupled with the fact that Uwharrie sites usually reflect more intense and permanent occupations imply an increasing population that was becoming more and more adapted to the fertile floodplains of the Piedmont (Woodall 1990:83, 91). From this widespread pattern of Uwharrie adaptation emerged the riverine-focused, nucleated settlements that characterized the last half of the Piedmont Village Tradition.

An exception to the riverine-focused settlements typical of the Uwharrie phase is the Hunting Creek site (31De155) in Davie County. This rich site is situated atop a hill approximately 1,500 feet from the nearest water source. Excavations have uncovered several burials, cultural features, and a midden area. Although Hunting Creek has received considerable attention from amateur and professional archaeologists, there are no written reports describing the results of the excavations.

FIGURE 4.10. *A Uwharrie Fabric Marked pot from the Forbush Creek site in Yadkin County (top) and a Uwharrie Net Impressed pot from the Trading Ford site in Rowan County (bottom).*

The Haw River Phase (A.D. 1000–1400)

The Haw River phase is restricted to the north central Piedmont. Pottery styles during the first half of the phase are typologically similar to Uwharrie phase ceramics, and settlements consisted of small scattered hamlets. Still, seeds of change were sown during the first half of the Haw River phase that would culminate in permanent, nucleated village settlements across much of the Piedmont at the end of the Late Woodland period.

The Hogue site (31Or231b/31Or233), located on the Eno River near Hillsborough, is one of four sites situated within a broad U-shaped bend of the river. These four sites—Hogue, Wall (31Or11), Jenrette (31Or231a), and Fredricks (31Or231)—span some 700 years of occupation within an area of approximately twenty-five acres. The Hogue and Wall sites were occupied during the Late Woodland period and clearly demonstrate the transition from small, scattered settlements to compact, palisaded villages.

The Hogue site, the earlier of the two, was first tested by the Research Laboratories of Anthropology in 1984. More extensive excavations were carried out during the summer of 1989. These tests and excavations revealed a dispersed settlement that was separated by a large wooded ditch. In 1989, the two sections of the site were named "Hogue East" (Or231b) and "Hogue West" (Or233). In addition to these two concentrations of artifacts and features, other pits dating to the Hogue site occupation were uncovered while the adjacent Jenrette and Fredricks sites were being excavated, both of whose primary occupations date to the Contact period (ca. A.D. 1650–1710).

Although postholes were found scattered across the Hogue site excavations, no clear house patterns could be discerned. Features consisted of large, basin-shaped pits whose function was unclear, cylindrical storage facilities that were subsequently filled with refuse deposits, and human burials. The burials were perhaps the most interesting discovery at Hogue. They were clustered in the eastern portion of the site in what appeared to be a cemetery. The skeletal remains were poorly preserved, but all seemed to have been placed in the graves in a flexed position. No burial offerings accompanied the remains, although large rocks were sometimes placed near the feet of the deceased. The placement of the burials in a cemetery may have begun during the Uwharrie phase, as evidenced by the concentration of primary interments described at the Forbush Creek site. Large rocks were also placed near the feet of some of the Forbush Creek burials.

Similarly, continuity between the Uwharrie and early Haw River phases can be seen in the ceramics from the Hogue site. Here, the most popular vessel form was a large, undecorated, conical-shaped jar with a straight or slightly constricted neck. Most often the surfaces of these vessels were finished with a net-

FIGURE 4.11. *A Haw River Net Impressed jar from a small site along Morgan Creek in Orange County.*

wrapped paddle. After a careful study of the Hogue site pottery, archaeologists have determined that it is a late manifestation of the Uwharrie series and is ancestral to the Haw River series pottery that became popular during the latter half of the Haw River phase (Ward and Davis 1993:408).

Surveys and excavations at late Haw River phase sites have revealed settlements similar to that of the Hogue site—with the exception of the cemetery. Most appear to represent small dispersed households, indicated archaeologically by low artifact densities and a low frequency of postholes and pit features. These settlements are frequently found along the ridges and knolls bordering the narrow floodplains of secondary streams (Ward and Davis 1993) (fig. 4.11).

Typical pit features are fairly large cylindrical storage facilities that were filled with soil and refuse once they were no longer used for storage. Evidence of agriculture has been found in all the Haw River phase storage facilities excavated so far. This evidence consists primarily of maize kernels and cupules, but beans, squash seeds, and sunflower seeds also have been recovered. In addition to domesticated plant food remains, these pits usually contained charred fragments of acorns and hickory nuts, alongside a variety of animal bones, including deer, squirrel, and rabbit. This evidence suggests that although domesticated plants—particularly corn and beans—began to be an important food staple during the first half of the Late Woodland period, wild food resources also continued to be important (Gremillion 1989; Holm 1994; Ward and Davis 1993).

The Dan River Phase (A.D. 1000–1450)

In the upper Dan River drainage of the northern Piedmont a cultural pattern identified as the Dan River phase emerged at the same time as the Haw River phase in the central Piedmont. Although archaeologists do not know for sure why, a much larger resident population occupied the Dan River valley during the Late Woodland period than the Eno and Haw River drainages. It has been speculated that the extensive bottomlands along the Dan and its tributaries offered more access to good agricultural soils and, therefore, attracted larger numbers of people. Still, it was not until after the thirteenth century that these groups aggregated into substantially larger villages (Ward and Davis 1993:418).

Excavations at the Powerplant site (31Rk5), located on the south side of the Dan River in Rockingham County, North Carolina, and at the Leatherwood Creek site in Henry County, Virginia, suggest that early Dan River phase settlements were very similar to those of the Haw River phase. A linear community of houses and associated features were loosely strung out parallel to the banks of the river. Surveys and excavations also indicate that artifact densities at these sites are relatively low, at least compared to those found on later sites (Gravely 1983; Ward and Davis 1993).

Large storage pits occur frequently on early Dan River phase sites. When found by archaeologists, these pits usually contain secondary deposits of refuse, reflecting their use as garbage receptacles after they were no longer suited for storage. Subsistence remains from the Powerplant site indicate a mixed economy of hunting, gathering, and agriculture. Although animal and plant food samples from this site were comparatively small, they did represent a wide variety of resources, and evidence of maize was recovered from almost every pit feature. The presence of beans and sunflower seeds, along with corn, clearly indicates the importance of agriculture on the Dan River after A.D. 1000 (Gremillion 1989; Holm 1994; Ward and Davis 1993).

A single burial placed in a simple oval pit was excavated at the Powerplant site. The body was flexed and not accompanied by burial offerings—at least any that had been preserved. The pit form and body disposition were similar to Haw River phase burials; however, the single interment contrasts with the group burials uncovered at the Hogue site (Ward and Davis 1993:237).

Dan River phase pottery was first recognized by Joffre Coe and Ernest Lewis, who thought it was the product of the historic Sara Indians (Coe 1952; Coe and Lewis 1952; Lewis 1951). More recent investigations have shown that the pottery described by Coe and Lewis was not made by Historic tribes but rather by their ancestors several centuries earlier. During the first half of the Dan River phase, Uwharrie influences are clearly evident. Crushed quartz was used as the tempering agent, and vessel interiors were usually heavily scraped. Most vessel surfaces were net impressed, but other techniques such as cordmarking, smoothing, corncob impressing, and brushing were also used (fig. 4.12). Most of the pots were formed into large storage and cooking vessels. Decorations consisted of notches along the lip, incised or brushed lines around the neck, or sometimes fingernail pinches or punctations in the neck area (Ward and Davis 1993:418–19) (fig. 4.13).

During the last half of the Dan River phase, settlement size and density increased dramatically over that of the early Dan River phase. Many of these settlements were located along the banks of the Smith and Mayo Rivers in southern Virginia, as well as along the Dan River in North Carolina. Although few Dan River sites in North Carolina have been excavated, many such sites were investigated in Virginia during the 1960s and 1970s (Davis and Ward 1991; Gravely 1983). The Late Prehistoric component at Lower Saratown (31Rk1) on the Dan River in Rockingham County, and sites such as Belmont, Koehler, and Stockton in Virginia, suggest that these settlements consisted of circular, stockaded villages from one to two acres in extent (Coleman and Gravely 1992; Davis et al. 1997a, 1997b; Ward and Davis 1993). Located within the stockades were from fifteen to twenty households represented by circular house structures with associated storage pits, burials, and hearths. These formed rings adjacent to the stockades and encircled open, central plazas where community activities took place. Late Dan River phase villages were located on the wide alluvial terraces of the Dan River and its major tributaries.

As mentioned earlier, the increase in size and occupational intensity seen during the latter half of the Dan River phase was associated with rapidly growing populations relying more and more on the cultivation of corn. It also seems likely that the rise of large fortified communities may be partially related to an increase in Iroquois raids from the north into the Eastern Siouan heartland. Internal strife probably also increased as villages vied for access to good crop lands.

Most (80–90 percent) of the late Dan River phase pottery is net impressed,

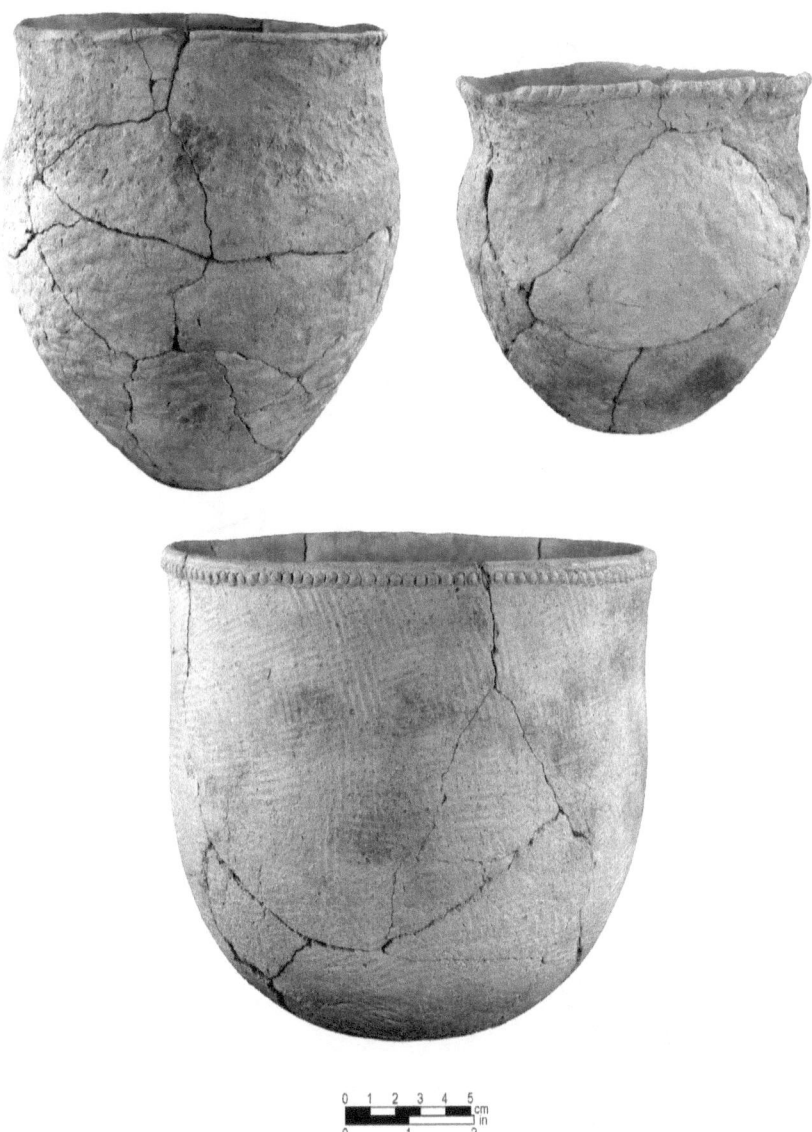

FIGURE 4.12. *A group of three pots found with a burial along Dan River in Rockingham County. The top two vessels are Dan River Net Impressed, and the bottom pot is Pee Dee Complicated Stamped.*

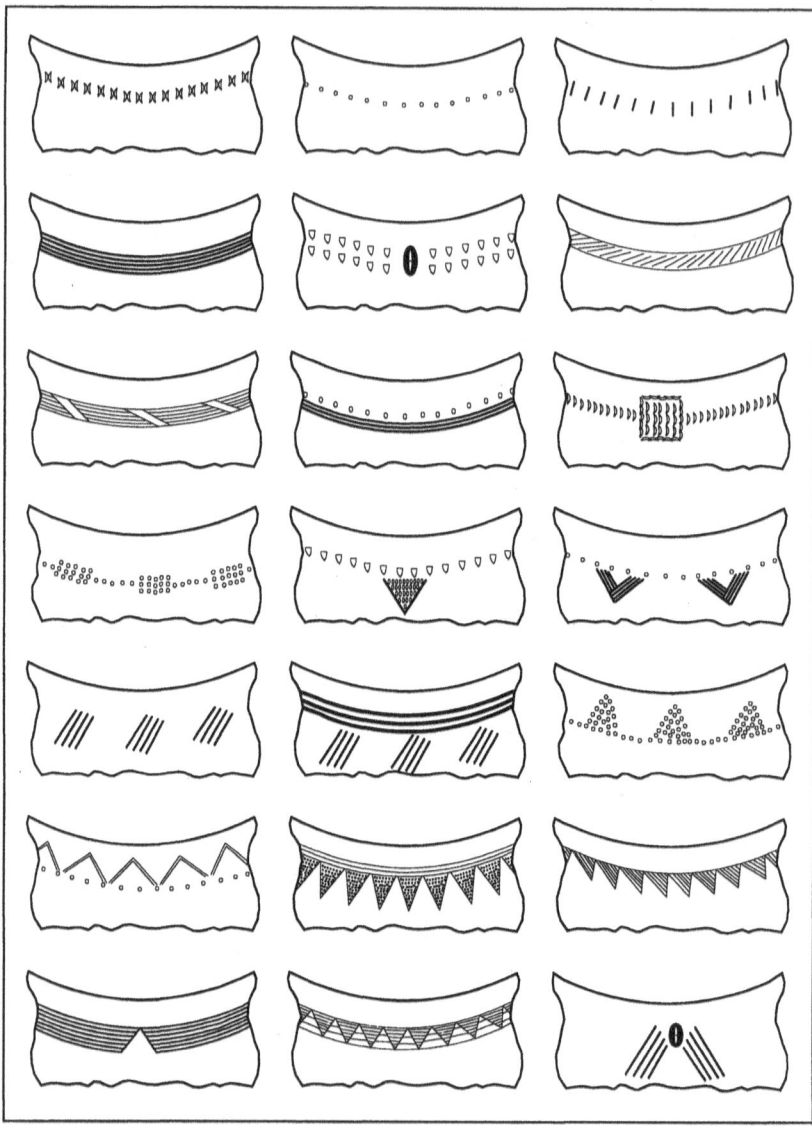

FIGURE 4.13. *Some Dan River pottery decorations found in the upper Dan River drainage. They were applied to the vessel neck and shoulder using fingertips, sticks, and sharp-pointed instruments.*

although a few sherds display cordmarked, cob-impressed, or smoothed surfaces. The interiors of most vessels usually were heavily scraped, but sand replaced crushed quartz, which was used during the early Dan River phase, as the most popular tempering agent. Large storage and cooking jars with constricted necks and flaring rims continued to be made along with smaller bowls.

Vessel decoration increased in popularity and variety over that of the early Dan River phase. Finger pinches, stick incisions, and reed punctations were applied in bands around the shoulder area, while lips were commonly notched, incised, or punctated with reeds (Ward and Davis 1993:419).

One of the most striking features of the Dan River phase is the variety of ornaments and tools made from bone, shell, and clay. Awls, pins, needles, fishhooks, beamers, gouges, antler flakers, antler picks, and turtle carapace bowls and cups, as well as a variety of beads, represent some of the bone artifacts (fig. 4.14). The edges of freshwater mussel shells were serrated and used as scrapers. The marine whelk was carved and ground into long columella beads, shorter barrel and disk beads, gorgets, and pendants. Marginella and olive shells were also used to make a wide variety of beads. Clay, in addition to its use in the manufacture of pots, was fashioned into cups, spoons, dippers, beads, and a variety of smoking pipes (Ward and Davis 1993:419).

The Donnaha Phase (A.D. 1000–1450)

Since 1973, archaeologists at Wake Forest University have been conducting surveys and excavations in the Great Bend area of the Yadkin River valley. Initially, this research focused on excavations at the well-known Donnaha site located on the west side of the Yadkin River in Yadkin County. Although this large, rich site was occupied throughout most of the Woodland period, the main occupation appears to have occurred during the Late Woodland period and is related to the Dan River phase (Woodall 1984).

The Donnaha site is characterized by a difficult and complex stratigraphy exacerbated by modern flooding and looting by relic collectors. In 1973, exploratory excavations were undertaken to determine the site's limits and stratigraphy and to begin to interpret the nature of the features and burials. To this end, a series of two-meter squares were randomly selected for excavation after the site's limits were determined by a walk-over survey. In 1975, excavations continued at the site in order to enlarge the sample of features and burials, and to try and identify house patterns (Woodall 1984:12–14).

The Donnaha excavations recovered "hundreds of thousands" of ceramic, bone, stone, and shell artifacts. "To write that artifacts were abundant at Donnaha would be an illustration of understatement" (Woodall 1984:61). The nonceramic artifact assemblage from Donnaha, particularly the array of shell and bone tools, is very similar to that found on Dan River phase sites in the Dan River valley. Although much of the pottery also is clearly related to ceramics of the Dan River phase, an assortment of earlier and later materials has also been recognized (Woodall 1984).

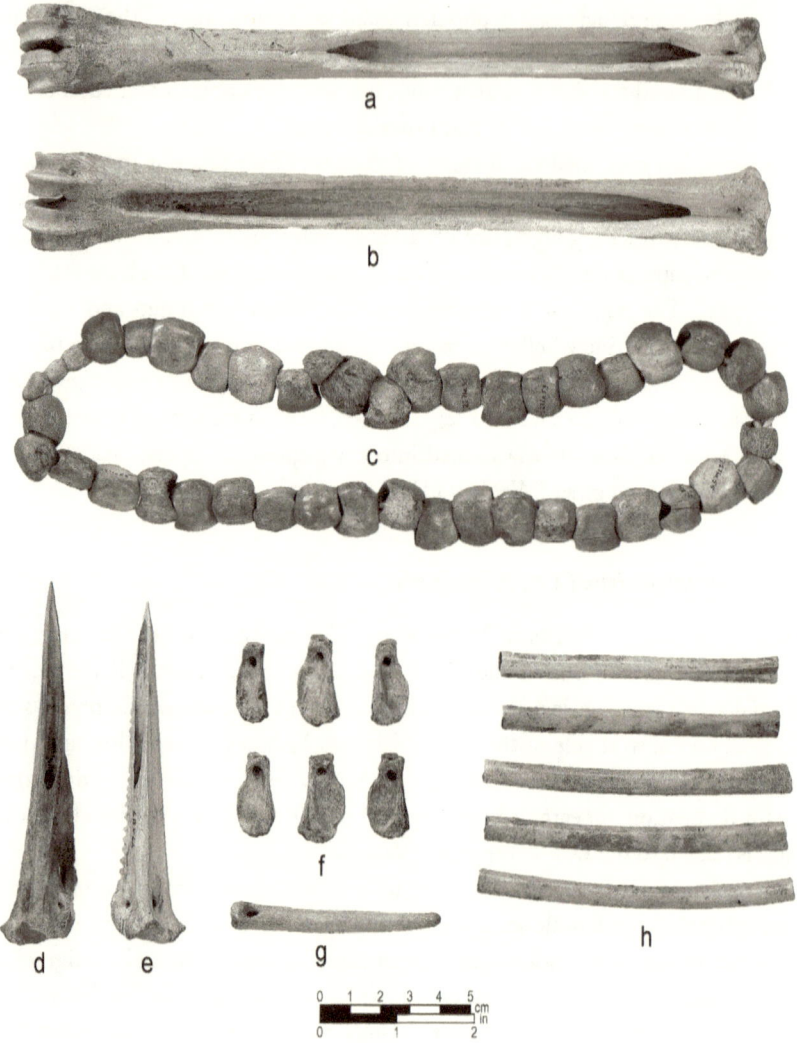

FIGURE 4.14. *Bone tools and ornaments from Dan River and Hillsboro phase sites: beamers (a–b), barrel-shaped beads (c), awls (d–e), drilled turkey wing-phalanx beads (f), antler pin (g), and tubular beads (h).*

No definitive house patterns were identified at Donnaha, although partial posthole alignments suggest that some of the burials might be associated with small houses or enclosures. Numerous trash-filled pits and nineteen human burials were excavated. The trash pits contained high densities of mussel shells. All of the burials were flexed and placed in oval or circular pits. Several contained a variety of shell and bone beads. Marginella shells were apparently sewn on burial garments, whereas tubular-shell beads and cut-disk beads made of bone and shell were strung and worn as necklaces. Conch shell gorgets were found with two individuals (Woodall 1984).

Although no remains of corn—either kernel or cob fragments—were identified during the early phases of the research at Donnaha, Gregory Mikell, a Wake Forest graduate student, later identified numerous carbonized cob fragments from pit features (1987). Ned Woodall, the archaeologist in charge of the Donnaha excavations, hypothesized that maize was introduced into a fledgling horticultural system based on squash and other native crops. Corn increased horticultural productivity and caused populations to grow, which, in turn, placed additional pressures on food resources. This cyclical process led to a greater reliance on the production of cultivated crops and the need for well-drained, fertile levee soils. As native farmers had to travel farther and farther to find good soils, they eventually established smaller, autonomous villages, and the population of the upper Yadkin valley began to stabilize (1984:107).

This settlement model is similar to the one proposed for the Dan River valley, where the increased reliance on maize agriculture resulted in population increases during the Dan River phase. However, rather than the population growth resulting in the fragmentation of large villages, the Dan River data suggest that smaller, more dispersed groups coalesced into larger, more compact settlements. In reality, both processes, fragmentation and coalescence, were probably responsible for Late Prehistoric settlement patterns in the upper Yadkin and Dan River valleys.

Since the Donnaha excavations, surveys and excavations by Wake Forest University have extended up the Yadkin River valley almost to the edge of the Blue Ridge escarpment, and south of the Great Bend area to the Davie County line. Whereas the early research focused on subsistence and settlement patterns, the most recent efforts have been directed toward identifying the size and extent of sociopolitical entities. So far, research indicates that there is insufficient stylistic variability, at least in the Dan River–like ceramics of the upper Yadkin valley, to isolate and identify social and political units above the village level. Even within villages, a lack of ceramic variability suggests that pottery-making was not regulated by kinship or group affiliations (Woodall 1987). However, at sites on the upper Yadkin near the Blue Ridge escarpment, the ceramics clearly reflect a blending of traditions from both the mountains and the Piedmont. This blending points to a high degree of social interaction between the two regions along the zone of their interface (Woodall 1990).

The Hillsboro Phase (A.D. 1400–1600)

The Hillsboro phase was defined by excavations conducted in the north central Piedmont. Although small, scattered settlements similar to those of the Haw River phase continued to dot the landscape during the Hillsboro phase, a few sites dating to the first half of the phase represent compact, nucleated villages with relatively large populations. The best example of this kind of community is the Wall site on the Eno River at Hillsborough. Wall has a long excavation history, beginning in 1938 when Joffre Coe launched the first Siouan project with funds provided by Eli Lilly, the pharmaceutical magnate, and the Indiana Historical Society.

Coe's objective was to locate and excavate Historic villages of the Piedmont Siouan tribes that had been described by early explorers like John Lawson and John Lederer. At that time, the Wall site was thought to be the Occaneechi village that John Lawson visited in 1701 and described in his journal published in 1709 (Lefler 1967).

The 1938 excavations consisted of a 100' trench that varied in width from 5 to 10 feet. The trench uncovered several archaeological features and a portion of a circular house but no Historic artifacts other than a few specimens screened from the plowzone. In 1940 and 1941, as part of the statewide Works Progress Administration (WPA) archaeological project, Robert Wauchope directed excavations at the Wall site, uncovering an extensive area of approximately 12,000 square feet. Wauchope's work revealed several houses, multiple stockade alignments, burials, and other pit features—but still no evidence of the Historic Occaneechi settlement (Petherick 1987:30) (fig. 4.15).

In 1983, excavations were resumed at the Wall site as part of the Research Laboratories of Anthropology's newly organized Siouan project, which was designed to study culture change in the Piedmont as a consequence of early European-Indian interaction. After reviewing Lawson's journal, the RLA staff felt that Coe and Wauchope were correct in assuming that the Occaneechi village should be located in the same vicinity as the Wall site. By using more refined screening techniques, the researchers thought they could recover small trade artifacts that the earlier excavators may have missed. However, it soon became apparent during the course of the 1983 fieldwork that the only European-made artifacts at the site were restricted to the plowzone and dated to the late, not early, eighteenth century. In 1983, radiocarbon samples obtained from charcoal found in Wall site features confirmed that the site was occupied during the middle of the fifteenth century (Ward and Davis 1993:412).

It is estimated that the Wall site covers approximately 1.25 acres, of which one-fourth has been excavated (fig. 4.16). These excavations have uncovered

FIGURE 4.15. *View of Robert Wauchope's 1941 excavation at the Wall site showing the circular wall alignment of House D marked with stakes. (Courtesy of the Research Laboratories of Archaeology)*

seven circular houses that average almost 35 feet in diameter. Two smaller "special purpose" structures that may have served as cribs or sheds also have been identified. In addition, eight burials and seventy-three other pit features have been excavated. All the structures and features are contained within one of five stockade alignments. Coincident with the stockades is a thick midden deposit that surrounds the ring of houses. The Wall site was probably occupied by a population of 100 to 150 people for less than twenty years (Petherick 1987; Ward and Davis 1991).

Most of the "features" at the Wall site were large postholes that were assigned numbers during the early years of excavation. True pit features rarely occurred; however, a few large, shallow, basinlike facilities were uncovered, which have been interpreted as communal roasting pits. These pits may have been used to prepare food for large feasts that marked communitywide ceremonies and celebrations. Typically, they contained large amounts of plant and animal food refuse, as well as charcoal, ash, and fire-cracked rocks. These deposits suggest that after the facilities were used as roasting pits, they became handy garbage receptacles.

Most of the Wall site burials were placed in what archaeologists call shaft-and-chamber pits. These were usually formed by digging a cylindrical shaft into the subsoil and then excavating a tunnel-like chamber off to one side at the

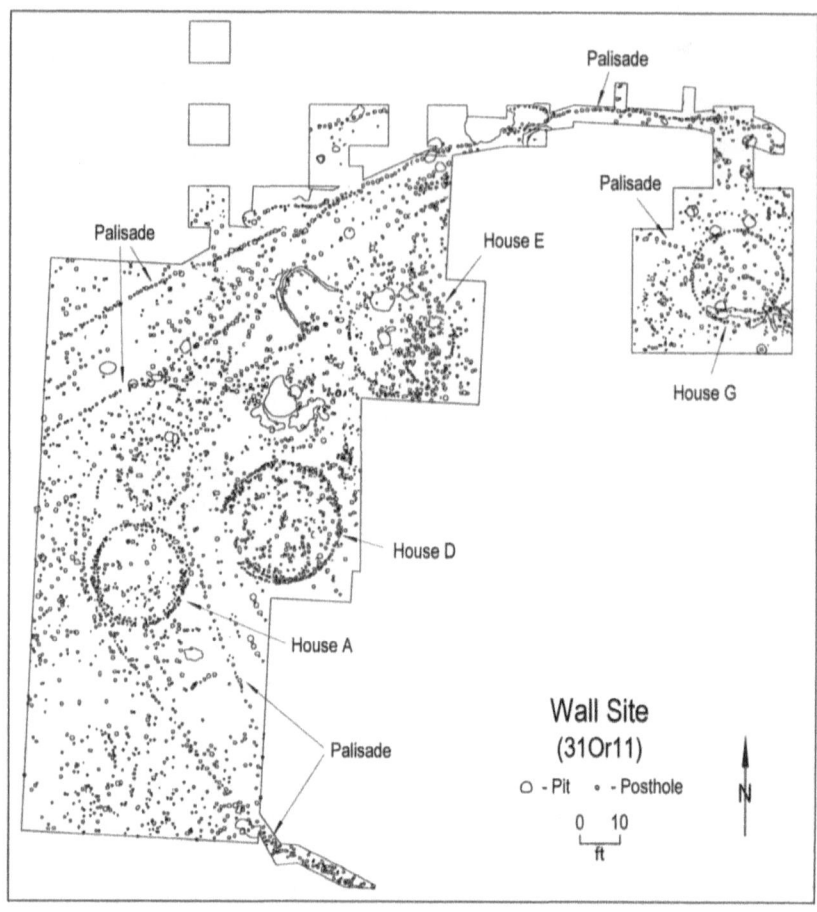

FIGURE 4.16. *Excavation plan of the Wall site showing pits and posthole patterns of houses and palisades.*

bottom of the shaft. The bodies of the deceased, after being placed in a flexed or fetal position and wrapped in mats, were placed in the chambers. The chambers were then sealed—sometimes with timbers, sometimes with large stones—and the shaft was then filled with the soil removed during the excavation of the pit. Two of the graves from the Wall site also contained upper layers of fill rich in food remains and other refuse, similar to the fill found in the roasting pits. This similarity in richness and content has led to the suggestion that feasting may have been an important aspect of the mortuary ritual (Ward 1987; Ward and Davis 1993:412).

At the Wall site, all the burials were oriented with their heads pointing in an eastward direction and usually located within or just outside houses. Grave offerings consisted of small clay pots that probably contained food remains to sustain the deceased during their journey to the other world. Often shell beads were sewn on the burial garments or strung and placed on the bodies as jewelry. Engraved shell gorgets were sometimes hung around the necks of children (Ward 1987:108).

The mixed subsistence base that developed during the Haw River phase continued to provide sustenance for the Wall site inhabitants during the early Hillsboro phase. The rich bottomlands contained within the broad U-shaped bend of the Eno were planted in fields of corn, beans, and squash. The edges of cultivated plots provided wild fruits and berries, while the surrounding hardwood forest produced seasonal supplies of acorns, hickory nuts, and walnuts. The primary source of meat was the white-tailed deer. Small mammals, turtles, fish, wild turkeys, and passenger pigeons supplemented the venison and added variety to the diet (Holm 1987:245; Ward and Davis 1993:411).

Although continuity can be seen between Haw River and Hillsboro phase subsistence practices, discontinuity characterizes the two ceramic assemblages (fig. 4.17). Only about 1.5 percent of the pottery sample from the Wall site displayed attributes characteristic of the Haw River phase, such as net-impressed, cordmarked, or brushed surfaces. Instead, almost 75 percent of the Hillsboro phase pottery had simple-stamped surfaces. The remainder were check stamped or plain. Temper consisted of medium-to-fine sand or finely crushed feldspar. These ceramic differences, in conjunction with the nucleated community pattern, strongly suggest that the early Hillsboro phase population of the Wall site probably moved into the Eno valley from outside the area, much like the Pee Dee Indians did in the southern Piedmont.

Ceramics typical of those found at the Wall site were found alongside net-impressed and complicated-stamped pottery at late Hillsboro phase sites. The net-impressed sherds represent the last gasp of the ceramic tradition that began during the Uwharrie and Haw River phases. The complicated-stamped specimens are typologically similar to the Caraway series pottery found at the Poole site (31Rd1) in Randolph County, which is discussed in detail in the following section. We suggest that the presence of complicated-stamped and net-impressed pottery, along with plain and simple-stamped sherds, like those found at Wall, is indicative of increased contacts between local groups and those living in adjacent regions (Ward and Davis 1993:98).

In contrast to the early Hillsboro phase Wall site, late Hillsboro phase sites show more affinities to the earlier Haw River phase settlements. At sites like George Rogers (31Am220) and Edgar Rogers (31Am167) in Alamance County, the resident population seems to have been dispersed. There is no evidence of stockades. These and other late Hillsboro phase sites are not located on the

FIGURE 4.17. *Hillsboro phase pots and vessel sections from the Wall site.*

broad floodplains of major streams but rather along valley margins or adjacent uplands of small tributary streams. Although similar in form to Haw River phase settlements, feature and artifact densities are much greater, reflecting a more intense occupation. At the George Rogers site, a portion of a circular house wall, similar to houses at the Wall site, was uncovered. Also, the large, shallow basinlike features, first identified at the Wall site as roasting pits, continued to be used during the late Hillsboro phase. These facilities were used to prepare the same array of wild and cultivated foods as those at the Wall site (Ward and Davis 1993:410).

Only one grave has been found that dates to the late Hillsboro phase. At the Edgar Rogers site, a shallow rectangular pit contained the remains of a child whose head was pointing to the east. Like some of the burials found at the Wall site, the upper layer of burial fill was comprised of a rich organic soil containing mussel shells and animal bones, similar to the fill of nearby roasting pits (Ward and Davis 1993:412).

The Early Saratown Phase (A.D. 1450–1600)

This phase was defined by data collected from excavations of Early Upper Saratown, or the Hairston site (31Sk1), located on the Dan River near its confluence with Town Fork Creek. Extensive looting took place at the site during the mid-1960s but was followed by formal excavations by the Research Laboratories of Anthropology during the summer of 1981 (Wilson 1983).

Early Saratown phase sites are fewer in number than the preceding Dan River phase sites, but they are larger in size and evidence a more intense occupation. This settlement shift is indicative of a stable population that joined together in fewer but larger villages. The heart of the Hairston site covers 2.5 acres and contains an extensive midden and numerous pit features. It is clearly visible as a large, dark, circular soil stain after fall plowings and was one of the most intensively occupied sites in the Dan River valley (Ward and Davis 1993:420).

During the 1981 excavations, forty features and six human burials were uncovered. The majority of the features were large, cylindrical or bell-shaped storage pits. Earth ovens, shallow basins, and hearths were also found. Although similar to earlier features of the Dan River phase in form, the fill of the Hairston facilities was considerably richer in refuse, particularly food refuse.

Faunal remains suggest the exploitation of a wide range of resources from a variety of habitats. White-tailed deer and black bear were followed in importance by raccoon, beaver, turkey, and mountain lion. Numerous remains of turtles were also found. Compared with Dan River phase faunal remains, the Early Saratown phase samples represent a much broader based subsistence orientation (Wilson 1983:540).

Although no ethnobotanical samples from Early Saratown phase sites have been analyzed, corn and other agricultural pursuits probably increased in importance during this period. The size and intensity of the Hairston site occupation suggest that the increased reliance on agriculture that began during the Dan River phase continued and probably reached its peak just before contacts with the first Europeans. This same trend can be seen to the south during the Haw River and Hillsboro phases (Ward and Davis 1993:420).

While only six burials were excavated at the Hairston site, they contained a rich array of grave goods, in stark contrast to burials of the earlier Haw River and Dan River phases. All but one of the individuals were subadults. Four were

FIGURE 4.18. *Citico-style shell gorgets from the Hairston site.*

placed in shaft-and-chamber pits, whereas two were interred in simple pits. The shaft-and-chamber burials were accompanied by the most grave offerings, including hundreds of bone and shell beads, bone awls, shell hair pins, serrated mussel shells, three "rattlesnake"- or "Citico"-style gorgets, and a single pottery vessel (Wilson 1983:379–85). Contact with a copper bar gorget preserved a piece of a pine bark covering over one burial (Ward and Davis 1993:420) (fig. 4.18).

Early Saratown phase pottery has been described as the Oldtown series (Wilson 1983). This is a well-made ware with a fine sand–tempered paste and smooth interiors. The majority of the sherds have smooth or burnished surfaces, followed in popularity by net-impressed surfaces. Minority surface finishes include simple stamping, complicated stamping, corncob impressing, cordmarking, and brushing. Decorations include rim notching, finger pinching, and stick punctation similar to Dan River phase ceramics. New decorative techniques include rim castellations, lip burnishing, and the application of filleted strips. Vessel forms include bowls and jars. Almost half of the bowls display a carinated or cazuela-type rim, suggesting influences from the Catawba drainage to the south. Southerly influence in the Oldtown series is also indicated by the presence of burnishing, carved-paddle stamping, and the use of appliquéd, notched rim fillets for decoration (Ward and Davis 1993:421).

The Southern Piedmont

The southern Piedmont region is archaeologically unique within North Carolina. During Late Woodland times, the cultures located between the Uwharrie Mountains and the border between North and South Carolina did not participate in the Piedmont Village Tradition. They were influenced by a very different cultural tradition called South Appalachian Mississippian. Between A.D. 1000 and 1400, Mississippian-influenced societies developed from the coast of Georgia to the mountains of North Carolina. Known archaeologically as Etowah, Wilbanks, Savannah, Pisgah, Irene, and Pee Dee, these politically complex cultures built mounds for their elite, participated in an elaborate ceremonialism, and sometimes ruled over large territories. In the southern North Carolina Piedmont, the most obvious expression of the South Appalachian Mississippian tradition is the Pee Dee culture. And the most obvious archaeological site relating to the Pee Dee culture is the Town Creek site (31Mg2, 31Mg3) located on the Little River in Montgomery County (Coe 1952, 1995; Oliver 1992; Reid 1965).

The southern North Carolina Piedmont is also unique in the history of North Carolina archaeology. It is here that the first formal excavations were organized and launched by North Carolina archaeologists. Excavations in the southern Piedmont began an unbroken tradition of research that gradually spread across the state and is manifest today in a multitude of public and private programs.

A Brief History of Early Excavations

The Poole site, located on Caraway Creek near Asheboro, was the first site in the southern Piedmont to be scientifically excavated. The Poole site is also known as Keyauwee, the name of one of the Indian villages that John Lawson visited in the vicinity of present-day Asheboro in 1701. These early excavations were carried out by members of the Archaeological Society of North Carolina during June and July 1936. As announced in the society's *Bulletin*, "The Archaeological Society of North Carolina is making preparation for a two to three weeks excavation of a village site in Randolph County, North Carolina, starting June 14, 1936. This site is believed to be the location of the Indian village 'Keyauwee' visited in 1701 by John Lawson, then surveyor general of North Carolina. Soon after his visit the village was abandoned and its exact location remains much of a mystery today. It is hoped that this excavation will yield sufficient evidence to determine the culture of its inhabitants, if not definitely to prove it to be the 'Keyauwee' village" (Winston 1936a:13).

Officially, this expedition was led by Dr. James Bullitt of the University of North Carolina Medical School. Dr. Bullitt was assisted by Rev. Douglas Rights of Winston-Salem, Mr. Harry Davis of the North Carolina State Museum, and Mr. Joffre Coe of Greensboro (Winston 1936a:14). To support the Keyauwee expedition, the Society raised $143.50 in contributions from its membership. As of August 1, the total expenditures for the project were $89.90 (Winston 1936b:16–17).

Joffre Coe was listed as an assistant to Dr. Bullitt in the announcement of the Keyauwee project. In reality, he was much more. Because Coe was the only member of the 1936 crew who had formal archaeological training, he was made field director and put in charge of the day-to-day excavations. Coe had received his training during the summer of 1935 when he worked at the Kincaid site in southern Illinois as a member of the University of Chicago's archaeological field school, under the direction of Thorne Deuel. However, he considered his training at Kincaid to be inadequate for the task he and the Society members faced at Keyauwee.

In November of 1935, Coe contacted Glenn Black, an archaeologist working for the Indiana Historical Society, and asked his advice on organizing the Keyauwee project and on field techniques that might be appropriate to use at the site. Black promptly answered Coe's letter, offering him his sympathies for attempting to set up the project on a shoestring budget and having to rely on unskilled, volunteer labor, but he failed to provide Coe with any tips that might be useful in the actual excavations. Coe was tenacious, however, and repeated his request for advice on excavation techniques the following month, describing in detail the situation at Keyauwee, where three burials had already been plowed out: "What is the best approach to dig where you have an acre field with about a foot of topsoil and burials in pits? Would you trench the field in several places or would you carry, say a twenty foot face across the area containing the burials?" (letter from Joffre Coe to Glenn Black, December 4, 1935, RLA files).

A month later, Black responded with a detailed description of how to lay out a grid and map the excavations. He also included a sketch of the grid system he used. A modified version of Glenn Black's grid system is still used today by the Research Laboratories of Archaeology.

One of the most beneficial outcomes of the Keyauwee project was that it laid the foundation for institutional support for North Carolina archaeology. Coe, James Bullitt, Harry Davis, Douglas Rights, and Guy Johnson of the University of North Carolina's Sociology Department were primarily responsible for organizing the Archaeological Society of North Carolina. Although Coe, Bullitt, and Johnson were all affiliated in one way or another with the University of North Carolina, the university administration at first offered little backing for the Society's fledgling excavation program. Johnson was able to persuade the university to loan the project a truck to haul the tools and specimens from Keyauwee. He also convinced the dean of administration, Robert House, to allocate a little space on campus for storing the artifacts from the excavation. University president Frank Porter Graham accepted Coe's invitation to view some of the artifacts and was apparently impressed—but not enough to commit anything to the archaeology program other than storage space in the corner of the basement of the Pharmacy building (RLA files).

With university support not forthcoming, the State Museum of the Department of Commerce and Development in Raleigh came to the rescue. The curator and later director of the museum was Harry Davis. Davis's interest in archaeology was whetted by the Keyauwee expedition, which he participated in as a volunteer "field assistant." During the course of the excavation he was favorably impressed by the young Joffre Coe: "The experience was quite valuable to me and my fellow diggers, and we did not even blister our hands at that. We certainly came away with better general knowledge on the subject, and all respect for the scientific methods of Joffre Coe" (RLA files).

Harry Davis soon became one of Coe's strongest supporters and a key player in developing the North Carolina archaeology program. Professor Johnson and Rev. Rights also were strong supporters of Coe and made it financially possible for him to attend the University of North Carolina. However, their backing of the archaeology program was channeled through the Archaeological Society, which, at the time, was barely able to support itself.

Davis's pivotal role in getting North Carolina archaeology off the ground is amply illustrated in the planning and organization of the first excavations at the Town Creek site. Following the Keyauwee work in 1936, the Archaeological Society, led by Douglas Rights, applied to the federal WPA for labor to excavate a large mound in Montgomery County, known at the time as the Frutchey mound, named after its owner, Mr. L. D. Frutchey (fig. 4.19). Rights and

FIGURE 4.19. *View of the Frutchey Mound at Town Creek in 1937, just prior to excavation. (Photo by Coe, 1937; from Coe 1995:62)*

Johnson, as well as Coe, felt the university should act as the co-sponsor of the project, with the Archaeological Society of North Carolina acting as the sponsor (Coe 1995:12).

The university administration, however, continued to be hesitant in becoming involved in archaeology, feeling that the general public might consider it to be too frivolous an undertaking during the hard times of the Great Depression. The administration was afraid that its involvement with the Town Creek excavations might prove to be a bad public relations move and adversely affect the university's efforts to squeeze funds from the financially strapped state legislature. When the WPA balked at the idea of the Archaeological Society acting as the project sponsor, and when the project failed to get university support, Mr. Davis arranged for the North Carolina Department of Conservation to serve as the official sponsoring agency of the 1937 WPA project at the Town Creek site (RLA files).

In March 1937, the project was approved by the WPA at the last minute. But, by this time, there was no WPA labor available in the counties around Town Creek. Again Mr. Davis came to the rescue. He managed to wrangle $300 from the budget of the State Museum to support the excavations. With this money, a few borrowed tools, and an old, broken-down car, Coe dropped his classes at the University of North Carolina and began the first excavations at Town Creek. Davis also arranged to get a few helpers—mostly high school students and volunteers—for Coe. From these humble beginnings in 1937, excavations at Town Creek would continue off and on for the next fifty years (Coe 1995; RLA files).

Before the 1937 excavations began, Mr. Frutchey donated the mound and two acres of land around it to the state. Additional land was later purchased, and Town Creek became a state historic site in 1955 under the administration of the Department of Archives and History. By 1962, the mound, the temple atop the mound, one of the stockades surrounding the site, and two structures within the enclosure had been reconstructed. The Town Creek site remains today North Carolina's only state historic site dedicated to its native population. A recent publication by Joffre Coe (1995), with contributions by several of his former students who worked at the site, provides a long-awaited account of the Town Creek excavations, excavations that have achieved almost mythic status over the years. As Jefferson Reid wrote in 1967, "The scope of the information collected thus far staggers both mind and imagination, especially, as it is now being called from the inert into publication" (ix).

The Pee Dee Culture

The people who lived at the Town Creek site during its heyday have been referred to as the Pee Dee Indians and their unique lifestyle, the Pee Dee culture (Coe 1952, 1995; Oliver 1992; Reid 1967). The site itself is located on the west bank of the Little River near its confluence with Town Fork Creek, in Montgomery County. A few miles downstream the Little River flows into the Pee Dee, which becomes the Great Pee Dee as it cuts through northeastern South Carolina to empty into the Atlantic Ocean.

Excavations revealed that the mound at Town Creek was constructed over an early rectangular structure that has been described as an earth lodge (Coe 1995:65–72). The walls of the structure were formed by individual posts set in holes (fig. 4.20). Earth was then piled in an embankment around the walls and over the roof to create the earth lodge. Eventually this structure collapsed. Its remains and the surrounding area were covered, creating a low earthen mound that served as a platform upon which a temple or town house was erected. This structure ultimately burned. Its charred remains also were covered by a thick layer of soil that served to enlarge and heighten the original mound. A second structure, identical to the first, was built atop the new mound (79–82).

The mound at Town Creek faced a large plaza or public area where public meetings and ceremonial activities took place. Several structures, including some that may have served as burial or mortuary houses, were constructed around the edge of the plaza. The mound, plaza, and habitation zone were

124 WOODLAND PERIOD: PIEDMONT

FIGURE 4.20. *Troweling the top of subsoil at the base of the Frutchey Mound inside the rectangular pre-mound earth lodge. The wall postholes and parallel entryway trenches have been excavated. (Photo by Coe, 1937; from Coe 1995:71)*

enclosed by a stockade made of closely set posts. Evidence of five episodes of stockade building has been found. All but the latest stockade stood before the mound was constructed (Coe 1995:87, 265) (fig. 4.21).

Although not visible like the mound, equally impressive is the large number of burials at Town Creek. A total of 563 burials are thought to be associated with the Pee Dee culture. Several of these graves are clustered in mortuary areas. Most individuals were interred in simple pits with their bodies arranged in a loosely flexed position. A few were buried with their bodies fully extended, and a small number of individuals appear to have been reburied as bone bundles. The bodies of several infants and small children were tightly wrapped and placed in large pottery vessels—called burial urns—which were then buried. A few of the Pee Dee burials were richly adorned with a variety of exotic artifacts made from copper imported from the Great Lakes area and shells from the coast. Copper artifacts include copper-covered wooden ear spools and rattles, pendants, sheets of copper, and a copper ax (fig. 4.22). Beads, gorgets, and pins were fashioned from conch shell (Coe 1995:232, 269).

It is apparent that the Pee Dee culture of Town Creek represented quite a departure from the Piedmont Village Tradition to the north. It was so different, in fact, that in 1952, Pee Dee culture was described as being "one of the best archaeological records of the movement of a people in the Southeast" (Coe

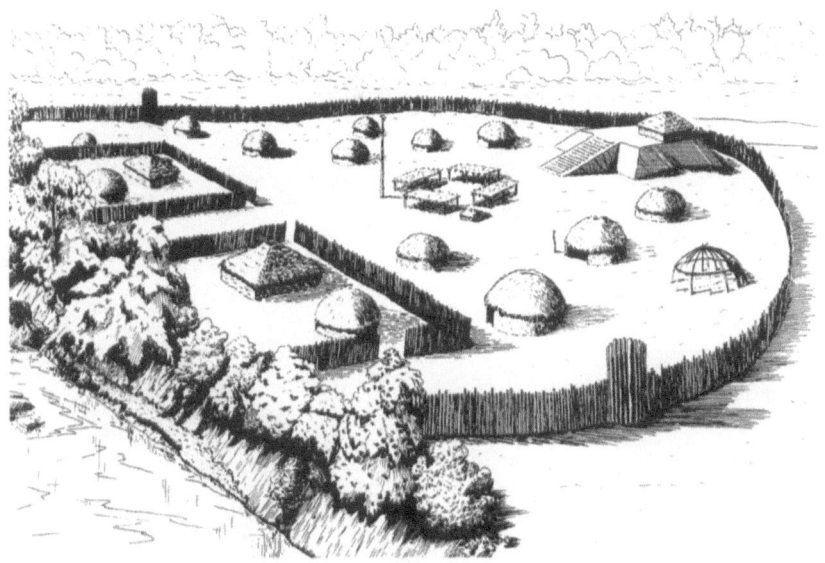

FIGURE 4.21. *An artist's conception of the Pee Dee village at Town Creek. (Drawing by Barton Wright, 1951; from Coe 1995:98)*

1952:308). The people who built Town Creek were seen as invaders from the south who traveled up the Pee Dee River valley and introduced an entirely new and alien way of life on the southern North Carolina Piedmont. At the time, it was thought that this new culture arrived around A.D. 1550 and had disappeared by 1650, like "a beam of light flashing across a dark sky" (309).

Today, archaeologists know that Pee Dee culture is considerably earlier than originally thought and that it was not introduced by invaders from the south who moved en masse into the North Carolina Piedmont. Pee Dee is better viewed as a regional center of South Appalachian Mississippian that interacted and evolved with other regional centers scattered from the Coastal Plain of Georgia and South Carolina to the western North Carolina mountains.

In 1967, Jefferson Reid, a graduate student at the University of North Carolina, analyzed pottery samples from various contexts within the mound at Town Creek for his master's thesis. Reid was interested in determining if temporal differences could be discerned within the Pee Dee ceramic assemblage. His most informative samples came from the humus layer beneath the mound and from refuse deposits along the flanks of the mound. Reid pointed out the obvious temporal differences between these two contexts but cautioned that the ceramic samples from each resulted from very different sets of activities. Therefore, the variability between the samples might not only be an expression of temporal differences but functional differences as well. Specifically, the pre-

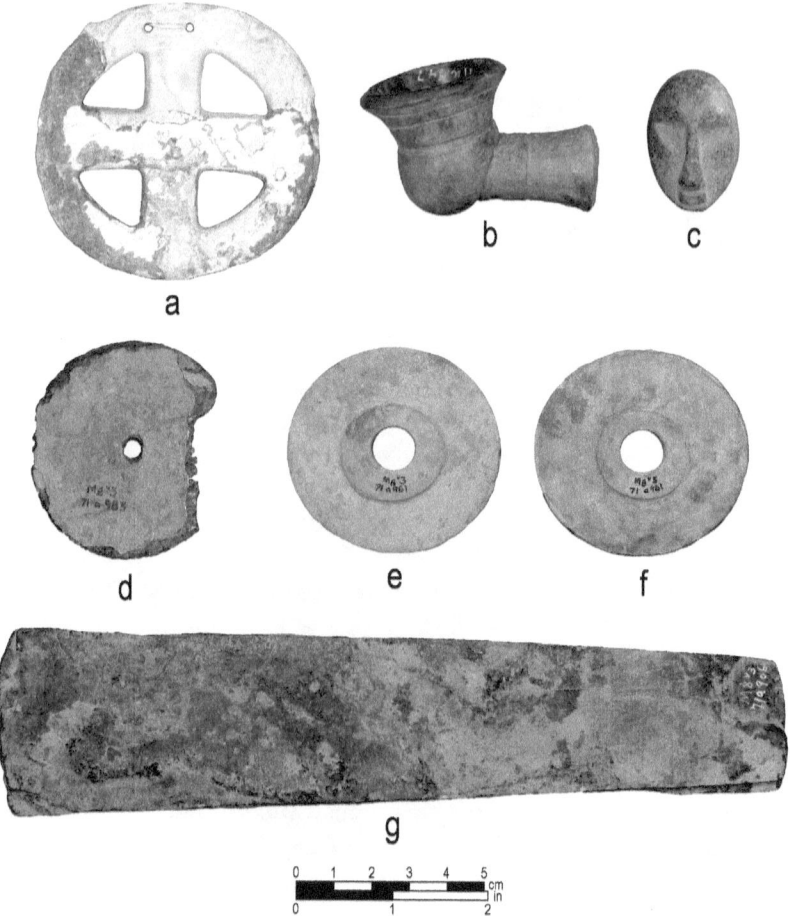

FIGURE 4.22. *Carved shell gorget (a), clay pipe (b), carved stone face (c), copper-coated wooden earspool (d), ground-stone earspools (e–f), and copper ax (g) found at Town Creek.*

mound humus sample could represent a wider range of domestic activities, whereas the sherds from the mound flank resulted from a narrower range of activities associated with ceremonial behaviors that took place in the temple atop the mound (1967:57, 1985:26).

Nevertheless, Reid was able to recognize several differences between the two samples, which he interpreted as being temporal. Sherds from the earlier humus zone were most often from hemispherical bowls and jars with complicated-stamped surfaces. The most popular design was formed by a series of concentric circles. The filfot-cross design was next in popularity. Decorations were rare except for the occasional addition of nodes and punctations along the vessel rims. In contrast, pottery from the later refuse sample indicated that the filfot cross replaced concentric circles as the most popular surface finish. Cazuela bowls became more popular, as did plain and burnished surface treatments. Vessel decoration also increased in frequency and variety (1967:83).

In addition to the concentric-circle and filfot-cross designs, several other varieties of Pee Dee complicated-stamped pottery were recognized by Reid. Sometimes the concentric circles were quartered by intersecting perpendicular lines. Chevrons connected by concentric arcs created an arc-angle design, and diamond motifs split by a single line often occurred in his samples. Herringbone, nested squares, and line-block designs were also popular (1967:10–19).

Another popular surface finish found at Town Creek is called textile wrapped. Unfired pottery vessels were wrapped with strips of fabric or textiles while still wet. The entire surface of the wrapped vessel was then paddled, which pushed the textile into the wet clay. When the material was peeled off, the textile impressions remained. This kind of surface treatment is unique to Pee Dee pottery. At Town Creek it follows complicated-stamped designs and burnished surfaces in popularity and appears to occur late in the Pee Dee ceramic chronology (Coe 1995:153; Oliver 1992:247; Reid 1967:8, 80).

Reid recognized strong similarities between Pee Dee pottery and pottery from other South Appalachian Mississippian sites in South Carolina and Georgia, including the Hollywood site on the Georgia side of the Savannah River, the Mulberry site near Camden, South Carolina, and the Fort Watson Mound in Clarendon County, South Carolina (1967). However, the ceramics most similar to the Town Creek pottery came from the Irene site, located on the bluffs overlooking the Savannah River near Savannah, Georgia (Caldwell and McCann 1941) (fig. 4.23).

Except for Reid's work, no attempt has been made to divide the Pee Dee ceramic assemblage from Town Creek into more discrete chronological units. The most recent analysis by Coe separated Pee Dee pottery from earlier and later wares but did not attempt to refine the chronological position of the various Pee Dee types. Coe (1995:167) did observe, however, that Pee Dee pottery developed from Savannah wares commonly found in the coastal regions of Georgia and South Carolina.

In addition to pottery, an obvious similarity between Town Creek and other South Appalachian Mississippian sites can be found in the way the construction of the mounds evolved. At the Irene and Beaverdam Creek sites on the Savannah River, earth lodges, or earth-embanked structures, were covered to create platform mounds in a fashion similar to the construction sequence at Town Creek (Anderson 1994; Caldwell and McCann 1941). The earth-lodge-to-

FIGURE 4.23. *Small Pee Dee pots from Town Creek (top and middle rows) and a Pee Dee Complicated Stamped vessel from the Leak site (bottom row).*

platform-mound sequence also was followed in the North Carolina mountains at the Garden Creek Mound No. 1—a Pisgah phase site—in Haywood County (Dickens 1976).

Many archaeologists consider the Irene site to bear the closest relationship to Town Creek (Coe 1952; Ferguson 1971; Oliver 1992; Reid 1967). The primary mound at Irene was built in eight stages. The first four building episodes involved earth-embanked structures, similar in form to the earth lodge at Town Creek. The only difference is the Irene structures were not covered with earth. The next three construction phases created a series of successively larger platform mounds upon which wall-post structures were built. These buildings were similar to the town houses or temples that stood atop the two mound stages following the earth lodge construction at Town Creek. After the seventh construction stage, the Irene mound was abandoned for a period of time.

The final mound-building episode was completely different from the previous stages. The old, flat-topped, rectangular mound was first covered with a layer of shell and sand, and then capped with a layer of clay. These additions greatly increased the size of the mound and transformed its shape from rectangular to circular, and its top from flat to round. This final construction stage was not designed to provide a platform for a building but rather to provide a matrix for human burials (Anderson 1994:174–80; Caldwell and McCann 1941:8–20). The platform mound at Town Creek did not undergo a similar transformation.

The first seven construction phases of the Irene mound took place during the Savannah I/II and III phases, dating from A.D. 1150 until about A.D. 1300. Based on surface finishes, the Savannah wares have been broken down into several types, including fine cordmarked, check stamped, complicated stamped, and burnished plain. The complicated-stamped type exhibits much variety in design, including concentric circles, figure eights, figure nines, barred circles, and diamonds. This type is believed to have developed around A.D. 1200 (Anderson, Hally, and Rudolph 1986:42–44). All of the Savannah types occurred in the occupation layers of the first six construction stages of the mound. However, Savannah Complicated Stamped pottery was not associated with the occupation zone of the seventh and last addition to the platform mound (Anderson 1994:174; Caldwell and McCann 1941:2).

The burial mound stage saw the arrival of a new ceramic ware called Irene. Three types comprise Irene ware—plain, incised, and a distinctive complicated-stamped motif in the form of a filfot cross. The Irene phase is believed to date from around A.D. 1300 to 1400 (Anderson, Hally, and Rudolph 1986:44).

Many of the Savannah and Irene complicated-stamped motifs, sometimes with slight variation, are duplicated in the Town Creek type defined as Pee Dee Complicated Stamped (fig. 4.24). Concentric circles, barred circles, and nested

FIGURE 4.24. *Etowah (a), Savannah (b–d), Irene (e–h), and Pisgah and Early Lamar (i–k) design motifs found on complicated-stamped pottery from Town Creek. (Drawings based on Reid 1967:11, 13).*

diamonds, as well as the Irene filfot cross, frequently occur in Pee Dee ware. However, cordmarked and check-stamped finishes have been found only rarely at Town Creek (Coe 1995:153; Reid 1967:71).

It is also interesting to note that several Pee Dee complicated-stamped motifs and textile-wrapped finishes are not found in Savannah and Irene wares. The nested-block, line-block, herringbone, and arc-angle designs reflect influences from the Pisgah and early Lamar phases (Dickens 1976; Hally 1994). Similarities also have been noted between the Pee Dee nested-diamond motif and pottery from the Etowah Mounds in north central Georgia (Ferguson 1971:124).

Without a more detailed chronological breakdown of the pottery from Town Creek, it is difficult to dovetail the sequence of cultural developments there with other South Appalachian Mississippian sites. It does seem clear, however, that the Pee Dee culture at Town Creek did not appear "like a beam of light" but rather evolved over a period of at least 200 years, beginning around A.D. 1200.

The form of mound at Town Creek and the way it evolved, taken in conjunction with the existing ceramic data, suggest that it was being built and modified at about the same time platform mounds were evolving during the Savannah II/III and Pisgah phases. The widespread presence of filfot-stamped pottery is evidence that Town Creek also was occupied later during the Irene phase. Although no burial mound was constructed at Town Creek, the large number of burials around the plaza may reflect sociopolitical and ceremonial changes similar to those documented at Irene. At both sites, burial of the dead may have become more important than the construction of elevated temples for a priestly elite (cf. Anderson 1994:292).

Archaeologists now believe that the fourteenth century saw the decline of many South Appalachian Mississippian centers like Irene and Town Creek. As the temple mounds were abandoned, burial practices changed to reflect a more egalitarian society. The shift from government by an elite to government by public consensus also is seen in the increased use of large public council houses rather than priestly temples atop mounds (Anderson 1994:293). In the Savannah River valley this decline in chiefly power is viewed, at least in part, as a consequence of prolonged drought conditions that caused a significant decline in agricultural production (Anderson 1995:327). The large number of burials at Town Creek may mean that the Pee Dee Indians faced a similar fate.

The Town Creek site, like a powerful magnet, has drawn the attention of archaeologists for over sixty years. With only mild hyperbole, it could be said that the mound on the banks of the Little River has been the center of the archaeological universe in the southern North Carolina Piedmont. However, since the 1980s, the focus of archaeological excavations has shifted away from Town Creek to outlying Pee Dee villages without mounds.

Joseph Mountjoy of the University of North Carolina at Greensboro recently reported on excavations at a large village site with a substantial Pee Dee component on the Deep River in Moore County. This site, called the Payne site (31Mr15), is located some thirty miles northeast of Town Creek (1989:7). Based on radiocarbon dates from three pit features—two that contained Pee Dee ceramics and one that contained "post-Pee Dee" pottery—Mountjoy concluded that Pee Dee culture arrived in the south central Piedmont sometime between A.D. 980 and 1160 (1989:19).

A similar conclusion also has been reached by Billy Oliver, an archaeologist with the North Carolina Office of State Archaeology. Excavations at the Leak (31Rh1) and Teal (31An1) sites in Richmond and Anson Counties, respectively, have allowed Oliver to tentatively propose three phases of development within Pee Dee culture. The earliest of these is the Teal phase, dating between A.D. 950 and 1200. These dates are based on radiocarbon assays from the Teal site and the Payne site (1992:240–47).

During the Teal phase, Pee Dee complicated-stamped pottery was accompanied by fine-cordmarked and simple-stamped types called Savannah Creek. Subsistence was based on hunting, fishing, and farming. Although nothing is known of their domestic structures, these early Pee Dee inhabitants built rectangular structures with rounded corners within which they conducted rituals and ceremonies. Infants and adults that had been cremated at death were sometimes buried in large clay urns similar to those that contained only children at Town Creek. Other graves consisted of primary interments in subterranean pits, and these sometimes contained more than one individual (Oliver 1992:243).

The Teal phase was followed by the Town Creek phase, which began around A.D. 1200 and ended around A.D. 1400. As previously discussed, this was the time when the mound was constructed at Town Creek and the site became the ritual and ceremonial center of the Pee Dee. At the Leak site, the filfot-cross motif and textile-wrapped vessels were the most popular pottery styles during the Town Creek phase (Oliver 1992:249). Urns continued to be used occasionally as burial containers, and the deceased were also placed in excavated pits. However, except for the elaboration of ritual activities evidenced by the construction of the mound at Town Creek, life for the Pee Dee continued much as before. Hunting, fishing, and gathering wild plant foods were important, but the mainstay of the subsistence system was maize agriculture (249).

As Town Creek's importance as the ritual and ceremonial center of the Pee Dee began to wane around A.D. 1400, the Leak site grew in size and importance. Oliver believes that the Leak phase, which began at this time, may have lasted until A.D. 1600. However, this assessment is based on uncorrected radiocarbon assays. While calibrated and uncalibrated dates closely correspond to the early end of the Pee Dee chronology proposed by Oliver, they begin to diverge significantly during the later end, particularly after A.D. 1500. When these dates are calibrated to make them consistent with calendrical dating, the Leak phase, for example, ends closer to A.D. 1500 than 1600. This "compression," or pushing the later end of the Pee Dee sequence back at least 100 years, is important because it allows time for the development of the Late Woodland Caraway phase, which followed Pee Dee in the southern Piedmont.

The Leak phase saw an increase in the popularity of complicated-stamped, plain, and textile-wrapped pottery styles, and cazuela bowl forms. Inhabitants of the Leak site lived in oval houses, and subsistence practices changed little during this time. The large fertile bottoms surrounding the site were planted in corn and beans. Fish and mussels were gathered from the Pee Dee River, and deer and other wild game were hunted. A variety of wild plant foods were collected as they became seasonally available (Oliver 1992:251–53).

Although some archaeologists (Coe 1952, 1995; Mountjoy 1989; Oliver 1992) believe that Pee Dee culture represents a foreign way of life introduced by a people who invaded from the south, many others, including us, see Pee Dee as an invasion of ideas, not people. Pee Dee is one of several regional expressions of the South Appalachian Mississippian tradition. Although contacts between people living at sites like Irene and Town Creek certainly happened, "invasions" or other large-scale group movements are not necessary to explain the spread of temple-mound ceremonialism and complicated-stamped pottery—the hallmarks of the South Appalachian Mississippian period. It seems more likely that local centers were tied into a vibrant communication network that facilitated the free flow of information, as well as the exchange of nonlocal goods and raw materials. These regional ties continued to be strong after the downfall of most of the mound centers, and they can be seen in the subsequent development of Lamar culture, whose spatial distribution overlaps that of the South Appalachian Mississippian tradition (Ferguson 1971; Hally 1994).

There is also a long-held view that Town Creek was a very special place where the Pee Dee Indians were allowed to visit but not live. Oliver (1992:60), for example, states: "Other than priests and their attendants, few people actually lived at Town Creek. Instead, people traveled from surrounding villages to participate in periodic religious, social, and political events held at Town Creek." The fact that the Town Creek site was special and important in the ceremonial activities of the Pee Dee who lived in the surrounding area cannot be disputed. However, it seems doubtful that the site was only occupied on a permanent basis by a small cadre of religious specialists. Evidence from other South Appalachian Mississippian sites clearly indicates occupations by large residential populations on a permanent basis (Anderson 1994; Dickens 1976). And at Town Creek, large amounts of domestic refuse, numerous postholes representing a maze of overlapping structures, and multiple stockade alignments also suggest a substantial residential population, as does the large number of burials. If Town Creek was the home of only a handful of high-ranking priests, they must have had voracious appetites and the itch to constantly move and rebuild their houses and surrounding stockades.

The Caraway Phase (A.D. 1500–1700)

The Caraway phase was first recognized at the Poole, or Keyauwee, site (31Rd1) mentioned previously for its role in the early history of North Carolina archaeology. Keyauwee is located on Caraway Creek in Randolph County, west of Asheboro. Before the 1936 excavations, the site had been disturbed by plowing, and several features and burials were exposed on the ground surface. Recognizing the disturbance, members of the state archaeological society conducted "preliminary" excavations at Keyauwee during the spring of 1935. They removed a burial richly adorned with a variety of shell beads that had been partially plowed out (Winston 1936a:13).

The more formal excavation strategy in 1936 was to explore simultaneously two areas of the site, designated Area A (fig. 4.25) and Area B. This kept the cadre of shovel-happy volunteers separated and thus minimized the risk of lost toes and fingers. For similar reasons, many archaeologists use a similar strategy today in their field school excavations. This approach also permitted the simultaneous sampling of two distinct areas of the site. Burials were concentrated in Area A, located in the eastern part, whereas pits containing village refuse were concentrated in Area B, located in the western portion of the site (Coe 1937:8–9). Still, the richest pit feature was uncovered in Area A, and a single burial was excavated in Area B (Coe 1937:Plates II and III).

A total of twelve skeletons were found in eight burial pits. It was reported that two graves contained two individuals and one contained three. All burials were shallow, and most had been badly disturbed by plowing and erosion (Coe 1937:11). Photographs of the burial excavations show that the "multiple" burials resulted from later graves intruding into previously dug burial pits. The individual pit outlines probably had been obliterated by erosion, or went unrecognized by the inexperienced excavators. All of the individuals were placed in their graves in a flexed position; two were children and the rest were adults at the time of death. A variety of artifacts were found associated with the burials, including bone and shell beads, shell gorgets, stone discoidals, and a stone pipe (11–14) (see fig. 4.6).

In addition to the burials, several other pits also were excavated. These were located in both excavation areas, but none was in the northern part of Area A where the burials were concentrated. The most interesting pit was located south of the burials in Area A. This large, shallow, oval pit measured some 6 feet in diameter and 10 inches deep, and it contained a rich assortment of refuse

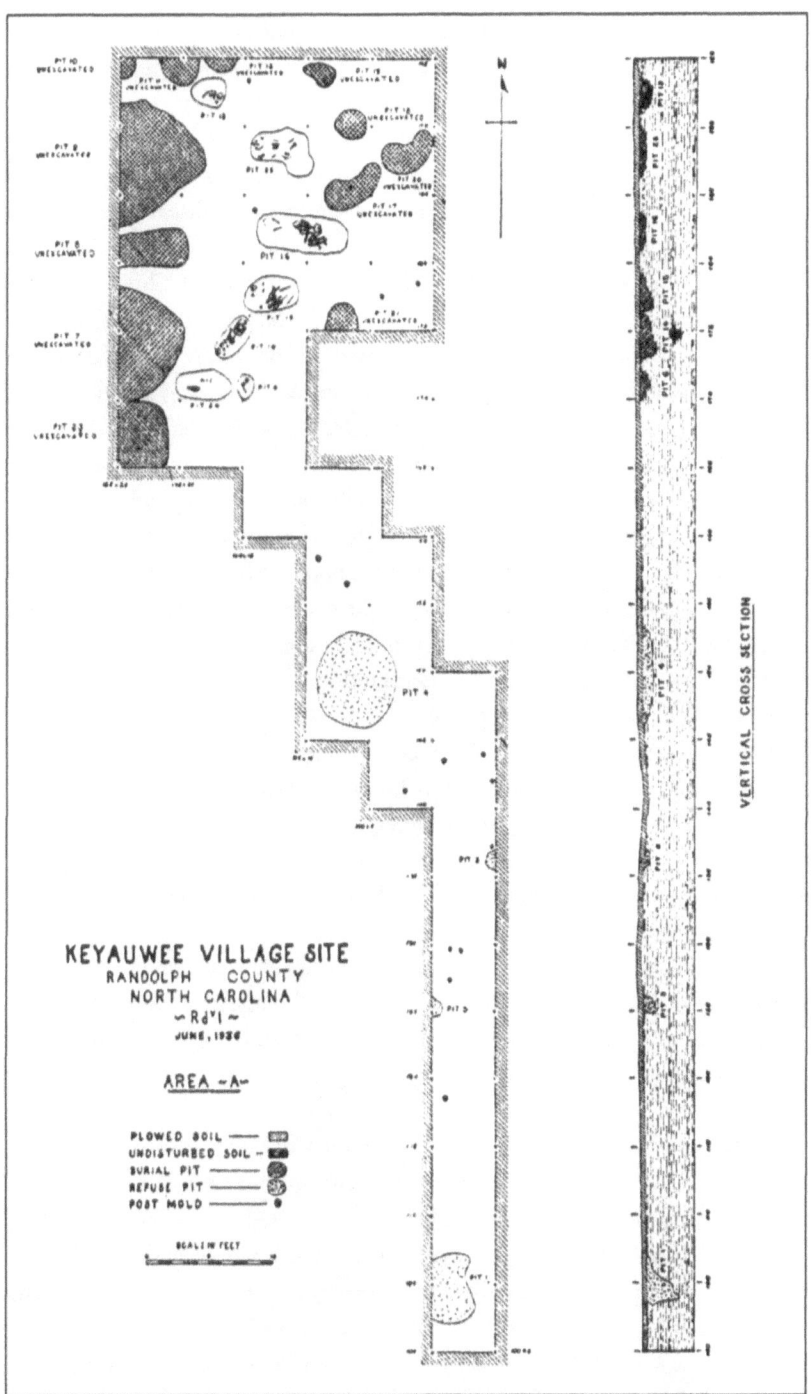

FIGURE 4.25. *Excavation plan of Area A at the Keyauwee site. (From Coe 1937)*

including pottery sherds, animal bones, ash, charcoal, and fire-cracked rocks. It was also the only pit that produced evidence of European contact—138 glass beads and kaolin trade pipe fragments (Coe 1937:15; RLA files).

But what intrigued Coe, the archaeologist in charge of the day-to-day excavations, most about this feature was the presence of thirty-seven fragments of human bone mixed in with the animal bones and other refuse. "This suggests that within historic times the people living at this site practiced cannibalism in some form," Coe wrote in 1937 (15). This assessment sparked a brief but lively debate between Coe and Rev. Douglas Rights. At the fall 1936 North Carolina Archaeological Society meeting, Coe reported on the results of the Keyauwee excavations and discussed the possibility of cannibalism being practiced. Apparently Rights said nothing at the meeting, but a few days later he wrote Coe and suggested that the presence of human bones in the pit was probably the result of some kind of disturbance, not cannibalism. Coe responded the same day he received Rights's letter and informed him that he stood behind his initial interpretation. He still considered the human bones to be evidence of cannibalism during the Historic period because "[t]he evidence gathered shows several things: 1. A low shallow pit, 4 to 5 feet in dia and 6 to 8 inches deep. 2. In the bottom of the pit there were scattered at random numerous fire cracked rocks, showing that at one time the pit contained fire. 3. The contents of the pit were mainly broken, cracked, charred, and calcined animal bones. 4. Occurring under the same conditions were a few human bones, several skull fragments, one half of a lower jaw, a few finger bones, and several other small fragments. Some of the human bones were burned - charred. 5. Scattered through the pit were small glass trade beads" (letter from Joffre Coe to Douglas Rights, October 10, 1936, RLA files).

Coe did not change his mind. When the preliminary report on the Keyauwee excavations was published in the *Bulletin of the Archaeological Society of North Carolina* in 1937, he concluded, "Evidence . . . would suggest that the people who lived at this site practiced some form of cannibalism during historic times" (16).

After re-examining the human bones from the Contact period feature, we are inclined to agree with the Rev. Rights—the bones got into the fill through some kind of disturbance or inadvertent mixing, not as food refuse. With the large number of burials disturbed by plowing and the disturbances by the inhabitants themselves, it is not surprising that some pieces of human bone from burials would get mixed with the refuse in feature fill, especially in a pit that was dug late in the site's occupational history. Also, it should be remembered that Coe was the only "experienced" excavator on the site in 1936, and the record does not show who actually excavated the feature in question. Moreover, none of the human bones appeared to us to have been burned or charred. The exuberance of youth has a way of creating its own reality, particularly when challenged by the wisdom of age.

Based on recent information gathered during the course of the Research Labs' Siouan project, most of the materials recovered during the 1936 excavations appear to date to the Late Woodland, and not the Contact, period (Ward and Davis 1993). Excavations at several Contact period sites have shown that some categories of trade artifacts, particularity small glass "seed" beads, are ubiquitous and occur in virtually all the features on these sites (see Chapter 7). Their presence in one pit and absence from all the others excavated at Keyauwee strongly suggest that most of the features and burials did not date to the time of European contact. Also, the shell and bone artifacts associated with the Keyauwee burials are very similar to grave goods found at sites dating to the Hillsboro, late Dan River, and Early Saratown phases (Ward and Davis 1993).

What all this boils down to is that some of the types that have been described as Caraway (Coe 1964:34; 1995:160–66) may date to the time of John Lawson's visit. However, Caraway phase ceramics represent types spanning some 300 years, and most seem to date to around the beginning of the sixteenth century.

Although a formal type description of Caraway ceramics has never been published, they have been described as representing the culmination of the Badin, Yadkin, Uwharrie, and Dan River ceramic traditions with an overlay of some Pee Dee influence. Caraway is the southern Piedmont's version of the widespread Lamar style. Smoothed or burnished surfaces predominate and are followed in popularity by complicated-stamped and simple-stamped surface treatments. A few sherds display brushed, corncob-impressed, and net-impressed surfaces (Coe 1964:33–34, 1995:160–65; Coe and Lewis 1952). Based on recent research at Lower Saratown, the Wall site, and the Hairston site, the smoothed and burnished types probably date later than those with stamped surface treatments (Ward and Davis 1993).

By the end of the Late Woodland period, the Caraway phase inhabitants of the southern Piedmont had returned to the mainstream of the Piedmont Village Tradition. Only a few vestigial stylistic ceramic traits and abandoned villages remained to hearken the accomplishments of the Pee Dee. Although the South Appalachian Mississippian tradition, as expressed by Pee Dee culture, was brief and not widespread in the Piedmont, it dominated cultural developments in the North Carolina mountains throughout the Late Prehistoric period.

5. The Woodland and Mississippian Periods in the Appalachian Summit Region
The Search for Cherokee Roots

Although the Appalachian Summit region was the focus of some of the earliest excavations in North Carolina, it was the last region of the state to be investigated scientifically. During the late nineteenth and early twentieth centuries, the Smithsonian Institution's Bureau of Ethnology, the Valentine Museum of Richmond, Virginia, and the Museum of the American Indian–Heye Foundation of New York sponsored digs into several mounds in the western part of the state. These excavations were conducted before the development of rigorous field methods and were designed primarily to retrieve artifacts to be exhibited in museums (see Chapter 1). This early work also contributed to the final demise of the "Mound Builder Myth"—the notion that the mounds had been constructed by an ancient race of people unrelated to the American Indian.

Still, the primitive nature of the early excavations meant that precious little information was retrieved that could be used to understand the development of the ancient cultures of the region and their connections to the Cherokee Indians living there today. Although more sophisticated techniques were used during the Peachtree mound excavations, carried out by the Smithsonian Institution in 1933 and 1934, this project also failed to shed much light on questions regarding the origins and development of Cherokee culture (Setzler and Jennings 1941). As late as 1955, some archaeologists still regarded the Cherokees as recent arrivals, not long-term residents of western North Carolina (Webb 1938; Lewis and Kneberg 1946; Caldwell 1955).

In January 1965, Joffre Coe presented a proposal to the National Science Foundation for a three-year research program whose goal was to establish "the ecological and cultural base of the Cherokee Nation" (Coe 1965). This proposal followed several years of archaeological surveys in the North Carolina mountains, beginning in 1935 when Coe investigated portions of Transylvania County while he was a student at Brevard College. In 1941, Harold E. Johnston surveyed and recorded 130 sites in Buncombe County as part of the statewide Works Progress Administration (WPA) project. In 1952 and 1953, Stanley South found twenty-seven sites in Watauga County. Survey efforts in the western counties intensified between 1961 and 1964 and continued after the Cherokee project was funded in 1965. In 1964, Bennie Keel conducted limited excavations at five sites in Swain, Jackson, Cherokee, and Clay Counties (Holden 1966; Keel 1976:15). All of this work laid the foundation for the extensive excavations that took place between 1965 and 1971 in Buncombe, Haywood, and Macon Counties.

Although many of the results of the Cherokee project research remain unpublished, several master's theses and Ph.D. dissertations were written during the course of the project. Two dissertations—Roy Dickens's "The Pisgah Culture and Its Place in the Prehistory of the Southern Appalachians" and Bennie Keel's "Woodland Phases of the Appalachian Summit Area"—were revised and subsequently published in 1976 by the University of Tennessee Press. These two important studies outlined the cultural chronology for the Appalachian Summit region that is still used today.

Although the Cherokee project was under the overall direction of Joffre Coe, Bennie Keel supervised much of the day-to-day fieldwork. During the course of the project, Coe and Keel were fortunate to have the assistance of several outstanding students, including Roy Dickens, Brian Egloff, Keith Egloff, Leland Ferguson, Patricia Holden, and Jefferson Reid. Like Dickens and Keel, these and other students also contributed to the archaeological interpretation of Cherokee archaeology through their theses and dissertations (e.g., Dickens 1970; B. Egloff 1967; K. Egloff 1971; Ferguson 1971; Holden 1966; Keel 1972) (fig. 5.1).

The Woodland Period

While Piedmont Woodland cultures were characterized by continuity and gradual internal change, the Woodland period of the North Carolina mountains was a time of increasing cultural diversity stimulated by ideas from outside the region. And much that is known about the Early and Middle Woodland periods in the Appalachian Summit is the result of research conducted in eastern Tennessee by archaeologists from the University of Tennessee at Knoxville. While the University of North Carolina's Cherokee project established

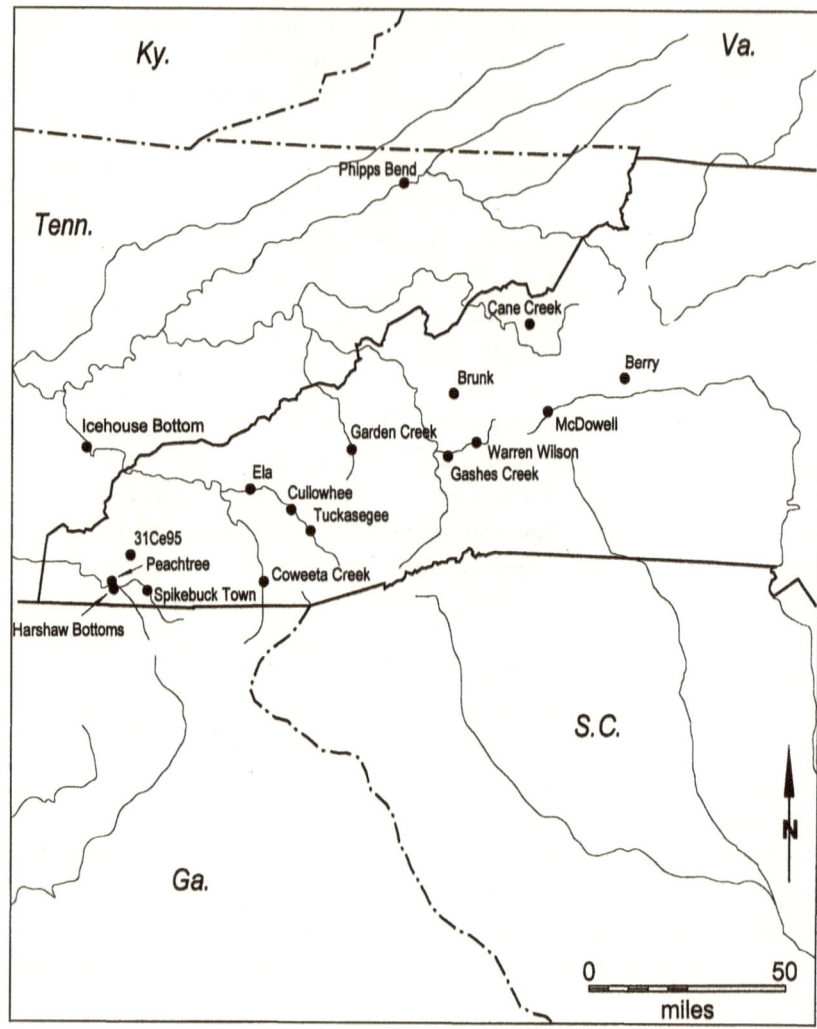

FIGURE 5.1. *Map of the North Carolina mountains showing Woodland and South Appalachian Mississippian sites discussed in the text.*

the chronological and stylistic markers for the Woodland period, the Tennessee research filled in details regarding settlement, subsistence, and overall cultural change and adaptation.

The Early Woodland Period (1000–300 B.C.)

In addition to locating sites for excavation, one of the early achievements of the Cherokee project surveys was to establish a ceramic typology. The basic typological framework for pre-Cherokee pottery was formally described by Patricia Holden (1966) and subsequently refined, using excavated samples, by Keel (1972). Holden studied just over 1,000 potsherds that she collected during a countywide survey of Transylvania County. At several sites, Holden noted the occurrence of a ceramic complex with cordmarked and fabric-impressed vessel surfaces that was similar to the Piedmont Badin series. She described this pottery as the "Early Series" and attributed it to the Early Woodland period. Though crude, this early pottery was well made and resistant to weathering (Holden 1966:61).

While Holden was conducting her survey of Transylvania County, Roy Dickens was beginning his excavations at the Warren Wilson site in nearby Buncombe County. This large, stratified village site, located along the Swannanoa River on the campus of Warren Wilson College, would be excavated extensively over the next eighteen years. Throughout this period, field supervisors were provided by the University of North Carolina, while Warren Wilson College provided most of the student labor force.

Although the main occupation at the Warren Wilson site dates to the South Appalachian Mississippian Pisgah phase (A.D. 1000–1450) and is represented by artifacts in the plowed soil, as well as numerous postholes and pits that intrude into the deeper soil horizons, an undisturbed stratum containing Holden's Early Series pottery and other artifacts lies just below the plowzone. Artifacts excavated by Dickens from this stratum, along with similar excavated samples from the Garden Creek site (31Hw2) in Haywood County, were analyzed by Bennie Keel in the early 1970s as part of his doctoral research. With added information from excavated contexts, Keel was able to refine and expand Holden's Early Series ceramics and incorporate them in his definition of the Swannanoa pottery series, named for the Swannanoa River that flows by the Warren Wilson site (1976:230–31).

The Early Woodland Swannanoa series pottery defined by Keel has crushed quartz or coarse sand added as a tempering agent. One of the most distinguishing characteristics noted by Keel is the thickness of the vessel walls, which range from 7 mm. to 22 mm. In addition to the cordmarked and fabric-impressed surface finishes originally described by Holden, Keel included check-stamped, simple-stamped, and plain surfaces as minority wares in his definition of the Swannanoa series (Keel 1976:115–16). The latter three surface treatments are thought to have occurred late in the Swannanoa phase. At the Warren Wilson site, a few steatite sherds were found in association with Swannanoa pottery, suggesting continuity with cultures of the preceding Late Archaic period.

Stylistically, Swannanoa series pottery is similar to Kellog ceramics from northern Georgia and Watts Bar pottery of eastern Tennessee (fig. 5.2). The

FIGURE 5.2. *A partially reconstructed Swannanoa Fabric Impressed pot from the Gashes Creek site (see fig. 5.1).*

latter two ceramic series appear to have begun around 700 B.C. (Chapman and Keel 1979:159). However, radiocarbon dates from the Phipps Bend site (40Hw45) in northeastern Tennessee place the beginning of the Swannanoa ceramic series there at around 1000 B.C. (Eastman 1994b:86–87; Lafferty 1981:501). Swannanoa phase pottery is also very similar to the Vinette wares of eastern New York State, which date to the same general time period and is the earliest pottery in the Northeast (Ritchie 1969). This overlap suggests that the earliest ceramic technology to reach the Appalachian Summit may have developed in an intermediate area between eastern New York and northeastern Tennessee (Lafferty 1981:506).

The Swannanoa phase is also characterized by small, stemmed projectile points, called Swannanoa Stemmed and Plott Stemmed by Keel (1976:194–97) and Gypsy points by Billy Oliver (1985:206) (fig. 5.3). All three "types" represent the last gasp of the stemmed-point tradition that began at the close of the Early Archaic period. Although Oliver (1985:207) regards Swannanoa Stemmed points as the lineal descendants of an earlier Gypsy type, there are no strong typological or stratigraphic grounds to support this view. It is equally plausible that these three "types" are simply the result of modifications from recycling and refurbishing.

Like other varieties of Early Woodland stemmed points, the Swannanoa phase points also were found stratigraphically associated with a large triangular point type named "Transylvania Triangular" (Keel 1976:211). These triangular points appear to be associated with the introduction of the bow and arrow during the Swannanoa phase.

Although several kinds of Swannanoa phase features were found at the Warren Wilson site, large hearth areas composed of clusters of fire-broken rock were the most common. Some were over 5 feet across and contained multiple layers of tightly packed fire-cracked or fire-clouded quartz cobbles. Sometimes the hearth rocks were widely scattered around a central core area. These hearths stand in marked contrast to the relatively small, circular pit hearths of the preceding Late Archaic period (Simpkins 1984:57). Other Swannanoa features included large, boat-shaped pits and several postholes, although no house structures were defined. At the Phipps Bend sites, large straight-sided and bell-shaped storage pits also were used during the Swannanoa phase (Lafferty 1981:350–51).

Evidence of the Swannanoa component at the Warren Wilson site has been found in all areas of the site that have been excavated. We do not know if these Early Woodland inhabitants occupied the site year-round, but they were there in sufficient numbers for enough time to create an extensive, well-defined archaeological deposit. The Late Archaic zone is similar in its spatial extent; however, Swannanoa phase features and artifacts are much more numerous.

Our present knowledge of Swannanoa subsistence practices in North Carolina is limited. In an analysis of carbonized plant remains from Swannanoa features at the Warren Wilson site, Dan Simpkins found only hickory, walnut, and acorn shells, and no evidence of cultigens or seed plants (1984:211–12). Although Simpkins's sample was small, consisting of a little over nine grams of

FIGURE 5.3. *Early Woodland Swannanoa Stemmed projectile points from the Warren Wilson site (bottom row) and Middle Woodland triangular points from the Warren Wilson site (middle row, left two specimens) and Garden Creek Mound No. 2 (top row and middle row, right two specimens).*

charred plant material, the dominance of arboreal nut crops is consistent with patterns of Archaic and Early Woodland subsistence patterns identified to the west along the lower Little Tennessee River, and at the Phipps Bend sites in northeastern Tennessee. This pattern reflects the continuation of economic pursuits begun several millennia earlier (Chapman and Shea 1981; Lafferty 1981:524). Likewise, available settlement data also suggest the continuation of Archaic lifeways. Working with survey data from the upper Watauga valley, Burt Purrington found that small Swannanoa settlements occurred frequently along ridge tops and within upland valley settings. Purrington hypothesized that because of the lack of preference for alluvial floodplains, incipient horticulture probably was not an important feature of Swannanoa subsistence (1983:133).

At first glance, this study appears to contradict the archaeobotanical record from eastern Tennessee, where Jefferson Chapman and others have documented the use in Early Woodland times of gourds, squash, and sunflower, as well as seedy plants such as maygrass, knotweed, chenopodium, and marsh elder. The seedy plants probably were being harvested from disturbed areas around Early Woodland campsites, and Chapman (1985:61) believes that marsh elder was being purposefully cultivated.

The Swannanoa occupation at the Warren Wilson site, situated on the fertile floodplain of the Swannanoa River, is not unique. Keel (1976) also found buried Swannanoa phase remains at the Tuckasegee (31Jk12) and Garden Creek sites, also located on floodplains. The lack of floodplain sites in Purrington's survey may simply reflect the fact that such sites are deeply buried and often not visible on the surface. If this is the case, then the small upland sites that he recorded probably reflect only part of the overall settlement system and most likely represent temporary, seasonal camps that were used for hunting and collecting activities. In light of Chapman's observations regarding Early Woodland subsistence in eastern Tennessee, it is likely that if Simpkins's archaeobotanical samples had been larger, he should have found more variety, including small seed-producing plants, in the Swannanoa phase plant food inventory.

Unfortunately, animal bones have not been preserved at the Warren Wilson site, so there is no direct evidence of the kinds of animals that were being hunted. However, based on the large numbers of projectile points and cutting and scraping tools that were found, hunting clearly was an important subsistence activity, and, in all likelihood, the white-tailed deer was the principal meat source.

Animal bones were preserved in Swannanoa features excavated at the Phipps Bend sites. There the primary animals hunted were deer, elk, and turkey. Of less importance were smaller mammals such as raccoon, squirrel, and beaver. Freshwater shellfish were also part of the diet. During the slightly later Long Branch phase, small mammals increased in importance relative to larger animals, and, at the same time, the use of aquatic species in the diet declined (Lafferty 1981:523).

Given available evidence, pottery-making stands out as the principal trait distinguishing the Swannanoa phase from earlier Archaic cultures. And the similarity of Swannanoa pottery to Early Woodland ceramic complexes in Piedmont North Carolina, eastern Tennessee, and northern Georgia indicates that this innovation did not appear in isolation but was part of a technological revolution of regional scope.

While subsistence information is sparse on North Carolina sites, it seems likely that the slow process toward an economy based on intensive seed collecting and gardening was well under way. The occupational intensity at sites such as Warren Wilson suggests that subsistence practices were sufficient to allow larger and more stable communities than existed earlier.

The Middle Woodland Period (300 B.C.–A.D. 800)

Archaeologists currently recognize two distinct phases of occupation during the Middle Woodland period in the North Carolina mountains: the Pigeon phase (300 B.C.–A.D. 200) and the Connestee phase (A.D. 200–800). The ceramic series that provide markers for these phases were originally defined by Patricia Holden after her survey of Transylvania County (1966). Although radiocarbon dates were lacking, Holden recognized connections between Pigeon ceramics and the widespread Deptford tradition centered in Georgia, and she also recognized that Connestee was later and more closely related to pottery types from eastern Tennessee, like Candy Creek (1966:84–85). Subsequent research in western North Carolina and eastern Tennessee has added considerably to our understanding of the Pigeon-Connestee chronology and Middle Woodland connections with areas outside the Appalachian Summit region (Chapman 1973; Keel 1976; McCollough and Faulkner 1973; Schroedl 1978).

However, archaeologists know much more about Connestee than they do about Pigeon. Keel's remark (1976:226) more than twenty years ago that little is known about the Pigeon phase other than the ceramics unfortunately is still true today. This is because a pure Pigeon component has not yet been isolated on a site. At Warren Wilson, Garden Creek, Tuckasegee, and other sites that have been excavated, the Pigeon phase artifacts have been found in the plowzone, or in deposits mixed with artifacts from later components. However, even in these contexts, Pigeon ceramics have been easy to identify.

Several attributes make Pigeon pottery distinctive, including: (1) the use of fairly abundant amounts of crushed quartz as temper; (2) the predominant use of check stamping as a surface treatment; (3) the use of large tetrapodal supports on the vessel base; and (4) an "iridescent sheen" on the interior surface that Keel (1976:49) regarded as unique to Pigeon series pottery in the Southern Appalachians. Vessel forms include simple bowls and subconical and necked jars. In addition to check-stamped surfaces, they may be plain, simple stamped, brushed, or complicated stamped. The latter three vessel surfaces occurred infrequently within the potsherd sample analyzed by Keel (256–60) (figs. 5.4 and 5.5).

Pigeon series pottery reflects a dramatic break with the cordmarked and fabric-impressed ceramics of the Swannanoa phase. Rather than looking to the north for possible connections, we must now turn to the south where carved wooden paddles were first used to stamp the surfaces of pottery vessels. As Holden recognized in 1966, the Deptford tradition of Georgia is the closest stylistic relative to Pigeon. Keel (1976:228–29) postulated a Middle Woodland "interaction sphere" involving northern Georgia, southwestern North Carolina, and eastern Tennessee to explain the spread of simple- and check-stamped pottery in the region.

Ceramic ties between these areas became more pronounced during the subsequent Connestee phase and continued after complicated-stamped ceramics became vogue throughout the remainder of Georgia and northern Florida (Keel 1976:228). Since the Cherokee project, several sites have been found in western North Carolina that contain significant amounts of complicated-stamped pottery similar to the Swift Creek and Napier styles that were popular in central and northern Georgia during the Middle Woodland period.

In eastern Tennessee, the Long Branch and Patrick phases are at least partially contemporaneous with the Pigeon phase. Here, however, limestone-tempered, fabric-impressed pottery continued to be the most popular type. Only a small percentage of the Tennessee materials are check stamped. The differences between the early Middle Woodland ceramic traditions in western North Carolina and eastern Tennessee reflect varying degrees of southern and northern influences, with southern connections being stronger in North Carolina than in Tennessee (Chapman and Keel 1979; Davis 1990).

Other artifacts that are probably associated with the Pigeon phase include small side-notched and triangular projectile points, expanded-center bar gorgets, grooved axes, celts, flake scrapers, ceramic pipes, and a variety of hammerstones (see fig. 5.3). The likely occurrence of these types of artifacts during the Pigeon phase is based on the fact that similar specimens are found in both the preceding Swannanoa and later Connestee phases (Keel 1976:229).

Pigeon components have been found on sites situated in a variety of ecological zones such as floodplains, upland valleys, coves, and ridgetops. Most of the

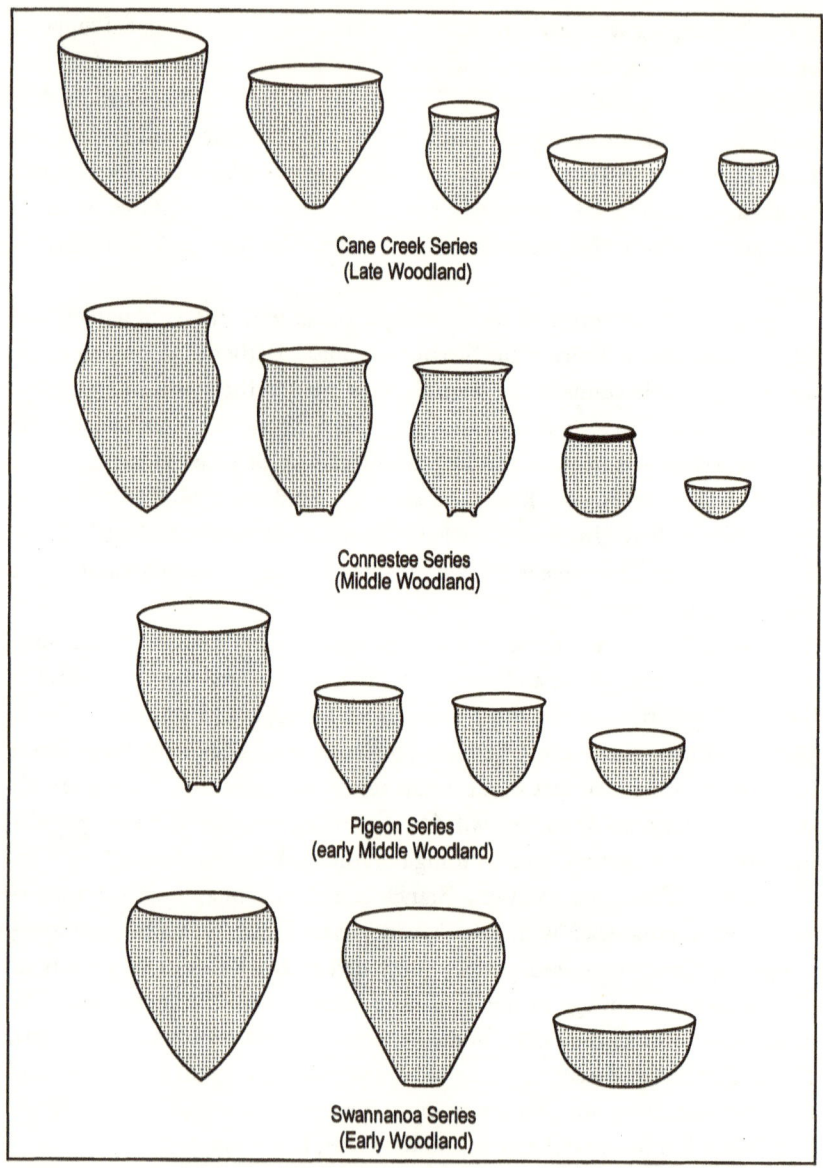

FIGURE 5.4. *Evolution of Woodland pot forms in the Appalachian Summit region. (Based on Keel 1976:249, 258, 262; Keel and Egloff 1984:15)*

FIGURE 5.5. *Connestee Plain (top row), Connestee Simple Stamped (second row and third row, left), and Pigeon Check Stamped (third row, right, and bottom row) potsherds from Garden Creek Mound No. 2.*

FIGURE 5.6. *Remnant of the Connestee phase secondary mound at Garden Creek Mound No. 2 (looking west). (Photo from Keel 1976:76)*

sites located away from floodplain environments are thought to represent hunting camps or other kinds of temporary food-collecting stations. Purrington's research in the upper Watauga valley suggests that Pigeon settlement patterns may reflect a shift toward greater use of fertile bottomlands. He feels that this shift is a consequence of an increasing reliance on horticulture (1983:136).

The Connestee phase (A.D. 200–800) defines the second half of the Middle Woodland period. Although Connestee series pottery was first defined by Holden in Transylvania County (1966:67), much of what we now know about the Connestee phase resulted from the excavation and analysis of the Garden Creek Mound No. 2 in Haywood County (Keel 1972, 1976) and investigations at the Icehouse Bottom site (40Mr23) in eastern Tennessee (Chapman 1973).

The Garden Creek mound was a relatively small, earthen platform mound that had been previously explored in 1880 by Mr. and Mrs. A. J. Osborne. The Osbornes were hired by Mann Valentine and his sons, of Richmond, Virginia, to procure Indian relics for their museum (see Chapter 1). Their casual digging into the mound caused minor damage compared to what happened in 1965. In that year, the landowner decided the large "bump" on his property was ideally suited to provide fill dirt, which he needed to prepare an adjacent house lot for sale. About half the mound was destroyed before archaeologists arrived on the scene, convinced the owner of its archaeological significance, and secured his permission to excavate the remaining portion (Keel 1976:73–74).

Excavations revealed two strata beneath the plowzone that represent distinct and successive stages of mound construction (fig. 5.6). Both mound stages were built and used during the Connestee phase and served as low platforms for public buildings. The first mound measured approximately 40'×60' and was a little less than 2 feet high. A second construction stage covered this mound, creating a tumulus that measured 80'×60' and was estimated to have been between 7 and 9 feet high. Because of the disturbance to the mound, neither of the structures they supported could be defined in any detail (Keel 1976:78–89).

The mound strata overlay a midden zone deposited by inhabitants of a village that predated the mound construction but also dated to the Connestee phase. An almost square structure, measuring 20'×19.5', was identified at the base of the pre-mound midden. This structure was defined by a pattern of postholes with a distinctive sandy fill. Some of these postholes also contained Connestee phase potsherds (Keel 1976:95).

The most notable features within the mounds were rock-filled pit hearths, similar to those found at the Warren Wilson site. At Warren Wilson, these facilities were used during the Late Archaic and Early Woodland periods. However, at the Garden Creek site, they were clearly associated with the Middle Woodland Connestee phase. Several pit hearths and clusters of fire-cracked rocks also were found on the pre-mound surface. In addition to large numbers of fire-cracked and modified cobbles, the hearths contained ash, charcoal, burned bones, broken pottery, and other refuse. The function of these hearths within the context of the mounds is unclear. Although several burials were excavated at Garden Creek, none were interred during the Connestee phase; instead, they were later, intrusive burials that dated to the Pisgah phase (Keel 1976:78–101).

Connestee series pottery consists of relatively thin-walled vessels that are tempered mostly with fine sand but may contain an occasional fragment of crushed quartz. Small tetrapodal supports are sometimes found attached to flat-bottomed jars. Hemispherical bowls and conical jars without supports are also part of the vessel assemblage. The exterior surfaces of these pots are usually plain, brushed, or simple stamped. Other minor surface treatments include cordmarking and fabric marking, as well as check stamping and complicated stamping. There is a clear developmental relationship between Connestee ceramics and pottery of the preceding Pigeon phase (Keel 1976:247–55).

The most interesting artifacts recovered from Garden Creek Mound No. 2 were those made of nonlocal, "exotic" materials or exhibiting nonlocal artistic styles. These artifacts demonstrate connections with other Middle Woodland groups living in eastern Tennessee and Ohio. They include clay figurines with human and animal forms, prismatic stone blades made from chert and chalcedony, cores from which these blades were struck, copper sheets, beads, and a copper pin. Many of these specimens appear to have originated in the Hopewell region of Ohio. In addition, several potsherds were found that appear to repre-

152 WOODLAND AND MISSISSIPPIAN PERIODS: MOUNTAINS

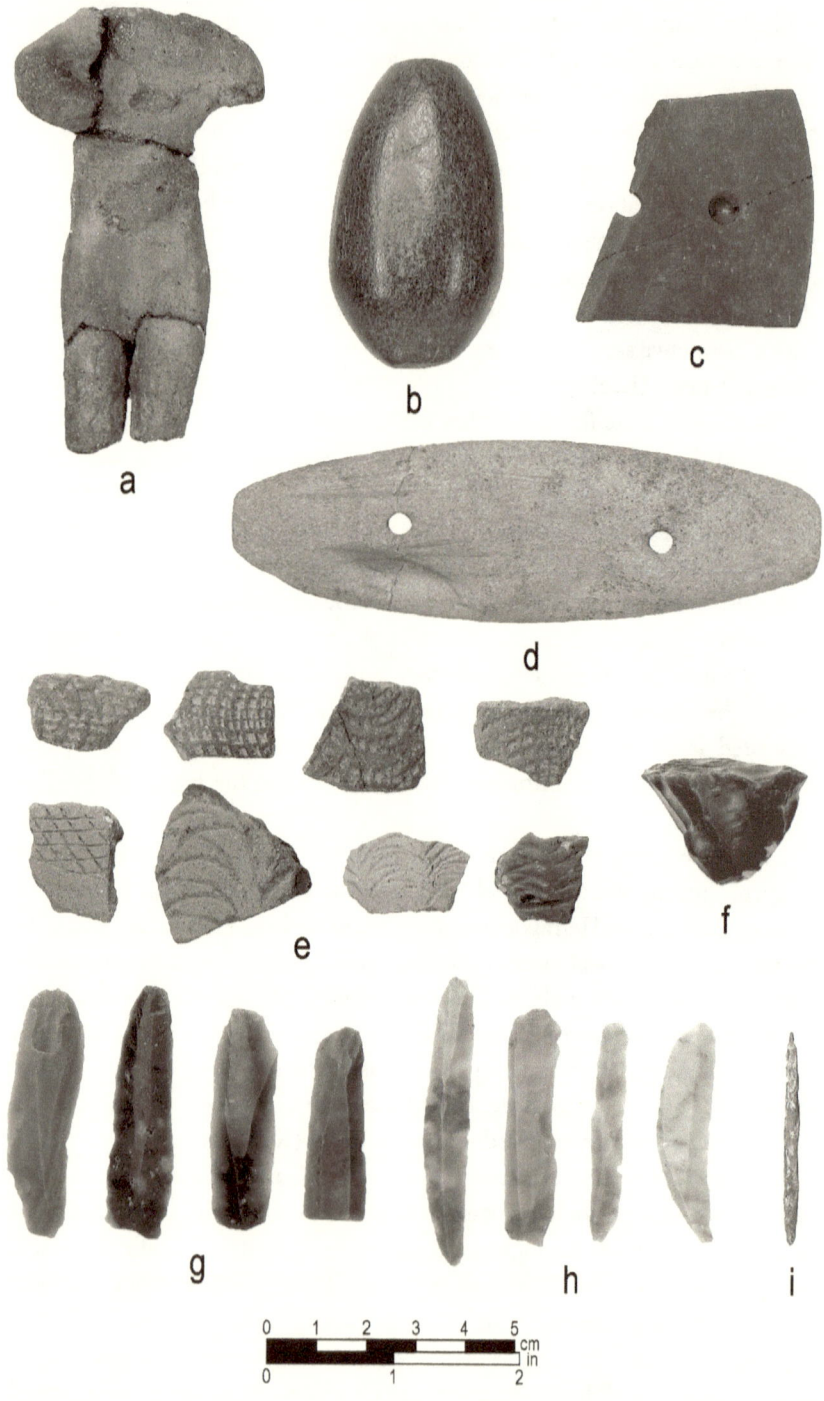

sent imported wares from the Ohio Hopewell area and eastern Tennessee. These artifacts were found in the upper portion of the pre-mound midden and in the fill that was used to construct the two mound stages (Keel 1976:117–49) (fig. 5.7).

Chapman and Keel believe that these foreign artifacts are evidence of interaction between Hopewell and Connestee peoples, precipitated by the abundant mica resources of the western North Carolina mountains. Mica, a material highly valued by Hopewell peoples, lured their traders down from the Ohio Valley. They traveled on ancient trails through eastern Tennessee into North Carolina and from there to other regions of the Southeast. Along the way, the traders swapped their exotic wares for raw materials not found in their native region (1979:161). In a microwear analysis of Hopewell blades from the Garden Creek and Icehouse Bottom sites, Larry Kimball (1992) found that these tools were used for a variety of cutting tasks, and that at least two of the Garden Creek specimens were used to cut soft stone such as mica.

The Icehouse Bottom site, located approximately seventy-five miles west of Garden Creek in eastern Tennessee, contained a rich midden that was created at about the same time the Garden Creek Mound No. 2 was constructed. Here, too, fragments of Hopewell pots and prismatic blades made of Ohio Flint Ridge chalcedony were found together with cut sheet mica and sand-tempered Connestee ceramics from western North Carolina. The Connestee pottery was found alongside the locally made limestone-tempered ceramics of the Candy Creek series. Both series share a number of surface treatments, including simple stamping, smoothing, cordmarking, and check stamping. Numerous radiocarbon dates from the Icehouse Bottom site place the Connestee–Candy Creek component in the fifth century A.D. (Chapman and Keel 1979:159–60; see also Cridlebaugh 1981:177–81).

Although the Icehouse Bottom and Garden Creek sites share many traits, there is one glaring difference—there is no mound at Icehouse Bottom. Mounds also are not commonly associated with known Connestee sites in western North Carolina. However, a number of Middle Woodland mounds have been found throughout the Southeast, and most have in common the presence of exotic artifacts generally associated with the Hopewell cultures of the Illinois and Ohio River valleys. Some, like the Tunacunnhee Mounds in northwestern

FIGURE 5.7. *Selected artifacts from Garden Creek Mound No. 2 (a–c, e–i) and the Warren Wilson site (d): clay figurine (a); stone plummet (b); stone pendant or gorget fragment (c); stone bar gorget (d); Hopewell dentate rocker-stamped, incised, and plain rocker-stamped potsherds (e); chert polyhedral core (f); chert prismatic blades (g); Ohio chalcedony blades (h); and native copper pin (i).*

Georgia, contain stone in their construction, whereas others, like the Mandeville site mounds in southwestern Georgia, were earthen constructions (Jefferies 1979; Smith 1979).

The Mandeville site is particularly interesting because one of the mounds (Mound A) is a platform mound similar to the Garden Creek Mound No. 2. The stratigraphy within Mound A indicated a change in ceramic styles from a preponderance of check- and simple-stamped pottery in the lower levels to more complicated-stamped wares in the upper levels. Betty Smith, who reanalyzed the Mandeville materials for her dissertation at the University of Georgia, saw this change as representing not two separate traditions but rather the evolution of a single tradition of the Early Swift Creek phase (1979:182). Mound B at the Mandeville site contained a number of Hopewell trade artifacts, including copper-covered panpipes, copper ear spools, ceramic figurines, platform pipes, and prismatic blades. Smith also noted strong affinities between Mandeville and Santa Rosa–Swift Creek sites in northwestern Florida, particularly with respect to the nonburial assemblage of lithic and ceramic artifacts (184).

Since Keel's work at the Garden Creek Mound No. 2, other Connestee sites have been tested and excavated in the Appalachian Summit region. Most of these excavations have been the result of cultural resource management studies, and only small areas have been exposed (e.g., Baker and Hall 1990, 1992; Hall and Baker 1993; Robinson 1989). There are, however, exceptions where large site areas have been explored. One of these, the Ela site (31Sw5) located on the Tuckasegee River in Swain County, revealed numerous Connestee features and structures. Most of the somewhat poorly defined circular structures are believed to represent domestic dwellings. Two larger circular posthole configurations are interpreted as possible public buildings or town houses. The domestic buildings lacked internal hearths, but large rock-filled pit hearths, like those found at Garden Creek, were located nearby. This site dates to the last half of the seventh century A.D. (Wetmore 1990; Robinson, Moore, and Wetmore 1994).

In general, Connestee sites are larger and reflect a greater occupational intensity than earlier Woodland sites within the Appalachian Summit region. Connestee sites usually are located in the floodplains of major streams, may cover several acres, and contain numerous features and structures. Small, temporary Connestee campsites also are found in a wide range of surrounding environmental zones. Although corn agriculture had not arrived on the scene at this time, the cultivation of indigenous small-grain seed plants had increased in importance. Still, hunting, gathering, and fishing continued to provide the mainstay of the Connestee diet.

Until recently, most of the radiocarbon dates for the Connestee phase have come from Tennessee. These dates, as mentioned earlier, place Connestee no later than the sixth century A.D. (Chapman and Keel 1979:160; Cridlebaugh 1981:177–79). And although Keel obtained a date of A.D. 805 ± 85 years from the Garden Creek Mound No. 2 site, he dismissed it in 1976 as being too late (Keel 1976:23). However, recent radiocarbon dates from North Carolina sites suggest that the Connestee phase might extend into the Late Woodland period, perhaps as late as A.D. 1000. (We should also point out that this was the original terminal date suggested by Keel in his 1972 dissertation, prior to his revising it for publication in 1976.) However, current data are inconclusive regarding the timing of the end of the Connestee phase, and much of the recent research needs to be published before the radiocarbon assessments can be evaluated.

Additional research is also needed to begin breaking Connestee phase assemblages down into finer chronological units. It is hoped that with the new radiocarbon dates, researchers will be able to identify variability within the various ceramic assemblages that can be used to date more accurately individual Connestee sites and components. One way to begin this task might be to look at the frequency of pottery types derived from outside the Appalachian Summit region and compare these with the frequency distributions of the local Connestee types.

The current evidence suggests that cultural influences during the Middle Woodland period entered the North Carolina mountains from two geographically distinct sources: the Hopewell centers to the north, and the Swift Creek area of southern and central Georgia. Although a small amount of Swift Creek Complicated Stamped pottery was found at the Garden Creek site, the main focus of most Connestee studies has been on the identification of Hopewell artifacts and connections to the north. Several Connestee sites recently have been found that contain significant amounts of Swift Creek Complicated Stamped and some later Napier Complicated Stamped pottery (cf. Robinson 1989). One of these, 31Ce95, in Cherokee County, produced only Swift Creek Complicated Stamped types along with plain sherds (Ward 1977a). Significant quantities of Swift Creek and Napier pottery also have been reported from Middle Woodland sites along the lower Little Tennessee River in eastern Tennessee (Chapman 1973, 1980; Cridlebaugh 1981; Schroedl 1978). The presence of these Georgia pottery types provides clear evidence that the North Carolina mountains and the greater Appalachian Summit region were involved in southern as well as northern "interaction spheres" (fig. 5.8).

It is plausible that these outside influences mark recognizable temporal boundaries. In other regions of the Southeast—particularly northern Florida—vigorous cultural traditions developed at the same time as Hopewell in the Midwest. These traditions continued as Hopewell influences diminished, and

FIGURE 5.8. *A Middle Woodland Swift Creek pot found on Bird Creek in Haywood County in the late 1800s.*

they set the stage for the later development of Mississippian culture (cf. Brose 1979). It is reasonable to assume that the influence of these Mississippian precursors continued to be felt in the North Carolina mountains after the Hopewell climax, culminating in the rise of the South Appalachian Mississippian tradition (Ferguson 1971). We hypothesize that the artifacts and ideas derived from the Hopewell area may be more typical of the first half of the Connestee phase and that the Swift Creek–Napier ceramic styles, with their southerly origins, may be more typical of the last half of the Connestee phase. Support for this hypothesis has been found at the Harshaw Bottom site (31Ce41) in Cherokee County. Here, early Swift Creek and Connestee ceramics were found together in the same excavated contexts. These ceramics have been radiocarbon dated to around A.D. 600 (Robinson 1989; Robinson, Moore, and Wetmore 1994).

The Late Woodland Period (A.D. 800–1100)

At present, the cultural dynamics and stylistic markers of the Late Woodland period in the Appalachian Summit region are poorly understood. Currently, only ideas, suggestions, and hypotheses can be offered to fill the void between the Middle Woodland period and the beginning of the Mississippian period. Once the Connestee phase is broken down into finer stylistic and chronological units, our understanding of this gap should increase substantially.

One excavated site that appears to have been occupied during the Late Woodland period is the Cane Creek site (31Ml3) in Mitchell County. This site is located near Loafers Glory, one of the most poetically named communities in the state. During late March 1964—before excavations began at the Garden Creek site in nearby Haywood County—Bennie Keel and graduate student Brian Egloff of the University of North Carolina conducted brief salvage excavations at the Cane Creek site. Before Keel and Egloff arrived, the landowner had dug into several areas of the site where he thought Indian graves were located. The targeted areas appeared as dark circular patches of earth in the freshly plowed field. Keel and Egloff believed that the organically rich stains indicated the locations of houses.

Working in rain, sleet, and snow for two weeks, the archaeologists placed excavation units in two of the house areas and tested other portions of the site that did not contain dark soil. While little was found outside the house areas, excavations where the dark soil was exposed uncovered three burials, eleven features, and numerous postholes, and yielded more than 4,000 artifacts (Keel and Egloff 1984).

At least two things stand out about the Cane Creek site: (1) the homogeneity of the ceramic assemblage; and (2) the large number of bone and shell artifacts. Keel and Egloff noted that out of a collection of over 3,700 potsherds, only eight were not classified in the same pottery series, which they named the Cane Creek series. The people living at Cane Creek made their pots from clays to which they added sand and occasional fragments of crushed quartz and hornblende as temper. Most potsherds had plain, smoothed, or brushed surfaces; the remainder were either fabric impressed, simple stamped, or check stamped. Vessel rims were frequently notched, and some incising was noted (1984:14–22). The similarities between the Cane Creek series and the Connestee series are obvious.

Comparing the Cane Creek pottery with that from the Garden Creek site, Keel and Egloff observed two distinct differences: (1) the Cane Creek pottery sample included a higher percentage of plain sherds; and (2) it lacked any evidence of tetrapodal supports. They suggested that these attributes are late and cautiously placed the Cane Creek material at the end of the Connestee phase, or around A.D. 1000 (1984:24).

We might add that the well-preserved assemblage of bone tools, including awls, pins, fishhook blanks, and cut deer mandibles, may also indicate a Late Woodland date. In Piedmont North Carolina, these artifacts first appear during the Late Woodland Uwharrie phase.

The burial data also point to the Late Woodland period. Although badly disturbed by plowing and the landowner's relic-collecting activities, two adult skeletons were found that were flexed and apparently placed in simple oval pits. The remains of an infant, placed in the same pit as one of the adults, were wrapped in a garment beaded with marginella shells and a necklace of shell disk beads was around the neck (Keel and Egloff 1984:6). This pattern of mortuary behavior—the lavish adornment of children with shell beads and other ornaments—is not seen until after A.D. 1000 on the North Carolina Piedmont, and it is a typical pattern found throughout the Southeast between A.D. 800 and 1200 (Steponaitis 1986:384).

While the archaeological evidence from the Cane Creek site may help us to identify and understand better the Late Woodland occupation of the North Carolina mountains, it only serves to heighten the seeming disparity between Woodland cultures and the Mississippian-influenced cultures that appeared shortly after A.D. 1000. With the current, limited data base for the Late Woodland period, it is easy to speculate about a transitional archaeological complex bridging the gap between the Connestee and Pisgah phases, as well as other Mississippian phases, and to thus argue that the Historic Cherokee were the product of an extremely long sequence of cultural development in the mountains. However, if the data are correct in this chronological placement of the Cane Creek site, then the emergence of Mississippian culture appears even more abrupt and a hypothesis of extended, in situ cultural evolution becomes more tenuous and complicated. For this reason, understanding what happened during the Late Woodland period in the mountains is critically important to understanding the origins of the South Appalachian Mississippian tradition with its complicated-stamped ceramics, stockaded villages, substructure mounds, and agricultural economy.

The South Appalachian Mississippian Tradition

One of the most important sites excavated during the course of the Cherokee project, the Warren Wilson site (31Bn29), was not on the original list of candidates proposed for study. Although we have previously discussed the Late

Archaic and Woodland components at Warren Wilson, the main occupation at the site took place during the Pisgah phase (A.D. 1000–1450) of the South Appalachian Mississippian tradition.

During the 1965 fall semester at the University of North Carolina, Chapel Hill, a student in Joffre Coe's "North American Archaeology" class brought in a shoe box filled with potsherds and other artifacts for Coe to look at. The student had collected the specimens from the bottomland along the north bank of the Swannanoa River on the campus of Warren Wilson College. A check of the Research Laboratories' site files revealed that the material came from 31Bn29, a site recorded by Harold E. Johnston in 1941. The variety of pottery in the collection piqued Coe's interest.

In December, Coe dispatched Roy Dickens to the Warren Wilson campus to inspect the site. College officials were notified of Dickens's impending visit, and they decided to make sure he found something and did not return to Chapel Hill with a negative report. To this end, they plowed the site as deeply as possible in order to bring to the surface a fresh assortment of artifacts. Dickens was indeed impressed. Unfortunately, the plowing not only churned up a considerable collection of potsherds and other artifacts; it also ripped through intact house floors and the tops of several pit features. In one of the areas where cultural materials were concentrated, Dickens excavated a 10' square test pit to see if any undisturbed deposits remained. At the base of the plowzone, a line of distinct postholes was clearly visible.

The following summer, excavations began in earnest at Warren Wilson and would continue every summer until 1977 (Dickens 1976). No work was carried out at the site in 1978, but excavations resumed in 1979 and continued until 1985. Today, approximately half of the palisaded Pisgah village has been uncovered.

In addition to having the distinction of being the most extensively excavated site in western North Carolina, Warren Wilson also has the distinction of being the most reported site studied during the Cherokee project. It was the subject of four doctoral dissertations (Dickens 1970; Keel 1972; Runquist 1979; and Ward 1980) and a master's thesis (Simpkins 1984). As mentioned earlier, Dickens's and Keel's dissertations were revised and published in 1976. The Warren Wilson site also has been the focus of numerous articles published in professional journals—too many to cite individually here.

Another important Pisgah phase site excavated during the course of the Cherokee project is the Garden Creek site, which was also reported by Roy Dickens (1970, 1976) and Bennie Keel (1972, 1976). The Garden Creek site covers some twelve acres and, at one time, contained three low platform mounds. We discussed the smallest mound (31Hw2), which was constructed during the Middle Woodland Connestee phase, earlier in this chapter. The largest mound, designated Garden Creek Mound No. 1 (31Hw1), was built during the Pisgah phase and is associated with a village midden about five acres in extent. This mound was completely excavated by crews from the Research Laboratories of Anthropology between 1965 and 1967. A third mound, which was apparently constructed prior to the Pisgah phase, was extensively excavated by the Heye Foundation in 1915 (Dickens 1976:69; Heye, Hodge, and Pepper 1918).

In some respects, data from the extensive excavations at Warren Wilson and Garden Creek Mound No. 1 make the Pisgah phase one of the best understood cultural complexes in the Appalachian Summit region (Purrington 1983:144). However, as will be demonstrated shortly, some of the ideas and interpretations gleaned from these excavations may have been stretched beyond their limits to include areas of the region to which they may not necessarily apply.

The Pisgah Phase (A.D. 1000–1450)

Ceramics recognized today as belonging to the Pisgah series were first recognized by William Henry Holmes in 1884, at the height of the Smithsonian Institution's mound explorations. The collection Holmes studied came from a site near Newport, Tennessee (Holmes 1884:440–41). Although ceramics similar to those identified by Holmes had been found widely scattered throughout the Appalachian Summit region for several years, the Pisgah ceramic series was not formally described until 1966, when Patricia Holden presented the first typological description of Pisgah pottery in her master's thesis at the University of North Carolina (1966:72–77).

The following year Brian Egloff (1967) recognized a few Pisgah sherds in his analysis of ceramics from historic Cherokee towns. However, it was the excavations at the Warren Wilson and Garden Creek sites that allowed Roy Dickens (1976) to present a detailed description not only of Pisgah ceramics but also of Pisgah houses, features, burials, subsistence practices, and ceremonial activities. Although other Pisgah sites have been excavated since this study (e.g., Dickens 1980; Moore 1981; Purrington 1983), Dickens's work remains the definitive statement on the Pisgah phase and the arrival of the South Appalachian Mississippian tradition in the Appalachian Summit.

Pisgah settlements are characterized by a variety of sizes, ranging from small farmsteads to fairly large nucleated villages that sometimes have substructure platform mounds. Smaller sites tend to be clustered around the larger villages with mounds. No matter the size, these settlements are almost always located in floodplain environments. Only small, temporary hunting or collecting camps have been found in nonriverine settings (Dickens 1978:131; Purrington 1983:145). Most Pisgah sites are located in the eastern and central portions of the Appalachian Summit, and the largest concentrations of sites are found in the Asheville, Pigeon, and Hendersonville intermontane basins (Dickens 1978:134–35).

One exception to the pattern of floodplain settlement is the Brunk site, located in northern Buncombe County. At Brunk, a fairly dense collection of artifacts, including a large number of pottery sherds, was found scattered over a half-acre area at the head of a mountain cove. Test excavations revealed several postholes that may have formed part of a house-wall alignment (Moore 1981). Although not as large as a floodplain village, the dense concentration of artifacts and structural remains suggests that the Brunk site represents more than a temporary campsite.

At this point, it is not known whether the Brunk site represents a typical component of the Pisgah settlement system that has not been generally recognized or an anomaly. We suspect the latter since numerous surveys have been carried out in a variety of nonfloodplain environments that have not turned up sites similar to Brunk (Bass 1977; Coe 1983; Purrington 1975, 1983).

Warren Wilson seems to be a typical, middle-sized Pisgah village (fig. 5.9). It covers approximately three acres and is surrounded by at least seven distinct palisade lines. Based on excavation results through 1969, Dickens (1976:50) felt the multiple palisades reflected an expanding village population. More recently, using excavation data obtained after 1968, it has been suggested that an inner series of palisades may have served as a wall to separate the central plaza from the surrounding habitation area. The central area may have been reserved for ceremonial and political activities—much like the "square grounds" of historic Cherokee villages (Ward 1986) (fig. 5.10).

Two parallel lines of postholes that form an outer band of palisades may represent a double-walled enclosure that served to protect the inhabitants of the village. These two outer palisades are thought to have been in use at the same time because of the narrow distance separating them, and the fact that the lines run parallel to one another around the entire excavated area, without ever crossing (Ward 1986:18). Even with this more static spatial interpretation, the village still probably expanded over time, as Dickens suggested, because one house structure was excavated beyond the known limits of the palisades. Also, surface artifact scatters are quite dense for at least 100 feet beyond the limits of the excavated area of the site.

Based on the Warren Wilson excavations, we know that Pisgah phase houses were roughly rectangular and measured about 20 feet on a side (fig. 5.11). Walls were constructed by setting individual posts in holes. Most houses had central hearth basins with prepared clay collars. Half of the Warren Wilson structures had parallel entry trenches in which small saplings were placed and bent over to create a tunnel-like entrance. All houses had central support posts in their

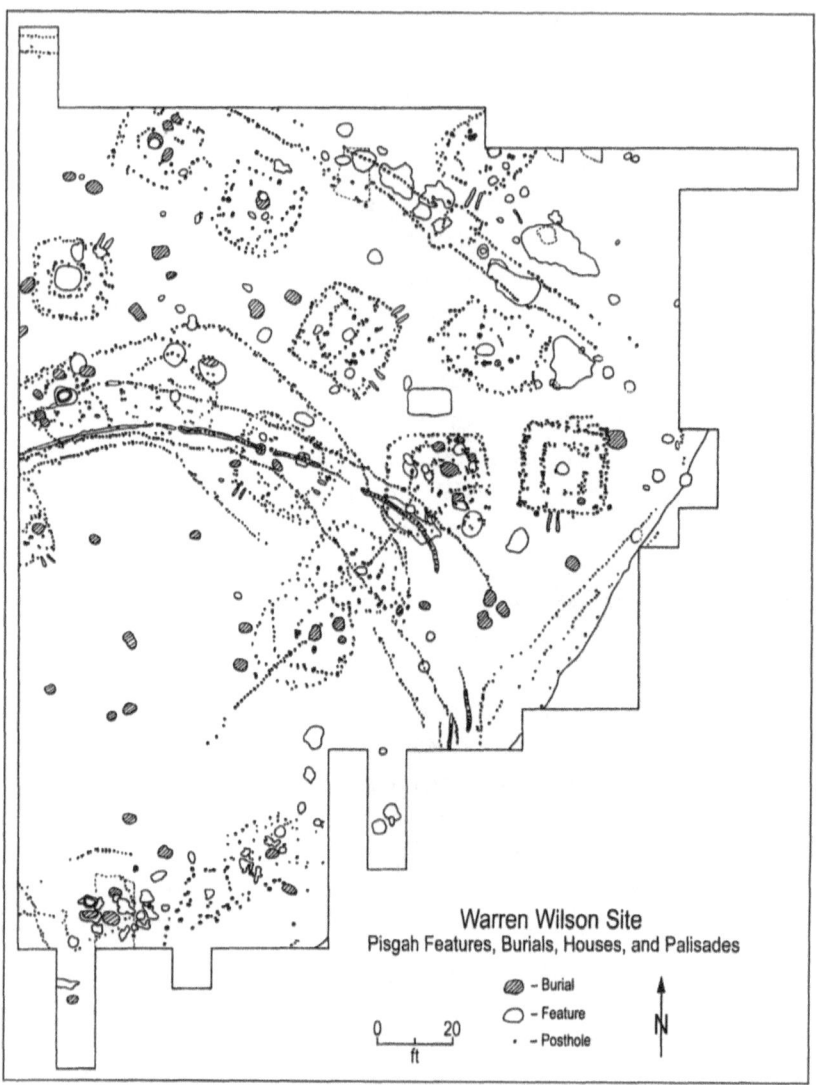

FIGURE 5.9. *Excavation plan of the Warren Wilson site through the 1982 excavation season showing features, burials, houses, and palisades associated with the Pisgah phase occupation. Only postholes associated with architectural features are shown.*

interiors, and some also contained rows of interior posts that were used to form partitions (Dickens 1976:33–34; Ward 1980:119–37).

Although very little fired-clay plaster or "daub" was found at Warren Wilson, given the cold winters common in the Appalachian Summit, the walls were probably finished with cane wattle and sealed with clay, at least during the

FIGURE 5.10. *An artist's conception of the Pisgah village at the Warren Wilson site. (Drawing by Frank Weir, 1970; from Dickens 1976:95)*

winter months. The absence of this plaster in the archaeological record is probably best explained by the fact that none of the structures was destroyed by fire. Because the clay was not fired and hardened, the plaster has not been preserved.

The most striking pit features at Warren Wilson were large, shallow depressions located around the edge of the village near the outer palisades. These facilities sometimes measured over 10 feet long and 5 feet wide, but they usually were less than a foot deep. Often the bottoms were partially or completely lined with a thin layer of clay. Most contained a rich assortment of artifacts, food remains, charcoal, and fire-cracked rocks. These facilities have been interpreted as roasting pits, perhaps used to prepare large quantities of food for communitywide celebrations (Ward 1980:108–10).

Several pit hearths also have been found. These were smaller than the roasting pits and are thought to have been used to heat sweat lodges, since they were found inside either small structures or posthole clusters that may have acted as supports for temporary coverings when the pits were in use. These roughly circular pits usually contained layers of tightly packed, fire-scarred or -cracked cobbles, charcoal, and sometimes burned timbers (Ward 1980:112).

Perhaps the most interesting aspect of the Pisgah phase features at Warren Wilson is the near absence of storage pits. Although a few small, clay-lined pits

FIGURE 5.11. *View toward the entrance of a rectangular Pisgah dwelling at the Warren Wilson site showing excavated wall posts (outer alignments), interior support and partition posts (inner alignment), parallel entryway trenches, and pits. This house measured 22 feet square and had a central hearth. (Photo from Dickens 1976:42)*

have been tentatively interpreted as storage facilities, only two definite subterranean storage facilities have been found at the Warren Wilson site (Ward 1985:86). Apparently Pisgah people preferred aboveground cribs and granaries over subterranean pits. The use of such storage facilities has been documented for the Historic Cherokees and other southeastern Indians (Lefler 1967:23; Swanton 1946:380). However, this pattern stands in sharp contrast to that of the Piedmont Siouans, who made extensive use of underground storage.

Some scholars have suggested that storage pits are associated with groups who abandoned their villages periodically, whereas aboveground facilities, like cribs, are more likely to be found in villages that were occupied year-round. Pits could be easily concealed and their contents protected by hiding their location. Because aboveground facilities could not be easily hidden, someone would have to be around at all times to protect their prized contents from thieves and looters (DeBoer 1988; Ward 1985).

Sixty-one human burials were excavated at the Warren Wilson site. Most of these graves were placed inside or adjacent to houses. The bodies were flexed in a fetal position and probably wrapped with mats or furs before interment. Most were buried with their heads oriented in a westward direction. Burial was made in simple, straight-sided pits or shaft-and-chamber pits (fig. 5.12). The latter

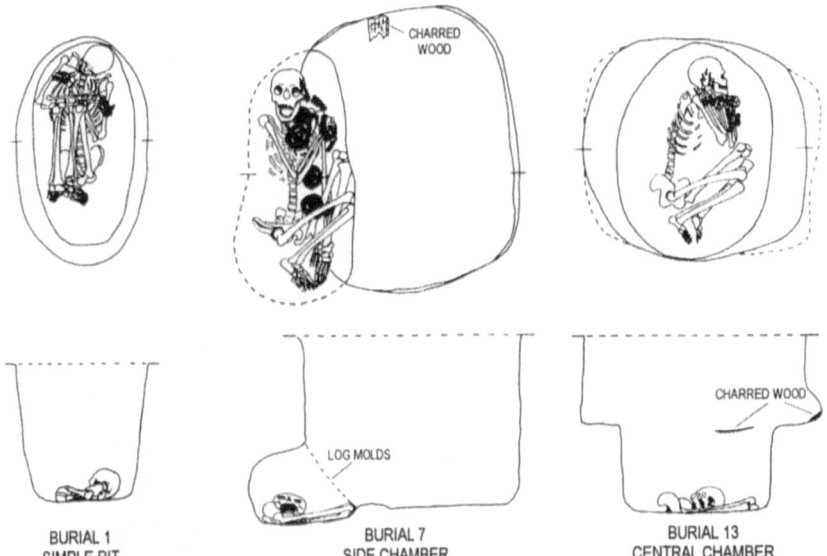

FIGURE 5.12. *Types of Pisgah phase burials found at the Warren Wilson site (top row, plan view; bottom row, profile view). The funerary objects shown with Burial 7 include four cut-mica disks, eighteen small mica disks, a conch shell filled with red ocher, two columella bead bracelets, and a bone awl. Items found with Burial 13 include two columella bead bracelets and two columella ear pins. (From Dickens 1976:104)*

graves consisted of two types: pits with central chambers and pits with side chambers. Central-chamber graves were created by digging a cavity for the body at the base of the pit shaft, leaving a ledge that could support logs or other coverings over the chamber. Side-chamber graves were formed by excavating a cavity beneath the pit wall at the base of the shaft. After the body was placed in the chamber, the cavity was sealed, sometimes with large, flat river cobbles (Dickens 1976:125; Wilson 1986:53).

Funerary objects, when present, usually consisted of ornamental items made from shell (e.g., beads, gorgets, and ear pins), animal bone (e.g., turtle-shell rattles and beads), or mica (e.g., plates and disks). The most common funerary objects were columella beads strung to form bracelets or necklaces. Only two burials contained nonornamental artifacts: a small conch shell, a conch-shell bowl, bone awls, red ocher, fish scales, and panther claws (Dickens 1976:127; Wilson 1986:54–55).

Burial clusters associated with some houses had grave offerings, whereas other household grave clusters did not. Dickens concluded that this pattern of distribution probably reflects the acquisition and use of sumptuary goods by higher-ranking households or kinship groups. Dickens also noted that only children received conch-shell gorgets, a further indication that social ranking was hereditary (1976:128).

Within the burial clusters where grave goods were found, one older male (Burial 7) received the most elaborate array of funerary objects found among all the burials from the site. These included the panther claws mentioned above, cut mica, columella bead bracelets, and other artifacts. It is believed that this individual may have been a chief-priest or shaman (Dickens 1976:128).

Compared to earlier and later pottery used in the Appalachian Summit, Pisgah types stand out and are easily distinguishable. Two traits in particular set Pisgah sherds apart: collared rims and rectilinear complicated-stamped vessel surfaces. Although thickened and unmodified rim forms also occur on Pisgah vessels, collared rims predominate. This rim form was created by adding a thick strip of clay or "collar" above the neck to create the rim and lip. These collars were usually decorated with punctations, incisions, and castellations (figs. 5.13 and 5.14).

This type of rim treatment has no precedent in western North Carolina or the surrounding area; however, similar forms have been found in the Iroquois area of western New York State and southwestern Ohio (Griffin 1966; Kelly and Neitzel 1961; MacNeish 1952). Dickens (1976:200) believed that the closest relatives to Pisgah rims came from the Oliver phase in southern Indiana. Whether they were derived from New York, Ohio, or Indiana may be debatable, but one thing is certain: Pisgah rims show no relationship to the simple, flaring, or straight rims of the preceding Connestee phase pottery. Nor do the complicated-stamped designs commonly found on the surfaces of Pisgah vessels show close affinities to local antecedent types. Most of the complicated-stamped designs that occur in Connestee ceramics are related to Swift Creek types from central and southern Georgia and do not appear to have evolved directly into designs commonly found on Pisgah vessels. However, the southern influences that appeared during the Connestee phase appear to have continued and intensified during Pisgah times.

Connections to Pisgah rectilinear complicated-stamped designs may be found in the Napier, Etowah, and Woodstock ceramic traditions of northern Georgia, whereas the roots of later and more varied Pisgah designs, including curvilinear complicated stamping, may be found in the Wilbanks and Savannah-Irene traditions of Georgia (Dickens 1976:198–99, 1979:17). This is not to say that Pisgah culture was not evolving along its own independent trajectory. It had its own distinct evolutionary history and, as Ferguson (1971:261) has pointed out, the specific designs on Pisgah pottery, although generally related to Georgia types, are unique to the North Carolina mountains. At the same time Pisgah

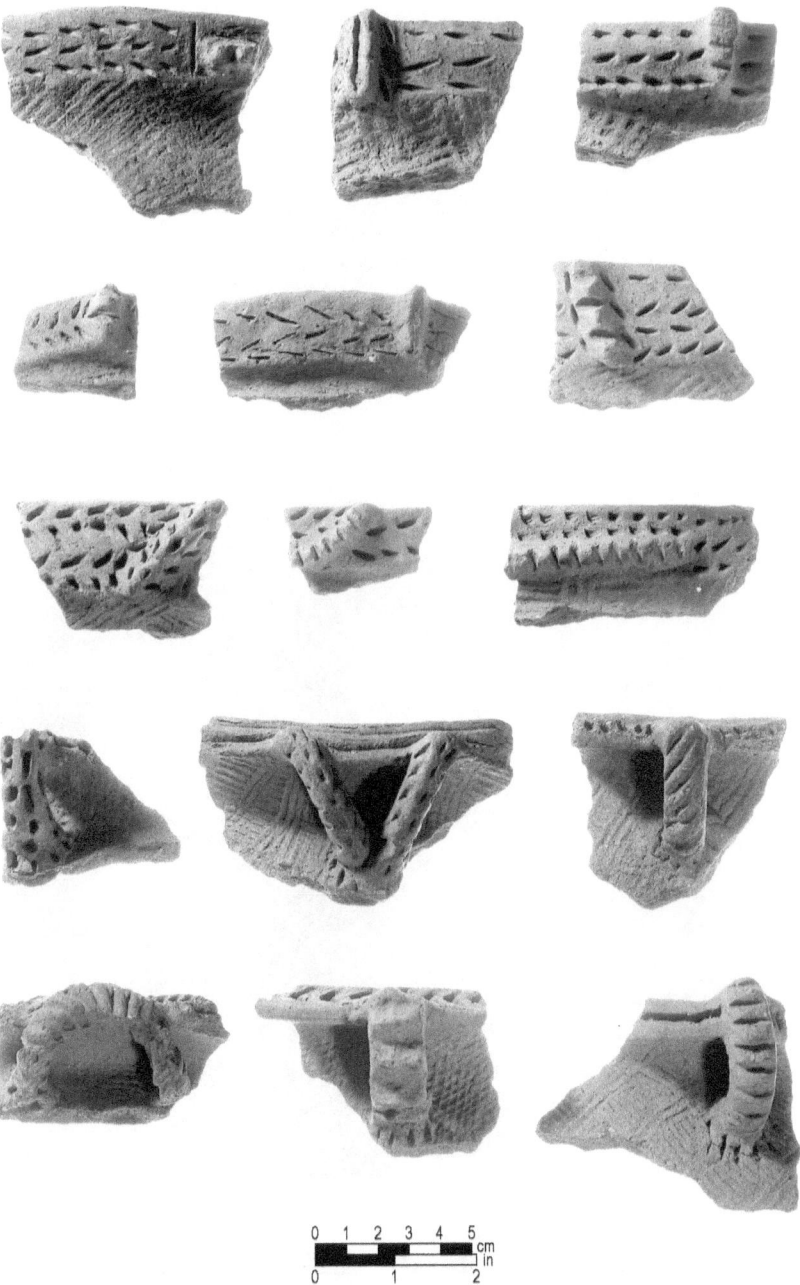

FIGURE 5.13. *Collared rims and thickened rims from Pisgah jars with lug handles (top three rows and bottom row, far left) and loop handles (fourth row and bottom row, right two specimens).*

FIGURE 5.14. *A Pisgah Check Stamped bowl with a castellated rim from Jackson County (top) and a Pisgah Rectilinear Complicated Stamped jar with a collared rim from Haywood County (bottom).*

potters received inspiration from the south, they were also being influenced by ideas from the Midwest. These two areas of influence gave Pisgah pottery its distinctive attributes.

The relative influence of northern and southern ceramic traditions on Pisgah pottery is nowhere more obvious than in Pisgah-like ceramics from the northwestern mountains of North Carolina. There, decorated and collared Pisgah rims have been found on vessels with fabric- and net-impressed surfaces, similar to indigenous Woodland types found locally and further east in the Piedmont. Differences in temper are also apparent. Instead of the sand temper usually found in Pisgah pottery, the northern variety is usually tempered with large fragments of crushed quartz and steatite (Purrington 1983:143; Senior 1981:127).

Apparently the influences from the south that resulted in complicated-stamped surface treatments did not penetrate beyond the central mountains. Instead, the rim forms originating in the Midwest were grafted onto a local ceramic tradition in the northwestern mountains. It should also be noted that these rims were not as ornate as those in the central Pisgah heartland (Purrington 1983:144). Other differences in settlement patterns and community structure have also been noted and will be discussed below.

After studying a large collection of Pisgah ceramics from western North Carolina and surrounding states, Dickens postulated that the Pisgah phase could be divided into early and late subphases. He characterized the early subphase (ca. A.D. 1000–1250) by the presence of fine-element, rectilinear complicated-stamped designs reflecting relationships with pottery types from the Etowah site in northern Georgia. The later subphase (A.D. 1250–1450) was characterized by the occurrence of bolder and more varied rectilinear complicated-stamped designs as well as curvilinear designs similar to those of the Wilbanks, Savannah, and Pee Dee ceramic series. Thickened or collared rims decreased in popularity over time, and inslanted cazuela-like rims with incised decorations were introduced during the last half of the Pisgah phase (Dickens 1976:209). These developments continue to point to a flow of ideas from the south into the central North Carolina mountains, a flow that continued as the Lamar phase of north Georgia merged with local ceramic traditions to form the Protohistoric/Historic Qualla phase. Other artifacts that reflect this influx of new ideas include clay pipes, polished stone discoidals, and stone celts (fig. 5.15).

Like other Woodland and Mississippian cultures in North Carolina, Pisgah folks took full advantage of their natural environment by consuming a variety of wild animal and plant foods. Deer and bear were the most important animals in the diet, and they also contributed skins for clothing and containers, as well as bones from which to make tools. The wild turkey followed in importance by providing meat, bones for tools, and feathers for clothing and decoration.

FIGURE 5.15. *Qualla clay pipes from Peachtree (top left) and Cullowhee (top right); Pisgah pipes from the Warren Wilson site (middle row); and Qualla stone discoidal and celt from Tuckasegee (bottom row).*

Smaller animals such as squirrels, rabbits, opossum, and raccoons were also used in a variety of ways. And fish and turtles were taken from the rivers and streams (Dickens 1976; Runquist 1979).

One of the most unusual archaeological finds at the Warren Wilson site consisted of a large number of toad (*Bufo* sp.) bones contained within a single feature. This large, shallow pit, which may have been used as an earth oven, was subsequently filled with refuse from food preparation and consumption activities. The uppermost fill zone of the feature contained what appeared to be a single deposit of almost 14,000 toad radii/ulnae (Runquist 1979:322). These forearm bones were found concentrated in a small area, mixed with numerous other animal bones, particularly deer. Runquist (285) suggested that the Pisgah people may have processed the toads for medicinal or hallucinogenic purposes. A similar find was made at the Qualla phase Coweeta Creek site (31Ma34) in Macon County.

As mentioned earlier, most Pisgah sites are located in the floodplains of major streams, where their inhabitants were able to take advantage of the fertile, friable soils that are normally found there. In these bottoms, Pisgah people planted fields of corn, beans, squash (or pumpkin), and sumpweed. Dickens (1976) estimates that half of Pisgah subsistence was derived from agricultural produce. This marks a major shift in the importance of agriculture from the preceding Connestee phase. Pisgah people also took advantage of the natural bounty offered by the surrounding forests. They collected acorns, hickory nuts, walnuts, and butternuts, as well as a wide variety of fleshy fruits (Yarnell 1976:217).

Pisgah ceremonial practices are best illustrated at the Garden Creek site complex (31Hw1, 2, 3, 7, and 8) located in Haywood County. This cluster of sites covers some twelve acres and is located on the south side of the Pigeon River, near its confluence with Garden Creek. Garden Creek Mound No. 1, the largest of the mounds, was constructed during the Pisgah phase and was associated with a large village designated 31Hw7 (Dickens 1976; Keel 1976).

Between 1965 and 1967, Garden Creek Mound No. 1 was completely excavated (fig. 5.16). At the time of the excavation, the mound stood only about 7 feet high and measured 150 feet east-west and 130 feet north-south. Initially, the plowed soil was stripped to reveal a rectangular mound with a ramp on the east side. Atop the mound were the remnants of two eroded house floors and numerous intrusive postholes, pits, and burials.

Both buildings were located on the west side of the mound summit, whereas seven burial pits were located on the east side. The earlier structure was the larger of the two and measured 28 feet square. The later structure, which contained two sets of entry trenches, measured only 15 feet square. Both struc-

FIGURE 5.16. *Two views of the Garden Creek Mound No. 1 during excavation: excavating an east-west exploratory trench to the mound center (top, looking west) and the exposed remains of Earth Lodge 1 at left and Earth Lodge 2 at right (bottom, looking west). (Photo from Dickens 1976:85)*

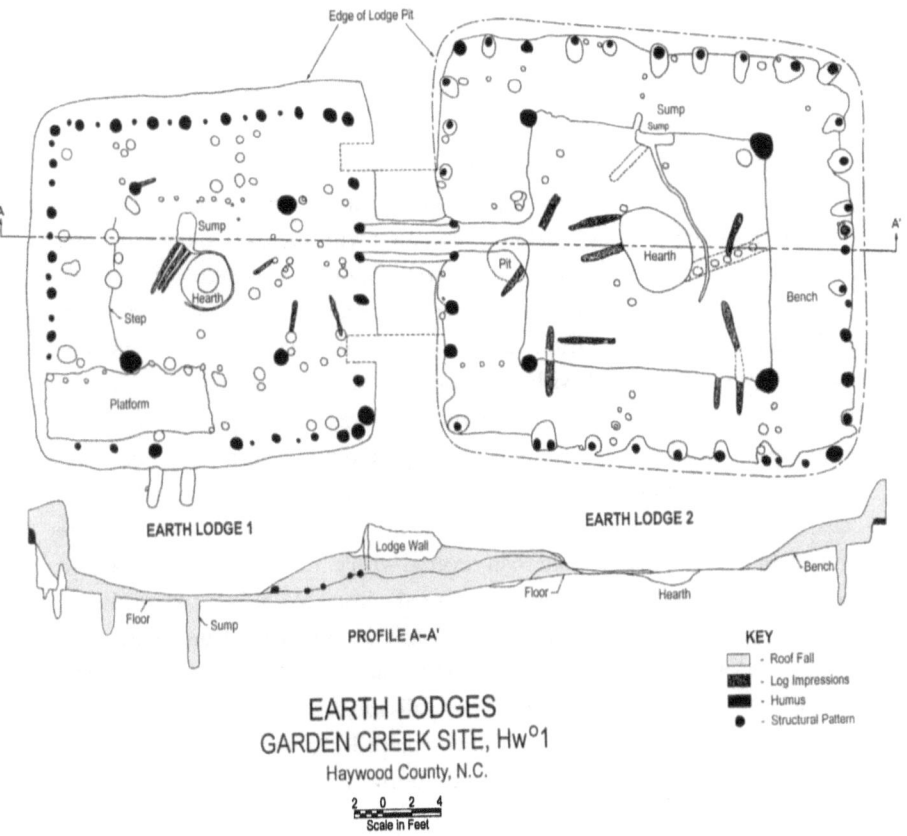

FIGURE 5.17. *Excavation plan of the paired earth lodges at the Garden Creek Mound No. 1. (Based on Dickens 1970:209)*

tures were encircled by an enclosure that probably followed the perimeter of the mound summit.

Although these structures and features dating to the Pisgah phase represent the latest preserved record of activity on the mound summit, artifacts contained in fill that had been plowed and eroded from the top of the mound dated to the subsequent Qualla phase (Dickens 1976:75–79; Keel 1976:69). This mound "outwash" probably represents the remains of superimposed town house floors like those found at the Coweeta Creek site, discussed later in this chapter.

After the Garden Creek Mound No. 1 was completely excavated, archaeologists were able to work out the following sequence of events. Initially, two semisubterranean, earth-embanked buildings were constructed at about the same time. These side-by-side earth lodges were connected by a common passageway (fig. 5.17). The larger of the two structures measured 28 feet square and had a clay bench along all four walls. The smaller structure was 20 feet square, and it had a clay bench along the wall adjacent to the vestibule entryway. Entrance to the larger earth lodge was gained through the passageway from the smaller structure (Dickens 1976:85–86).

After the earth lodges were built, several rows of posts were placed adjacent to them, forming a 42'×60' rectangle. These posts probably supported a large, arborlike building that was used in conjunction with the earth lodges, perhaps for communal gatherings during the warmer months (Dickens 1978:123). At some point, the earth lodges began to deteriorate, and a layer of boulders was placed along their western flanks and over the entire area of the post rows. The boulder layer was covered with soil from the village midden, almost to the height of the earth lodge roofs. The midden soil was then capped with a layer of clean yellow clay. The roofs of the earth lodges did not receive a clay cap.

Construction had been attempted on this surface, but the earth lodge roofs collapsed before it was completed. The depressions created by their collapse were filled with midden soil and then covered with a thin clay cap. At this point, the elevated surface of the mound measured some 50'×70'. However, it was still not stable, as the fill continued to settle in the large depressions. This settling required another layer of clay before construction could begin on a new temple. Finally, the two structures, the palisade, and the burials mentioned above were placed on this surface, which escaped plowing and erosion. However, evidence of later use of the mound during the Qualla phase was plowed and eroded away (Dickens 1976:87).

Although seven burials intruded from the top level of the mound, a total of twenty-four were found during the course of the mound excavation. All the burials date to the last half of the Pisgah phase. Most of the individuals were interred in simple pits; however, six were placed in shaft-and-chamber pits with the chambers dug off to one side. All the bodies were flexed, and most of the heads were oriented in a westward direction. Over 50 percent of the burials were accompanied by grave goods—compared with only 30 percent at the Warren Wilson village site. As was the case at Warren Wilson, most of these artifacts were made from shell, the most popular being columella beads, tubular shell beads, shell gorgets, and shell ear pins.

Dickens (1976:130) noted that one burial contained three ground-stone disks while another was accompanied by two ground-stone celts. He interpreted the presence of ground-stone artifacts in the burials as being more related to the succeeding Qualla phase, thus reinforcing the late Pisgah affiliation of the Garden Creek Mound No. 1. Except for the presence of these ground-stone artifacts, the kind and quantity of the grave goods from the mound did not differ appreciably from those accompanying the village burials at Warren Wilson. This suggests that people buried in the mound were of no higher status than those buried in the village. Of course, mound burial itself may be the best indicator of higher status.

Mound Structure and Political Complexity

The form and structure of Garden Creek Mound No. 1 and Mound No. 2 suggest fundamental differences in the evolution of political organization and ceremonial practices during the Connestee and succeeding Pisgah phases. The earlier Mound No. 2 did not have an earth lodge at its base but rather started out as a low clay platform to support a wall-post structure. After this building burned—perhaps in an intentionally set fire—a layer of soil was laid down to provide the foundation for another wall-post structure. Within the fill of both mound stages, numerous hearths, including rock-filled basins, and refuse pits were found. No Connestee phase burials were associated with the mound (Keel 1976:78–101).

The purpose and function of this mound is unclear, except for the fact that it served as a slightly elevated platform for a structure. And it is believed that this building served a public or ceremonial purpose. The large number of refuse pits and hearths suggests that food preparation and consumption were important activities, perhaps associated with communal feasting.

Instead of continuing the Connestee tradition of platform mound construction, Pisgah people initially built earth lodges in which they conducted rituals and carried out their civic responsibilities. After these earth lodges collapsed or were destroyed, their remains were covered by elevated platform mounds constructed of soil, upon which temples or chiefly residences were placed. These mounds, like the earth lodges, reflect political and ritual changes associated with the South Appalachian Mississippian tradition; moreover, they do not derive from earlier Middle Woodland mound-building.

Although archaeologists have recognized fundamental differences in how Middle Woodland and Mississippian platform mounds were used, they are still not sure how the early platform mounds functioned within Woodland societies. Not only are they very different from Mississippian platform mounds, but they also exhibit considerable variability among themselves. The surfaces of some were kept clean with no evidence of structures; others are topped with thick middens and postholes indicating habitation; and still others have produced evidence that suggests that mortuary activities took place atop the mounds (Jefferies 1994:82–83). The discontinuity in the development of Connestee and

Pisgah public architecture emphasizes the distinctions noted earlier between Connestee and Pisgah ceramics, as well as other areas of divergence in subsistence, settlement systems, and demography (Purrington 1983:144–45).

Although the Pisgah mound at Garden Creek is not like earlier Middle Woodland mounds, it is very similar to the Town Creek mound, as well as other South Appalachian Mississippian mound sites in Georgia and South Carolina. One of the most obvious similarities is the use of earth lodges or similar structures as public buildings prior to their being covered with soil to create pyramidal mounds upon which temples or chiefly residences were built. This earth-lodge-to-temple-mound construction sequence was followed at Town Creek (see Chapter 4), perhaps at the Peachtree site in Cherokee County, and also at the Tugalo, Irene, and Beaverdam Creek sites in the Savannah River drainage of Georgia. Earth lodges have also been reported beneath mounds at the Dallas, Davis, and Hixon sites in Tennessee, as well as at the Wilbanks, Horseshoe Bend, Log Swamp, and Eastwood sites in northern Georgia (Anderson 1994; Ferguson 1971; Lewis and Kneberg 1941; Rudolph 1984; Wauchope 1966).

Many researchers believe that this shift in public architecture also may mirror a shift in sociopolitical organization. It has been suggested that earth lodges probably served as council houses wherein several representatives of an egalitarian society met to negotiate consensus decisions. The later construction of elevated mounds to support temples or chiefly residences reflects a change to a more hierarchical form of political organization centered around a class of hereditary elites who ruled, to varying degrees, by decree (Anderson 1994:308; DePratter 1983:209).

The size and complexity of polities comprising the South Appalachian Mississippian tradition exhibited considerable variability. Some were represented by large centers with multiple mounds, whose leaders controlled large territories, whereas other groups were represented by relatively small villages, often without mounds, whose influence did not extend beyond the immediate vicinity. Also, as some ceremonial and political centers declined in power and importance, others rose. Platform mounds might have been abandoned in one area as chiefly power waned, while in other areas, mound construction and additions continued until the time of first European contacts (see Hally 1996; Steponaitis 1986:391–92). The North Carolina Pisgah and Qualla phase cultures were at the low end of the scale of sociopolitical complexity during the period of major Mississippian influence across the Southeast.

The reasons for the collapse of many of the complex Mississippian chiefdoms is mostly a matter of speculation. Some researchers have proposed that in some regions, climatic conditions changed, creating weather patterns that were no longer favorable for intensive corn agriculture (Anderson 1994:286). Others have suggested that good agricultural soils became scarce commodities as populations increased. Limited accessibility to these soils caused increased hostilities and warfare, which eventually led to the collapse of the chiefdoms (Larson 1972:391). At the Irene site, located at the mouth of the Savannah River, chemical analyses of human skeletal remains indicate that there was a marked change in diet between the earlier Savannah and later Irene phases. A decrease in corn consumption by the later inhabitants indicates that agricultural food production declined through time, at least in this region (Anderson 1994:293).

Smaller regional polities located away from the centers of political control may have revolted under the burden of being forced to pay increasing amounts of tribute to support a distant power. This unrest was no doubt exacerbated as rival chiefdoms competed to extend their spheres of influence and control.

Disease may have played a role in the political decline of some Mississippian chiefdoms. Just as sanitation and health deteriorated in the densely packed communities of Medieval Europe, similar conditions may have arisen within the concentrated populations surrounding many of the major Mississippian political and religious centers. The large numbers of burials at sites like Town Creek in North Carolina and Irene in Georgia may reflect higher than normal mortality rates during the fourteenth and fifteenth centuries, before the arrival of Old World pathogens.

For whatever reason or reasons, most archaeologists today see Mississippian chiefdoms as inherently unstable political entities that were in a constant state of change—"cycling" through periods of emergence, expansion, and fragmentation. Few chiefdoms lasted more than 100 years (Hally 1996:123).

In North Carolina, the construction of platform mounds took place during the Pisgah and Qualla phases. Some of these mounds continued to be used into the Historic period, when town houses were constructed on their summits. These town houses were built with few additions or modification to the mounds themselves (Dickens 1979:24). It is also likely that town houses have a long history in the Appalachian Summit region and were important public meeting places at the same time temples and chiefly residences were being erected atop platform mounds. At many sites, civil and ceremonial activities may have been carried out solely in town houses.

William Bartram, traveling through Cherokee territory in the 1770s, described the typical town house as "a large rotunda, capable of accommodating several hundred people; it stands on the top of an ancient artificial mount of earth, of about twenty feet perpendicular, and the rotunda on the top of it being above thirty feet more, gives the whole fabric an elevation of about sixty feet from the common surface of the ground. But it may be proper to observe, that this mount, on which the rotunda stands, is of a much ancienter [*sic*] date than the building, and perhaps was raised for another purpose" (Van Doren 1928:297).

Unfortunately, earlier plowing, erosion, and looting by relic collectors obliterated the upper portions of the platform mounds that have been excavated in western North Carolina. These activities destroyed the evidence of any Qualla structures that may have been built atop these mounds. Plowing and erosion also have been responsible for transforming the pyramidal shapes of the substructure platforms into low conical rises that are sometimes hard to recognize as artificial mounds, even by the practiced eye of the archaeologist. This "flattening out" or "melting" of the mounds also has often caused the latest cultural materials to be concentrated on the surface around many mound sites, sometimes giving the false impression that they were used almost exclusively at the end of the Qualla phase (cf. Egloff 1967; Hally 1994:147).

Lamar Culture and the Qualla Phase (after A.D. 1350)

The Qualla phase of western North Carolina is best understood when placed within a broader regional context. Most archaeologists working in the Southeast consider Qualla to be a manifestation of the widespread Lamar culture that is found across the northern half of Georgia and Alabama, most of South Carolina, and eastern Tennessee—as well as the western one-third of North Carolina. Not only does Lamar cover a wide geographical area, but it also spans a long period of time, from around A.D. 1350 until 1800 (Hally 1994:147). Early and Middle Lamar periods fall within the last half of the South Appalachian Mississippian tradition.

Lamar culture was first recognized and formally described by A. R. Kelly in 1938 when he reported on excavations at the Lamar site near Macon, Georgia. This site was one of several along the Ocmulgee River in central Georgia that were the focus of extensive excavations funded by various federal relief programs between 1933 and 1941 (Kelly 1938; Hally 1994). During this same time, similar federal programs were sponsoring excavations at the Peachtree, Town Creek, and Wall sites in North Carolina.

Kelly considered Lamar to be a late pre-European contact culture that represented a blending of local and intrusive Mississippian cultural traits. Since Kelly's report, the geographical and temporal range of Lamar has been greatly expanded.

David Hally of the University of Georgia has defined three somewhat arbitrary periods within Lamar culture that can be recognized by gradual changes in pottery styles, particularly those from central and northern Georgia: Early Lamar (A.D. 1350–1450); Middle Lamar (A.D. 1450–1550); and Late Lamar (A.D. 1550–1800). Within each of these periods, several local phases have been identified (1994:147).

Early Lamar ceramics are typified by a variety of well-executed complicated-stamp motifs, including the filfot cross, figure nine, and figure eight. Incised decorations are rare and, when present, consist of simple designs incorporating one or two lines. The rim area is often decorated with individual nodes or appliquéd strips of clay that are pinched, notched, or punctated (Hally 1994:147).

Incised decorations increase in frequency and variety during the Middle Lamar period. Finer lines were incorporated in more complex motifs. In contrast, the application of complicated-stamped designs became more sloppy, and the designs themselves were not as finely executed as those of the Early Lamar period. Appliqué strips were used to thicken jar rims. Sometimes rims were folded over to create the same effect. The rims were usually decorated by pinching the edges between the fingers (Hally 1994:147).

The Late Lamar period saw a continuation of the trend toward refining complex incised-design motifs, at least in parts of Georgia. Complicated-stamped pottery was joined by pottery with a variety of other surface finishes, including brushed and check stamped. Notched rim fillets were often added for decoration (Hally 1994:147). According to Hally's chronology, the Qualla phase of the Appalachian Summit, as it is currently defined, falls within the Middle and Late Lamar periods and is contemporary with the Tugalo and Estatoe phases of north Georgia (Hally 1986:111–12).

As a result of research conducted during the Cherokee project, Roy Dickens initially subdivided Qualla into early and late phases (1979:12). The Early Qualla phase (A.D. 1450–1650) was seen as the period following the Pisgah phase and preceding the time of sustained European contacts. The Late Qualla phase (A.D. 1650–1838) was believed to date from the beginning of direct interaction between Europeans and Cherokees until the Removal, when many Cherokees were forced from their mountain homeland.

Dickens also recognized a discontinuity in the distribution of Pisgah and Qualla sites in the Appalachian Summit area. Most Pisgah sites are located in the eastern and central mountains, within the French Broad and Pigeon River drainages. Qualla sites, on the other hand, are concentrated in the western and southern mountains, within the Little Tennessee and Hiwassee drainages. Settlements of both phases are found in the central mountains along the Pigeon, Tuckasegee, and Oconaluftee Rivers. This almost complementary distribution of Pisgah and Qualla sites led Dickens (1978:132) to state, "If Pisgah and Qualla do indeed represent a cultural continuum, then the site distributions indicate a major occupational shift in the late prehistoric or protohistoric times."

Several surveys have confirmed Dickens's observation that the evidence for Pisgah sites is slight in the western portion of the Appalachian Summit region. A survey of the upper Hiwassee River valley recorded forty-seven Qualla sites and only two sites with small Pisgah components (Dorwin, Tiger, and Bistline 1975). A similar survey along the Valley River between the towns of Andrews and Murphy in Cherokee County found fourteen sites with Qualla components. Only one of these also produced a small number of Pisgah potsherds (Ward 1977a). A recent analysis of pottery from a sample of sites discovered during the course of the Cherokee project's survey of Cherokee County found only a single Pisgah sherd (Farmer 1997). Likewise, two large mound sites, Peachtree and Spikebuck Town, located in Cherokee and Clay Counties, respectively, have produced only a trace of Pisgah ceramics. Qualla pottery is the dominant type at these and other mound sites in the area; however, at the Peachtree mound, the only mound to have been excavated in the southern and western mountains, pottery similar to that of the Dallas phase was also recovered. And, graves lined with large stone slabs, like those of the Mouse Creek phase, were present (cf. Setzler and Jennings 1941:Plates 15–17, 42–44; Sullivan 1987). Dallas and Mouse Creek were Mississippian cultures of eastern and southeastern Tennessee that date between A.D. 1300 and A.D. 1600 (Sullivan 1995:xx).

Current evidence suggests that the Pisgah phase did not make a significant cultural impact in the North Carolina mountains west of the Tuckasegee drainage. Although the archaeological complex representing the inhabitants of the region during this time is presently not known, it seems unlikely that the lower Little Tennessee and Hiwassee River valleys were abandoned between A.D. 1100 and 1450. Nearby areas of eastern Tennessee and northern Georgia contained large populations, and the large platform mounds, like Peachtree and Spikebuck Town, point to the presence of a sizable population in the western North Carolina mountains, at least during the last half of this period. We suggest that an as-yet-unrecognized early Qualla (or Lamar) phase culture was thriving in the western mountains at about the same time Pisgah influence was being felt in the central portion of the Appalachian Summit. Once detailed studies of Qualla ceramics from the western mountains are completed and more excavated samples are analyzed, archaeologists will probably find that this early Qualla phase is characterized by pottery related to that of the Wilbanks phase of northern Georgia, the Dallas phase of eastern Tennessee, and other ceramic series described as Early Lamar (Hally 1994:147).

It is also possible that an Early Qualla phase will be recognized in other portions of the Appalachian Summit region. Regardless of what this Early Qualla phase material resembles, the view of a simple Pisgah-to-Qualla developmental sequence throughout the North Carolina mountains is no longer tenable. In fact, this sequence may be the exception rather than the rule and a historical consequence of which sites were chosen for excavation during the Cherokee project.

Given the likelihood that a pre-1450 Qualla or Qualla-like phase will be identified, "Early Qualla," as originally defined by Dickens, is referred to here as the Middle Qualla phase, beginning around A.D. 1450. And because significant contacts between Cherokees and European traders did not begin until the eighteenth century, we prefer to extend the ending date of the Middle Qualla phase to A.D. 1700.

Ceramics of the Middle Qualla phase are characterized by jars with flaring rim forms, usually adorned with a notched appliqué strip added beneath the lip. Often the lips of the vessels appear to have been thickened by folding excess clay under the lip and around the rim. However, careful examination usually reveals the addition of a strip of clay that was carefully applied to the edge of the lip and molded onto the U-shaped constriction created by a flaring rim. Although most Qualla and Pisgah rims are quite different in form, they share a tradition of having clay added to the rim area of vessels for the purpose of providing a background for decoration.

Middle Qualla phase vessels were most often stamped with a carved wooden paddle. Rectilinear-stamped and curvilinear-stamped designs occurred, with the latter having become more popular during the last half of the phase. Concentric circle, figure nine, parallel undulating line, chevron, and rectilinear line block or herringbonelike designs were popular motifs. Often these designs were blurred by a partial smoothing of the vessel surface (Egloff 1967).

Dickens (1979:24) has suggested that carved-paddle stamped motifs were not as well executed during the Late Qualla phase as they were during the Middle Qualla phase. Although this statement may be true as a general trend, a casual inspection of Middle and Late Qualla ceramics suggests that much of the pottery made during the beginning of the Late Qualla phase was well made, with clean, boldly executed design motifs.

Cazuela bowl forms, with their sharply carinated shoulders, made their debut during the Middle Qualla phase (fig. 5.18). Incised designs were executed in a variety of motifs around the broad cazuela bowl shoulders. These incorporated curvilinear and rectilinear elements, both of which were sometimes concatenated in an interlocking fashion. For example, some scrolls and embedded line blocks alternate to form an intricate pattern. In some cases, the incised decora-

FIGURE 5.18. *Middle Qualla vessels from the Coweeta Creek site. The bottom two vessels are cazuela bowls with incised designs between the rim and shoulder; the top two vessels are jars with incised, punctated, and applied-clay decorations.*

tions on vessel shoulders are repeated in the complicated-stamped designs that were applied to the vessels' bodies. The incised designs of the Middle Qualla phase appear most similar to the motifs characteristic of the Middle Lamar Tugalo phase of northern Georgia (Hally 1994:153).

Burnishing, check stamping, and cordmarking were minority surface finishes during the Middle Qualla phase, with burnishing being the most popular. Although never as popular as the complicated-stamped motifs, the frequency of check-stamped and cordmarked pottery appears to have increased during the Late Qualla phase. Dickens (1979:26) and Egloff (1967:38–43) have suggested that both techniques gained in popularity as incising and burnishing became less popular.

In general, later Qualla and Lamar cultures appear to have been more egalitarian than earlier ones. Although still governed by chiefs, their authority was grounded in community consensus rather than fiat. The town house, previously described, became the focal point of the community where the decision-making process was opened up to a large segment of the population, which was represented by clan leaders (Anderson 1994:293; Ferguson 1971).

Although some Early and Middle Qualla phase platform mounds were probably constructed and used as summits upon which chiefs resided, other Middle and Late Qualla phase mounds were not purposely constructed but resulted from a very different process. They were formed as successive town house structures were built at the same location. The rubble and debris from earlier structures formed the foundations for later ones, and additional soil was added only to flatten and smooth the ground surface so that new buildings could be erected. After a period of time, the successive building episodes created a low mound whose elevation was fortuitous to its purpose.

One of these Middle Qualla phase town house mounds is known as the Coweeta Creek site, located in Macon County. The site is located on the west bank of the Little Tennessee River, near its confluence with Coweeta Creek. During the course of the Cherokee project, between 1965 and 1971, the mound at Coweeta Creek was completely excavated by UNC archaeologists (fig. 5.19). These excavations also uncovered a portion of the village associated with the earliest town house construction phase at Coweeta Creek (Egloff 1971) (fig. 5.20).

When the Coweeta Creek site was first visited by UNC archaeologists, the mound was not visible. In 1965, not knowing a mound was present, a small-scale test excavation was planned at the site. However, after a portion of a large, circular town house was uncovered that summer, the decision was made to continue the excavations the next year and to make Coweeta Creek a prime target of the Cherokee project (Egloff 1971:47).

When the excavations were completed in 1971, six separate town house floors, stacked one atop the other, had been carefully peeled away. Each floor was separated from the preceding one by only a few inches of sand and refuse. European trade artifacts, consisting mostly of glass beads, were found in association with all but the earliest town house floors (Egloff 1971:62). The absence

FIGURE 5.19. *Two views of the Coweeta Creek mound during excavation: view with the plowzone, sand floor, and daub fall removed, revealing Structure 1 (top, looking northeast) and Floor 3 of Structure Group 1 (bottom, looking northwest). (Courtesy of the Research Laboratories of Archaeology)*

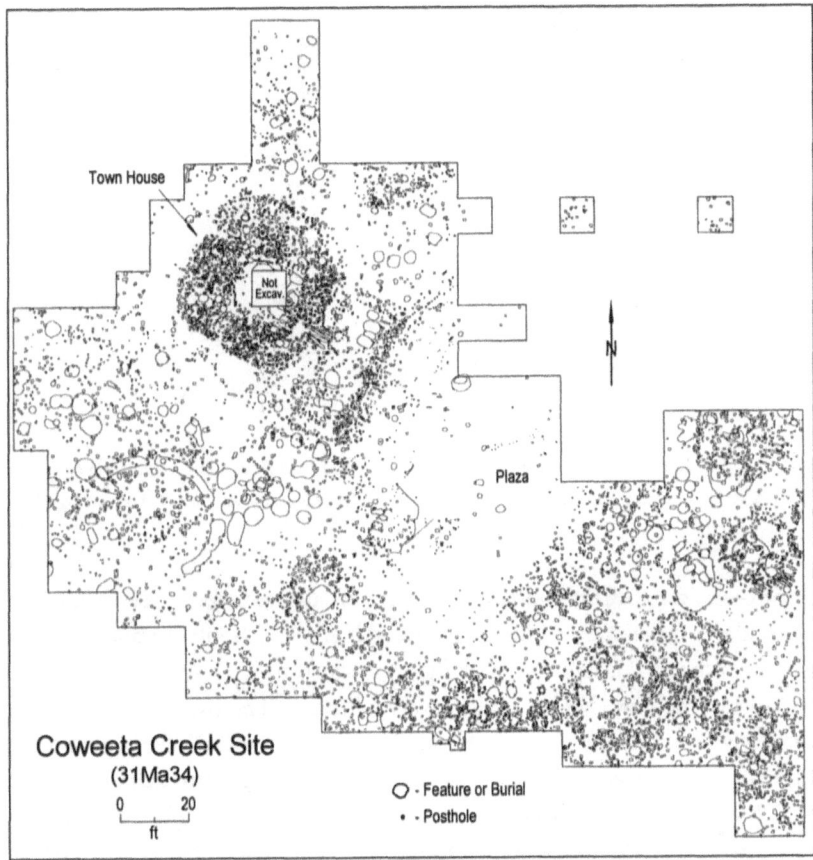

FIGURE 5.20. *Excavation plan of the Coweeta Creek site showing the town house and dwellings surrounding the village plaza. (Drawing by Christopher Rodning, 1998; courtesy of the Research Laboratories of Archaeology)*

of iron cutting tools, clothing fasteners, ornaments made of copper and brass, or other European-made goods stands in contrast to the trade assemblages found on Late Qualla sites in North Carolina and Overhill Cherokee sites in eastern Tennessee (Schroedl 1986; Setzler and Jennings 1941).

The earliest town house at Coweeta Creek was constructed on the ground surface. It was square in outline, with rounded corners, and measured approximately 36 feet on a side. A vestibule entrance was evidenced by parallel trenches oriented perpendicular to the town house wall. The roof was supported by large, interior support posts that surrounded a central, puddled-clay hearth.

Except for the latest structure, which was roughly circular, all of the subsequent town house floors were of similar size and orientation as the first one. In

FIGURE 5.21. *An artist's conception of the mound and town house at Coweeta Creek. (Drawing by Frank Weir, 1970; courtesy of the Research Laboratories of Archaeology)*

most cases, the hearths and entry trenches of later structures were rebuilt directly above those of the earlier structures. All of the vestibule entrances opened to the southeast (Dickens 1978:124; Egloff 1971:61).

Most of the town houses appear to have burned. The two structures represented by Floors 2 and 3 were particularly well preserved. As the town houses burned, roof beams, timbers, and boards fell onto the prepared clay floors and the charred remains of benches and other interior furnishings. The benches, arranged around the walls, were covered with cane mats, fragments of which were also charred and preserved. The clay-lined, or "daubed," walls collapsed and covered the floors and charred debris from the roofs. This layer of fire-hardened clay sealed the underlying remains in an excellent state of preservation. After a town house burned, enough soil was brought in to just cover the remains and create a smooth, flat surface. A new town house was then constructed on top of this layer (Egloff 1971:61) (fig. 5.21).

The Middle Qualla phase houses excavated at the Coweeta Creek site were identical in size and shape to Pisgah phase houses uncovered at the Warren Wilson site. They were rectangular in outline, they averaged a little over 20 feet on a side, and they had vestibule entrances and interior supports surrounding centrally located clay hearths (Dickens 1978:123).

Although the Coweeta Creek excavations failed to uncover remains of a stockade surrounding the village, one may have been present. Only a small area was excavated at the edge of the site, where a stockade was suspected. Unfortunately, this area was severely eroded (Dickens 1978:131). The internal arrangement of the village, with houses clustered around the plaza and mound, suggests that it probably was enclosed by a stockade, much like the Warren Wilson site discussed earlier in this chapter.

At Coweeta Creek, the excavated village area predated the later stages of town house construction. None of the houses or associated features and burials contained European trade artifacts. Such artifacts were present on the floors of all the town houses comprising the mound, except the earliest one. This distribution suggests that during the Middle Qualla phase, villages tended to consist of nucleated arrangements of domestic structures around a centrally located town house and plaza. After European contact, Qualla settlements appear to have become more dispersed. However, the continued use of the Coweeta Creek mound and a town house during the Historic period indicates a strong sense of community even though people may have lived some distance apart.

Eighty-three burials were excavated at the Coweeta Creek site. These contained the remains of eighty-seven individuals who were placed either in simple, straight-sided, oval-to-rectangular pits, or in pits with cylindrical shafts and side chambers. Most were oriented with their heads to the southeast. Twenty-nine individuals were accompanied by funerary objects. Artifacts of shell, including a variety of small and large cut-shell beads, olivella beads, and ear and hair pins, occurred most frequently. Engraved gorgets, pendants, and masks made from conch shells accompanied some of the burials (fig. 5.22). Stone and clay pipes, pottery vessels, rattles, red ocher, and freshwater pearls also were found with the burials.

Most of the graves were placed in the village area, often associated with houses and, in some cases, beneath or near hearths. No European trade artifacts were found with any of the burials, reinforcing the idea that the village and the earliest town house construction predate the time of European contact.

A cluster of nine graves was present in the central area of the superimposed town house floors and associated with the two earliest construction phases: Floor 5 (n = 1) and Floor 6 (n = 8). All but two of these individuals were adults and included six males and one female. Two of the male burials were accompanied by conch-shell face masks. One child grave contained shell pendants and beads, whereas the other contained shell ear pins, a shell mask gorget, freshwater pearls, and a pottery vessel (Rodning 1996).

Two additional groups of burials were found on either side of the town house entrances, on the flank of the mound. Although no European grave goods were found in any of these burials, all are thought to date to the period of the latest constructions on the mound, a time when European trade artifacts frequently

FIGURE 5.22. *Middle Qualla hairpins (top left), mask (top right), and gorget (bottom) made of marine shell from Coweeta Creek.*

occurred on the town house floors (Egloff 1971:69). The absence of European artifacts in the graves may reflect a conservatism in maintaining traditional mortuary rituals.

The more northern cluster of graves beside the town house entrance contained the remains of two adult males, one adult female, and a small child. All were accompanied by a varied assortment of burial goods, including stone pipes, gorgets, and shell beads and pins. One of the adult males displayed a uniquely rich assortment of grave associations, including: a quiver of seven arrows represented by small triangular stone arrow points and the dark stains of their rotted shafts; four shell pins; a string of olivella beads; two strands of large and small cut-shell beads; fourteen freshwater pearls; a split-cane basket represented by organic stains on the bottom of the burial pit; several pieces of cut mica; and a clay "gaming" disk that covered the individual's left eye orbit. The body was placed in a flexed position, in a straight-sided, oval pit (Egloff 1971; Rodning 1996).

The more southern cluster of graves beside the town house entrance contained the remains of four adult males, one adult of undetermined sex, and a very young child. Only the child burial contained grave goods, which consisted of shell beads and a shell pendant (Rodning 1996).

The presence of burials associated with the various town houses strongly suggests that these individuals were important members of the community. Both males and females were represented, as well as children. However, most of the town house burials were males. And the graves with the most elaborate offerings were all adult males. This pattern suggests that men most often filled the roles of town leaders. A study of mortuary data from the area of the village surrounding the Coweeta Creek mound found that female burials there were more elaborate than those of males. This pattern suggests that females filled the roles of clan leaders (Rodning 1996:55).

Because burials were associated with various construction stages of the mound, the death of important town leaders may have affected the schedule of town house and mound construction. This interpretation is reinforced by the fact that most of the town houses seem to have been purposefully burned before new ones were built. It is likely that these cycles of destruction and construction followed the death and burial of important community leaders in the floors of the town houses.

During the Middle Qualla phase, farming continued to be the most important subsistence activity. Fertile alluvial soils were used to grow corn, beans, squash, pumpkins, and gourds. Seasonally available nuts, fruits, and berries were collected, and several species of wild animals were hunted and trapped to provide a varied and balanced diet.

Comparing the animal remains from the Coweeta Creek site with those from the Warren Wilson site, Jeannette Runquist noted that the two sites were very similar in that deer provided the overwhelming bulk of the meat that was eaten. However, Runquist also noted that black bear and toad remains were much more abundant at Coweeta Creek (1979:336).

We mentioned earlier that a large number of toads were represented in a food preparation facility at Warren Wilson and that the toads may have been used for hallucinogenic or medicinal purposes. An even larger number of toad remains (7,106 bone elements) were found at the Coweeta Creek site. Most of these, as well as a large percentage of the remains of black bear, were contained in a single pit feature. Because this pit was located near the town house mound, Runquist suggested that both species may have been important in Qualla ceremonies (1979:337).

The Eastern Fringe of the Appalachian Summit

Questions concerning the chronological and cultural relationships between the Pisgah, Qualla, and Lamar phases recently have been addressed indirectly by surveys and excavations within the Catawba River valley, an area outside the traditional mountain homeland of the Cherokees. From its headwaters, the Catawba flows in an easterly direction in McDowell, Burke, and Catawba Counties before turning southward near Statesville and flowing toward the North Carolina–South Carolina border, in the vicinity of Rock Hill, South Carolina.

The territory along the south-flowing leg of the Catawba has been known historically as the homeland of the Catawba Indians (Hudson 1970; Merrell 1989). Who occupied the upper Catawba River valley is less clear, although archaeologists believe that during the time of the Pisgah and Qualla phases, the people who lived in Burke and McDowell Counties show affinities to both the Prehistoric Cherokee and Catawba Indians (Keeler 1971; Moore 1987).

This similarity is manifest at two Late Prehistoric archaeological sites— the McDowell site and the Berry site (Moore 1987). During 1971, portions of Burke and McDowell Counties were surveyed by Robert Keeler, a UNC–Chapel Hill student who was conducting research for his undergraduate honors thesis. Keeler also analyzed several large, privately owned artifact collections during the course of his study.

In 1977 one of the sites Keeler had recommended for excavation, the McDowell site (31Mc41), was tested by UNC archaeologists. This site is comprised of a village and low mound located on the south side of the Catawba River, near the town of Marion. The small-scale excavation uncovered a few pit features and several postholes. A 5′ square excavation unit in the top of a 2′ rise, thought to represent the remains of the mound, verified that it was in fact artificial and created by dumping basket loads of soil. The internal structure of the mound indicated that it was created as a substructure platform, similar to the Garden Creek Mound No. 1, and was not the result of successive stages of town house construction, like the Coweeta Creek mound (Ward 1977b).

Excavations resumed at the McDowell site in 1986 and uncovered a Pisgah-like house and a large burned structure, 40 feet in diameter, adjacent to the mound. Because of its size and placement near the mound, this building is thought to represent the remains of a town house (Moore 1987).

The majority of the ceramics from the McDowell site are tempered with particles of crushed steatite or soapstone. This soft rock could easily have been quarried from local outcrops. Crushed quartz and fine sand also were used as tempering agents. The most notable quality of the McDowell site pottery is its similarity to Pisgah phase ceramics. An analysis of sherds from the 1977 excavations revealed that the most popular surface finish consisted of rectilinear complicated-stamped motifs identical to those of Pisgah pottery. The distinctive folded or "collared" Pisgah rim form with punctated designs also frequently occurred in the ceramic sample (Ward n.d.).

The ceramics, substructure mound, and Pisgah-like house leave little doubt that Pisgah phase people of the Appalachian Summit and the inhabitants of the McDowell site were closely related. This relationship is further supported by radiocarbon dates that place the McDowell site occupation in the fifteenth century, coinciding with the last gasp of the Pisgah phase (Eastman 1994a:34; Moore 1987).

The Berry site (31Bk22) is located north and east of the McDowell site in Burke County on Upper Creek, a tributary of the Catawba River. It consists of the remnant of an earthen mound and an associated village. According to local tradition, the mound once stood 12 feet high before it was bulldozed by the landowner to obtain fill dirt. The Berry site, like the McDowell site, has a long history among Indian artifact collectors as a favorite collecting spot. It was also visited by Keeler, who recommended that it be excavated (1971).

In 1986, a 10' wide trench was excavated into the remains of the mound and a block excavation was opened adjacent to it. What was left of the mound consisted of basket-loaded fill, indicating that, at least during its early history, the mound served as a substructure platform for a temple or elite residence (Moore 1987). For years, local collectors referred to the Berry site mound as a "refuse mound" because of the large amounts of bone, shell, and other refuse found around it. This concentration of debris suggests that during its later history, town houses may have been constructed atop the mound in a fashion similar to the Coweeta Creek mound. Unfortunately, evidence to verify this interpretation was destroyed by the bulldozer before archaeologists arrived on the scene.

Although tempered primarily with steatite, pottery from the Berry site is very different from the McDowell site ceramics. Curvilinear complicated-stamped motifs are much more common than rectilinear designs, and the distinctive "collared" Pisgah rim form is absent. In addition to the curvilinear complicated-stamped designs, other Lamar- and Qualla-like attributes dominate the assemblage. These include notched rim folds or appliqué strips, burnished surface treatments, and the presence of carinated bowls decorated with a variety of incised motifs (Moore 1987; Ward n.d.). Moore believes that this ceramic assemblage is very similar to the Lamar period Tugalo phase of northeast Georgia (1987:9).

Radiocarbon dates place the main Berry site occupation in the fifteenth century, making it contemporary with the Pisgah-related occupation of the McDowell site (Eastman 1994a:34; Moore 1987:4). This temporal overlap presents a problem if the traditional view of Pisgah phase preceding and being ancestral to the Qualla phase is accepted. There is no question that the McDowell site represents the easternmost extension of Pisgah influence, and it is equally clear that the Berry site pottery is closely related to Qualla and Lamar ceramics.

If the radiocarbon dates are accepted at face value, and there is no reason to doubt them, then we are again forced to re-examine the traditional view of the Pisgah-to-Qualla developmental relationship. Although stylistic similarities and stratigraphic evidence support this developmental sequence in the central Appalachian Summit region, this sequence is not found throughout the region. Pisgah influence is virtually absent in the southwestern mountains of North Carolina, where we have postulated the presence of an as-yet-unidentified Early Qualla phase temporally coeval with at least the last half of the Pisgah phase. It also appears that a similar situation occurred in the eastern foothills, in the upper Catawba River valley. Here, strong Lamar influences from the south may have spread into the Catawba drainage at the same time Pisgah influences were spreading eastward across the Blue Ridge and into the foothills. The distribution of Pisgah phase sites covers a relatively restricted area, extending from the Nolichucky River in eastern Tennessee, along the French Broad and Pigeon drainages in the west central North Carolina mountains, and into the upper Catawba River valley (Dickens 1978; Moore 1987).

Summary

At the conclusion of the Cherokee project in the 1970s, the cultural history of the Appalachian Summit region during the Woodland and Mississippian periods seemed clear. A straightforward sequence of development, beginning with the Early Woodland Swannanoa phase and culminating with the Qualla phase of the Historic period Cherokees, had been outlined. Much had been learned about the distribution, sizes, and types of settlements that characterized the various phases comprising the sequence. Temporally sensitive styles of pottery and other artifacts that could be used to order the phases in a fairly tight chronology had been identified.

At the time of the Cherokee project, comparatively little research had been conducted in the neighboring areas of Tennessee, Georgia, and South Carolina. For this reason, archaeologists were inclined to view the surrounding region from the pinnacles of the North Carolina mountains (cf. Anderson 1989:109). Today, this situation has changed. New information on the development of Woodland and Mississippian cultures has poured in from bordering states, forcing archaeologists, especially those of us from North Carolina, to refocus our perspectives, climb down from the mountains, and take another look at some of those ideas that once seemed so clear and straightforward.

6. The Woodland Period on the Coast and Coastal Plain

Archaeologists have long considered the North Carolina Coastal Plain to be comprised of distinct cultural and archaeological areas. These areas generally are seen to coincide with tribal and linguistic groupings recognized by anthropologists who have studied the ethnohistoric records (e.g., Boyce 1973; Mook 1944; Swanton 1946).

The Coastal Plain can be divided into northern and southern regions (cf. Herbert and Mathis 1996; Phelps 1983). The northern region extends from the Neuse River basin to the Virginia state line and encompasses the area occupied by Algonkian- and Iroquois-speaking groups at the time of the arrival of the first English colonists. The Algonkians lived in the eastern Tidewater zone of the northern coast, whereas the Iroquois, represented by the Tuscaroras, occupied the interior Coastal Plain. The southern Coastal Plain extends from just south of the Neuse River basin to the South Carolina state line and covers a territory that during the Contact period was occupied by Siouan-speaking tribes. The traditional Siouan territory extends from the coast westward to the fall line and into the Piedmont.

Some archaeologists have suggested that the central coast should also be recognized as a distinct region. This central region would be comprised primarily of the counties of Onslow and Carteret and would reflect an area of cultural overlap and transition between the northern and southern regions (Jones, Espenshade, and Kennedy 1997; Loftfield 1975, 1990).

For some purposes, it might be helpful to think in terms of a central coastal region. For example, if one is interested in studying ethnic boundaries and how they shifted over time, viewing the central coast as a separate cultural and geographic region might be appropriate. However, when trying to correlate ceramic sequences and phases for all of the coast and Coastal Plain, carving out a central coastal section only adds confusion, not clarity, at least given the current state of our understanding of the coastal ceramic chronology (Herbert and Mathis 1996:141).

Along the northern coast, the barrier islands known as the Outer Banks are separated from the shoreline by the broad, shallow estuarine waters of Pamlico, Croatan, Albemarle, and Currituck Sounds. The shoreline is broken into a plethora of large and small bays and peninsulas as the numerous rivers and streams, including the Neuse, Pamlico, and Chowan Rivers, empty into the sounds. In contrast, the southern coast is characterized by barrier islands lying close to the shoreline and is broken by the narrow mouths of the Newport, White Oak, Cape Fear, and New Rivers. In terms of the availability of estuarine resources, the northern coastal region would have provided far greater access than the southern coast. However, the southern coast offered an environment more protected from the extremes of wind and cold (Herbert and Mathis 1996; Phelps 1983).

A Brief History of Coastal Plain Archaeology

Professional archaeologists did not begin to show interest in the rich cultural remains along the North Carolina coast until after World War II. Between 1947 and 1953, the National Park Service sponsored excavations on Roanoke Island. These excavations, under the direction of J. C. Harrington, were undertaken in order to expose and reconstruct the remains of Fort Raleigh, the first English settlement in North Carolina and the home of the "Lost Colony" (see Chapter 7). Although numerous native artifacts were found while trenches were being excavated in the vicinity of the fort, archaeologists did not know how old the artifacts were or how they came to be buried there (Harrington 1962).

In 1954 and 1955, the Office of Naval Research sponsored an extensive archaeological survey of the northeastern coastal region, from Currituck Sound to the Neuse River. This research, under the direction of William Haag, was carried out as part of a program to develop the Cape Hatteras National Seashore Park. Haag was charged with finding sites that depicted the ancient history of the region; he also was directed to find evidence of the whereabouts of members of the "Lost Colony" after they abandoned Fort Raleigh. The latter goal dictated that Haag's survey focus on the Cape Hatteras area, where many believed the English settlers moved after leaving Roanoke Island (Haag 1958:24). Haag recorded a total of sixty-nine sites, most of which were located on Hatteras Island and along the north bank of the mouth of the Pamlico River.

Like most archaeological surveys along the coast, pottery sherds constituted the main body of Haag's data. Although he saw considerable variability in the way vessel surfaces were treated, he regarded temper as the most "culturally important" attribute. Pottery thought to be the earliest contained a mixture of sand and grit temper, whereas later ceramics were shell tempered (1958:107).

During subsequent surveys, Haag also collected artifacts from several sites along the southern coast; however, the results of these investigations were never published. In 1960, this gap in archaeological knowledge was filled by Stanley South, the archaeologist in charge of studying the ruins of the colonial town of Brunswick near Wilmington. South's survey of Prehistoric sites was supplemental to his main task as historical archaeologist at Brunswick Town. Still, in only four days, South collected artifact samples from eighty-one sites located in New Hanover and Brunswick Counties, North Carolina, and Horry County, South Carolina (1976:4).

South's research was guided by two hypotheses: (1) because of natural barriers and geographic proximity, a closer cultural relationship existed between native groups of the southern coast and groups to the southwest than between the southern Indians and those living north of the Neuse; and (2) because the ethnohistoric records indicated that the northern groups were Algonkian speakers and that the southern groups were Siouan speakers, the two regions should produce distinct cultural assemblages, at least during the Historic period (1976:3). To some extent, both hypotheses were confirmed, and, in the process of testing them, South developed a detailed ceramic chronology for the southern coastal region that is still used today (28–29).

In the early 1970s, Thomas Loftfield, then a Ph.D. candidate at the University of North Carolina, surveyed portions of the central coastal region. Loftfield was aided in the fieldwork by the late Tucker Littleton, an accomplished historian and amateur archaeologist from Swansboro who had also worked with Stanley South. Most of the sites Loftfield and Littleton studied were located in Onslow and Carteret Counties, in the New River basin. In addition to surface collecting and recording some 175 new sites, Loftfield and Littleton chose 5 sites for stratigraphic test excavations. Collections from previously recorded sites were also studied, and several exposed pit features were salvaged during the course of the survey work (Loftfield 1976:103–46).

Loftfield's study focused on developing a ceramic sequence for the central coastal region. Based on a seriation of pottery sherds from the surfaces of sites and small stratigraphic test excavations at the five sites mentioned above, he identified five chronologically distinct ceramic series: New River, Carteret, Onslow, White Oak, and Adams Creek (1976:103–46).

In 1970, David Phelps arrived at East Carolina University and began a vigorous program of archaeological research in the northern coastal region. Initially, his research sought to refine the basic chronological framework suggested by Haag and to develop an understanding of the cultural dynamics of the region. Because of the fragile coastal environment and the rapid encroachment of commercial and urban development, the East Carolina program also became very active in cultural resource–management studies (Phelps 1983:12).

By 1980, Phelps was able to present what he called an "initial model" of the culture history of the southern and northern coastal areas. By drawing on the work of South and Loftfield, and comparing it with his own research in the area north of the Neuse River, Phelps proposed a detailed ceramic chronology for the Woodland period and a sequence of phases that describes patterns of change and stability in settlement, subsistence, and mortuary behaviors. This model was considered applicable to the Tidewater and Coastal Plain regions from the Cape Fear drainage to the Virginia state line (1983).

While most recent archaeological studies have been carried out in the Tidewater and adjacent areas of the coast, some of the earliest research took place on sites located in the interior Coastal Plain. J. A. Holmes, a geologist with the U.S. Department of Interior's Bureau of Mines, was the first to report on the archaeological remains of the North Carolina Coastal Plain. In 1883, Holmes excavated and described the contents of four low sand burial mounds in Duplin County. In addition to his own work, Holmes described the excavation results of other investigators on similar mound sites in Sampson, Robeson, Cumberland, and Wake Counties (1883). He observed that the mounds in the Coastal Plain were very different from those that had been reported in the Appalachian Summit region by archaeologists working for the Smithsonian Institution (see Chapters 1 and 5). Holmes (1883:48) described the Coastal Plain mounds as "usually low, rarely rising to more than 3 feet above the surrounding surface, with circular bases, varying in diameter from 15 to 40 feet; and they contain little more than the bones of human (presumably Indian) skeletons, arranged in no special order."

In 1910, anthropologist Charles Peabody excavated and described a mound in Cumberland County similar to those described by Holmes. In addition to human skeletons, Peabody found several associated artifacts, including a celt, stone and clay pipes, arrow points, a shell gorget, pottery sherds, and deposits of red and yellow ocher. Peabody (1910:433) observed that the dense concentration of the bones, representing the remains of perhaps as many as sixty individuals in a space of only a few cubic feet, pointed to an episode of secondary deposition and to "suddenness or haste in their putting away greater than would be the case were there no emergency at hand; accustomed as one may be to extraordinary postures and careless deposition one is surprised at the extreme exemplification of these features here."

Following in Holmes's footsteps in 1961, Howard MacCord, an army officer

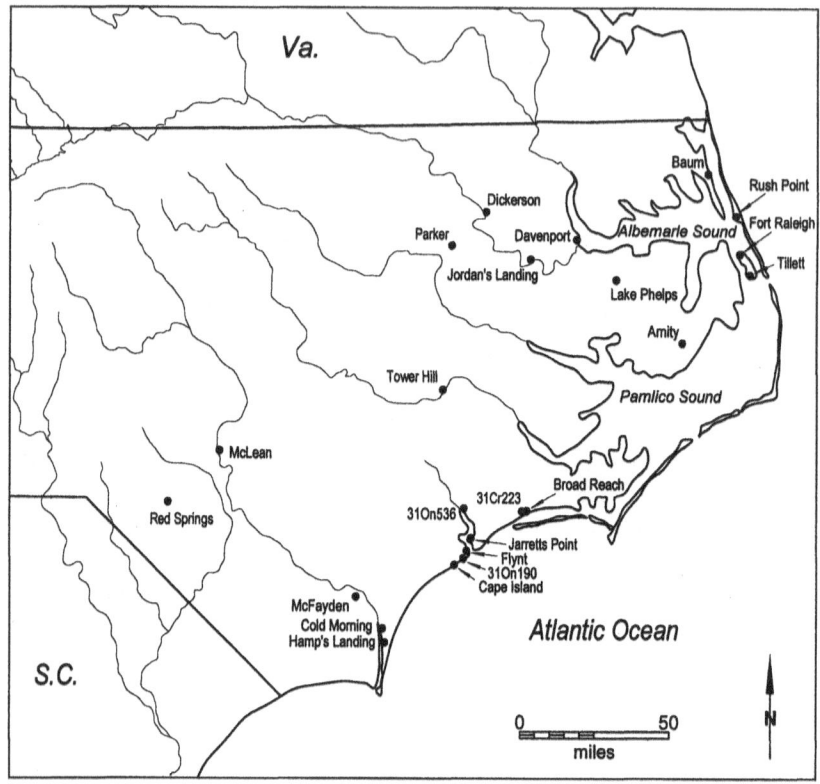

FIGURE 6.1. *Map of the North Carolina Coastal Plain showing Woodland sites discussed in the text.*

stationed at Fort Bragg, excavated a large sand mound in Cumberland County. The site, known as the McLean Mound (31Cd7), contained the remains of 268 individuals and numerous artifacts. The overwhelming majority of the burials consisted of incomplete bundles or clusters of bones. A few bones showed evidence of cremation (MacCord 1966; Stewart 1966).

The next year, Stanley South and members of the Cape Fear Archaeological Society conducted a two-day excavation at a similar mound, the McFayden Mound, located in Brunswick County. The McFayden Mound (31Bw67) is located about fifteen miles north of Wilmington, well away from the Tidewater region. Although the mound had been badly disturbed by relic collectors, it appeared to have been about the same size as the McLean Mound and to have contained a similar number of individuals. Most interments were represented by bundles of fragmented bones, and a few burned bones suggested cremation (Hogue 1977:3; South 1966:60).

In 1971, another burial mound similar to those described above was investigated briefly by members of the North Carolina Archaeological Society under the direction of J. Ned Woodall of Wake Forest University and David A. McLean of St. Andrews Presbyterian College. Bennie Keel and students from St. Andrews Presbyterian College also conducted excavations at the mound in 1971, as did Jeffrey Gordon and students from Pembroke State University. This mound was situated on the western edge of the Coastal Plain in Robeson County. Known as the Red Springs Mound (31Rb4), the site had been so thoroughly disturbed by looting that Keel (1970:22) could only conclude that it probably was similar to other Coastal Plain burial mounds and that there was little chance that any of the mound had survived the looters' destructive digging.

Nonetheless, sporadic excavations continued at the Red Springs (also known as the Buie Mound) between 1972 and 1974. The final excavations were conducted in the fall of 1974 and reported by Ruth Wetmore. Several concentrations of disturbed human bone and charcoal were found along with numerous artifacts. Most of the pottery recovered appeared to be related to Pee Dee and Irene ceramics (Wetmore 1978:64) (fig. 6.1).

The Early Woodland Period (1000-300 B.C.)

Most of what is known about the Early Woodland period comes from ceramic studies. During the preceding Late Archaic period, pottery made its debut along the North Carolina coast (see Chapter 3). Most of the earliest pottery is typologically similar to the early ceramics found along the Georgia and South Carolina coasts. Fiber-tempered Stallings Island pottery has been found as far north as the Tar and Chowan River drainages, but most potsherds of this type have been recovered south of the Neuse River. Thom's Creek pottery, which is thought to be roughly contemporary with Stallings ware, has a more restricted distribution in North Carolina and has only been reported from the southern coastal region (fig. 6.2). In the Middle Atlantic region, the earliest pottery is a steatite-tempered ware called Marcey Creek. Steatite tempering is virtually absent in the southern coastal region but occasionally has been found north of the Neuse River (Loftfield 1976; Phelps 1983; South 1976).

At the Davenport site (31Br28) in Bertie County, Croaker Landing sherds, containing a mixture of steatite and clay temper, have been recovered along with small, stemmed spear points. Croaker Landing pottery is probably contemporary with Marcey Creek (Egloff 1985; Mathis, personal communications).

FIGURE 6.2. *Early and Middle Woodland pottery from the southern Coastal Plain: Hanover Fabric Impressed (top row), Cape Fear Fabric Impressed and Cordmarked (second row), Hamp's Landing Simple Stamped (third row), and Thom's Creek Punctated (bottom row).*

The Deep Creek and New River Phases

At the beginning of the Early Woodland period, pottery made with a sand-tempered paste and with a cordmarked exterior began to be made throughout the coastal region. In the north, it is called "Deep Creek series" after the tributary of the Tar River where the pottery was first recognized by David Phelps at the Parker site (31Ed29). Here, a few fiber-tempered and early steatite-tempered sherds were found along with several of these sand-tempered sherds. Although test excavations failed to reveal stratified layers, Phelps believed that, based on typological grounds, the sand-tempered ware was later and dated to the beginning of the Early Woodland period. Most of the sand-tempered sherds had cordmarked surfaces, although a few were net impressed, simple stamped, and plain (Phelps 1981:79–86). The Deep Creek series is related to the Stony Creek series (Evans 1955) of southern Virginia (Phelps 1983:31). Although not found at the Parker site, large triangular points similar to the Roanoke Triangular type found by Coe (1964) and South (1959a) at the Gaston site in Halifax County are believed to be associated with Deep Creek ceramics (Phelps 1983:29).

In the southern coastal region, the New River pottery series is thought to date to the same time period as Deep Creek. This pottery is tempered with coarse sand, and, like Deep Creek, it is characterized by mostly cordmarked surfaces. Minority surface treatments are also similar, but a higher frequency of net impressing has been observed in the Deep Creek ceramic series (Herbert and Mathis 1996:145). Although some archaeologists consider the two pottery series to represent the same type (e.g., Phelps 1983), others prefer to keep them separate (e.g., Herbert and Mathis 1996).

Because few Early Woodland components have been isolated stratigraphically, the detailed studies needed to clarify interregional temporal relationships are not possible at this time. Consequently, the New River and Deep Creek series have the potential for evolving into distinct ceramic assemblages and should remain typologically separated (cf. Herbert and Mathis 1996:145).

Given the proximity of the southern coastal region to the vibrant Early Woodland ceramic traditions of Georgia and South Carolina, Thom's Creek, Deptford, and Mossy Oak influences should be visible here. However, current evidence suggests that the direction of most of the ceramic influence was from north to the south, not vice versa. The use of cordmarking and fabric marking on pottery vessels spread southward from North Carolina to become part of the carved-paddle-stamped tradition that evolved in Georgia and South Carolina. In particular, strong Deep Creek/New River influences have been observed in Deptford ceramics from South Carolina (Trinkley 1989:80). On the other hand, Early Woodland check-stamped and simple-stamped pottery rarely occurs in the southern coastal region of North Carolina, and only a few Thom's Creek potsherds have been reported. When these types do occur, they are usually restricted to New Hanover and Brunswick Counties (Herbert and Mathis 1996:143).

Only one radiocarbon date has been obtained for the Early Woodland period in the coastal region. This date is from one of several wooden canoes that were discovered in the shallow waters of Lake Phelps in Washington County. Fragments of a Deep Creek Net Impressed pot were found in the canoe. Wood from the canoe yielded a calibrated radiocarbon age of 1120 ± 60 B.C. (Eastman 1994a:19). This date is earlier than what most archaeologists believe to be the beginning date of the Deep Creek phase. It is also problematic because it is associated with a net-impressed pottery vessel. Net impressing is thought to have occurred late in the Deep Creek pottery sequence (Phelps 1983:31). Pottery similar to Deep Creek also has been found in the northern coastal region of South Carolina, and there it has been radiocarbon dated to between 120 B.C. and A.D. 210 (Trinkley 1990:16). Clearly, more radiocarbon dates are needed before the temporal brackets of the Deep Creek and New River phases can be firmly established along the coast.

Hamp's Landing

At the Hamp's Landing site (31Nh142) located on Cape Fear River, archaeologists found limestone-tempered pottery with plain, faint thong-marked, cord-marked, fabric-impressed, and simple-stamped surfaces (fig. 6.2). The limestone used as a tempering agent was derived from crushing calcareous marl. Although the Hamp's Landing site lacked clear stratigraphic layers, the Hamp's Landing pottery was concentrated in the lower excavation levels, which also contained Thom's Creek sherds. In contrast, the upper excavation levels contained a majority of Middle Woodland Hanover and Cape Fear series sherds (Hargrove and Eastman 1997; Herbert and Mathis 1996).

Although no radiocarbon-datable material was associated with the Hamp's Landing pottery at the type site, excavations at a site on Topsail Island (31On190) uncovered a large, shallow pit that contained forty-eight sherds from a single Hamp's Landing vessel. This feature was radiocarbon-dated to 1945 B.C. (Jones, Espenshade, and Kennedy 1997:100). If this date is correct, Hamp's Landing pottery is temporally related to Thom's Creek ware and falls at the end of the Late Archaic period.

The limestone-tempered or marl-tempered pottery from Hamp's Landing and elsewhere along the southern coast currently poses more questions than it answers. The archaeologists working on Topsail Island felt that the radiocarbon date was too early for the Hamp's Landing sherds. They also believed that the type of temper might not be as important as the size, shape, and density of tempering materials. If these attributes are considered, Hamp's Landing pottery is similar to the grog-tempered Hanover ware of the Middle Woodland period (Jones, Espenshade, and Kennedy 1997:101). And by giving the stratigraphy at the Hamp's Landing site precedent over the radiocarbon date from Topsail Island, it would seem that a transitional, Early-to-Middle Woodland time span is probably more accurate than the Late Archaic radiocarbon date for Hamp's Landing ceramics (Hargrove 1993:20).

Writing in 1983, David Phelps noted that little was known about Early Woodland settlement and subsistence (32). Today, Phelps's observation still rings true. Almost no Early Woodland subsistence remains have been recovered, and there is no evidence to suggest that plant domestication, one of the hallmarks of the Early Woodland period, was important. Based on settlement pattern studies, it has been suggested that the rich marine/estuarine environment led to the continuation of an Archaic subsistence cycle based on fishing, hunting, and gathering (Jones, Espenshade, and Kennedy 1997:8; Phelps 1983:32).

The Middle Woodland Period (300 B.C.-A.D. 800)

The Mount Pleasant Phase

More Middle Woodland sites have been studied than Early Woodland sites. In the northern coastal region, the Mount Pleasant phase dates to the Middle Woodland period, whereas in the southern coastal region, the Cape Fear phase has been tentatively defined as Middle Woodland (Phelps 1983; South 1976). Mount Pleasant pottery is tempered with sand and varying amounts of grit and pebble-sized particles. Surface finishes include fabric impressed, cordmarked, net impressed, and smoothed. Sometimes incising occurs on smoothed vessel surfaces (Phelps 1983:32). Mount Pleasant pottery is similar to Early Woodland Deep Creek ware and is probably a direct descendant of the Deep Creek ceramic tradition (Herbert and Mathis 1996:146). Although the Mount Pleasant phase is believed to have begun around 300 B.C., so far there are no radiocarbon dates earlier than A.D. 162. The latest dates for Mount Pleasant fall around A.D. 800 (Eastman 1994a; Phelps 1981, 1983).

In addition to the sand-grit-tempered pottery of the Mount Pleasant phase, a few shell-tempered potsherds resembling the Middle Woodland Mockley series of Delaware and Virginia have also been found in the northern coastal region (Egloff 1981; Herbert and Mathis 1996). These potsherds usually have cordmarked, net-impressed, or plain surfaces, and they are rarely found south of Albemarle Sound, with most occurring along the Chowan River and Currituck Sound (Herbert and Mathis 1996:147).

Sites that contain Mount Pleasant ceramics have been found in the Tidewater as well as the inner Coastal Plain of the northern coastal region. According to Phelps (1983:33), the number of sites along the major streams and estuaries and on the coast increases during the Mount Pleasant phase. Most coastal sites are marked by shell middens and appear to represent seasonal encampments where marine and estuarine resources were gathered. Mount Pleasant sites also often contain small quantities of other subsistence remains, such as the bones of deer, raccoon, rabbit, turkey, and turtles, and charred fragments of hickory nutshell; however, the exploitation of these resources was secondary to shellfish collecting and fishing (Phelps 1984:63). At the Rush Point site (31Dr15), located on Colington Island, freshwater mussel shells were carried onto the island by seasonal Mount Pleasant inhabitants whose main interests were the nearby oyster beds (Phelps 1981:44). Although these shell midden sites often cover large areas, they probably were occupied at any one time by fairly small groups of individuals comprising extended family units (Phelps 1983:33). The large size of the shell middens resulted from repeated occupations over a long period of time. Many sites were not only used during Middle Woodland times but also during the Late Woodland period as well (cf. Mathis 1993a; Phelps 1984). In some areas along the coast where shellfishing was particularly pervasive and intense, it is often difficult to tell where one site ends and another begins. In these situations, archaeologists have been forced to use arbitrary boundaries such as roads to separate artifact collections from individual "sites" (South 1976:8).

Archaeologists believe that people of the Mount Pleasant phase were beginning to settle into more permanent villages at the same time they were spending part of the year collecting shellfish along the coast. These sedentary settlements are thought to have arisen as domesticated plants gained importance in the subsistence cycle. However, none of these sites has been sufficiently excavated to understand how large they were or what they might have looked like (Phelps 1981:51, 1983:35).

During the Mount Pleasant phase, mortuary practices included primary burial and cremation. Flexed and semiflexed graves have been found at sites located in the inner Coastal Plain as well as the Tidewater region. At the Jordan's Landing site (31Br7), located in Bertie County on the Roanoke River, a flexed burial was found accompanied by seven small triangular arrow points. These points were included as grave goods, the only instance of grave offerings so far found with Mount Pleasant burials in the northern coastal region. At the Baum site (31Ck9) in Currituck County, the cremated remains of an individual who had been wrapped in a grass mat were uncovered overlaying an earlier flexed grave (Phelps 1983:33).

The Cape Fear Phase

The Cape Fear phase of the southern coastal region presents a more varied picture of Middle Woodland life than does the Mount Pleasant phase to the north. Two distinct ceramic traditions are found in the south: a grog-tempered series called Hanover and a sand-tempered series called Cape Fear (Herbert and Mathis 1996; South 1976) (fig. 6.2). South originally defined the Hanover series as being "sherd" tempered. Here, we follow Herbert and Mathis (1996:147) and use the term "grog" to refer to either particles of crushed sherds that were added to clay to make new pots or particles of fired clay lumps that were purposefully added to the potter's clay. It is often difficult to tell the difference between the two types of clay tempers. The surfaces of Hanover series vessels were either stamped with a cord-wrapped or fabric-wrapped paddle or smoothed (Herbert and Mathis 1996:147; South 1976:16).

Pottery that is identical to the Hanover series but from Onslow and Carteret Counties has been called "Carteret" by Loftfield (1976:154). Today, most archaeologists working on the North Carolina coast lump the two series together under the Hanover rubric (Herbert and Mathis 1996; Phelps 1983).

Sites that contain Hanover series pottery are widespread in the southern coastal region. They occur on the banks of rivers and creeks that drain into the sounds, and they also occur along the estuarine shorelines, as well as around the edges of inland swamps and pocosins. As is the case north of the Neuse River, most all sites that contain evidence of a Late Woodland occupation also contain earlier, Middle Woodland artifacts.

Settlement studies suggest that during the Middle Woodland period in the southern coastal region, a pattern of widespread resource utilization with an intense focus on the estuarine environment developed (Loftfield 1987). Unfortunately, subsistence data other than shellfish remains are almost totally lacking. No evidence of horticulture has been found on Middle Woodland sites in this region, and sites that contain the remains of terrestrial animals like deer are extremely rare. However, it is hard to imagine that people living along the coast restricted their diet to oysters, clams, and wild plants. Equally difficult to fathom is their failure to use the hides of deer and smaller mammals for clothing, containers, and coverings, and their bones for awls, needles, fishhooks, and other tools. In all likelihood, the sites so far excavated by archaeologists represent short-term occupations for the very specific purpose of procuring and processing marine resources, especially shellfish.

Only circumstantial evidence exists for Middle Woodland houses. At the Broad Reach site (31Cr218) in Carteret County, oval or circular posthole patterns have been uncovered near archaeological features that appear to be associated with Hanover pottery. These posthole patterns suggest structures measuring around 15 feet in diameter (Mathis 1997). If these represent houses, and they were used during the Middle Woodland period, they probably represent semipermanent shelters that were constructed while their occupants were busy oystering and fishing.

At the Broad Reach site, a primary burial containing the flexed remains of two individuals was found that also contained a number of artifacts, including pieces of two Hanover pottery vessels. At least eight turtle shells (six stacked together in a bundle), a deer antler and leg bone, a beaver tooth, and a conch shell comprised the remainder of the inventory. Archaeologists working at 31Cr223 in Carteret County also found a mass cremation, thought to be of Middle Woodland age, that contained the mixed remains of at least ten individuals. Marginella-shell beads and perforated canine teeth were associated with the cremation (Mathis 1993a, 1993b, 1997). These data suggest that Middle Woodland folks also died while visiting their estuarine fishing camps or were brought there for burial. In either case, they were supplied with a variety of grave goods made from animals not taken from the sea. These grave associations reinforce the importance of land animals, although they were not an important part of the subsistence cycle while Middle Woodland peoples were shellfishing and fishing.

Cape Fear series pottery is similar to that of the Mount Pleasant series, although Cape Fear potsherds occasionally contain larger quartz particles along with coarse-sand temper. Like Hanover, Cape Fear vessels were finished with cord-wrapped or fabric-wrapped paddles (Herbert and Mathis 1996:149). South also observed net impressing as a rare surface finish on Cape Fear sherds (1976:18).

Sand Burial Mounds

In the past, archaeologists have considered most of the widespread, low, sand burial mounds of the southern inner Coastal Plain to be associated with the Cape Fear phase. These mounds, mentioned at the beginning of this chapter, share many characteristics. They are usually circular in outline, low in profile, and contain secondary burials and cremations (Phelps 1983).

Secondary burials represent individuals whose flesh had been partially or wholly removed prior to interment. After death, bodies were placed in charnel houses or sometimes on scaffolds where they lay for a period of time to decompose. Periodically, the charnel houses were cleaned out to make room for more bodies. Bones were collected in bundles, and these bundles were then buried in mounds or other mass graves. Although archaeologists have never identified the remains of a charnel house or scaffold, charnel houses are well-known from the descriptions of early settlers along the coast (Mook 1944).

Most sand burial mounds are between 25 and 50 feet in diameter, and they usually are about 3 feet high, although some have been reported to have been as high as 15 feet before being plowed down. All of these mounds are described as being located on low sand ridges some distance away from habitation sites. The number of individuals interred in such mounds ranges from 10 to over 300 (Holmes 1883; MacCauley 1929; MacCord 1966; Peabody 1910; South 1966).

Unfortunately, most of the sand mounds share another trait—they were severely disturbed by relic collectors before being observed by professional archaeologists. As a consequence, comparative data are often unreliable or nonexistent. The most thoroughly studied sand mound in North Carolina is the McLean Mound, located near the Cape Fear River in Cumberland County (fig. 6.3). In 1961, Howard MacCord, then an army officer stationed at Fort Bragg, excavated a 1,400-square-foot area in the center of the mound. Although not an archaeologist by profession, MacCord was aided and advised by several professional archaeologists, including Joffre Coe, Stanley South, and C. G. Holland. The excavated materials were curated by the Research Laboratories of Anthropology, and the skeletal remains were studied by T. Dale Stewart of the U.S. National Museum (MacCord 1966:4).

The mound contained a large number of individuals represented by extremely fragmentary remains. MacCord reported removing skeletal elements representing over 300 individuals contained in 268 "numbered burials" (1966:4, 13). Most of the burials consisted of poorly preserved bundles of bones that often contained skeletal elements of more than one individual. Some contained bones from cremations conducted prior to interment (MacCord 1966; Stewart 1966).

Also found in the mound were numerous artifacts thought to be grave offerings. Some were purposefully placed with individual burials, while others were randomly scattered throughout the mound. These offerings included bone and shell beads, chipped-stone and antler arrow points, pottery sherds, animal bones, celts, abrading stones, and paint pigments. Of particular interest were the fragments of at least twenty-five stone smoking pipes, eight of which could be reconstructed (fig. 6.4). All were made from a chloritic schist except one, which was carved from steatite. Some of these pipes are very similar to the platform pipes that are known from Middle Woodland Hopewell sites in the Ohio Valley. A radiocarbon date of A.D. 970 places the McLean Mound at the very end of the Middle Woodland period or at the beginning of the Late Woodland period (MacCord 1966).

Although group burials or ossuaries are known to have occurred along the Tidewater region of the southern North Carolina coast, there are no mounds comparable to the McLean Mound and the other sand mounds of the inner Coastal Plain. Most of the pottery analyzed by MacCord was sand tempered and had fabric-impressed surfaces. Cordmarking was not reported, but many sherds were described as having smoothed or burnished surfaces, a trait not

208 WOODLAND PERIOD: COAST AND COASTAL PLAIN

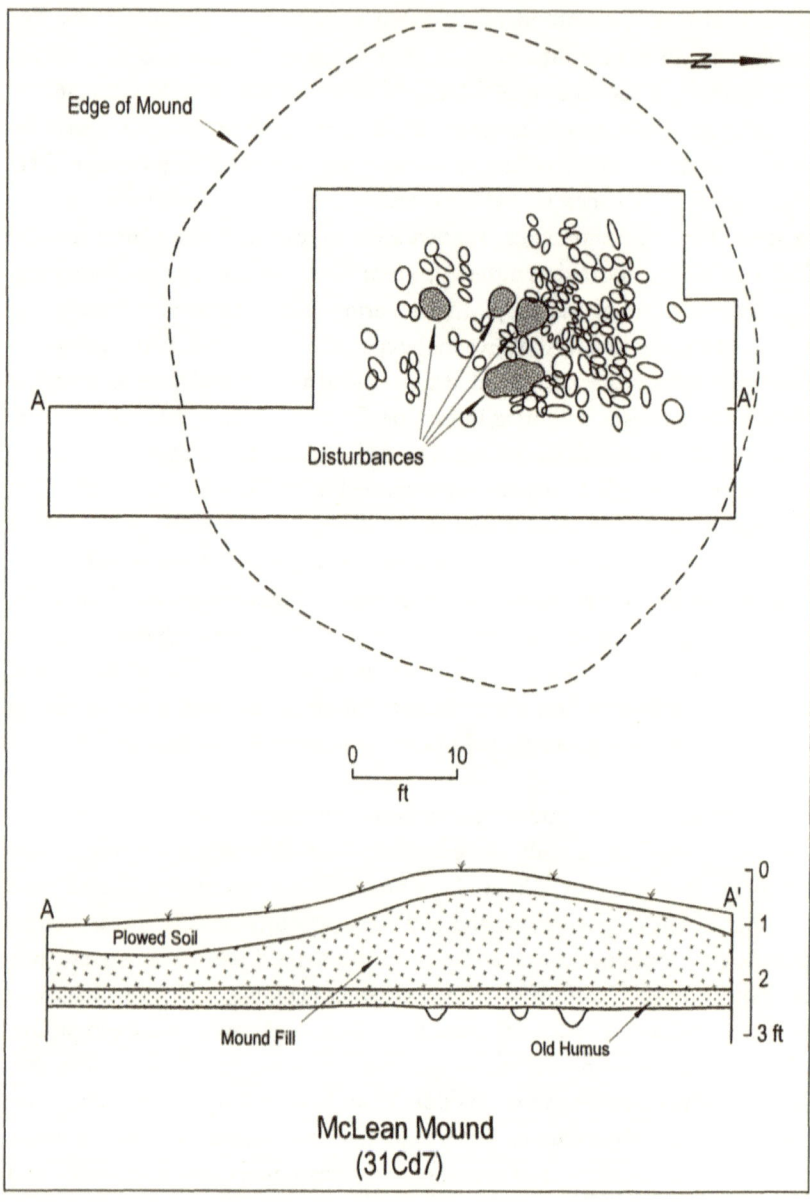

FIGURE 6.3. *Plan and profile drawings of the McLean Mound excavation showing burials found at the 12–20-inch level. (Based on MacCord 1966:9, 13)*

FIGURE 6.4. *Stone platform pipes and small clay pots from the McLean Mound.*

reported for Cape Fear ceramics. Wetmore also found smoothed and burnished pottery, similar to Pee Dee and Irene types, at the Red Springs Mound in Robeson County (1978). Rather than assigning the sand burial mound complex of the inner coastal region to the Middle Woodland Cape Fear phase, we prefer to see it as a distinct but yet unnamed Late Woodland cultural phenomenon, extending southward into the Coastal Plains of South Carolina and Georgia (Trinkley 1989:83).

The Late Woodland Period (A.D. 800-1650)

Along the entire length of the coastal Tidewater region of North Carolina, the Late Woodland period is marked by the introduction of shell-tempered pottery. Exactly when shell tempering became popular is open to debate. One group of radiocarbon dates places shell-tempered ceramics a little earlier than A.D. 800, whereas another group of dates marks its beginnings after A.D. 800 (Eastman 1994a; Loftfield 1979; Phelps 1983). However, by A.D. 1000 shell-tempered ceramics were being made from Currituck Sound to at least as far south as Pender County. In the northern coastal region, the practice continued into the Historic period. In the southern coastal region, the latest dates so far obtained fall in the middle of the fifteenth century (Eastman 1994a; Herbert and Mathis 1996).

Late Woodland people of the inner Coastal Plain made pottery that was more similar to the ceramics of their Middle Woodland ancestors. Instead of crushed shell, small pebbles were added as a tempering agent. These particles often protrude both interior and exterior vessel surfaces. If vessel walls were particularly thin, fine sand was used instead as a tempering agent (Phelps 1983:43).

During the Late Woodland period, physical, cultural, and linguistic differences emerged that can be traced to the ethnohistorically documented tribes who occupied the coast at the time of European contact. The region from the Tidewater coast to the barrier islands was dominated by Algonkian-speaking groups. Their territory extended from Tidewater Virginia to at least as far south as Onslow County. These Algonkian speakers were responsible for most of the shell-tempered pottery made along the coast.

In the northern coastal region, the Algonkians were bordered on the west by the Iroquois-speaking Tuscarora tribes. The Tuscaroras made pebble-tempered pottery and occupied the inner Coastal Plain from the fall line to the Tidewater.

In the southern coastal region, the neighbors of the Algonkians and Tuscaroras were Siouan-speaking peoples related to the hill tribes of the Piedmont. At present, the pottery of the coastal Siouans is poorly understood. Current evidence suggests that those living along the Tidewater made shell-tempered ceramics, while Siouan tribes occupying the inner Coastal Plain followed the ceramic traditions of their Iroquois neighbors (Crawford 1966; Eastman, Lautzenheiser, and Holm 1997; Ward and Wilson 1980).

The Colington Phase

The Late Woodland Colington phase coincides with the distribution of shell-tempered ceramics associated with the coastal Algonkians living north of Onslow County. Most of the surfaces of Colington series pottery are fabric impressed, followed in popularity by simple stamped, plain, and incised (fig. 6.5). Incised decorations were often placed near the vessel rim. Punctations were also used, but not as frequently.

According to Phelps (1983:36–37) and Egloff (1985:235–36), Colington pottery is closely affiliated with the Townsend series and the Roanoke Simple Stamped ceramic type of southeastern Virginia. The latter was found at the bottom of a ditch excavated at Fort Raleigh on Roanoke Island and in a pit containing colonial artifacts at the trading post site of Kiotan in Hampton, Virginia (Blaker 1952; Harrington 1948). As in the Piedmont, simple stamping appears to mark the end of the Late Woodland period and the beginning of the Historic period (see Chapter 7).

A variety of stone, bone, and shell artifacts also have been found at Colington phase sites. Small triangular arrow points, polished celts, abraders, and grinders were fashioned from stone; fishhooks, punches, awls, and pins were made from animal bones; and conch shells were used for hoes and picks. Marginella-shell beads are common, and freshwater pearls and a copper disk bead have also been reported (Phelps 1983:39).

The nature of Colington phase settlements is difficult to characterize. During the 800 or so years that currently comprise the phase, a great deal of variability in the size, function, and distribution of settlements probably existed. At the time of earliest European contact, the Algonkians were organized into a number of ranked societies or chiefdoms, each with a hereditary ruler who lived in the capital village of his territory. It has been estimated that the average Algonkian town at the end of the sixteenth century contained between twelve and eighteen longhouses and held a population of roughly 120–200 individuals (Gardner 1990; Potter 1982).

These towns were situated along the major streams, sounds, and estuaries

FIGURE 6.5. *A Colington Fabric Impressed pot found in an ossuary at the Garbacon Creek site in Carteret County.*

where a variety of subsistence tasks, including farming, hunting, gathering, fishing, and shellfish collecting, could be carried out. Separate, seasonal shellfishing and fishing camps also have been reported (Phelps 1981:54; 1983:39).

Although it is not presently known to what extent this pattern persisted throughout the Colington phase, it is doubtful that the ranked chiefdoms observed by early Europeans arose full-blown out of the relatively small, geographically dispersed Middle Woodland societies. As was the case elsewhere in North Carolina, the amalgamation and concentration of people into larger villages with some degree of permanence probably followed closely on the heels of an increased reliance on cultivated crops, particularly corn. Although a radiocarbon date from a site recently excavated in Onslow County (31On536) places maize cultivation as early as A.D. 1050, it probably did not become important until sometime later (Davis and Child 1996). And the ranked societies with their capital villages and paramount chiefs probably did not evolve until after A.D. 1200 or perhaps even later.

In the Chesapeake Bay area of Virginia, the beginning of the Late Woodland period (A.D. 900–1300) was a time of population dispersal with a proliferation of intermediate-sized settlements. This pattern is seen as resulting from the gradual incorporation of agricultural pursuits into the overall subsistence economy. As domesticated crops became more important, people moved into new territories where soils were well suited for agriculture. After A.D. 1300, populations began to cluster around a few large villages, with small satellite communities relating to more specialized activities such as shellfishing (Potter 1982; Turner 1992). A similar pattern of settlement evolution may have taken place during the Colington phase.

Although there is little archaeological evidence to inform on the internal organization of Colington phase villages, there are excellent descriptions of Algonkian communities located in the northern coastal region. These were provided by the early English explorers of the Raleigh expeditions carried out between 1584 and 1587. In addition to the written descriptions of Thomas Harriot, the artist John White made detailed watercolor drawings depicting the people and their customs (Hulton 1984). A set of replicas of White's drawings was later given to Theodor de Bry to engrave for illustrations in Harriot's book, *A briefe and true report of the new found land of Virginia*, published in 1590 (Quinn 1985:157).

White's drawings provide us with two quite different village arrangements. The village of Pomeiock, located on the mainland side of Pamlico Sound near Lake Mattamuskeet, consisted of a tight cluster of longhouses surrounded by a stockade (fig. 6.6). Eighteen houses formed a concentric circle within the stockade and surrounded a central open plaza. In the center of the plaza, White drew a large fire surrounded by a dozen or so individuals. Other small groups of people were depicted in various poses outside the longhouses (Quinn 1985:188–89).

The village of Secoton, located on the south bank of the Pamlico River, was drawn as an open settlement of longhouses (fig. 6.7). Some thirteen structures are shown, although more appear to have been present. Some of the houses are aligned along a wide central path, whereas others appear scattered in the surrounding woods. Individuals are depicted in various activities including praying, dancing, and eating. Three cornfields with crops in various stages of maturity are shown. A bird-watcher's hut was drawn in the field containing the ripe corn ready for harvest (Quinn 1985:185–87).

Most of what is known regarding the houses of the Colington phase also

FIGURE 6.6. *A drawing by John White in 1585 of the coastal Algonkian village of Pomeiock. (© The Trustees of the British Museum)*

comes from the ethnohistoric records provided by members of the Raleigh expeditions (Quinn 1985). Excavations at the Amity site (31Hy43) in Hyde County provide the only archaeological information on Colington phase structures (Gardner 1990). White's drawings and Harriot's narrative describe small and large longhouses. Some of the smaller structures probably served as storehouses. The larger structures were residences for multiple family groups. The buildings were usually made by placing small poles in the ground in parallel rows to form walls. The tops of these were bent and tied together to create an arborlike configuration. Other poles were lashed horizontally to create a framework upon which mats or bark coverings were attached. The larger longhouses ranged from 36'×8' to 72'×36' (Quinn 1985:189).

The Amity site is located east of Lake Mattamuskeet. Discovered in 1985, the site was originally thought to represent the remains of John White's Pomeiock. Using mechanical equipment, a large area of the site was stripped of plowed soil. After the area was shovel-skimmed, two longhouse structures and a portion of a stockade were identified. One of the longhouses measured 46'×21', whereas the other measured 30'×20'.

FIGURE 6.7. *A drawing by John White in 1585 of the coastal Algonkian village of Secoton. (© The Trustees of the British Museum)*

Although the house patterns and palisade generally fit the longhouse descriptions at Pomeiock, radiocarbon dates and European trade artifacts suggest a seventeenth-century rather than a sixteenth-century date for their construction. Also, archaeologist Paul Gardner considered the site to be too small—containing only two or three houses—to be the remains of Pomeiock. Instead, Gardner suggested that it was a seasonal farmstead occupied during the late spring and fall, at which time corn and other crops were planted and harvested. The inhabitants may have spent the summers along the coast collecting shellfish and other marine resources. The winters would have been devoted to hunting deer farther inland (Gardner 1990:72–73).

Most authorities agree that two traits stand out in defining Algonkian culture. One is the construction of longhouses described above. The other is the practice of burying large numbers of individuals in mass graves or ossuaries. In the northern coastal region, this custom reached its most elaborate expression during the Colington phase. The typical Colington phase ossuary contained between twenty and sixty individuals. Prior to burial, the deceased were placed in charnel or burial houses where they reached various stages of decomposition. Periodically, the bodies were removed from the houses. When placed in the ossuary pit, the skeletal remains were in various stages of articulation, depending on how much time an individual corpse may have spent in the charnel house. Some of the remains were fully articulated, others were represented by disarticulated bundles of one or more individuals, and still others were represented only by scattered bone fragments. The ossuaries were not located far from villages, and male and female, both young and old, were all buried together in a shallow pit, seldom accompanied by grave goods (Loftfield 1990:116; Mathis 1993a:4; Phelps 1983:40–42).

However, not all burials of the Colington phase were placed in ossuaries. At the Tillett site (31Dr35) in Dare County, three pit burials were found with associated Colington phase ceramics. One appeared to be a badly disturbed bundle burial, another contained partially disarticulated remains of a single individual, and the third contained a semiflexed individual. Burial forms other than ossuaries were probably common during the Colington phase, but because ossuaries have received the most archaeological attention, their importance in the overall Algonkian mortuary complex has probably become exaggerated (Mathis 1993a:3; Phelps 1984:30–35).

The White Oak Phase

The Late Woodland White Oak (Loftfield 1976) or Oak Island phase (South 1976) of the southern coastal region, extending roughly from the Neuse River basin south to the Cape Fear, contains many of the same cultural traits as described for the Colington phase. People lived in longhouses, exploited the estuarine environment, made shell-tempered pottery, and buried their dead in ossuaries. There is also evidence that, at least as far south as Onslow County, these people were Algonkian speakers (Loftfield 1990).

Shell-tempered pottery of the southern coastal region was first described by Stanley South after his 1960 archaeological survey of Brunswick and New Hanover Counties, North Carolina, and Horry County, South Carolina. South named the ceramics "Oak Island" and recognized cordmarked, net-impressed, fabric-impressed, and plain surface finishes (South 1976:21). Most potsherds had plain surfaces, followed by cordmarking and net impressing. Only 1 percent of his sample had fabric-impressed surfaces. South later surveyed two islands in the mouth of the White Oak River that produced an abundance of fabric-impressed sherds, which he described as White Oak Fabric Impressed (South 1962:26).

Tom Loftfield, working primarily in Onslow and Carteret Counties, redefined the term "White Oak" and used it to refer to shell-tempered pottery that had fabric-impressed, smoothed and plain, cordmarked, simple-stamped (or "thong-marked"), and net-impressed surfaces (1976:157–63). Sites producing Oak Island and White Oak ceramics are located close to saltwater sources and usually have dense middens of oyster or clam shells (198; South 1976:5).

Today, most researchers see few differences between South's Oak Island and Loftfield's White Oak ceramic series. Because of the historic precedence of South's types, some have suggested that White Oak be dropped and only Oak Island be used to refer to the shell-tempered ceramics of the southern coast (Phelps 1983:48). Although Oak Island and White Oak have been used interchangeably, there are some differences between these two series and the Colington ceramic series. Incised decorations, common in Colington pottery collections, have not been reported from the southern coast, except at the Cold Morning site, which will be discussed later. Burnishing has been found on a few southern coastal sherds but rarely on Colington pottery. There are numerous radiocarbon dates that place White Oak in the temporal range between A.D. 800 and A.D. 1500 (Eastman 1994a:25–26).

Some archaeologists believe that many of the potsherds from the southern coast that were originally identified as "shell tempered" are actually limestone or marl tempered and related to the Middle or Early Woodland Hamp's Landing series rather than the Late Woodland White Oak series. It is often difficult to distinguish the two tempering agents when the shell or limestone has leached out, leaving only holes in the potsherds. Simple stamping, cordmarking, and net impressing are seen as surface finishes that fit better in the Early or Middle

Woodland periods than in the Late Woodland period. When these surfaces are found on pottery that is also classified as "shell tempered," some researchers believe these potsherds may actually be limestone tempered (Herbert 1997:17–18; Herbert and Mathis 1996:151).

In the case of simple stamping, some of the shell-tempered sherds may be misidentified, but others are not. Careful studies reveal that simple-stamped sherds are sometimes tempered with shell and sometimes with limestone (Eastman, personal communication 1998). As mentioned earlier, simple stamping does occur in the Late Woodland shell-tempered Colington series of the northern coastal region. It may occur earlier on the southern coast, but it also may be a Late Woodland surface treatment here.

Recently, archaeologists have encountered a significant number of fabric-impressed sherds that contain both shell and grog temper. Although at first appearance they would seem to represent a transitional type between Hanover and Oak Island, radiocarbon dates suggest an early-fifteenth-century date for this ware, placing it late in the White Oak phase (Herbert and Mathis 1996:152).

Unlike the northern coastal region, several longhouses have been excavated on southern coastal sites. All of the structures have been dated to the Late Woodland White Oak phase. Two basic styles are represented: a small rectangular form averaging around 24' × 12'; and a larger style sometimes over 50 feet long and 18 feet wide. The largest house, discovered at the Broad Reach site in Carteret County, was partitioned by an interior wall (Loftfield and Jones 1995:130; Mathis 1997:4) (fig. 6.8).

The sandy nature of coastal soils makes the identification of houses difficult. The postholes that have been identified suggest that the posts used to construct house walls were small, rarely over four inches in diameter. They were closely spaced, and house walls show little evidence of rebuilding and repairs (Loftfield and Jones 1995:133).

Mass secondary ossuary burial is also a trait of the White Oak phase. At the Flynt site (31On305) in Onslow County, the bundled and randomly mixed remains of at least 150 individuals were uncovered. The Jarretts Point ossuary (31On309), also in Onslow County, appears to have been very similar in size and form. Although over half of this ossuary was destroyed prior to excavation, the remains of between thirty-seven and sixty-eight individuals were identified. These were contained in fifteen distinct clusters, consisting mainly of long bones and crania. Hand and foot bones were scattered throughout the clusters. A cremation was observed in the center of the bundles. Both ossuaries were radiocarbon dated to the fourteenth century (Loftfield 1990:119; Ward 1982:5).

In addition to these large ossuaries, smaller group burials have been observed at the Broad Reach site. One grave contained nine adults represented by dis-

WOODLAND PERIOD: COAST AND COASTAL PLAIN 219

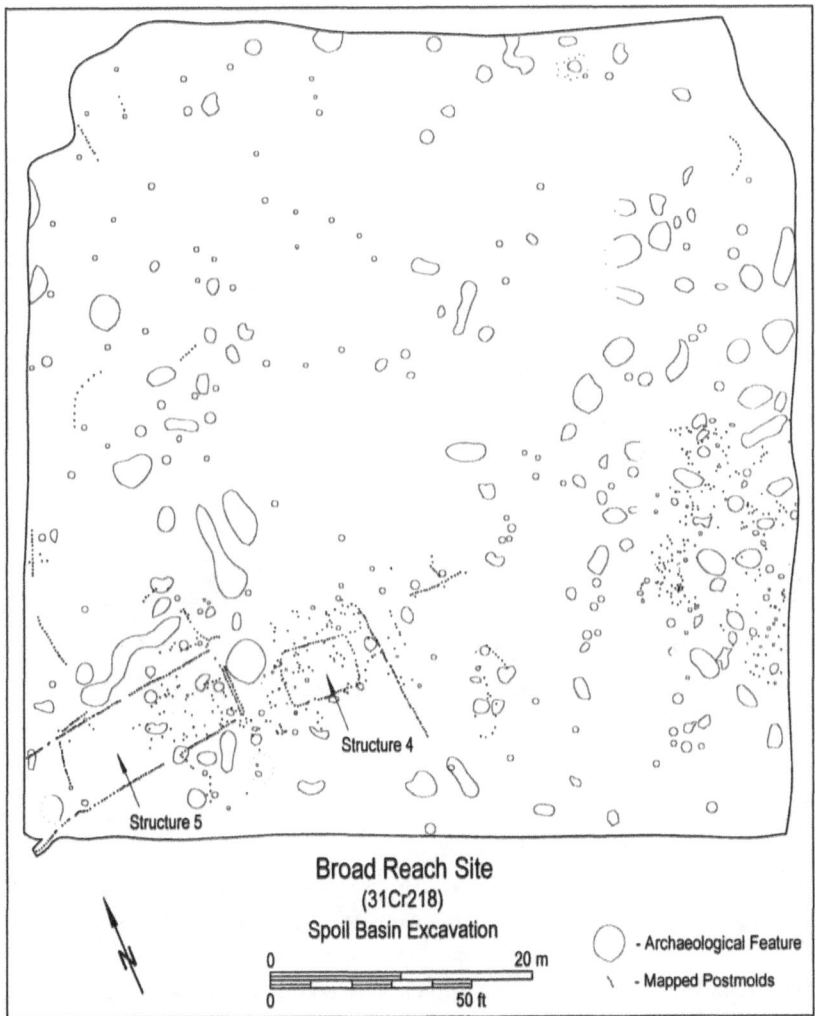

FIGURE 6.8. *Excavation plan of the spoil basin at the Broad Reach site showing pits, postmolds, and house patterns. (Courtesy of Mark A. Mathis)*

tinct, articulated bundles (fig. 6.9). These bundles were covered by a layer of clam shells. Several large potsherds, which were believed to have been used to excavate the burial pit, were found around the edge of the shell mantle. Unlike other White Oak ossuaries, which seldom contain artifacts, two of the Broad Reach bundles were accompanied by grave goods. One contained two shell-tempered White Oak pottery vessels, a small ground-stone cup, cut-shell disk beads, clusters of marginella-shell beads, the remains of a small dog, and a turtle carapace. The other bundle contained a large number of marginella-shell beads.

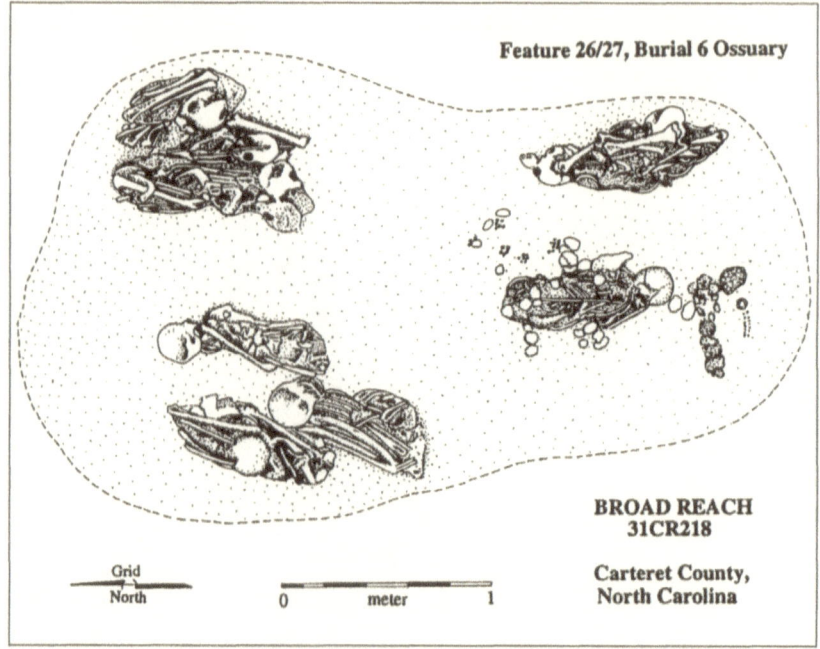

FIGURE 6.9. *Drawing of the Late Woodland ossuary designated Burial 6 at the Broad Reach site. (From Mathis 1993b:45)*

This grave has been dated to about the same age as the Flynt and Jarretts Point ossuaries (Mathis 1993a:4; Monahan 1995).

Another, smaller group burial was also discovered at Broad Reach. This grave contained the randomly mixed remains of from four to six individuals and a cremation. None of the bones was clustered or articulated. Associated artifacts included eight copper beads, which were randomly distributed among the bones (Mathis 1993a:5).

A few of the White Oak phase graves at Broad Reach were made in individual pits. Some of these contained individuals in a flexed position, whereas others contained secondary bundles of bones. Three contained individuals that appear to have been partially disinterred after burial.

The two distinct types of ossuaries at Broad Reach may reflect differences in the social standing of the individuals interred. The larger ossuary with the clustered bundles and elaborate grave offerings appears to represent a higher status group than the smaller, fragmented burials without grave offerings. It is also possible that differences in social rank may be represented within an ossuary population (Mathis 1993a:5). This would seem to be the case with the larger ossuaries that contain fifty or more individuals.

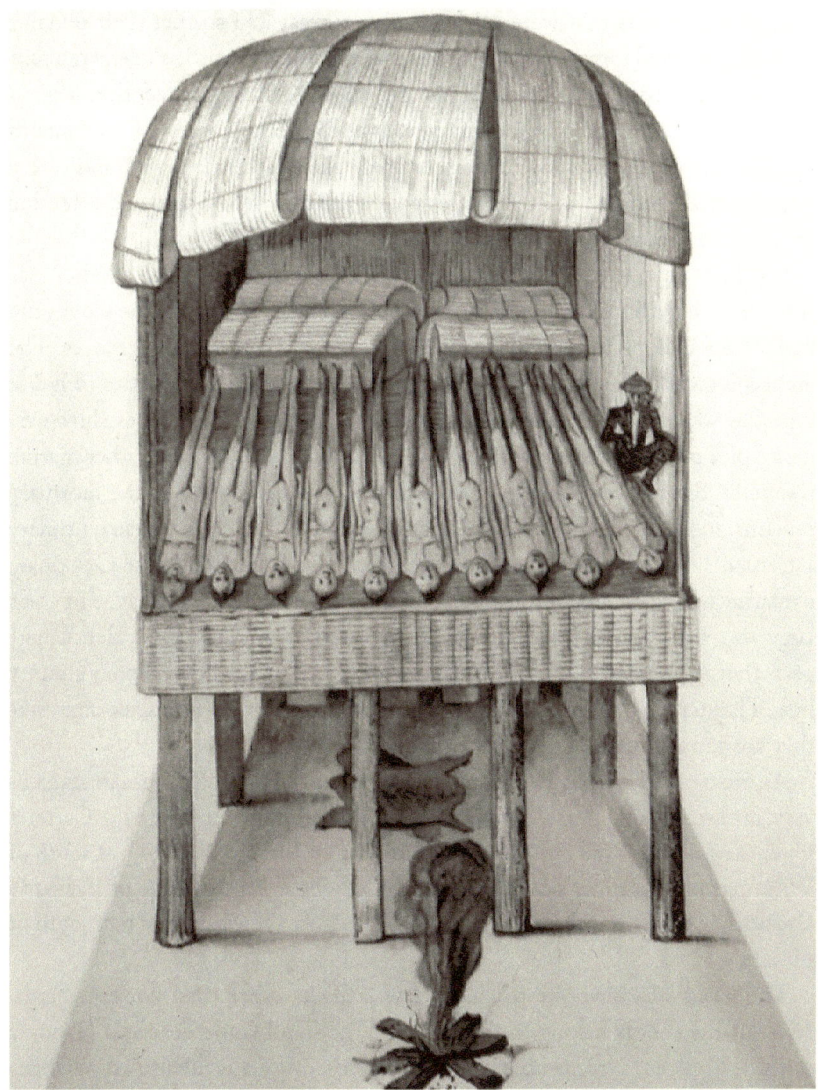

FIGURE 6.10. *A drawing by John White in 1585 of a coastal Algonkian charnel house. (© The Trustees of the British Museum)*

As mentioned earlier, the condition of bones placed in ossuaries was, in part, determined by how long and in what fashion the bodies were treated after death and prior to burial. If the skeleton was placed on a simple scaffold for a long period of time, its completeness and condition would be quite different from that of a body placed in a well-constructed and -maintained charnel house like the one depicted by John White (Hulton 1984:68) (fig. 6.10). If some individuals were placed in pits that were subsequently re-excavated so that their remains could be removed for mass burial, this too would affect how the skeletal remains appear in the ossuary. Mark Mathis (1993a:6–7) has suggested that a good indicator of the status of an individual may be the completeness of the remains that end up in the ossuary. More complete skeletal remains may indicate a higher social status since it indicates an increased level of care and attention given to the remains prior to burial.

Just how far south did the territory of the coastal Algonkians extend? Although we have noted minor distinctions between the pottery of the Colington and White Oak phases, there are many more similarities than differences. The archaeological and ethnohistoric records also show many similarities in house types, as well as village size and internal organization. Both phases show evidence of a mixed economy with a heavy reliance on shellfish and other marine resources. Similarities also exist in the size, form, and content of the mortuary remains, including large and small ossuaries, bundle burials, and a few primary interments. And finally, when the skeletal remains from the White Oak phase ossuaries had been analyzed, they appeared to be Algonkian because of their large size and robusticity (Loftfield 1990; Ward 1982). Current evidence suggests that Algonkian culture spread as far south as the Onslow-Pender County line. This territory overlaps areas of the Colington and White Oak phases as they are currently used by archaeologists.

An ossuary excavated in New Hanover County contained human remains very different from those described from ossuaries in Onslow and Carteret Counties to the north. The Cold Morning site (31Nh28) is located just south of Wilmington on a relict sand dune that lies on the northwest side of Barnard's Creek. The creek empties into the Cape Fear River a few hundred feet south of the site.

The Cold Morning site produced few artifacts other than pottery sherds. Most of the sherds belong to the Middle Woodland Cape Fear and Hanover series. However, a concentration of potsherds originally identified as shell-tempered Oak Island/White Oak was found in the vicinity of a small ossuary that contained the remains of fifteen individuals, including a fetus. Except for the fetal bones, which were found together, the remains were randomly scattered throughout the ossuary without any evidence of skeletal articulation. The only artifacts found within the bone matrix were a few pottery sherds. Two of these were identified as White Oak, and one was classified as Cape Fear. A radiocarbon date of A.D. 950 was obtained from bone in the ossuary. This date places the interment at the beginning of the Late Woodland period.

In light of the recent discovery of limestone-tempered pottery at Hamp's Landing, which is located only a short distance from the Cold Morning site, the "shell-tempered" White Oak sherds associated with the Cold Morning ossuary were re-examined. The voids in the sherds are blocky rather than platelike and are more likely indicative of marl or limestone tempering than shell tempering. However, the date for the ossuary is considerably later than the Early or Early/Middle Woodland affiliation recently suggested for Hamp's Landing (Hargrove and Eastman 1997). Either the radiocarbon date is erroneous or the use of limestone for tempering pottery was not restricted to one time period. Given the close association between the ceramics and the ossuary, the date is probably correct. Also, similar mass burials have not been reported from Early Woodland or Middle Woodland contexts. A high percentage (89 percent) of plain and smoothed marl-tempered sherds, and the frequent use of incising (28 percent) for decoration also argue in favor of a Late Woodland date for the ossuary and associated pottery. Although incising has not been found elsewhere on the southern coast, it is present in the ceramics of the Late Woodland Colington phase of the northern coastal region. The Cold Morning data, therefore, suggest that the use of marl or limestone for temper was not restricted to the Early Woodland or Middle Woodland periods.

The small size of the ossuary and the lack of bone bundles stands in contrast to the mass graves found farther north in Onslow County. Aside from the seemingly unique pottery associated with the Cold Morning ossuary, the biggest difference between it and others excavated along the North Carolina coast lies in the skeletal remains themselves. A comparative study of cranial morphology revealed strong similarities between the Cold Morning population and Siouan populations from the Piedmont. Marked differences were noted when the Cold Morning crania were compared with specimens from Onslow and Pender Counties identified as Algonkian (Coe et al. 1982:88).

The Cold Morning site tells us that by A.D. 1000, the people living south of the Cape Fear River were physically very different from the coastal peoples identified as Algonkians to the north. How different these people were culturally, we do not know. The two groups appear to have participated in different ceramic traditions and practiced group burial, but in different ways. Historically, the native people living in the vicinity of the Cold Morning site were referred to simply as the "Cape Fear Indians," and we know little about them other than the fact that they seem not to have been numerous and were probably affiliated with the Waccamaw Siouan tribes (Swanton 1946:206).

The Cashie Phase

Turning from the Tidewater coast to the inner Coastal Plain, we find that a great deal of archaeological research has been conducted in the northern half of the region, but very little work has been done south of the Neuse River. At the time of European contact, the northern region of the inner Coastal Plain was the home of the Iroquois-speaking Tuscaroras, who occupied the territory from the Neuse River to the North Carolina–Virginia state line. Their northern neighbors were the Meherrin and Nottoway tribes who also spoke an Iroquoian language. Their southern and western neighbors spoke a Siouan language. Along the eastern edge of their territory, the Tuscaroras were in close contact with the coastal Algonkians.

Archaeologically, the Late Woodland period in the Tuscarora homeland is known as the Cashie phase (A.D. 800–1650). Radiocarbon dates place this phase between A.D. 673 and A.D. 1444 (Eastman 1994a:25). Ceramics of the Cashie phase have fabric-impressed, simple-stamped, and plain surface finishes. Incised lines, punctations, and finger pinching were used to decorate Cashie pots, and these usually were applied around the vessel rim. The most distinguishing feature of Cashie pottery is the paste, which is usually tempered with small pebbles. These pebbles are often large enough to extrude through the interior and exterior vessel surfaces. In some cases, where vessel walls are particularly thin, sand instead was added as a tempering agent (Phelps 1983:43).

Most of what is known about the Cashie phase comes from long-term excavations by East Carolina University archaeologists at the Jordan's Landing site (31Br7) in Bertie County. The site is located on the north bank of the Roanoke River, near Williamston, and covers approximately three acres. Although no house patterns were found, numerous pit features, hearths, and burials were uncovered. One of the most interesting archaeological features at the site is a large ditch that represents a borrow pit used to mine soil that could be banked against the surrounding village stockade. This ditch became the village dump, and over time it was filled with refuse (Byrd 1997:16; Phelps 1983:45–46).

Evidence from Jordan's Landing indicates a mixed subsistence economy based on agriculture, hunting, gathering, and fishing. Corn, beans, and probably other crops as well were harvested to complement a diet of deer, bear, turkey, opossum, and other terrestrial animals. The river provided a bounty of fish, turtles, and freshwater mussels (Byrd 1997; Phelps 1983).

During the Historic period, the Tuscaroras often abandoned their villages during the winter to establish hunting camps for harvesting deer. Although hunting parties may have periodically left the Jordan's Landing village during the winter season, it does not appear that it was ever entirely abandoned. Participation in the European deerskin trade probably precipitated the movement of entire Tuscarora villages during the latter part of the seventeenth century. However, before trade relations were established with Europeans, Tuscarora villages like the Jordan's Landing site appear to have been occupied year-round (Byrd 1997:67).

By definition, most Cashie phase burials are ossuaries in that they contain the remains of more than one individual. However, they are quite different from the large ossuaries of the coastal Algonkians. The Cashie ossuaries typically contain the remains of two to five individuals. Once the flesh was removed from the bodies, the skeletal remains were bundled together and buried. David Phelps interprets Cashie burials as representing family units rather than the multi-family community unit represented by the larger Algonkian ossuaries (1983:46). However, it should be noted that at least one of the burials (Burial 1) at the Broad Reach site seems to fit the Cashie pattern more closely than the White Oak or Colington ossuary patterns (Mathis 1993a:6).

Marginella-shell beads are commonly found in association with Cashie burials. Only one ossuary, the Dickerson site (31Br91), failed to produce any. It appears that sometimes the beads were strung together; however, they also occur randomly scattered within the burials. As few as 200 and as many as 2,000 individual shells have been found in Cashie graves (Phelps 1983:46; Mathis 1990).

During the early 1960s, an archaeological survey of Lenoir County was conducted by Robert Crawford, a University of Florida graduate student. During the course of the survey, Crawford worked closely with archaeologists at the Research Laboratories of Anthropology. He recorded fifty-three sites and conducted test excavations at the Tower Hill site (31Lr1), which is located just east of Kinston, on the north side of the Neuse River. Crawford removed the plowed soil from two 10'×10' squares and excavated several pit features that intruded into the subsoil (1966).

Based on this small excavation, three ceramic series were proposed. The earliest pottery, named the Grifton series, was characterized by clay or grog temper and a fabric-impressed exterior surface treatment. This series shows a clear relationship to the Middle Woodland Hanover series found along the southern coast. Grifton ceramics were replaced by a crushed-quartz or coarse sand–tempered ware called Lenoir series. Lenoir series potsherds have a variety of surface finishes that included cordmarked, fabric impressed, and simple stamped. Crawford believed that Lenoir pottery was Middle Woodland in age and related to the Gaston series in the Roanoke Rapids Reservoir described by Coe and South (Coe 1964; South 1959a). The final series identified by Crawford (1966) was named the Tower Hill series. Although many of the basic Lenoir series attributes continued, Tower Hill pottery appeared to have a more compact, fine sand–tempered paste, and the fabric impressions on the sherds were somewhat finer.

Recently archaeologists affiliated with Coastal Carolina Research, Inc., re-analyzed pottery from one of the largest and richest features Crawford excavated. The Coastal Carolina researchers also submitted charred hickory nutshells from the feature for radiometric dating. After their re-analysis, it was concluded that the Lenoir and Tower Hill series should be combined and viewed as part of the Cashie series (Eastman, Lautzenheiser, and Holm 1997).

The interior Coastal Plain south of the Neuse River is probably the least archaeologically understood region in North Carolina. This is particularly true for the Woodland period. Except for sporadic cultural resource–management surveys and the sand mound excavations previously discussed, very little research has been conducted here. A basic ceramic chronology has not yet been worked out, and almost nothing can be said about settlement patterns and subsistence practices. It is ironic that today this region contains the largest number of Native Americans east of the Appalachian Summit.

Summary

The coastal region of North Carolina has received more archaeological attention—and archaeological dollars—than any other area of North Carolina. Yet today it is arguably the least understood of all the major physiographic regions in the state. It should be quickly added, however, that major strides have been made over the last few years, especially along the southern coast, to bring coastal research up to par with that of the rest of the state.

Some of the reasons the coast has lagged behind can be found in the context of the archaeological research itself. The outer coastal fringe is the most fragile and changing environment in North Carolina. It is also the region most threatened by commercial development. Because of these internal and external environmental conditions, the overwhelming majority of archaeological research has been directed toward salvaging threatened sites, whether they be ossuaries washed out by the latest storm or villages about to be bulldozed for housing and other commercial developments. Under these circumstances, it has been difficult to develop regional research designs that address specific questions and gaps in the archaeological record (cf. Phelps 1983:12). Nonetheless, over the last ten years, an enormous amount of data has been generated. Archaeologists working along the coast are now beginning to tighten ceramic chronologies, recognize regional cultural variability, and understand stability and change in subsistence adaptations.

Archaeologists excavating coastal sites face problems that are similar in kind to those faced by archaeologists working elsewhere in the state and the Southeast. However, the coastal environment exacerbates many of the everyday frustrations fieldworkers face. Good stratigraphic separation of temporally distinct cultural levels is virtually unknown along the coast because of the nature of the soils and how they were formed. Pottery sherds and other artifacts easily migrate up and down in these sandy soils. Also, the forces of aeolian deposition often churn up artifacts and sometimes reverse the laws of superposition. On most coastal sites, chronological separation of cultural components, when it occurs, is based more on the horizontal placement of archaeological deposits than the vertical superposition of artifact-bearing soils.

Rapid water percolation and leaching quickly dissolve organic deposits and fade the outlines of pit features and postholes, making it difficult to detect architectural and community patterns. Although the preservation of organic remains such as animal bones is enhanced on sites with shell middens, the middens themselves are a stratigraphic nightmare. Artifacts move through the shell matrix as easily as through sand. A millennia of tree falls, animal burrowing, and the digging and shuffling of repeated human inhabitants leave a confused and often convoluted record to frustrate even the most laid-back coastal archaeologist.

During most of the Woodland period, the coastal Tidewater region of North Carolina was marked by continuity, and the cultural changes that occurred were of a gradual nature. Except for the changes that marked the shift from the Middle to the Late Woodland period, changes in technology, subsistence, and political organization seem almost imperceptible and reflect few outside influences. However, differences between the cultural patterns of the Middle and Late Woodland periods are sharp, and some archaeologists believe shell-tempered pottery, ossuary burials, and longhouses mark the arrival of Algonkian speakers from the Chesapeake region (Mathis 1997). Nonetheless, the Late Woodland period from A.D. 800 until the first contacts with Europeans was more a time of stability and continuity than one of disruption and change. Similarly, there appear to be few differences between the Early Woodland and Late Archaic cultural traditions, and, throughout the Early Woodland period, cultural changes that can be recognized in the archaeological record were gradual, without disruption.

As a result of this cultural continuity, material culture changed relatively little. Consequently, the artifact complexes of the various phases presently recognized along the coast are remarkably similar. Pottery alone has provided a means for detecting subtle differences in these complexes that might have more important cultural meaning; however, much work needs to be done before a cultural sequence with the sensitivity of that of the mountains and Piedmont can be worked out. This sequence probably will have to rely heavily on non-ceramic traits such as mortuary practices, house types, village layouts, and settlement patterns. Unfortunately, these kinds of data cannot be obtained easily from reconnaissance surveys and salvage excavations.

7. The Contact Period
Tribes, Traders, and Turmoil

The time of contact between Indians living in North Carolina and Europeans arriving from Spain and England varied considerably across the state. The dates of the first arrivals of early explorers from the Old World do not necessarily herald the beginnings of significant changes in the histories of North Carolina's Indian tribes. The traditional territories of some tribes afforded them relative isolation, and they managed to avoid contacts with the newcomers for several years, even decades, after their arrival from Europe.

After Columbus landed in the Bahamas in 1492, over thirty years passed before a European set foot on North Carolina soil. In the spring of 1525, an expeditionary party sent out by Lucas Vázquez de Ayllón, under the command of Pedro de Quejo, sailed along the Atlantic Coast from Andrews Sound in southern Georgia to the Delaware Bay area. During the voyage, Quejo's party made several landfalls to explore possible sites for settlement by Ayllón's colony. Some of the areas explored were located along the North Carolina coast (Hoffman 1994:40).

The expedition of Hernando de Soto, embarking from La Florida in 1539, arrived in what is now west central North Carolina in the spring of 1540. According to some scholars, the first town de Soto described in North Carolina was Guaquili, located near Hickory in Catawba County. His army then may have traveled west over the Blue Ridge and north into Tennessee before heading south into northern Georgia (Hudson et al. 1984:73–75) (fig. 7.1).

In 1566, the Spanish fort of Santa Elena was established on the southern end of Parris Island, off the southern South Carolina shore. From there, Juan Pardo led two expeditions in 1566 and 1568 that roughly retraced de Soto's route through western North Carolina.

During the first expedition, Pardo built a small fort near present-day Marion

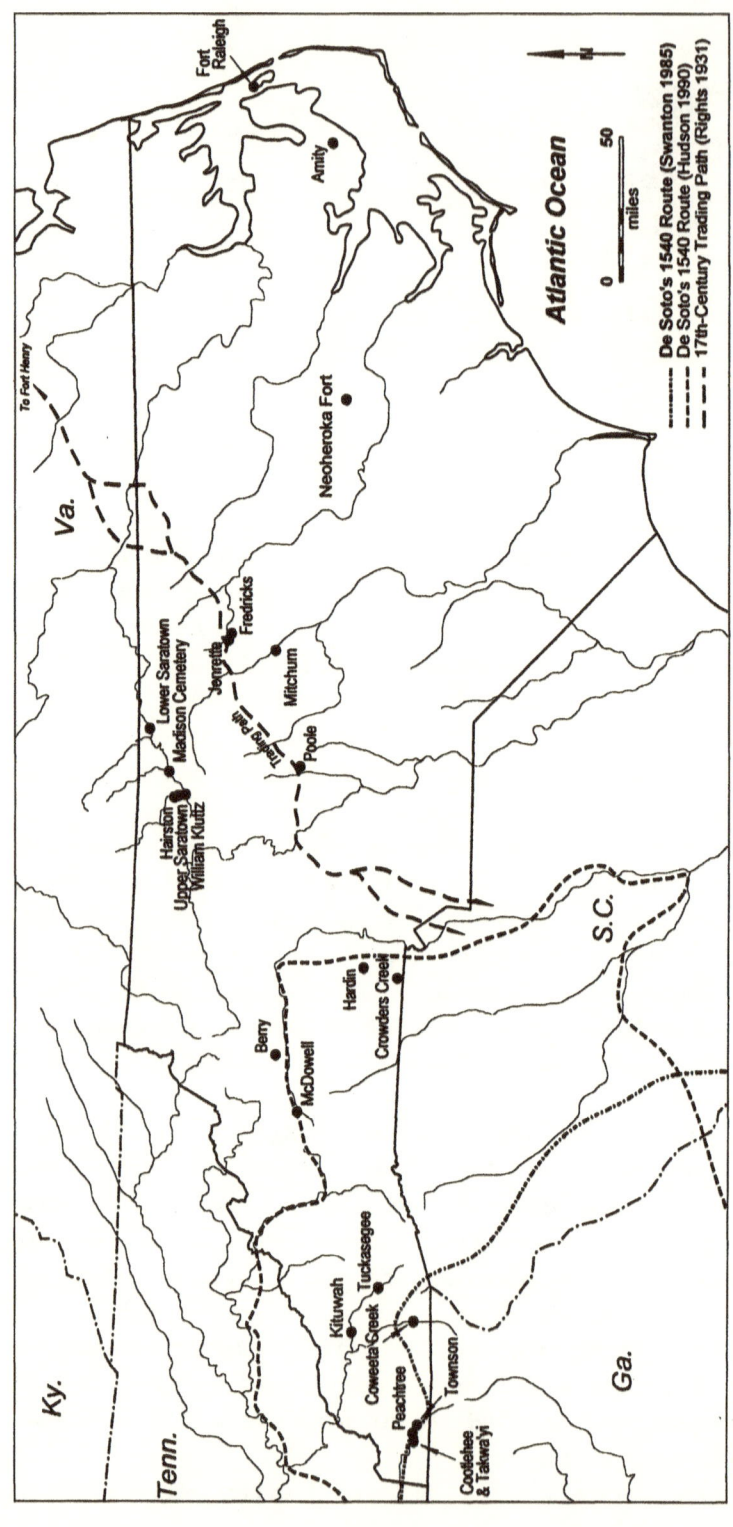

FIGURE 7.1. Map of North Carolina showing Contact period sites discussed in the text, proposed routes of Hernando de Soto and Juan Pardo through the western part of the state, and the trading path from Virginia.

in McDowell County and left it garrisoned with thirty men. The fort was under the command of Sergeant Hernando Moyano de Morales. Moyano was befriended by local Indians, and he and his men joined with them in raids against rival tribes (Hudson 1990:26–27).

Although several Indian towns were visited by the Spaniards while they were in North Carolina, none have been located with any degree of accuracy, and the routes taken by de Soto and Pardo through the interior Southeast are themselves the subject of debate among southeastern archaeologists (e.g., Boyd and Schroedl 1987; Larson 1990).

Debate also revolves around the impact the Spanish expeditions had on the native populations of the Southeast. Some archaeologists believe that the newcomers introduced Old World diseases that triggered waves of epidemics, or "pandemics." This view sees diseases like smallpox spreading rapidly and unabated throughout the Southeast, destroying a large portion of the native population and causing a widespread cultural collapse (Dobyns 1983; Smith 1987).

Other researchers have taken a more cautious view and see the impact of Old World diseases as being governed by a number of local factors such as native population densities, the intensity of interaction between natives and newcomers, and geographic and topographic factors related to population isolation. They believe that some areas may have suffered severe depopulation as a consequence of the Spanish expeditions, whereas other areas may have escaped the scourge of Old World diseases altogether (Milner 1980; Larsen 1994; Ward and Davis 1991). More will be said about this issue later, but for now we can state that there is no archaeological evidence to indicate that the sixteenth-century Spanish expeditions into North Carolina had any impact on the Indians living along the presumed paths taken by de Soto and Pardo.

Not to be outdone by the Spanish, Sir Walter Raleigh organized three expeditions between 1584 and 1587 in what proved to be a futile effort to establish an English colony on Roanoke Island, situated in the narrow neck of Croatan Sound. After a reconnoitering voyage in 1584, led by Arthur Barlowe and Philip Amadas, Raleigh sent a larger fleet the following year under the command of Sir Richard Grenville. Ralph Lane was appointed deputy governor of the colony and was in charge once the party landed on Roanoke Island. Soon after landing, Grenville returned to England for additional supplies.

After building a fort on the island, Lane and his men, around 100 in all, explored the surrounding territories. During these explorations, they seem to have gone out of their way to anger their native hosts. Lane chose to settle petty disputes and frivolous conflicts with force rather than diplomacy, killing several Indians during the course of his stay. Almost a year passed, and Lane began to give up hope of Grenville's return. As luck would have it, Sir Francis Drake stopped by the Roanoke colony for a visit on his way to England, after having spent the winter in the Caribbean attacking Spanish ships. Lane and his party were happy to accept Drake's offer of a ride home. The long-awaited supply fleet commanded by Grenville landed soon after Lane had left with Drake. Finding the settlement abandoned, Grenville left fifteen men and supplies with orders to hold the fort and surrounding territory in the name of Mother England. Unfortunately, Grenville was not aware of the public relations debacle that Lane had created with the local Indians (Powell 1989:42).

In 1587, John White, who had been a member of Lane's expedition, returned with 150 men, women, and children to establish a permanent colony. Remembering the hostile environment that Lane had created with the local Indians, White was not surprised when his party found only the bones of one of the men left on the island by Grenville (Powell 1989:43; Quinn 1985).

After settling the colonists in their new home, John White returned to England for more supplies. Because of England's ongoing war with Spain, White was unable to gain passage back to Roanoke until 1590. And when he did, he found even less evidence of his colony than he had earlier found of Grenville's contingent—no bones or bodies but only the letters "CRO" carved on a tree near the shore (Morton 1960:3).

As with the earlier Spanish expeditions in western North Carolina, the early English explorations do not seem to have had any measurable impact on the native cultures of the northeast coast. However, these early contacts did make the Indians aware of the contentious nature of the English, and they set the stage for the bloody encounters that took place during the first half of the seventeenth century.

Although conflict and strife between native peoples and Europeans often erupted in armed hostilities and ended in death during the early 1600s, it was not until the latter half of the seventeenth century that North Carolina's Indians felt the brunt of the European presence in their land. And the initial advance of English explorers, traders, and settlers into the backcountry of North Carolina came from Tidewater Virginia and not coastal North Carolina.

In 1644, fearing that their hunting territories would be overrun, tribes affiliated with the Pamunkey attacked and killed several hundred Virginia settlers who had ventured westward from the Tidewater region. This uprising, known as the Second Pamunkey (or Powhatan) War, was soon put down, and by 1645, several forts had been established along the falls of the major streams north and south of the settled James River to protect its English residents. Fort Henry was established south of the James, at the falls of the Appomattox, for the security of settlers in the southern region of the colony (Morton 1960:155–57).

Fort Henry, and the town of Petersburg, which sprang up around the fort, became the jumping-off point for the exploration of the Carolina backcountry south and west of the Virginia settlements. In addition to searching for a short route through the Blue Ridge Mountains to the "South Seas of China and India," the early explorers from Virginia also were interested in finding an untapped supply of furs and skins that could be exchanged for their guns and trinkets. By 1670, a steady stream of traders and packhorses had begun to pour into the heart of North Carolina, from Albemarle Sound to the eastern edge of the Blue Ridge.

The traders not only brought strange new tools, weapons, and ornaments; they also carried new germs that caused epidemic diseases, diseases that most North Carolina Indians had managed to escape during the earlier Spanish visits. After traveling through the heart of North Carolina in 1701, John Lawson observed that there was not the "sixth Savage living within 200 miles of our Settlements as there were fifty years ago" (Lefler 1967:252).

Throughout most of the seventeenth century, the Indian trade was dominated by Virginians. Men like Abraham Wood and William Byrd I, headquartered at Fort Henry, made handsome profits before the Piedmont populations became so decimated by disease, warfare, and slave raids that they could no longer supply the peltry that had become fashionable in Europe. By the end of the seventeenth century, the center of trade had shifted from Petersburg, Virginia, to Charleston, South Carolina. The Charleston traders focused their attention on the remote interior tribes that had been only indirectly affected by the Virginia trade. They established direct contacts with tribes as distant as the Choctaws and Chickasaws of Mississippi and western Tennessee, and the Creeks of Georgia and Alabama.

The Charleston traders also opened up the Appalachian Summit region in western North Carolina and brought the Cherokees into the web of colonial commerce (Martin 1994:310). And as had happened in the Piedmont and in the coastal region earlier, this new arrangement did not bring peace and prosperity but instead created turmoil and strife. The last half of the eighteenth century for the Cherokees was a time of political intrigue and warfare that culminated in 1838 with the tragic removal of many Cherokee families from their mountain homes.

The Contact Period in the Central Piedmont (A.D. 1600-1710)

Although interest in the Contact period began early in the development of North Carolina archaeology, it was short lived. The 1936 excavations at the Poole site (31Rd1), thought to be a historic Keyauwee village visited by John

Lawson in 1701, were followed by surveys and excavations along the Dan, Eno, and Yadkin Rivers between 1938 and 1941 as part of the first Siouan archaeological project. The goals of this project were to locate and identify historic Siouan villages that had been described by the German explorer John Lederer in 1670, the Virginia traders James Needham and Gabriel Arthur in 1673, the English surveyor John Lawson in 1701, and the Virginia colonel and surveyor William Byrd in 1728 (Coe 1964; Rights 1947).

Almost fifty years passed before the results of the first Siouan project research were scrutinized. And over thirty years lapsed before excavations were resumed at a Piedmont village site that had been occupied after the time of first contacts with Europeans.

On a cold January day in 1972, Bennie Keel and Keith Egloff, archaeologists with the University of North Carolina's Research Laboratories of Anthropology, visited the seventeenth-century village of Upper Saratown, located on the Dan River in Stokes County. When they arrived, they discovered a teenaged pothunter looting a grave. After lecturing the looter, the archaeologists salvaged the partially disturbed burial and returned to Chapel Hill. The following summer, Keel led a small UNC field crew that began systematic excavations at Upper Saratown. The purpose of these excavations was to try to save as much of the village as possible, before it was completely destroyed by pothunters whose appetites had been whetted by the rich funerary offerings placed with many of the Sara burials. These excavations continued every summer until August 1981.

The Upper Saratown excavations sparked memories of the 1938–41 Wall site excavations conducted by Joffre Coe and Robert Wauchope. Based on Douglas Rights's reconstruction of John Lawson's route through the Piedmont, Wall was thought to represent the Occaneechi village visited by Lawson in February 1701 (Rights 1947). In 1982, a cursory look at the artifacts that were found at the Wall site raised doubts that it had been occupied during the Contact period. Very few Historic artifacts were recovered, and those that had been found came from the disturbed plowzone and dated to the late eighteenth and early nineteenth centuries.

In 1983, a new program of Siouan research was organized by archaeologists at the University of North Carolina. The overall goal of this project was to study culture change in the Piedmont during the Contact period. The research was designed to explore the question of what happened to the native inhabitants as European explorers, traders, and settlers moved into the North Carolina backcountry during the last half of the seventeenth century and early eighteenth century.

Initially, excavations were resumed at the Wall site to determine if, in fact, it was Occaneechi Town. Fine-grained recovery techniques were used to see if things like small glass trade beads had fallen through the screens of the earlier investigators. These excavations also failed to recover European trade artifacts from undisturbed contexts. Even more convincingly, charcoal samples collected at the site in 1983 yielded radiocarbon dates that placed the Wall site occupation in the fifteenth or early sixteenth centuries.

Realizing that Rights's reconstruction of Lawson's route to Occaneechi Town was probably correct, other areas of the large field containing the Wall site were tested in 1983 for evidence of Indian occupation. During this search, a few English kaolin pipe stems and aboriginal potsherds were found in a small garden plot about 100 yards west of the Wall site. Subsurface tests in a grassy area adjacent to the garden uncovered evidence of intact cultural features. Upon excavation, these turned out to be graves that comprised a cemetery associated with a Contact period Indian village. This site, named Fredricks, was completely excavated between 1983 and 1986. The age of the associated trade artifacts and the site's location left little doubt that it was the Occaneechi village visited by Lawson in 1701.

After 1986, Siouan project excavations were expanded to include other Late Prehistoric and Contact period sites located in the Dan and Haw River drainages, and additional sites were excavated along the Eno River. By 1990, fourteen Siouan sites had been excavated by UNC's Research Laboratories of Anthropology, and extensive surveys of all three drainages had been completed (Simpkins 1985; Simpkins and Petherick 1986; McManus and Long 1986). These investigations led to the development of a detailed cultural chronology and allowed archaeologists to study processes of culture change in the central and northern Piedmont during the Contact period (Ward and Davis 1993). The results of the Siouan project research are summarized below, beginning with the investigations along the Eno and Haw Rivers and ending with the Dan River excavations.

The Mitchum Phase (A.D. 1600–1670)

Information on the Mitchum phase was obtained from excavations conducted at the Mitchum site (31Ch452) during the summer of 1983 and the fall of 1986. The site is located in northern Chatham County on a low alluvial terrace adjacent to the Haw River. Archaeologists believe that the Mitchum site and the Mitchum phase can be attributed to the Sissipahaw Indians who lived along the Haw River during the last half of the seventeenth century. Although John Lawson did briefly mention the "Sissipahau" Indians, he did not visit a Sissipahaw village as he crossed the Haw River in February 1701 (Lefler 1967:60). Lawson's failure to take advantage of Sissipahaw hospitality may reflect their early cultural disintegration at the beginning of the Contact period. Trade artifacts suggest that the Mitchum site probably was occupied around 1650 and abandoned before Lawson's journey (Davis and Ward 1989; Ward and Davis 1993).

Excavations at the Mitchum site revealed a small stockaded village covering less than 1.5 acres. One oval-shaped house, measuring 18' × 24', was uncovered. The wall posts of the house were set in individual holes and showed little evidence of rebuilding. The structure was probably a dome-shaped wigwam covered with bark or skins, since no evidence of clay plaster or daub was found.

Most Mitchum phase features were poorly defined. The only functional categories recognized at the Mitchum site were storage pits, smudge pits, and hearths. Two burials were excavated. In each, the body was flexed and placed in a shaft-and-chamber pit like those of the earlier Haw River and Hillsboro phases. However, unlike these earlier phases, glass trade beads and brass ornaments, rather than shell beads and ornaments, were placed with the dead (Ward and Davis 1993:413).

Pottery of the Mitchum phase developed out of the preceding Hillsboro phase and is very similar to pottery found at the Jenrette site on the Eno River. Sand and crushed feldspar were used as temper, and vessel forms consist primarily of small and medium-sized jars and bowls with smoothed exteriors, and large simple-stamped jars. The vessels were sometimes decorated by notching the lips and applying circular reed punctations to the lip, neck, or shoulder. The lips of simple-stamped jars were sometimes paddle stamped as well (Ward and Davis 1993:414).

Subsistence practices changed little as a consequence of contact with Europeans. Deer provided the main meat source and was supplemented by a variety of small mammals. Fish, turtles, and mussels were taken from the Haw River, and corn, beans, squash, and sunflowers were planted in the fertile soils along the river bottoms. Peach pits provide the only evidence of European influence on the Mitchum phase diet (Gremillion 1989:143).

The inhabitants of the Mitchum site obtained a limited variety of English items through trade, and these probably were supplied through an indirect trade network among native groups living in the region. The use of firearms was indicated by only a few gunflints, but no gun parts were found. Knives, hatchets, hoes, and other iron tools apparently were not available. Instead, the English trade inventory consisted mainly of ornaments—brass bells, rolled brass or copper beads, and mostly small, white and blue, glass beads.

Milder forms of non-native tobaccos, perhaps from the West Indies, may have been an important commodity in the English trade network. That a new kind of tobacco was introduced is suggested by the appearance, in relatively large numbers, of finely made clay pipes that resemble European kaolin pipes, except that they lack mold seams. These were found alongside more traditional pipe forms and suggest a change in smoking behavior after 1650. Prior to this time, native tobacco seems to have been used only in rituals or to commemorate important events. The use of tobacco, particularly milder, imported varieties, became much more widespread during the Mitchum and Jenrette phases and continued to increase in popularity during the last half of the seventeenth century. While the numbers and styles of pipes changed to reflect European influence, traditional pipes, in which native tobaccos were smoked in ceremonial and ritual settings, were still made (cf. Swanton 1946:383–84; Ward and Davis 1993:367–68).

The Jenrette Phase (A.D. 1600–1680)

Like the Mitchum phase, the Jenrette phase is defined from archaeological information obtained at a single excavated site, the Jenrette site (31Or231a). Jenrette is located in a large bend of the Eno River, just a stone's throw from downtown Hillsborough. It is situated next to the Fredricks site (31Or231), believed to be the remains of early-eighteenth-century Occaneechi Town (fig. 7.2). The Jenrette site may represent the remains of a village occupied by the Shakori Indians, who were visited by John Lederer in 1670 (Cumming 1958).

Excavation of the Jenrette site began in 1989 and was completed in 1998 (fig. 7.3). The stockaded village revealed by archaeologists covered a one-half-acre area and consisted of a ring of houses surrounding an open plaza; however, the architectural remains of only two houses were clearly identified. Many additional houses were no doubt present when the site was occupied, but their remains have been plowed and eroded away. Several pit features were found inside the stockade, but only four burials were found that can be attributed to the Jenrette phase. The small number of burials suggests that European diseases had not yet affected the Eno River population (Ward and Davis 1993).

Unlike most houses found on sites in the Piedmont (see Chapter 5), the Jenrette structures were built by placing wall posts in long trenches rather than placing them in individual postholes. Wall trenches were also used in house construction at the slightly later Fredricks site. The Jenrette houses are slightly larger than those at Fredricks, but they are smaller than Mitchum and Hillsboro phase structures. The larger house at Jenrette contained a little over 300 square feet of floor space, while the smaller one contained 220 square feet. Both had two or three large storage pits dug into their floors (Ward and Davis 1993:344) (fig. 7.4).

The ceramic assemblage from the Jenrette site is very similar to that of the

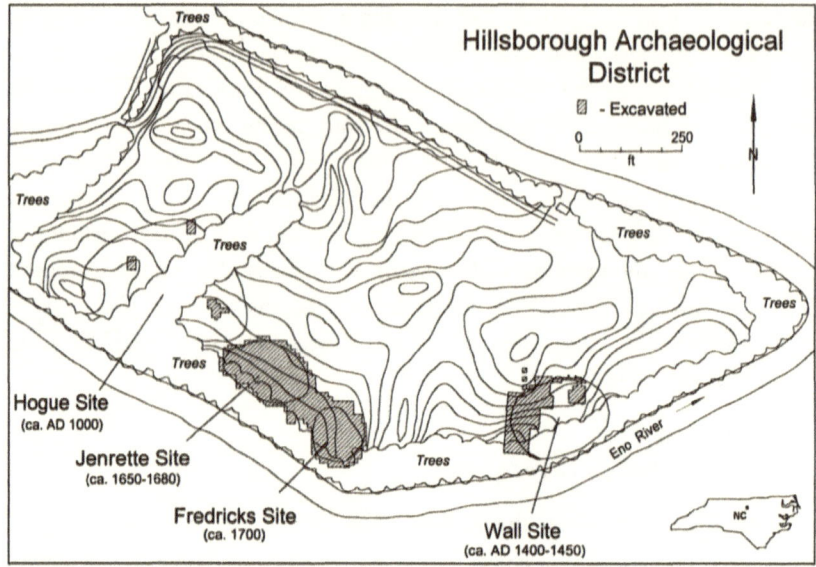

FIGURE 7.2. *A map of the Hillsborough archaeological district showing the locations of the Hogue, Jenrette, Fredricks, and Wall sites.*

Mitchum phase. Both comprise the Jenrette ceramic series; however, it is believed that the Jenrette pottery was made by Shakori, not Sissipahaw, potters. Almost half of the Jenrette phase sherds have plain or roughly smoothed exterior surfaces, while most of the remaining sherds are simple stamped. Minority surface treatments include brushed and cob impressed. The primary difference between Jenrette and Mitchum phase pottery is that Jenrette pottery is more often tempered with finely crushed quartz. Although similar to the earlier and ancestral Hillsboro series, Jenrette series vessels are heavier, have thicker walls, and are, in general, more crudely made (Ward and Davis 1993:415).

Faunal and ethnobotanical remains from the Jenrette site are similar to samples from sites occupied just prior to European contact, and they show no significant changes in subsistence practices and diet. Meat was obtained primarily from the white-tailed deer. Important wild plant foods included acorns, hickory nuts, and walnuts. Corn, beans, bottle gourds, and sumpweed were cultivated in the fertile fields along the Eno River. The river also provided a variety of fish, including gar, sucker, catfish, and sunfish, as well as turtles (Ward and Davis 1993:373). As was the case at the Mitchum site, peaches were the only non-native food harvested, and they were probably introduced earlier by native middlemen who were in contact with the Spanish settlements along the South Carolina and Georgia coasts.

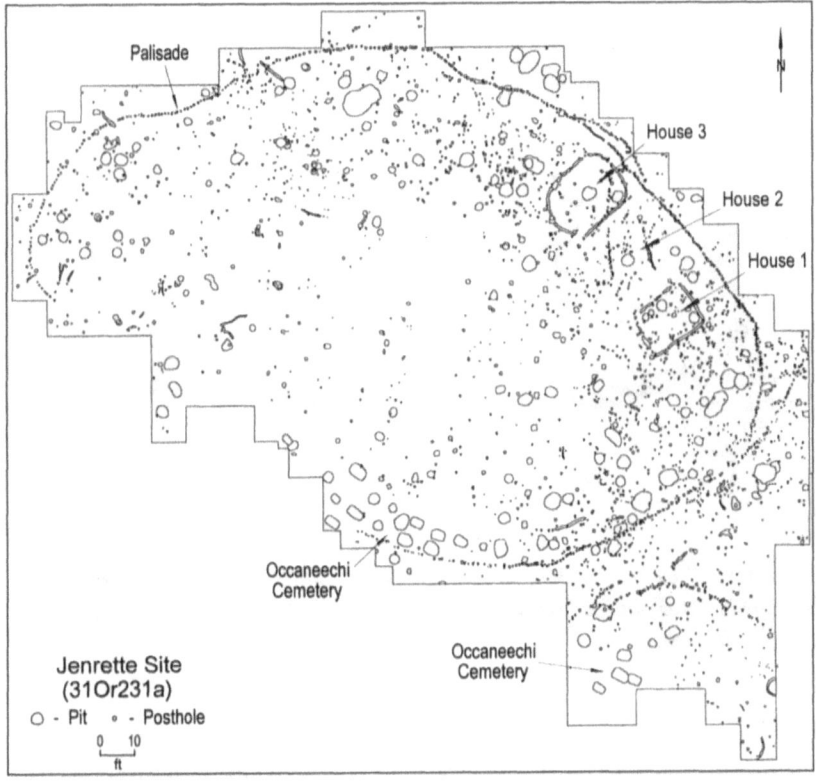

FIGURE 7.3. *Excavation plan of the Jenrette site showing pits, postholes, and the palisade. The two Occaneechi cemeteries are associated with the nearby Fredricks site.*

Most of the Jenrette phase features consisted of storage pits and large, basin-shaped food preparation facilities called "roasting pits" or "earth ovens." As mentioned previously, several storage pits were found inside the two houses. Several others were found within a 30′ band just inside the stockade and probably mark the locations of additional houses whose remains have been destroyed by plowing.

One thing common to all storage facilities found on sites in the Piedmont is that they were quickly filled once they were no longer used for storage. Often the soil removed while a new storage pit was being dug was thrown into the old facility. As this soil slumped, refuse was often added to fill the resulting depression. Sometimes these abandoned storage pits were completely filled with refuse that was produced over a short period of time (Ward and Davis 1993:415).

The large, shallow roasting pits at Jenrette are like those described earlier for the late Hillsboro phase and were usually located near the stockade. They are believed to reflect feasting activities associated with communitywide rituals and

FIGURE 7.4. *A wall-trench house (House 3) excavated at the Jenrette site. The house measured 16' ×22' and had two interior storage pits. (Courtesy of the Research Laboratories of Archaeology)*

celebrations, probably similar to the Busk ceremony celebrated throughout the Southeast. Similar facilities have been found at sites on the Dan River that date to the early Contact period; however, they have not been found on late Contact period sites in the Haw, Eno, or Dan River drainages. This may reflect a breakdown in community celebrations brought on by disease and depopulation during the last half of the seventeenth century.

The inhabitants of the Jenrette site buried their dead in both shaft-and-chamber and simple, straight-sided pits. Associated funerary objects reflect the beginnings of trade with the English and consist primarily of small glass beads that probably were sewn on burial garments. As was the case during the Mitchum phase, contacts between natives and Europeans were probably indirect and neither regular nor sustained. The nature of these contacts may explain the lack of evidence for epidemic diseases during the Jenrette phase.

The increased popularity of pipe smoking that took place during the Mitchum phase can also be seen in the Jenrette phase. Numerous fragments of terra-cotta pipes were recovered along with more traditional forms. Fine, rouletted designs, like those found on "Tidewater" pipes throughout the Middle Atlantic region, often occurred on the bowls of terra-cotta pipes from Jenrette (fig. 7.5). This style of pipe is also commonly found on sites dating to the

CONTACT PERIOD 241

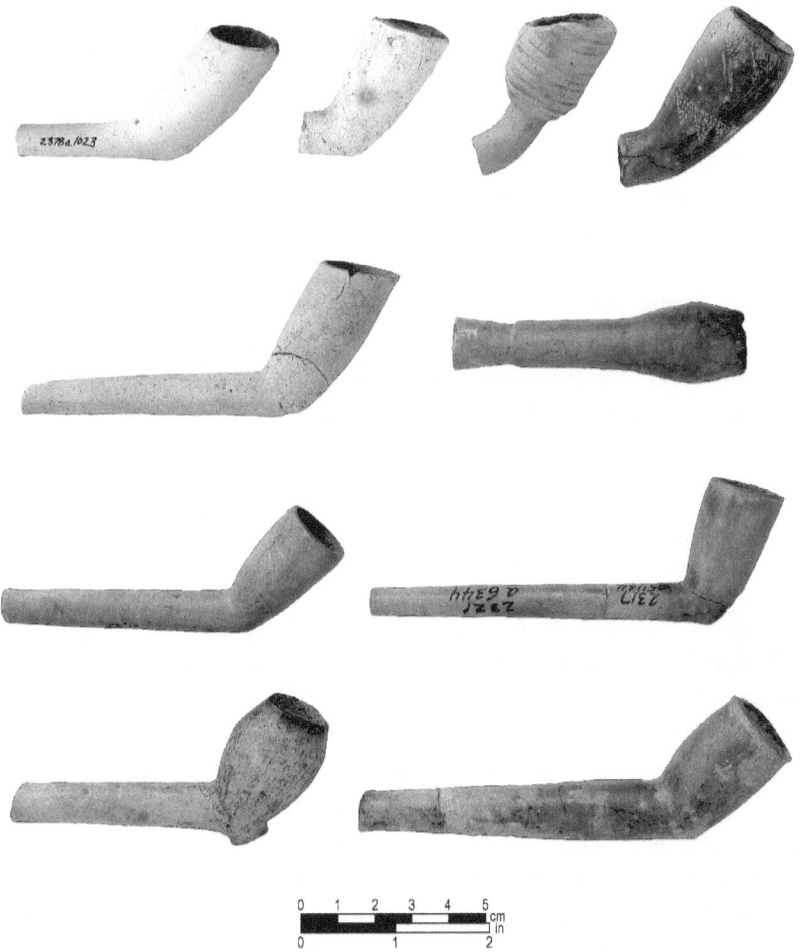

FIGURE 7.5. *Tobacco pipes found at Contact period sites in Piedmont North Carolina. The two specimens at the top left and the specimen to the left in the second row are English trade pipes; the specimen at the top right (from the Jenrette site) and the specimens in the third row are terra-cotta pipes with rouletted designs.*

Middle Saratown, Late Saratown, and Fredricks phases. Although archaeologists debate who made these pipes—African Americans, colonials, or natives—they are excellent horizon markers for the period between 1650 and 1700 in the North Carolina and Virginia Piedmont (Heite 1973; Kent 1984; Ward and Davis 1993).

During the Jenrette phase, small, triangular arrow points continued to be made. Many appear to have been casually shaped from small flakes with little effort. Other stone tools include drills, perforators, gravers, spokeshaves, scrapers, and a variety of used and retouched flakes. Ground-stone celts, chipped hoes, and milling stones were also used at Jenrette.

Bone and shell tools used during the Jenrette phase closely resemble those of the preceding Hillsboro phase. Disk beads were made from marine shells, and scrapers were formed by finely notching the edges of mussel shells. A number of animal bones were cut and split to create awls, needles, beamers, and other hideworking implements.

Boneworking and shellworking techniques show a strong affinity to toolmaking technologies used during the preceding Hillsboro phase. However, bone and shell tools were only rarely used during the later Fredricks phase, when iron hoes, knives, and other European-made tools took their place (Ward and Davis 1993:414).

The Fredricks Phase (A.D. 1680–1710)

The Fredricks phase defines the archaeological remains of the Occaneechis after they moved from the Roanoke valley to the Eno River, following Bacon's Rebellion in 1676. At present, the Fredricks site is the only site that can be assigned to this phase (Davis and Ward 1991). This site is believed to be the remains of "Achonechy Town," which was visited and briefly described by John Lawson in 1701 (Lefler 1967:61). The small stockaded village was completely excavated between 1983 and 1986 (figs. 7.6 and 7.7).

Although most native traditions appear to have remained intact during the Fredricks phase, trade between Piedmont Indians and the English intensified considerably during the last quarter of the seventeenth century. This intensification is seen primarily in the grave goods associated with the Occaneechi burials. Knives, tobacco pipes, hoes, kettles, and guns were added to the beads and ornaments common during the Mitchum and Jenrette phases (figs. 7.5 and 7.8). Shaft-and-chamber burial pits were abandoned in favor of rectangular, straight-sided graves dug with metal tools. Bodies were still flexed, but the burial pits were no longer placed in and around dwellings. Instead, the Fredricks site burials were carefully aligned and interred in three cemeteries located outside the stockade surrounding the small village.

The first cemetery to be discovered contained the remains of thirteen individuals and lay adjacent to the Fredricks site stockade. The second cemetery contained four graves and was located between the Fredricks and Jenrette site stockades. The third cemetery contained eight graves and was located just inside the stockade surrounding the Jenrette village. Although the village likely had been abandoned by the time of the Fredricks occupation, the alignment of

CONTACT PERIOD 243

FIGURE 7.6. *Excavation plan of the Fredricks site showing pits, postholes, houses, and the palisade.*

the graves suggests that the stockade wall may still have been standing at the time the burials were made. The cemeteries appear to have contained members of related families. Three families were interred in the first cemetery; one was interred in the second; and two were interred in the third. The existence of separate cemeteries may reflect the amalgamation of different ethnic groups forced to band together as a consequence of depopulation (Ward et al. 1996).

By the time of Lawson's visit, European diseases and warfare had decimated

FIGURE 7.7. *An artist's conception of the Occaneechi village at the Fredricks site. (Drawing by Orna Weinroth, © 1998)*

the Occaneechis and other Piedmont tribes. Archaeologically, this decimation is indicated by the small size of the settlement and a very high mortality rate. A single stockade of small posts, some placed in wall trenches, enclosed no more than ten to twelve houses of wall-trench and single-post construction. Probably fewer than seventy-five individuals lived in the village for less than a decade. The burial population of the three cemeteries accounts for a substantial portion of that population (Ward et al. 1996; Ward and Davis 1991).

Although the Fredricks phase represents a time of dramatic disruption and upheaval, a surprising degree of continuity is reflected in the subsistence data. As was seen during the Mitchum and Jenrette phases, the peltry trade and the introduction of European tools and trinkets seem to have had a minimal impact on the day-to-day subsistence of the Occaneechis. Deer, turkey, fish, turtle, and numerous small mammals were hunted and trapped. Only one bone each of a pig and a horse attest to the European presence (Holm 1987:245). The only evidence for the use of Old World plants during the Fredricks phase consists of a single watermelon seed and numerous peach pits (Gremillion 1987).

Fredricks phase pottery is represented by two types: Fredricks Plain and Fredricks Check Stamped (fig. 7.9). Fredricks Plain pottery is associated with a variety of vessel forms, including small and large jars and small bowls, whereas Fredricks Check Stamped pottery is almost exclusively associated with cooking vessels. The presence of check stamping indicates that the Fredricks series is

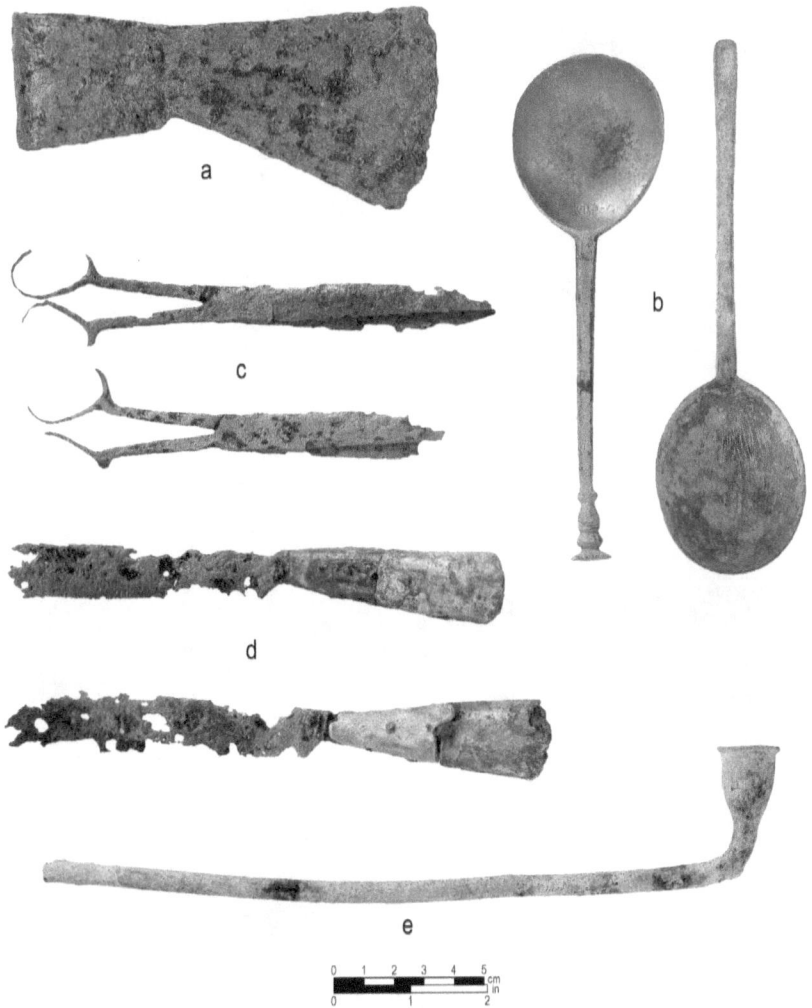

FIGURE 7.8. *European trade items found at the Fredricks site: ax (a), spoons (b), scissors (c), knives (d), and pewter tobacco pipe (e).*

more closely related to the Hillsboro series than to the Jenrette series. Unlike the Jenrette pottery, all the Fredricks pottery was tempered with sand, had thin walls, and lacked evidence of simple stamping. Furthermore, the homogeneity within the Fredricks series suggests that all the pottery recovered from the Fredricks site was made by one or a few potters (Ward and Davis 1993:416).

Although European-made weapons and cutting tools were available to the Occaneechis, they continued to make and use stone tools in styles that can be traced back several hundred years. Arrows were tipped with small triangular

246 CONTACT PERIOD

FIGURE 7.9. *Fredricks series pots from Occaneechi Town.*

points, and hideworking, woodworking, and plant-processing tasks were often carried out using stone tools. Drills, gravers, perforators, scrapers, and a variety of used and reworked flake tools were found at the Fredricks site, along with manos and milling stones. However, the Occaneechis do not appear to have been heavily engaged in boneworking or shellworking. Although numerous shell ornaments, including gorgets, columella beads, disk beads, wampum, and runtees, were found at Fredricks, these were probably manufactured by groups living along the Atlantic Coast and traded to the Occaneechis (Hammett 1987).

The North Central Piedmont during the Contact Period

The Middle Saratown Phase (A.D. 1620–1670)

The Middle Saratown phase represents the mid-seventeenth-century occupation of the upper Dan River drainage by the Sara, or Saura, Indians. This phase was defined from excavations at the Lower Saratown site (31Rk1) located on the Dan River, just below the mouth of the Smith River, and it marks the first arrival of European trade goods in the northern Piedmont. Although Spanish explorers traveled through the southwestern North Carolina Piedmont during the mid-sixteenth century (Hudson 1990), their visits left no discernible traces in the archaeological record of the Dan River drainage. Even the early-seventeenth-century English settlements on the lower James River meant little to the Piedmont tribes. It is doubtful that many of the Sara living along the Dan River during the Middle Saratown phase ever laid eyes on the English or felt the deadly sting of their diseases. The few beads and trinkets that found their way into Sara villages probably were passed along from Indian to Indian through traditional trade networks.

Settlement patterns during the Middle Saratown phase changed little from those of the preceding Early Saratown phase, discussed in Chapter 4. The Sara continued to occupy large, stockaded villages, and the population of the Dan River valley seems to have stabilized. Limited excavations at Lower Saratown uncovered two superimposed houses of single-post construction that were similar in size and shape to wall-trench and single-post houses built by the Occaneechi, Shakori, and Sissipahaw along the Eno and Haw Rivers.

Middle Saratown phase features are very similar to facilities found on other Protohistoric and Contact period sites in the Piedmont. Large, shallow roasting pits or earth ovens indicative of communitywide food preparation activities were common and usually were placed around the periphery of the village. These facilities do not appear to have been recycled and were usually filled with food remains and cooking debris. Circular storage pits and small, corncob-filled smudge pits also were common during the Middle Saratown phase. The large storage facilities, like those on other Piedmont sites, were quickly filled with soil and refuse after they were no longer suited for their primary purpose.

Although contact with European traders is indicated by the presence of glass and brass beads, European influence is not seen in the subsistence inventory.

The rich assortment of food remains from Lower Saratown points to a varied diet balancing wild plant and animal resources with indigenous crop production. As was the case during the Early Saratown phase, turtles, mussels, and fish from the Dan River provided an important supplement to the terrestrial diet of deer, turkey, and bear. Maize was abundant and ubiquitous. Beans also were grown, along with squash. However, sunflower and other common Eastern North American cultigens were not harvested (Gremillion 1989).

Pottery of the Middle Saratown phase closely resembles that found at the Hairston site (31Sk1), about thirty miles upstream in Stokes County. Most of the sherds had smoothed or burnished exteriors; many others had net-impressed surfaces. A few were cob impressed, check stamped, simple stamped, and complicated stamped. The most popular vessel form was a small jar with a smoothed surface. These vessels were infrequently decorated.

A variety of chipped-stone tools were used. These often were made from large, patinated flakes or from Archaic spear points scavenged from sites of much earlier settlements. Small triangular arrow points and bifacial drills were also frequently used. Other stone tools included chipped hoes, manos and milling stones, celts, numerous hammerstones, and large cobble choppers.

The rich boneworking and shellworking traditions begun during the Dan River phase persisted into the Middle Saratown phase. Numerous awls, beamers, antler flakers, needles, fish hooks, turtle carapace cups, and beads were manufactured from bone, whereas scrapers were made from freshwater mussels and large and small cut-disk beads were made from marine shells.

The single Middle Saratown phase burial found at Lower Saratown was placed in a shaft-and-chamber grave and indicates the continuation of this unique method of interment begun by the early Dan River phase. The occurrence of a relatively small number of grave goods, mostly rolled copper or brass beads, contrasts with the extensive use of shell beads and ornaments during the Early Saratown phase. However, a sample of one burial does not permit even a superficial comparison of mortuary practices between these two phases.

The Late Saratown Phase (A.D. 1670–1710)

By 1670, the flow of English-made goods reaching the Sara increased dramatically. It was also during the Late Saratown phase that European diseases struck with devastating force, making many of the excavated villages appear more like cemeteries than habitation sites. The Upper Saratown village, located near the confluence of the Dan River and Town Fork Creek, is the most extensively excavated Late Saratown phase site (fig. 7.10). As previously mentioned, excavations began here in 1972 and continued until 1981, uncovering numerous

CONTACT PERIOD 249

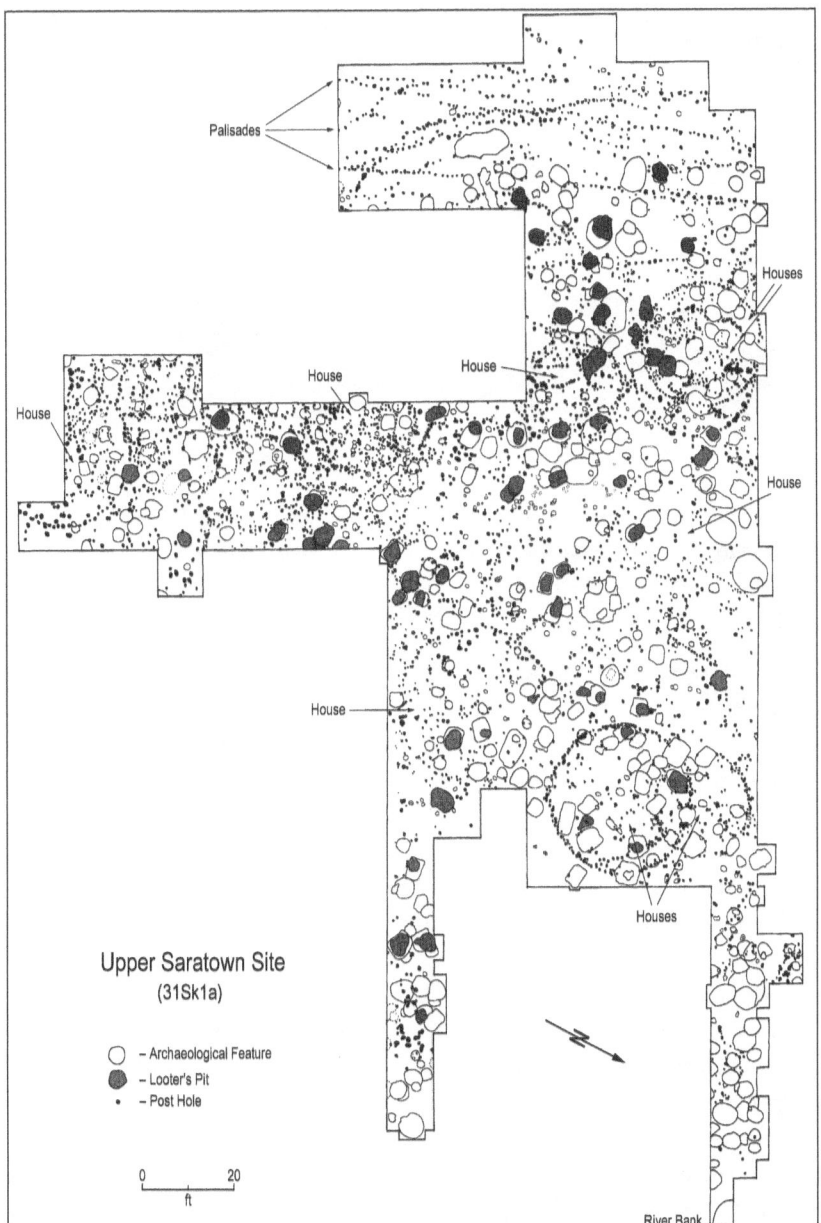

FIGURE 7.10. *Excavation plan of the Upper Saratown site showing pits, postholes, palisades, circular house patterns, and looter's pits. (Courtesy of the Research Laboratories of Archaeology)*

FIGURE 7.11. *A circular house excavated at the Upper Saratown site. This house measured 23 feet in diameter and was intruded by numerous burial pits. (Courtesy of the Research Laboratories of Archaeology)*

houses, pit features, and burials (Ward 1980; Wilson 1983). At the Madison Cemetery site, located about nine miles downstream near the confluence of the Mayo and Dan Rivers, an amateur archaeologist uncovered graves so tightly packed that he thought he was working in a cemetery rather than a habitation site (Gravely 1969:11).

The end of the Late Saratown phase is represented by the William Kluttz site, located less than one mile downstream from Upper Saratown and thought to have been occupied between about 1690 and 1710. Here, numerous shallow graves, clustered in a cemetery area, attest to the continuing devastation of alien diseases.

As evidenced at the Upper Saratown and the William Kluttz sites, Sara community patterns changed drastically during the Late Saratown phase. At Upper Saratown, which was occupied during the first half of the phase, the community consisted of a stockaded village occupied by between 200 and 250 individuals living in circular houses (fig. 7.11). Although no structures were found at the William Kluttz site, the distribution of artifacts and features suggest a very different community pattern by the close of the seventeenth century. By this time, communities no longer consisted of compact, stockaded villages; instead, they appear to have been comprised of widely dispersed households. Ceramic evidence further suggests that fragments of ethnically diverse Siouan tribes may have merged with the Sara at the William Kluttz site to form a dispersed refugee community.

The most characteristic type of Late Saratown phase feature consists of a large, deep, and almost perfectly circular storage facility. These pits were usually over 3 feet in diameter and often were as deep. Typically they contained stratified deposits rich in food remains and other domestic refuse. Large roasting pits or earth ovens also were frequently encountered at Upper Saratown. These are identical to those described for the late Hillsboro, Jenrette, and Middle Saratown phases. Usually these large cooking facilities were located around the edge of the village, near the stockade, and it is believed that they were used to prepare large amounts of food consumed during ritual celebrations (Eastman 1996; Ward 1980; Wilson 1977).

Late Saratown phase pottery has been described based on an analysis of rimsherds and vessels from the Upper Saratown village and an analysis of a large number of vessels and vessel sections from the William Kluttz site (Ward and Davis 1993:285–98; Wilson 1983:425–54). Pottery from both sites comprises the Oldtown series. Smoothed and burnished surface finishes were most popular, followed by net impressing, which accounts for less than 25 percent of the overall assemblage. In contrast to earlier Dan River phase net impressing, Oldtown Net Impressed sherds were paddled with a very fine, netlike material. Minority surface finishes include scraping, brushing, check stamping, simple stamping, and complicated stamping. Most of the pots used during the Late Saratown phase were large cooking or storage jars with slightly everted or flaring rims. These sometimes were decorated with notches on the vessel lip. Hemispherical and cazuela bowls also were found, and these were often decorated with incised lines and punctations (Ward and Davis 1993:425–26) (fig. 7.12).

The basic subsistence pattern described for the earlier Protohistoric and Contact period Siouan phases continued into the Late Saratown phase. A balance was struck between wild and domestic food resources. Corn, beans, squash, and gourds were cultivated, and peaches continued to be a popular Old World addition to the diet (Wilson 1977). Like other Siouan phases during the Contact period, there is no evidence that European animals played an important role in the subsistence cycle.

As with community patterns, mortuary patterns also reflect dramatic changes during the Late Saratown phase. At Upper Saratown and the Madison Cemetery site, graves were placed within and around houses. Usually, these graves were deep shaft-and-chamber pits, with the "central chamber" type occurring most frequently. Bodies were flexed and often accompanied by large amounts of European-made ornaments, particularly glass beads and copper trinkets (Navey 1982) (fig. 7.13). Toward the end of the Late Saratown phase, however, a drastic change in mortuary practice took place.

FIGURE 7.12. *Oldtown series pots from the Hairston site (top left) and Upper Saratown (top right and middle and bottom rows).*

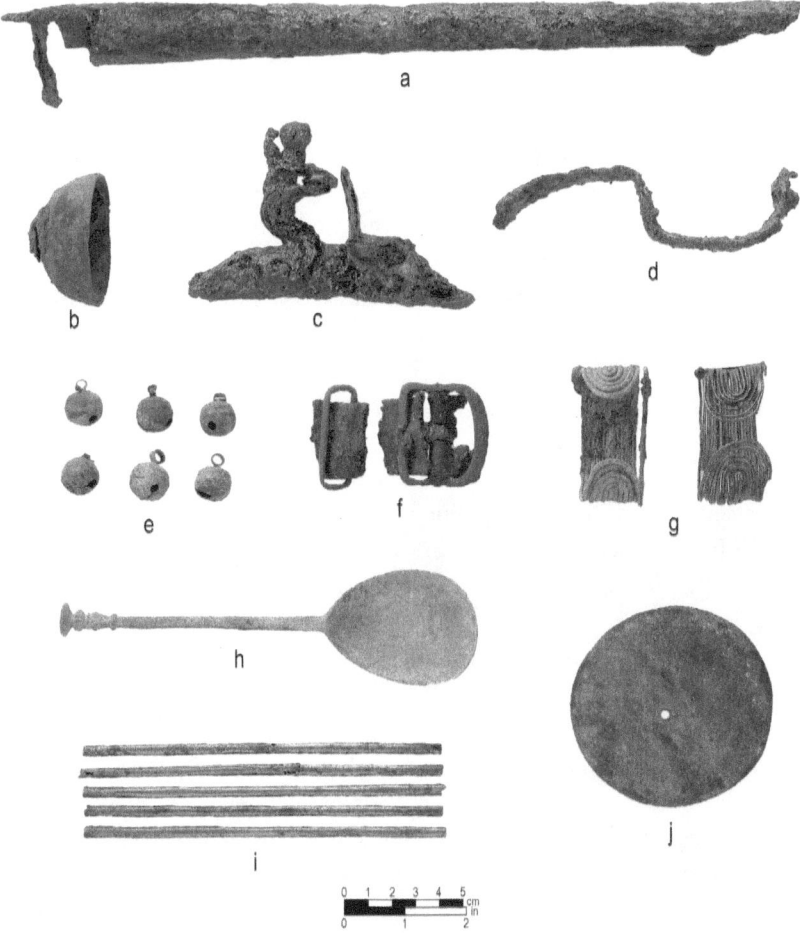

FIGURE 7.13. *European trade items found at Upper Saratown: bells (e), spoon (h), circular gorget (j), and brass tubular beads (i); and additional items from the nearby William Kluttz site: parts of flintlock pistol (a–d), buckle and leather belt fragments (f), and brass wire bracelets (g).*

Excavations at the William Kluttz site uncovered a cemetery containing numerous shallow pit burials. Most of these were subadult interments that did not contain any associated artifacts. Collectively, these graves suggest that sufficient energy to continue traditional mortuary practices could no longer be mustered within the community. The isolation of the dead in a cemetery also may indicate an increasing awareness of the contagiousness of the alien microbes, a lesson that was perhaps learned less than a generation earlier at Upper

Saratown. The fact that most of the dead were subadults further suggests that their deaths resulted from a single epidemic. Those adults who survived earlier epidemics at Upper Saratown would have developed some immunity to new waves of European diseases.

In addition to the cemetery burials, two individuals were placed in traditional shaft-and-chamber pits. One of these was a young adult male outfitted in European attire, with a pistol in his belt (fig. 7.13). Although most of the dead, at least those in the cemetery, seem to have received comparatively little attention, this grave suggests that some individuals still warranted special treatment.

Contact, Interaction, and Cultural Change in the Piedmont

Using the chronological framework presented above, we can now synthesize and review some of the more specific consequences of the interaction between the Piedmont tribes and Euro-Americans. This discussion will focus on four different but, in most cases, related topics: trade, intertribal relations, subsistence, and disease.

Trade

During the Jenrette and Middle Saratown phases, only a few glass and brass or copper beads found their way into the Piedmont villages. The scarcity of trade goods suggests that these items were exchanged through native intermediaries who operated within traditional trade networks. However, during the 1670s, the trade changed abruptly and dramatically. At this time, the Virginia traders began making regular trips into the backcountry searching for new markets.

The intensification and spread of the peltry trade is directly reflected in the Late Saratown and Fredricks phases. Literally thousands of glass beads, copper bells, and other ornaments—but few tools and weapons—have been recovered from Upper Saratown. At Occaneechi Town, guns, iron knives, hatchets, beads, and trinkets were obtained in quantity. Prior to 1676, the Occaneechis' role as middlemen in the Virginia trade had allowed them to control the flow of goods to the more remote groups like the Saras. And by controlling access to firearms and using intimidation when necessary, the Occaneechis were able to maintain their dominant position (Davis and Ward 1998; Merrell 1987). Abraham Wood, a prominent Virginia trader, noted that the Occaneechis' supply of arms and ammunition made them "the Mart for all the Indians for at least 500 miles" ("Virginias Deploured Condition" 1871:167).

The Occaneechis' stranglehold was broken by Bacon's Rebellion in 1676, and groups like the Saras began receiving the full inventory of goods offered by the English traders (Davis and Ward 1998). For example, the young adult male from the William Kluttz site was buried with a 1680 English military-issue pistol, tucked in a leather belt with a brass buckle that was used to hold up cloth trousers. After 1680, the Saras were no longer satisfied to deal strictly in glass beads and copper trinkets, for they had gained access to weapons and other utilitarian goods offered by the Virginia traders.

The introduction of iron tools and firearms, however, did not have a drastic effect on the traditional technologies of the Piedmont tribes. They were used alongside, but not in place of, their aboriginal counterparts. At Occaneechi Town, lead shot and gunflints were recovered from almost every excavation unit, but so were stone arrow points. Clay pots were still made, although copper kettles were available, and glass beads were worn and sewn on garments just as their shell counterparts had been earlier. Other than firearms, perhaps the only new technology introduced by the traders was the use of scissors, which were now needed to cut and shape the bolts of European-made cloth that were used to make clothing, bags, and other items that formerly were made from animal skins.

The peltry trade perhaps had a greater impact on traditional Siouan social structure than it did on their technology. Among the Piedmont tribes, individuals who could deal most successfully with the Virginia traders appear to have gained a level of prestige and influence not possible within the traditional social structure. Mortuary data from Occaneechi Town and the William Kluttz site suggest that, during the Fredricks and Late Saratown phases, these individuals were young adult males and adult females (Ward 1987; Ward et al. 1996). Mortuary evidence indicates that only adult females achieved positions of highest prestige during the earlier Middle Saratown phase (Navey 1982). These differences in status recognition appear to reflect the relative impact of trade on the social structures of the Saras and Occaneechis at the beginning and end of the Contact period (cf. Davis and Ward 1998).

The ethnohistoric documents also point to similar differences. John Lederer observed in 1670 that kinship was traced through the female line, and among the "remoter" tribes such as the Eno, the government was democratic. However, a "democratic" social order did not seem to be the norm among the tribes that had been heavily engaged in trade with the English. The Occaneechi, for instance, were said to have had two "kings" governing them when they lived on the Roanoke River and controlled the trade. And the nearby Saponis were ruled by an "absolute monarch" (Cumming 1958).

European Plants and Livestock

The Europeans not only brought new tools and strange weapons to the New World, they also filled their boats with horses, pigs, chickens, and other creatures unknown to Native Americans. They packed seeds of wheat, barley, and peaches to be planted in the fertile soils of their new home. How were these new plants and animals received by the Piedmont Siouans and what changes did they forge in the native subsistence cycle? Surprisingly, archaeological evidence has shown that new plants and animals were virtually ignored by most Piedmont Indians. Peaches and watermelons were planted, but the traditional trinity of corn, beans, and squash remained the mainstay of the diet (Gremillion 1989).

Old World animals were even less popular than Old World plants. The only evidence of their use comes from the Fredricks site, where one bone each of a pig and a horse were recovered (Holm 1987). As was the case with tools and trinkets, only those items that did not require a re-organization of the traditional ways of doing things were incorporated, and these were used alongside, not in place of, familiar native resources (Gremillion 1995).

Intertribal Relations

Stockaded villages such as the Hillsboro phase Wall site attest to the fact that intertribal conflict and warfare preceded the arrival of the Europeans. However, hostilities increased dramatically during the Contact period when Indian slaves and stolen deerskins could be traded for the prized kettles and guns of the foreigners. The knife-scarred skull of a scalp victim and a lead ball flattened against the fibula of a young woman in the Occaneechi cemetery at the Fredricks site are clear evidence of such hostilities. Often, these conflicts took the form of raids by larger, well-armed groups from as far north as New York and Pennsylvania. In 1701, John Lawson was forced to turn off the main trading path to Virginia and head due east toward the English settlements along Pamlico River after being warned of a "Sinnager" (Seneca) raiding party in the vicinity of Occaneechi Town (Lefler 1967:61).

Not only did the infusion of European goods and arms increase external threats, but the competition for foreign trade and a market for native slaves also heightened hostilities among the Piedmont tribes themselves. Whereas in the past blood feuds and revenge fueled the fires of conflict, the European presence introduced new motives and new ways of conducting warfare.

At various times during the latter half of the seventeenth century, groups such as the Wainokes, Occaneechis, and Tuscaroras were offered unprecedented opportunities, through trade and the acquisition of firearms, to obtain and exert considerable economic and political power. Each of these groups was located along the ever-advancing colonial frontier; therefore, each was in a position where it might control or at least influence contacts with more remote tribes. The Occaneechis, being positioned astride the principal trading path out of Fort Henry, were particularly successful in this respect. By controlling access to firearms and using intimidation when necessary, the Occaneechis were able to maintain their dominant position as middlemen. Significantly, when their downfall came in 1676, it was not at the hands of their deprived "trading partners" but by the superior forces of Nathaniel Bacon and his well-armed militia.

Disease

Without a doubt, the most devastating result of the European arrival on the North Carolina Piedmont was the introduction of new diseases for which the native populations had little or no resistance. Smallpox, measles, and other viral diseases swept across the region, killing and disabling thousands. The lack of biological resistance to the new diseases made them particularly deadly for the native tribes. Their devastation was accelerated during the late 1600s by increased population movements and expanded intertribal contact as native peoples adapted to the economic and political changes brought about by the trade. In short, the intensification and spread of traditional trade networks to accommodate the flow of European goods and deerskins also facilitated the rapid spread of deadly pathogens (Wood 1987:31).

There can be no argument concerning the final, disastrous result of the introduction of foreign diseases; however, there is considerable debate concerning the timing and spread of these diseases into the interior Southeast. Many researchers (e.g., Ramenofsky 1987; Smith 1987) generally support the position taken by Henry Dobyns (1983), who believes that waves of pandemics swept through the interior Southeast soon after the arrival of the first Spanish explorers into North America. According to Dobyns (13), diseases spread from population to population on their own momentum, without the necessity of face-to-face contacts between natives and foreigners. Others (e.g., Blakely and Detweiler-Blakely 1989; Henige 1989; Larsen 1994; Milner 1980; Snow and Lamphear 1989) have suggested that, instead of occurring as continent-wide pandemics on the heels of the Spanish entradas, the spread of Old World diseases depended on a number of local and regional factors. Population density, community size, and the degree and nature of the contacts between natives and foreigners all affected the timing, speed, and scope of the devastation caused by diseases such as smallpox, measles, and influenza. Both of these positions depend heavily on historical and ethnographic data.

In the Siouan project area of north central North Carolina, there is no ethnographic or archaeological evidence of epidemic diseases until the arrival of the Virginia traders in the last half of the seventeenth century. In 1670, John Lederer passed through southern Virginia and central North Carolina, visiting the villages of the Saponis, Occaneechis, Enos, Shakoris, Saras, and others, without mentioning any signs of population disruption or decline (Cumming 1958). Three years later, James Needham and Gabriel Arthur also traveled through the north central Piedmont without reporting any evidence of depopulation (Alvord and Bidgood 1912). Even John Lawson in 1701 was impressed with the numbers of people he encountered during the southern leg of his journey through Catawba country (Lefler 1967:46). However, as he moved northward and began to visit groups that had been intensively engaged in the Virginia deerskin trade, his observations changed. Here, Lawson described large vacant areas and small towns of "not above 17 houses." At Sapona on the Yadkin River, he noted for the first time the amalgamation of once distinct tribes into single villages as a consequence of depopulation (50–53). It was his experience with these more northern groups that led Lawson to remark that "there is not the sixth Savage living within two hundred Miles of all our Settlements, as there were fifty years ago" (232).

The archaeological record also points to a late arrival of epidemic diseases in the Siouan area. Late Hillsboro phase sites (ca. A.D. 1500–1600), which would have been occupied when the Spanish first arrived in the Southeast, consistently contain few burials and show no evidence of increased mortuary activity. Even after archaeologists auger tested extensive areas at sites such as Edgar Rogers and George Rogers and focused excavations in areas with a high concentration of subsurface pits, few burials were found (Ward and Davis 1993:29, 85). Nor is there any evidence of a breakdown or disruption of other cultural components during the Hillsboro phase. On the contrary, population density increased, subsistence practices became more intense and diverse, and ceramic and lithic technologies became more elaborate.

One could argue that cemeteries were located away from the habitation areas and that archaeologists have simply failed to find them. Some archaeologists also have suggested that the living were so weakened that they were unable to bury their dead and therefore they are not represented in the archaeological record (Ramenofsky 1987; Smith 1987). The first argument can never be completely dismissed because of the nature of archaeological data. However, the typical pattern of Siouan burial from Late Prehistoric times until the end of the Contact period was to place graves within or near domestic structures. These are the site areas that have been intensively sampled and excavated by archaeologists. During the Fredricks and Late Saratown phases, this pattern did change and graves were placed in cemeteries. Still, using the same subsurface testing strategy as employed at earlier sites, archaeologists were able to locate these cemeteries at the later sites (Davis and Ward 1987).

There is also ample archaeological evidence that the dead were buried even during the most virulent epidemics. At Upper Saratown and the Madison Cemetery sites, both of which were decimated by diseases during the late seventeenth century, individuals were buried in traditional shaft-and-chamber pits. Even at Occaneechi Town, where probably fewer than seventy-five individuals survived, deep graves were arduously dug into a stiff subsoil clay, and the dead were laid to rest with full, traditional ceremony.

Only at the William Kluttz site, which represents the last desperate gasp of the Saras on the Dan River, is there evidence that the decimation had become so great that it affected the burial of the dead. Here, children and subadults were interred in shallow, oval pits within a cemetery, apparently with little attendant ritual. Adult graves, however, were placed away from the cemetery in deep shaft-and-chamber pits. Burial goods indicate that these individuals were given their last rites in a traditional manner. Even during the worst of times, the dead were still buried, and more often than not, they too were laid to rest with full ceremony.

There is further evidence for the late arrival of epidemics on the Carolina Piedmont from excavations at sites occupied during the Jenrette and Middle Saratown phases (ca. A.D. 1600–1680). At the Jenrette site, almost 20,000 square feet of the stockaded village have been excavated, exposing numerous pit features but only four graves. Extensive auger testing and excavations at Lower Saratown uncovered only a single burial (Ward and Davis 1993). Both of these sites contained trade materials that suggest only indirect contacts between Indians and European traders.

This evidence alone may not be entirely convincing to some scholars, and contrary arguments can still be made with regard to the reliability of the excavation samples and the possibility of drastically altered mortuary patterns. However, when the burial density data from sixteenth-century and early-seventeenth-century sites are compared with that from late-seventeenth-century sites, the differences are so striking that they cannot be explained away by "sampling error." At Upper Saratown, the graves were so numerous that it was impossible for the archaeologists there to dig a 10' square excavation unit without uncovering the tops of one or more burial pits. At the Madison Cemetery site, the number and density of graves led a vocational archaeologist to mistakenly assume the site was a cemetery (Gravely 1969). The sheer numbers and concentrations of burials on sites postdating 1670, compared with the numbers at earlier sites, make it clear that diseases and not sampling error or burial practices were responsible for the dramatic differences between the earlier and later sites.

By studying the archaeological data from the Piedmont during the Contact period against the background of the ethnohistoric record, it is possible to create a composite picture of native cultures during the seventeenth century with a relatively high degree of clarity and focus. At first glance, this picture appears to be one of explosive and dramatic change. Yet, as one moves in for a closer look, it becomes clear that change was tempered by stability and that many native traditions persisted in the face of the devastation brought on by disease and depopulation. Nevertheless, except for a few scattered, isolated families whose relatives remain in the region today, the first Europeans to permanently settle in the North Carolina Piedmont found only abandoned villages and vacant fields.

The Contact Period in the Appalachian Summit

In 1935, President Franklin D. Roosevelt appointed a commission of scholars to examine the documentary and scientific evidence for reconstructing Hernando de Soto's 1539-43 route through the southeastern United States, including the southwestern North Carolina mountains. John R. Swanton, an anthropologist with the Smithsonian's Bureau of American Ethnology and the foremost authority on Indians of the southern United States, was appointed to head the commission. The results of the commission's study, which for the most part were the results of Swanton's individual efforts, were published in 1939 (Swanton 1985). This report represents one of the many remarkable achievements accomplished by Swanton, a founding father of southern Indian studies. As with many of Swanton's other works, the report has been reprinted and is still found on the shelves of modern scholars' bookcases, with pages dog-eared from frequent use.

During the early 1980s, Chester DePratter, Charles Hudson, and Marvin Smith of the University of Georgia, using information not available to Swanton, presented evidence suggesting a realignment of segments of the de Soto route as it had been reconstructed by the De Soto Expedition Commission. Much of this new evidence came not from the de Soto chronicles but from documents recording the day-to-day activities of the 1566-68 Juan Pardo expeditions through South Carolina, western North Carolina, and eastern Tennessee. Pardo and his men visited at least five of the same towns through which de Soto had traveled some twenty-seven years earlier. Although Swanton also used accounts of the Pardo expeditions to aid in orienting the commission's reconstruction of de Soto's route, he did not have access to the most detailed account of Pardo's explorations. This document, known as the Bandera (or "Vandera") account, did not become available to scholars until the early 1980s (Hudson et al. 1985; Larson 1990).

Juan de la Bandera, the official scribe of Pardo's second expedition in 1567–68, kept detailed notes on daily distances traveled, the names of the native chiefs they met, and descriptions of the local terrain. According to the Georgia scholars' interpretation, Bandera's narrative, when coupled with recent archaeological discoveries, provides firmly fixed reference points that can be used to accurately orient the alignment of de Soto's interior route, particularly through portions of South Carolina and western North Carolina (Hudson 1990; DePratter, Hudson, and Smith 1983).

Not all scholars accept the reconstructions of the routes followed by de Soto and Pardo as presented by DePratter, Hudson, and Smith. Tennessee archaeologists Clifford Boyd Jr. and Gerald Schroedl (1987:841) have questioned, among other things, the correlations of some of the key towns and political territories described in the narratives with known archaeological sites and cultural complexes.

After reviewing the Bandera documents, Lewis Larson, then state archaeologist of Georgia, concluded that Hudson, DePratter, and Smith had Pardo's heading from Santa Elena off by some 110 degrees. Larson argued that instead of leaving Santa Elena and heading north-northwest along the Broad River in South Carolina, Pardo headed in a south-southwesterly direction along the Georgia coast before making a turn west into the interior. Larson's research focuses only on the first leg of Pardo's journey, and he emphasized that he did not know what effect his findings might have on the remainder of Pardo's route—or de Soto's (Larson 1990:137). DePratter, Hudson, and Smith (1990:140) argue that Larson uses only selective maps and documents and ignores other evidence that supports their conclusion that Pardo headed in a northward direction from Santa Elena.

Although other scholars also have offered interpretations that differ from Swanton's reconstruction of the de Soto route (cf. Brain 1985), Hudson and his colleagues are alone in reinterpreting the entire route from Florida to Texas. The most noticeable thing about the different reconstructions, when viewed from an overall perspective, is not their differences but their congruity. In the heart of the Southeast, most scholars agree on the route de Soto's army took through Florida, Georgia, and Alabama. Divergence of opinion focuses on portions of the western alignment in Louisiana and Texas and the eastern segment running through South Carolina, North Carolina, and Tennessee (National Park Service 1989:fig. 1). The eastern segment is the one that concerns us—and other southeastern archaeologists—the most.

According to Swanton (1985:348c), de Soto passed through the very northwestern edge of South Carolina and the southwestern tip of North Carolina, on a north-northwesterly heading from the Georgia border. Once in North Carolina, the army turned sharply to the west and barely skirted the southeastern corner of Tennessee before turning southward near the Georgia-Alabama line. This reconstruction has de Soto entering North Carolina in the vicinity of Highlands, along the Jackson-Macon County line. He then traveled northwest toward the town of Franklin in Macon County. From Franklin, the expedition turned to the west in the direction of the present-day towns of Andrews, Marble, and Murphy in Cherokee County. The Spanish explorers then exited North Carolina by following the Hiwassee River into Tennessee.

According to Hudson and his colleagues (1984:73–75), de Soto's army traveled northward along the Wateree River through central South Carolina and crossed into North Carolina near the town of Gastonia. Following the Catawba River, they continued their northward trek toward Hickory, and then turned to the west on a heading that would have taken them to the vicinity of the present-day towns of Morganton and Marion in Burke and McDowell Counties. Following a trail that roughly paralleled Interstate 40, de Soto would have entered the Blue Ridge Mountains at Swannanoa Gap. From there, the expedition traveled northward, closely following the French Broad River. The army left North Carolina and entered Tennessee near the present-day community of Hot Springs in Madison County.

These two reconstructions of de Soto's path through North Carolina are based on detailed and tedious analyses of evidence from the various documentary sources, as well as more general archaeological information. A critical evaluation of the different interpretations of the documentary sources is well beyond our scope here. We can, however, offer a review of the relevant archaeological data.

Janet Levy of UNC-Charlotte and Alan May of the Schiele Museum have conducted excavations at the Crowders Creek (31Gs55) and Hardin (31Gs30) sites in the lower Catawba River drainage, near the North Carolina–South Carolina border in Gaston County. David Moore of the North Carolina Office of State Archaeology has studied the McDowell (31Mc41) and Berry (31Bk22) sites in the upper Catawba River drainage in McDowell and Burke Counties. All of these sites are located in the vicinity of de Soto's and Pardo's routes as proposed by Hudson, Smith, and DePratter. The Gaston County sites are located near the territory of Chalaque mentioned in the de Soto narratives. The

McDowell and Burke County sites are located in the vicinity of Guaquili (Guaquiri) and Xuala (Joara), two towns that were visited by de Soto and Pardo (Hudson, Smith, and DePratter 1984).

Radiocarbon dates from the four sites suggest that they were occupied during the fourteenth, fifteenth, and sixteenth centuries, although earlier dates also have been obtained. Most of the ceramic samples from the sites fall within the general Lamar style. The Gaston County pottery is similar to pottery from the Mulberry Mounds in South Carolina, whereas the upper Catawba ceramics are very similar to Pisgah and Qualla types (Levy, May, and Moore 1990:162–63).

Based on the ceramic assemblages and the radiocarbon dates, it seems likely that at least some of these sites were occupied during the period of the de Soto and Pardo expeditions. Direct evidence of Spanish contacts, however, is questionable. A small copper tube was recovered from the plowzone at the Hardin site. This has been described as a possible Spanish "lacing tip." The specimen might also represent a native-made tubular bead, a common artifact type found on late-seventeenth-century sites. An iron knife was found with an extended burial at the Berry site. Some authorities have dated the knife to the sixteenth century, whereas others have dated it to the eighteenth century. The extended form of the burial suggests the later date is probably correct. Very small fragments of iron from the plowzone at the McDowell site have been identified as possible fragments of chain mail; however, the fragments lack any diagnostic attributes of chain mail, and they are so fragmentary that they could represent almost anything (Levy, May, and Moore 1990:158–59).

Olive jar fragments from three vessels have been recently identified from excavated and surface contexts at the Berry site. Most of these small sherds are not temporally diagnostic; however, one sherd has been identified as Caparra Blue Majolica, which has a temporal range from 1492 to around 1600. A similar ceramic type was found at the site of de Soto's first winter camp in present-day Tallahassee, Florida. Another small sherd has been identified as a type similar to ceramics from the sixteenth-century Spanish fort of Santa Elena on the South Carolina coast. This evidence, as well as a handful of other artifacts from the Berry and McDowell sites, has convinced some archaeologists that the upper Catawba River valley was visited by de Soto and Pardo (Beck 1997; Moore and Beck 1994).

Equally tantalizing—and questionable—archaeological evidence exists to support the route reconstructed by Swanton and the De Soto Expedition Commission. Anne Rogers, an archaeologist at Western Carolina University, has identified several glass trade beads, believed to date to the sixteenth century, in privately owned artifact collections from the Cherokee County area in extreme southwestern North Carolina (Rogers, personal communication).

Local artifact collectors report that many of these specimens came from the Peachtree Mound site (31Ce1), excavated by the Smithsonian Institution in 1933 (see Chapter 1). Swanton believed that the Peachtree site was the remains of the village of Guasili, which was described by one of the de Soto chroniclers as having a mound. Although numerous European trade artifacts, including knives, scissors, copper bells, and glass beads, were found during the course of the Peachtree excavations, Jesse Jennings, who headed the excavations, felt that the European trade goods postdated the Spanish entradas (Setzler and Jennings 1941; Swanton 1985:202).

Today, we know that Jennings was generally correct in his assessment of the European artifacts. Most of the trade goods recovered during the Smithsonian excavations appear to date to the eighteenth century. Some of the glass beads, however, probably have a Spanish origin. The question is whether they were left by members of the de Soto and Pardo expeditions or were introduced later through trade with the Spanish colonies along the coasts of South Carolina and Georgia.

In 1673, James Needham and Gabriel Arthur noted that the Cherokees had earlier traded with a "white people which have long beardes and whiskers" and who lived in brick houses arranged in streets. These strangers also raised cattle and swine. When a Cherokee party of eight men and four women accompanied Needham to Abraham Wood's home in Virginia to set up trade relations with the English, they were reported to be carrying "bout sixty gunnes, not such locks as oures bee" (Alvord and Bidgood 1912:214). These guns were probably Spanish and either obtained through trade or raiding. While living with the Cherokee, Gabriel Arthur accompanied them on an eight-day march to the south and east to raid a Spanish town that was presumably located on the coast of South Carolina (19–20).

Apparently the Cherokee had ample opportunity to acquire Spanish goods, and their presence on archaeological sites does not necessarily prove or disprove that these sites represent villages that lay along the routes taken by the early explorers. Even if artifacts from the mid-sixteenth century are found in an undisputed archaeological context, there is no way of knowing if they were left there by Spaniards, or if they found their way into the archaeological record through a circuitous route of trade or inheritance.

What all this means is that the precise routes of the de Soto and Pardo expeditions through North Carolina may never be established with certainty. The existing documentary records are too vague and will always be subject to different interpretations. Much like religious texts, one's belief in the written word depends more on faith than fact. And the fragile and incomplete archaeological record appears to have little potential for clarifying matters.

Although it would be nice to erect monuments along the roadside, confidently tracing de Soto's trail through North Carolina, a more important anthropological and archaeological question is what impact did the early Spanish entradas have on the native populations of the state. This question is usually framed in terms of the disease issue. Did the armies of de Soto and Pardo spread waves of epidemics that wiped out significant portions of the native population? Or did their visits have only limited and isolated impacts on the towns and people they visited?

As mentioned earlier in this chapter, this question recently has been the subject of some debate among archaeologists, historians, and physical anthropologists. There is no doubt that the Spaniards and their African slaves introduced Old World diseases that had devastating effects on native populations in the Western Hemisphere. Lacking any immunity to diseases such as smallpox, measles, and certain kinds of influenza, American Indians often suffered high mortality rates when they came in contact with Old World germs. But did these new diseases sweep over most of the Southeast on the heels of the earliest Spanish explorations in Mexico and Florida? While some scholars say yes, others are more cautious and question whether or not widespread pandemics resulting in massive depopulation occurred during the period of initial contacts between Indians and newcomers.

After extensive research on Contact period native populations from Florida to Hawaii, paleoarchaeologist Clark Larsen has come to the conclusion (1994:143) that there is no clear dichotomy between pre-Contact and post-Contact populations in terms of overall health and well-being. His position does not deny the deadly impact of Old World diseases in some areas, but Larsen points out that before the arrival of Europeans, native populations were not free from devastating diseases, nor were they free from death and injury due to dietary stress and conflict.

It is also clear from the archaeological record that many of the complex cultures of the Southeast were in a state of decline and collapse long before Christopher Columbus's first voyage. As discussed in Chapter 5, many Mississippian centers were abandoned around the end of the fourteenth century. Large mound and village complexes such as Moundville in Alabama, Etowah, Irene, and the Lamar site in Georgia, and Town Creek in North Carolina were in a state of population decline or had been abandoned years before Columbus first laid eyes on San Salvador (Anderson 1994; Coe 1995; Ferguson 1971; Steponaitis 1983).

In the Appalachian Summit region, the evidence for massive depopulation during the sixteenth century is even less convincing than that seen at sites along de Soto's purported route. Just as in the Piedmont, no sixteenth-century sites have been found that suggest increased mortality due to epidemic diseases. Even those sites that have been regarded as possible candidates for towns visited by de Soto and Pardo have failed to yield evidence of unusually high mortality rates. At the Hardin, Crowders Creek, Berry, and McDowell sites, the remains of at least four structures and numerous pit features have been uncovered, but only two burials have been reported (Levy, May, and Moore 1990). This pattern is similar to that of Piedmont sites that date to the same time period, and it stands in sharp contrast to the numbers of burials found on late-seventeenth-century Piedmont sites like Upper Saratown, Occaneechi Town, and the Madison Cemetery site (cf. Ward and Davis 1991:180). However, only a half century later, the Cherokee would face the same devastation and disruption as their Piedmont cousins.

During the early eighteenth century, English traders began to push west through the Blue Ridge mountains of North Carolina into the Ridge and Valley province of Tennessee. They also made their way into the upper Piedmont of South Carolina and Georgia, searching for new markets for their guns and trinkets, as well as new supplies of peltry. Here, they found the Cherokees, a populous people who resided in a widely scattered collection of towns and communities that maintained a common identity through a shared language and culture (Gilbert 1943; Mooney 1975).

Although the Cherokees recognized a common cultural heritage that united them as one tribe, they also recognized clusters of settlements that were geographically, linguistically, and politically distinct. These were known as: (1) the Lower Settlements, located along the upper tributaries of the Savannah River in Georgia and South Carolina; (2) the Middle, Valley, and Out Settlements of western North Carolina, reaching from the Little Tennessee and Tuckasegee Rivers westward to the Hiwassee River; and (3) the Overhill Settlements of Tennessee, located along the upper Tennessee and lower Little Tennessee Rivers (Gilbert 1943:178).

Of these divisions, the Middle and Valley Settlements represented the cultural core of the Cherokees. Unlike the inhabitants of the Lower and Overhill Settlements, this group managed to retain a small portion of their native territory, along with much of their traditional culture. The Qualla Boundary, as the Eastern Cherokee reservation is referred to today, consists of a little over 56,000 acres of rugged terrain along the Tuckasegee and Oconaluftee Rivers in the heart of the Middle Settlements (Egloff 1967; Gilbert 1943).

As mentioned in Chapter 5, the Cherokee Archaeological Project focused research on Middle and Valley town sites between 1965 and 1971. This research, in conjunction with more recent work by Brett Riggs of the University of Tennessee, has resulted in a refinement of the Late Qualla phase, which archaeologically represents Cherokee culture during the Contact period (Dickens 1976; Riggs 1995).

The Late Qualla Phase (A.D. 1700–1838)

The first fifty years of the Late Qualla phase was a time of relative cultural and political stability for the Cherokee; however, they did not fully avoid the destructive turmoil brought on by warfare, disease, and trade. While contacts with Virginians and South Carolinians were established during the late 1600s, and the Spanish presence to their south had been felt for more than a century, the Cherokee remained somewhat isolated until the close of the Tuscarora War in 1713. As an ally of South Carolina during that war, the Cherokee were afforded an opportunity to attack their hereditary enemy, the Tuscarora. This alliance resulted in an unstable peace between the colony and the Cherokee, a succession of treaties designed to maintain that peace, and an economic relationship that grew stronger throughout the eighteenth century. While the benefits of trade kept this alliance from falling apart, it was severely strained by both sides because of relationships between the South Carolinians and the Creek and between the Cherokee and the French. By the late 1730s, European diseases had spread to Cherokee country, and a smallpox epidemic in 1738–39 was estimated by trader James Adair to have destroyed nearly half of the tribe. While this epidemic likely was most devastating to the towns in the upper Savannah drainage that were closest to South Carolina, the more remote Cherokee towns in western North Carolina probably also suffered severely (Mooney 1975:22–26).

With the onset of the French and Indian War in 1754, the Cherokees came under ever-increasing pressure to change their traditional ways, as the British and emerging Americans vied for control of the southern Appalachians. Although the Cherokee sided with the British against the French and their Indian allies, and even assisted in the retaking of Fort Duquesne under George Washington, many frontier settlers and colonial militiamen suspected the Cherokee's loyalty. In 1760, these suspicions and mistrust by both sides led to war along the Carolina-Cherokee frontier and the siege of Fort Loudoun in the heart of the Overhill Cherokee. Colonels Montgomery and Grant led punitive expeditions into the heart of the southern Appalachians, where they killed many Cherokees and burned numerous towns. During the American Revolution, similar expeditions were led by General Rutherford of North Carolina and Colonel Williamson of South Carolina in 1776 because of the Cherokee's alliance with the British. The Cherokee suffered greatly during these wars and lost much of the political and military power they possessed earlier. While the period following the Revolution was relatively peaceful compared to the previous thirty years, it was also during this period that the Cherokee began to lose control of their own destiny. Beginning with the Treaty of Hopewell in 1785 and culminating with the Removal of 1838, each new treaty between the Cherokee and the newly formed United States cost them more and more of their mountain homeland (Mooney 1975:29–40).

The pottery of the Late Qualla phase reflects the relative stability and conservatism that mark the beginning of this phase. No drastic changes occurred to clearly demarcate the Late Qualla ceramic tradition from pottery made during the preceding Middle Qualla phase. Instead, curvilinear, complicated-stamped designs gradually became more popular as rectilinear motifs declined. After the middle of the eighteenth century, all complicated-stamped designs became bolder in form and cruder in execution. Concomitantly, incised decorations and the burnishing of vessel surfaces decreased in frequency as cordmarking and corncob impressing became more popular methods of surface treatment (Egloff 1967:38–43).

Excavations at the Tuckasegee site (31Jk12), located in Jackson County, North Carolina, revealed a small circular structure and a large collection of Qualla ceramics. This site is thought to have been occupied during the first half of the eighteenth century. The ceramics recovered from the house floor conform to the above description, with the addition of brushing as a minority surface treatment (Dickens 1978:123; Keel 1976:45).

Another collection of Late Qualla phase pottery, dating to the last half of the phase, was excavated from the Townson site (31Ce15), located near the junction of the Hiwassee River and Brasstown Creek in Cherokee County. This site may represent a Cherokee village that was attacked by General Griffith Rutherford in 1776. A burned house was excavated at the site in 1964 by archaeologists from the University of North Carolina. Several mostly intact pottery vessels were found on the house floor (Dickens 1967) (fig. 7.14).

Although the pots varied in size and surface finish, their general form was very similar. Most were globular jars with broad shoulders and out-flaring rims. Some of the rims were folded, creating a rolled lip, and were unadorned. On other vessels, the folded rim formed a filletlike strip that was notched in much the same way as Middle Qualla rims. Instead of a notched, folded fillet, a thin, simple clay strip was sometimes added below the lip and decorated with vertical notches.

In general, the surface treatments found on the Townson site pottery are similar to those found on earlier Qualla pottery. Curvilinear and rectilinear designs were used. However, these were bolder in form and more crudely executed in comparison to similar surface finishes on earlier wares. Coarse

FIGURE 7.14. *Late Qualla pots from a burned house at the Townson site.*

cordmarked, simple-stamped, and check-stamped vessels also were found on the burned house floor.

All of the pots were made from clay that contained medium-sized or large particles of grit or crushed stone. This coarse tempering material added to the overall crude "feel" of the ceramics. Of course, the Townson site sample is too small and spatially restricted to provide a definitive statement regarding all Late Qualla pottery. Nevertheless, the attributes displayed fit well in an overall pattern that has been observed by other archaeologists working in the Cherokee area of western North Carolina (e.g., Dickens 1979; Egloff 1967; Riggs 1995).

The house excavated at Townson differs greatly from houses of the Middle Qualla phase and the structure excavated at the Tuckasegee site. Instead of being constructed of posts set individually in the ground, the walls of this rectangular house were formed by split rails, laid horizontally atop one another and anchored to four corner posts. Cracks between the rails were chinked with clay. The house measured approximately 18'×12', and, from the outside, it probably looked very much like a contemporary Euro-American log cabin. Inside, however, it retained the traditional, centrally located, puddled-clay hearth found in earlier Cherokee houses. Sadly, the charred remains of an old man who apparently was trapped in the burning structure during Rutherford's attack were found inside (Dickens 1978:123).

A structure very similar to the one uncovered at the Townson site was described in an 1825 letter from Lewis Williams to Archibald Murphey. The description was related to Lewis by his father, a colonial soldier who in 1776 had participated in an attack on an Overhill Cherokee village in eastern Tennessee: "The towns destroyed were irregularly built on various sites along the Tennessee river—The Houses were generally of an oblong figure, constructed by placing four posts in the ground, and extending rails representing the four sides of the square from one post to the other—The space on the sides between the rails were filled with reeds in the form of wattle or wicker work, and over these again on the inside was spread a coat of plaster—The roofs of the Houses were covered with bark peeled from the Trees at the proper season of the year—Thus constructed the Houses would be warm and comfortable in the winter" (Dickens 1967:34).

The earlier circular structure uncovered at the Tuckasegee site was defined by an outer ring of individually set wall posts. It measured 23 feet in diameter. An interior ring of roof support posts surrounded a central, puddled-clay hearth basin, similar to ones found in the Coweeta Creek town houses. The circular outline of the structure and the similarity in form of the hearth to those in the town houses led to an initial speculation that this structure also may have served as a town house (Coe and Keel 1965). However, because of its small size and the lack of evidence that rebuilding took place to form an accretional mound, this interpretation has changed over the years. Today, most scholars agree with Dickens's assessment that the Tuckasegee structure served as a domestic dwelling (Dickens 1978:123; Keel, personal communications 1996).

If this interpretation is correct, then the Cherokee during the Late Qualla phase built both circular and rectangular houses. According to the historical records, circular houses in the interior Southeast were used mainly as winter dwellings, whereas the rectangular form was used in the summer (Faulkner 1977). After an extensive study of European descriptions of Cherokee houses, Gerald Schroedl of the University of Tennessee concluded that the rectangular floor plan became the dominant form after 1776 (1986:227).

As house types changed during the Late Qualla phase, so did village configurations. The Townson site reflects a dramatic shift in settlement type from the compact, usually stockaded villages of the Middle Qualla phase. The site covers approximately fifty acres and is comprised of houses scattered along a terrace on the north side of the Hiwassee River. Although the overall extent of the Townson site is considerably larger than earlier Qualla sites (for example, the Coweeta Creek site covers only about three acres), the size of the resident population probably was not much greater than that of the earlier villages (Dickens 1978).

When the Townson site is plowed, it is possible to stand on U.S. Highway 64, which bisects the site, and view the dark oblong stains of earth that mark the locations of individual structures burned by the 1776 Rutherford expedition. These stains for the most part are separated by several hundred feet of light brown soil where small gardens were once tilled. In 1761, a British army captain described the nearby town of Nuquasee as being composed of houses separated by distances that could not be reached by a musket shot (Hatley 1989:228). This process of population dispersion intensified as acculturation and pressures to change increased. By the time the Cherokee were forcibly removed in 1838, most families lived in isolated farmsteads and small hamlets.

In the early 1990s, the water level of Hiwassee Reservoir on the Hiwassee River below Murphy was temporarily lowered by the Tennessee Valley Authority, and archaeologists from Appalachian State University conducted extensive surveys of the exposed land. Their research located over fifty Middle Cherokee residential sites dating between 1775 and 1838. Two basic settlement types were recognized during the study: (1) loosely clustered villages similar to those at the Townson site; and (2) more isolated farmsteadlike settlements. The clustered settlements were surrounded by small farmsteads and eventually were replaced by them just prior to Removal (Riggs 1995:1–3).

One of the clustered settlements, thought to be the village of Cootlehee, was defined by two large, dense artifact scatters. One of these areas contained as many as three rectangular structures, a possible town house, and numerous pit features. Artifacts recovered from the site included Late Qualla ceramics, gun parts, lead shot, glass beads, pieces of bottle glass, and brass kettle fragments. Another site, thought to be the settlement of Takwa'yi, was represented by seventeen household clusters spread out and spaced like those at the Townson site (Riggs 1995:3–4).

The farmsteads, in contrast, were evidenced on the ground surface by small, low-density scatters of artifacts where family cabins and outbuilding once stood. Some of these sites produced relatively large numbers of artifacts, including many non-native, commercially manufactured items. Others contained mostly native-made artifacts. Archaeologists believe that these differences may reflect varying degrees of acculturation to Western values and different intensities of participation of individual families in the colonial market economy (Riggs 1995).

During the Late Qualla phase, subsistence practices changed as European plants and animals were introduced. The latter appear to have been particularly important. Unlike the Siouan-speaking peoples of the Piedmont, the Cherokees readily adopted Old World animals, and most families kept horses, cows, pigs, and chickens. Horses increased in importance during the eighteenth century as the deerskin trade became an important economic pursuit among the Cherokee. These animals were invaluable in transporting large numbers of hides to the British markets as far away as Charleston, South Carolina. The Cherokees were so successful in breeding and raising horses that they supplied packhorses to the white traders during the height of the deerskin trade (Hatley 1989:236; Mooney 1975:26).

Although the Cherokee population became more dispersed during the Late Qualla phase, the town house continued to be the focus of public and ceremonial activities. And many of these town houses continued to be used and rebuilt at the same locations long after the surrounding villages had been abandoned. Moreover, the religious and ceremonial realms of Cherokee culture retained their traditional form and practice throughout Late Qualla times, even though many other aspects of daily life changed to accommodate newly introduced European goods and customs.

The Contact Period along the North Carolina Coast

Although the first European footprints on North Carolina soil were made by Spaniards, the first settlements were made by Englishmen. Sir Walter Raleigh's failed attempts to establish a colony on Roanoke Island between 1584 and 1590 represent the beginning of English colonization in the New World. The successful settlement at Jamestown on the lower James River in 1607 gave the English the toehold they needed to expand into new territories. However, even with the establishment of Jamestown, North Carolina's Indians were given a fifty-year respite before having to deal with the English again.

Around 1650, Virginia settlers began to push into the Albemarle region of northeastern North Carolina. By 1655, Nathaniel Batts had built a house on the west end of Albemarle Sound and had begun trading with the local Indians. By 1663, when the colony of Carolina was established, some 500 white settlers occupied the area between Albemarle Sound and the Virginia border (Powell 1989:52).

In 1662, Captain William Hilton explored the lower Cape Fear region looking for a suitable location for a settlement. He was dispatched by a group of Massachusetts Bay Puritans who wanted to move to a warmer climate. Acting on Hilton's advice, they established a small settlement on Cape Fear River in the winter of 1663. The Puritan settlement was short-lived and unpleasant. They departed abruptly, leaving a warning message at the point of the cape that advised others to stay away (Lee 1971:4–5).

Ignoring the Puritans' warning, a group of English colonists from Barbados established a small settlement on the west bank of Cape Fear River in 1664. This settlement thrived for a few years with as many as 800 inhabitants, but it too was doomed to failure. By 1667, the Cape Fear area was once again left to its native inhabitants (Lee 1971:5–6). Although Charles Town was a thriving port that served the southern portion of the Carolina colony after 1670, no further attempts were made to settle the lower Cape Fear until after the Tuscarora Indian War in the early 1700s (Gray 1997:71).

Meanwhile, the Albemarle region thrived as small farmers and merchants moved from southern tidewater Virginia onto the fertile sandy soils of northeastern North Carolina. At first these settlers faced few threats from the natives whose lands they encroached upon. However, in 1675 hostilities between Indians and whites spread throughout the English colonies and erupted in Albemarle County as the Chowanoc War. After a couple of years, the firearms of the colonists brought the Chowanoc to defeat, and those who survived were moved to a reservation located on Bennetts Creek in what is now Gates County (Lee 1963:16).

For the most part, the settlers of the Albemarle did not venture very far inland. They chose instead to find new lands and opportunities by spreading southward and staying near the coast. By 1675, the southern shore of Albemarle Sound was settled, and by 1691, newcomers were starting to settle along Pamlico River. The area of the Neuse was settled shortly after the beginning of the eighteenth century (Lee 1963).

The rapid encroachment of settlers on the territory south of the Albemarle sowed the seeds for the Tuscarora War, the worst conflict ever between colonists and natives. The North Carolina colonists were instructed by the Lords Proprietors to deal with the Indians as they saw fit, and they often appropriated tribal lands with little or no compensation in exchange. Resentment grew as prized hunting territories were declared off-limits to Indians who for countless generations had reaped their bounty. But land-grabbing was only part of the story. Though illegal, a lively trade in Indian slaves was carried out from Virginia to South Carolina. Charles Town, the center of the fur trade, was also the center of the native slave trade. Many Indian slaves were shipped to the West Indies, while others were traded throughout the colonies. In addition to this reckless disregard for Indian land and Indian freedom, many traders also lacked honesty and fairness in their everyday dealings with the Indians (Boyce 1973:16).

Relations became so bad that the Tuscaroras asked permission to leave North Carolina and move to Pennsylvania. Pennsylvania authorities agreed to the move, but only if the North Carolina government would agree to certify the past good behavior of the Tuscaroras. This certification was not granted. Left with little choice, the Indians turned to violence in an attempt to rectify what they perceived as an unbearable state of relations with the North Carolina colonists.

The Tuscaroras attacked on the morning of September 22, 1711, killing 130 colonists who lived along the Neuse and Pamlico Rivers. Most of the warriors were from southern or lower Tuscarora villages, and they were aided by several smaller tribes in the Neuse-Pamlico area. The northern Tuscarora villages remained neutral during the conflict, which lasted some three and a half years. In the end, 200 whites and nearly 1,000 Indians had been killed, and an equal number of Indians had been sold into slavery. Of those who were left, some 3,500 were forced from their homes. Most of these people emigrated north to Pennsylvania and New York (Boyce 1973:15; Lee 1963:23).

Although recent archaeological excavations have been conducted at Contact period sites on the coast and Coastal Plain, in general, the results of much of this research have not been reported at the time of this writing. At a site on Hatteras Island near Buxton, David Phelps has uncovered large numbers of European trade artifacts from an Algonkian village thought to be Croatan, the capital of the Croatan chiefdom.

The Amity site (31Hy43), excavated by Paul Gardner, also produced European trade artifacts. These consisted primarily of glass beads, pipe fragments, and a few glass arrow points. The site, located east of Lake Mattamuskeet, was originally thought to represent the remains of the village of Pomeiock. However, excavations revealed a small farmstead, comprised of two to three houses, that dated to the middle of the seventeenth century and not the end of the sixteenth century, when Pomeiock existed (Gardner 1990).

For the past several years, archaeologists from East Carolina University have focused their research on the historic Tuscarora. In addition to David Phelps's seminal work in the Coastal Plain, John Byrd has recently completed an intensive survey of the Contentnea Creek drainage in Greene County. This work has allowed Byrd to identify five of the six Historic Tuscarora communities reported to have been located along Contentnea Creek. These communities consisted mostly of scattered hamlets or farmsteads. Byrd (1996, 1997) estimates the Contentnea Creek population to have been around 5,000 individuals in 1712. The total Tuscarora population is believed to have been around 8,000.

During the Tuscarora War, the Tuscaroras built at least a dozen forts to protect individuals living in the dispersed hamlets. One of these, Neoheroka Fort (31Gr4), has been partially excavated by East Carolina archaeologists. Located near Snow Hill in Greene County, this was the last of the Tuscarora forts to be captured by the colonists. Excavations inside the fort have revealed a maze of bunkerlike structures interconnected by a series of tunnels. Archaeologists also found abundant supplies of foodstuffs, consisting primarily of corn, beans, and other plant foods. Relatively few animal food remains were found (Byrd 1997:7).

Pottery-making, subsistence, and patterns of settlement do not seem to have changed much during the first part of the Contact period. Ceramics similar to those of the Cashie, Colington, and White Oak/Oak Island phases of the Tidewater and Coastal Plain continued to be made. Longhouses were still constructed, and a mixed economy based on hunting, gathering, fishing, shellfishing, and agriculture continued after the first colonists arrived.

However, aboriginal life was rapidly disrupted as more outsiders moved in. Warfare, slavery, and epidemic diseases combined to decimate first the natives living near the coast and then those who lived within the interior Coastal Plain. In 1701, John Lawson observed that the coastal tribes were "very much decreas'd . . . and all other Nations of *Indians* are observ'd to partake of the same Fate, where the *Europeans* come" (Lefler 1967:17).

Summary

The Contact period was a time of sweeping and often devastating change among native cultures across North Carolina. Many thousands of people fell victim to war and disease, and many more were caught up in a firestorm of cultural change and disruption brought on by contacts with Europeans. However, North Carolina today is the home of the largest Native American population east of the Mississippi River. Some 85,000 individuals representing six recognized tribes and organizations are spread throughout the state, from the coast to the mountains. And much of the robust cultural diversity seen in the archaeological record of the last 12,000 years survives today in the tribal traditions of North Carolina's native peoples.

References Cited

Alvord, Clarence W., and Lee Bidgood, eds. 1912. *The First Explorations of the Trans-Allegheny Region by the Virginians, 1650–1674.* Cleveland: Arthur H. Clark Co.

Anderson, David G. 1989. "The Mississippian in South Carolina." In *Studies in South Carolina Archaeology: Essays in Honor of Robert L. Stephenson*, edited by Albert C. Goodyear III and Glen T. Hanson, 101–32. Anthropological Studies 9. Columbia: Institute of Archaeology and Anthropology, University of South Carolina.

———. 1990. "The Paleoindian Colonization of Eastern North America: A View from the Southeastern United States." In *Early Paleoindian Economies of Eastern North America*, edited by Barry Isaac and Kenneth Tankersley, 163–216. Research in Economic Anthropology, Supplement 5. Greenwich, Conn.: JAI Press.

———. 1994. *The Savannah River Chiefdoms: Political Change in the Late Prehistoric Southeast.* Tuscaloosa: University of Alabama Press.

———. 1995. "Paleoindian Interaction Networks in the Eastern Woodlands." In *Native American Interaction: Multiscalar Analyses and Interpretations in the Eastern Woodlands*, edited by Michael S. Nassaney and Kenneth E. Sassaman, 3–26. Knoxville: University of Tennessee Press.

Anderson, David G., and Glen T. Hanson. 1988. "Early Archaic Settlement in the Southeastern United States: A Case Study from the Savannah River Valley." *American Antiquity* 53:262–86.

Anderson, David G., David J. Hally, and James L. Rudolph. 1986. "The Mississippian Occupation of the Savannah River Valley." *Southeastern Archaeology* 5, no. 1:32–51.

Ayers, Harvard G., L. J. Loucks, and B. L. Purrington. 1980. "Excavations at the Ward Site, a Pisgah Village in Western North Carolina." Paper presented at the 37th Southeastern Archaeological Conference, New Orleans.

Baker, C. Michael, and Linda G. Hall. 1990. "The Bent Creek Archaeological Site: A Woodland Tradition Settlement within the French Broad River Basin." Ms. on file, Baker and Hall, Weaverville, North Carolina.

———. 1992. "Archaeological Testing of Three Buried Prehistoric Sites along the Swannanoa River in Central Buncombe County, North Carolina." Ms. on file, North Carolina Office of State Archaeology, Raleigh.

Bass, Quentin R. 1977. "Prehistoric Settlement and Subsistence Patterns in the Great Smoky Mountains." Master's thesis, Department of Anthropology, University of Tennessee, Knoxville.

Beck, Robin A., Jr. 1997. "From Joara to Chiaha: Spanish Exploration of the Appalachian Summit Area, 1540–1568." *Southeastern Archaeology* 16:162–69.

Binford, Lewis R. 1980. "Willow Smoke and Dogs' Tails: Hunter-Gatherer Settlement Systems and Archaeological Site Formation." *American Antiquity* 45:4–20.

Blakely, Robert L., and Bettina Detweiler-Blakely. 1989. "The Impact of European Diseases in the Sixteenth-Century Southeast: A Case Study." *Midcontinental Journal of Archaeology* 14:62–89.

Blaker, Margaret C. 1952. "Further Comments on Simple-Stamped Shell-Tempered Pottery." *American Antiquity* 17:257–58.

Blanton, Dennis B., and Kenneth E. Sassaman. 1989. "Pattern and Process in the Middle Archaic Period of South Carolina." In *Studies in South Carolina Archaeology: Essays in Honor of Robert L. Stephenson*, edited by Albert C. Goodyear III and Glen T. Hanson, 53–72. Anthropological Studies 9. Columbia: Institute of Archaeology and Anthropology, University of South Carolina.

Blanton, Dennis B., Christopher T. Espenshade, and Paul E. Brockington Jr. 1986. "An Archaeological Study of 38Su83: A Yadkin Phase Site in the Upper Coastal Plain of South Carolina." Ms. on file, Garrow and Associates, Inc., Atlanta, Georgia.

Boyce, Douglas W. 1973. "Tuscarora Political Organization, Ethnic Identity, and Sociohistorical Demography, 1711–1825." Ph.D. dissertation, Department of Anthropology, University of North Carolina, Chapel Hill.

Boyd, C. Clifford, Jr., and Gerald F. Schroedl. 1987. "In Search of Coosa." *American Antiquity* 52:840–44.

Brain, Jeffrey P. 1985. "Introduction: Update of De Soto Studies Since the United States De Soto Expedition Commission Report." In *Final Report of the United States De Soto Expedition Commission*, by John R. Swanton, xi–lxxii. Washington, D.C.: Smithsonian Institution Press.

Brose, David S. 1978. "Comments." *Current Anthropology* 19:729–31.

———. 1979. "An Interpretation of the Hopewellian Traits in Florida." In *Hopewell Archaeology*, edited by David S. Brose and N'omi Greber, 141–49. Kent, Ohio: Kent State University Press.

Broyles, Bettye J. 1966. "Preliminary Report: The St. Albans Site (46Ka27), Kanawha County, West Virginia." *West Virginia Archaeologist* 19:1–43.

———. 1971. *Second Preliminary Report: The St. Albans Site, Kanawha County, West Virginia*. Report of Archaeological Investigations no. 3. Morgantown: West Virginia Geological and Economic Survey.

Byrd, John E. 1996. "Preliminary Report of the Archaeological Survey of the Contentnea Creek Drainage." Report submitted to the Office of State Archaeology, North Carolina Division of Archives and History, Raleigh.

———. 1997. *Tuscarora Subsistence Practices in the Late Woodland Period: The Zooarchaeology of the Jordan's Landing Site*. North Carolina Archaeological Council Publication no. 27. [Raleigh]: North Carolina Archaeological Council.

Caldwell, Joseph R. 1955. "Investigations at Rood's Landing, Stewart County, Georgia." *Early Georgia* 2, no. 1:22–47.

———. 1958. *Trend and Tradition in the Prehistory of the Eastern United States*. American Anthropological Association Memoir no. 88. [Menasha, Wisc.]: American Anthropological Association.

Caldwell, Joseph, and Catherine McCann. 1941. *The Irene Mound Site*. Athens: University of Georgia Press.

Chapman, Jefferson. 1973. *The Icehouse Bottom Site—40Mr23*. Report of Investigations no. 13. Knoxville: Department of Anthropology, University of Tennessee.
———. 1975. *The Rose Island Site and the Bifurcate Tradition*. Report of Investigations no. 14. Knoxville: Department of Anthropology, University of Tennessee.
———. 1976. "Some Thoughts on Early Archaic Settlement and Subsistence Patterns in the Lower Little Tennessee River Valley." Paper presented at the 33rd Annual Meeting of the Southeastern Archaeological Conference, Tuscaloosa.
———. 1977. *Archaic Period Research in the Lower Little Tennessee River Valley—1975: Icehouse Bottom, Harrison Branch, Thirty Acre Island, Calloway Island*. Report of Investigations no. 18. Knoxville: Department of Anthropology, University of Tennessee.
———. 1978. *The Bacon Farm Site and a Buried Site Reconnaissance*. Report of Investigations no. 23. Knoxville: Department of Anthropology, University of Tennessee.
———. 1980. "The Jones Ferry Site (40Mr76)." In *The 1979 Archaeological and Geological Investigations in the Tellico Reservoir*, edited by Jefferson Chapman, 43–58. Report of Investigations no. 29. Knoxville: Department of Anthropology, University of Tennessee.
———. 1981. *The Bacon Bend and Iddins Sites: The Late Archaic Period in the Lower Little Tennessee River Valley*. Report of Investigations no. 31. Knoxville: Department of Anthropology, University of Tennessee.
———. 1985. *Tellico Archaeology*. Report of Investigations no. 43. Knoxville: Department of Anthropology, University of Tennessee.
Chapman, Jefferson, and James Adovasio. 1977. "Textile and Basketry Impressions from Icehouse Bottom, Tennessee." *American Antiquity* 42:620–25.
Chapman, Jefferson, and Bennie C. Keel. 1979. "Candy Creek–Connestee Components in Eastern Tennessee and Western North Carolina and Their Relationship with Adena-Hopewell." In *Hopewell Archaeology*, edited by David S. Brose and N'omi Greber, 157–61. Kent, Ohio: Kent State University Press.
Chapman, Jefferson, and Andrea B. Shea. 1981. "The Archaeobotanical Record: Early Archaic Period to Contact in the Lower Little Tennessee River Valley." *Tennessee Anthropologist* 6:61–84.
Claflin, William H., Jr. 1931. *The Stallings Island Mound, Columbia County, Georgia*. Papers of the Peabody Museum of American Archaeology and Ethnology, vol. 14, no. 41, Harvard University, Cambridge.
Claggett, Stephen R., and John S. Cable. 1982. *The Haw River Sites: Archaeological Investigations at Two Stratified Sites in the North Carolina Piedmont*. Report R-2386. Jackson, Mich.: Commonwealth Associates, Inc.
Clausen, C. J., A. D. Cohen, C. Emeliani, J. A. Holman, and J. J. Stipp. 1979. "Little Salt Spring, Florida: A Unique Underwater Site." *Science* 203:609–14.
Coe, Joffre L. 1934. "Planning an Archaeological Survey of North Carolina." *Bulletin of the Archaeological Society of North Carolina* 1, no. 2:11–14.
———. 1937. "Keyauwee—a Preliminary Statement." *Bulletin of the Archaeological Society of North Carolina* 4, no. 1:8–16.
———. 1949. "Excavating in a Parking Lot at Morrow Mountain State Park." *Southern Indian Studies* 1, no. 1:20–21.

———. 1952. "The Cultural Sequence of the Carolina Piedmont." In *Archaeology of the Eastern United States*, edited by James B. Griffin, 301–11. Chicago: University of Chicago Press.

———. 1964. *The Formative Cultures of the Carolina Piedmont*. Transactions of the American Philosophical Society, n.s., 54, pt. 5. Philadelphia, Pa.: American Philosophical Society.

———. 1965. "The Ecological and Cultural Base of the Cherokee Nation." Proposal submitted by the Research Laboratories of Anthropology to the National Science Foundation, Ms. on file, Research Laboratories of Archaeology, University of North Carolina, Chapel Hill.

———. 1983. "Through a Glass Darkly: An Archaeological View of North Carolina's More Distant Past." In *The Prehistory of North Carolina: An Archaeological Symposium*, edited by Mark Mathis and Jeffrey J. Crow, 161–77. Raleigh: North Carolina Division of Archives and History.

———. 1995. *Town Creek Indian Mound: A Native American Legacy*. Chapel Hill: University of North Carolina Press.

Coe, Joffre L., and Bennie C. Keel. 1965. "Two Cherokee Houses in Western North Carolina." Paper presented at the 30th Annual Meeting of the Society for American Archaeology, Urbana, Illinois.

Coe, Joffre L., and Ernest Lewis. 1952. "Dan River Series Statement." In *Prehistoric Pottery of the Eastern United States*, edited by James B. Griffin. Ann Arbor: Museum of Anthropology, University of Michigan.

Coe, Joffre L., H. T. Ward, M. Graham, L. Navey, H. Hogue, and J. H. Wilson Jr. 1982. "Archaeological and Paleo-osteological Investigations at the Cold Morning Site, New Hanover County, North Carolina." Report prepared for the Interagency Archeological Services (Atlanta) by the Research Laboratories of Anthropology, University of North Carolina, Chapel Hill.

Coleman, Gary N., and Richard P. Gravely Jr. 1992. "Archaeological Investigations at the Koehler Site (44Hr6)." *Quarterly Bulletin of the Archeological Society of Virginia* 47:1–41.

Crawford, Robert G. H. 1966. "An Archaeological Survey of Lenoir County, North Carolina." Master's thesis, Department of Anthropology, University of Florida, Gainesville.

Cridlebaugh, Patricia A. 1981. *The Icehouse Bottom Site (40Mr23): 1977 Excavations*. Report of Investigations no. 35. Knoxville: Department of Anthropology, University of Tennessee.

Cumming, William P., ed. 1958. *The Discoveries of John Lederer*. Charlottesville: University Press of Virginia.

Daniel, I. Randolph, Jr. 1994. "Hardaway Revisited: Early Archaic Settlement in the Southeast." Ph.D. dissertation, Department of Anthropology, University of North Carolina, Chapel Hill.

———. 1998. *Hardaway Revisited: Early Archaic Settlement in the Southeast*. Tuscaloosa: University of Alabama Press.

Daniel, I. Randolph, Jr., and J. Robert Butler. 1991. "Rhyolite Sources in the Carolina Slate Belt, Central North Carolina." *Current Research in the Pleistocene* 8:64–66.

———. 1994. "Rhyolite Sources in the Uwharrie Mountains, Central North Carolina." In "Hardaway Revisited: Early Archaic Settlement in the Southeast," by I. Randolph Daniel Jr., 286–323. Ph.D. dissertation, Department of Anthropology, University of North Carolina, Chapel Hill.
Daniel, I. Randolph, Jr., and R. P. Stephen Davis Jr. 1996. "Projectile Point Classification Project: The Classification of Projectile Points in Existing Archaeological Collections from North Carolina (Phase II)." Report submitted to the North Carolina Division of Archives and History, Raleigh.
Davis, John D. 1987. "Early Woodland of the North Carolina Piedmont: New Information from the E. Davis Site." Paper presented at the 44th Annual Meeting of the Southeastern Archaeological Conference, Charleston, South Carolina.
Davis, R. P. Stephen, Jr. 1990. *Aboriginal Settlement Patterns in the Little Tennessee River Valley*. Report of Investigations no. 50. Knoxville: Department of Anthropology, University of Tennessee.
Davis, R. P. Stephen, Jr., and I. Randolph Daniel Jr. 1990. "Projectile Point Classification Project: The Classification of Projectile Points in Existing Archaeological Collections from North Carolina." Report submitted to the North Carolina Division of Archives and History, Raleigh.
Davis, R. P. Stephen, Jr., Jane M. Eastman, Thomas O. Maher, and Richard P. Gravely Jr. 1997a. *Archaeological Investigations at the Stockton Site, Henry County, Virginia*. Research Report no. 14. Chapel Hill: Research Laboratories of Archaeology, University of North Carolina.
———. 1997b. *Archaeological Investigations at the Belmont Site, Henry County, Virginia*. Research Report no. 15. Chapel Hill: Research Laboratories of Archaeology, University of North Carolina.
Davis, R. P. Stephen, Jr., and H. Trawick Ward. 1987. "A Comparison of Plowzone and In Situ Site Structure at the Fredricks Site, a Siouan Village in Piedmont North Carolina." Paper presented at the 44th Annual Meeting of the Southeastern Archaeological Conference, Charleston, South Carolina.
———. 1989. "The Evolution of Siouan Communities in Piedmont North Carolina." Paper presented at the 46th Annual Meeting of the Southeastern Archaeological Conference, Tampa.
———. 1991. "The Evolution of Siouan Communities in Piedmont North Carolina." *Southeastern Archaeology* 10, no. 1:40–53.
———. 1998. "The Occaneechi and Their Role as Middlemen in the Seventeenth-Century Virginia–North Carolina Trade Network." In *Excavating Occaneechi Town: Archaeology of an Eighteenth-Century Indian Village in North Carolina*, edited by R. P. Stephen Davis Jr., Patrick C. Livingood, H. Trawick Ward, and Vincas P. Steponaitis, 244–49. CD-ROM. Chapel Hill: University of North Carolina Press.
Davis, Thomas W., and Kathleen M. Child. 1996. "Phase III Data Recovery at Site 31ON536 and Phase II Evaluation of the Prehistoric Component at Site 31ON534, Marine Corps Base Camp Lejeune, North Carolina." Ms. on file, North Carolina Division of Archives and History, Raleigh.
DeBoer, Warren R. 1988. "Subterranean Storage and the Organization of Surplus: The View from Eastern North America." *Southeastern Archaeology* 7:1–20.

DeJarnette, David L., Edward B. Kurjack, and James W. Cambron. 1962. "Stanfield-Worley Bluff Shelter Excavations." *Journal of Alabama Archaeology* 8, nos. 1–2.

Delcourt, Paul A., and Hazel R. Delcourt. 1979. "Late Pleistocene and Holocene Distributional History of the Deciduous Forest in the Southeastern United States." *Veroffentlichungen Geobotanischen Institutes der ETH, Stiftung Rubel (Zurich)* 68:79–107.

———. 1981. "Vegetation Maps for Eastern North America: 40,000 Years B.P. to Present." In *Geobotany: An Integrating Experience*, edited by R. Romans, 123–66. New York: Plenum Press.

———. 1983. "Late Quaternary Paleoclimates and Biotic Responses in Eastern North America and the Western North Atlantic Ocean." *Palaeogeography, Palaeoclimatology, Palaeoecology* 48:263–84.

DePratter, Chester B. 1983. "Late Prehistoric and Early Historic Chiefdoms in the Southeastern United States." Ph.D. dissertation, Department of Anthropology, University of Georgia, Athens.

DePratter, Chester B., Charles M. Hudson, and Marvin T. Smith. 1983. "The Route of Juan Pardo's Explorations in the Interior Southeast, 1566–1568." *Florida Historical Quarterly* 62:125–58.

———. 1990. "The Juan Pardo Expeditions: North from Santa Elena." *Southeastern Archaeology* 9: 140–46.

Dickens, Roy S., Jr. 1967. "A Note on Cherokee House Construction." *Southern Indian Studies* 19:35.

———. 1970. "The Pisgah Culture and Its Place in the Prehistory of the Southern Appalachians." Ph.D. dissertation, Department of Anthropology, University of North Carolina, Chapel Hill.

———. 1976. *Cherokee Prehistory: The Pisgah Phase in the Appalachian Summit Region*. Knoxville: University of Tennessee Press.

———. 1978. "Mississippian Settlement Patterns in the Appalachian Summit Area: The Pisgah and Qualla Phases." In *Mississippian Settlement Patterns*, edited by Bruce D. Smith, 115–39. New York: Academic Press.

———. 1979. "The Origins and Development of Cherokee Culture." In *The Cherokee Indian Nation: A Troubled History*, edited by Duane H. King, 3–32. Knoxville: University of Tennessee Press.

———. 1980. "Preliminary Report on Archaeological Investigations at the Plum Grove Site (40Wg17), Washington County, Tennessee." Ms. on file, Research Laboratories of Anthropology, University of North Carolina, Chapel Hill.

Dickens, Roy S., Jr., H. Trawick Ward, and R. P. Stephen Davis Jr., eds. 1987. *The Siouan Project: Seasons I and II*. Monograph Series no. 1. Chapel Hill: Research Laboratories of Anthropology, University of North Carolina.

Dillehay, Tom D. 1997. *Monte Verde: A Late Pleistocene Settlement in Chile*. Washington, D.C.: Smithsonian Institution Press.

Dobyns, Henry F. 1983. *Their Numbers Become Thinned: Native American Population Dynamics in Eastern North America*. Knoxville: University of Tennessee Press.

Dorwin, John T., Robert N. Tiger III, and E. Marian Bistline. 1975. "Upper Hiwassee River Survey: 1974–1975." Ms. on file, Department of Sociology and Anthropology, Western Carolina University, Cullowhee.

Drye, Carmen M. 1998. "An Analysis and Interpretation of the Archaic Projectile Point Sequence from Lowder's Ferry, Stanly County, North Carolina." *North Carolina Archaeology* 47:34–65.

Eastman, Jane M. 1994a. "The North Carolina Radiocarbon Date Study (Part 1)." *Southern Indian Studies* 42.

———. 1994b. "The North Carolina Radiocarbon Date Study (Part 2)." *Southern Indian Studies* 43.

———. 1996. "Searching for Ritual: A Contextual Study of Roasting Pits at Upper Saratown." Paper presented at the 53rd Annual Meeting of the Southeastern Archaeological Conference, Birmingham, Alabama.

Eastman, Jane M., Loretta Lautzenheiser, and Mary Ann Holm. 1997. "A Reevaluation of Ceramics from the Tower Hill Site (31LR1), Lenoir County, North Carolina." *North Carolina Archaeology* 46:109–20.

Egloff, Brian J. 1967. "An Analysis of Ceramics from Cherokee Towns." Master's thesis, Department of Anthropology, University of North Carolina, Chapel Hill.

Egloff, Keith T. 1971. "Methods and Problems of Mound Exploration in the Southern Appalachian Area." Master's thesis, Department of Anthropology, University of North Carolina, Chapel Hill.

———. 1981. "Ceramics of Coastal Virginia." Ms. on file, Virginia Research Center for Archaeology, Richmond.

———. 1985. "Spheres of Cultural Interaction across the Coastal Plain of Virginia in the Woodland Period." In *Structure and Process in Southeastern Archaeology*, edited by Roy S. Dickens Jr. and H. Trawick Ward, 229–42. Tuscaloosa: University of Alabama Press.

Evans, Clifford. 1955. *A Ceramic Study of Virginia Archeology*. Bureau of American Ethnology Bulletin no. 160. Washington, D.C.: Smithsonian Institution.

Farmer, Brenna. 1997. "The Prehistory of Cherokee and Clay Counties in the Appalachian Summit Region of Western North Carolina." Ms. on file, Research Laboratories of Archaeology, University of North Carolina, Chapel Hill.

Faulkner, Charles H. 1977. "The Winter House: An Early Southeast Tradition." *Midcontinental Journal of Archaeology* 2:141–59.

Ferguson, Leland G. 1971. *South Appalachian Mississippian*. Ph.D. dissertation, Department of Anthropology, University of North Carolina, Chapel Hill.

Figgins, Jesse D. 1927. "The Antiquity of Man in America." *Natural History* 27, no. 3:229–39.

Ford, James A., and Gordon R. Willey. 1941. "An Interpretation of the Prehistory of the Eastern United States." *American Anthropologist* 43, no. 3:325–63.

Futato, Eugene M. 1983. *Archaeological Investigations in the Cedar Creek and Upper Bear Creek Reservoirs*. Report of Investigations no. 13. Tuscaloosa: Office of Archaeological Research, University of Alabama.

Gardner, Paul S. 1990. *Excavations at the Amity Site: Final Report of the Pomeiooc Project: 1984–1989*. Archaeological Research Report no. 7. Greenville, N.C.: Archaeology Laboratory, East Carolina University.

Gardner, William M. 1974. *The Flint Run Paleoindian Complex: A Preliminary Report 1971 through 1973 Seasons*. Occasional Paper no. 1. Washington, D.C.: Archaeology Laboratory, Catholic University of America.

Gardner, William M., and R. Verrey. 1979. "Typology and Chronology of Fluted Points from the Flint Run Area." *Pennsylvania Archaeologist* 49:13–45.

Gilbert, William H., Jr. 1943. "The Eastern Cherokees." *Bureau of American Ethnology Bulletin* 133:169–413.

Goodyear, Albert C., III. 1974. *The Brand Site: A Techno-Functional Study of a Dalton Site in Northeast Arkansas.* Arkansas Archeological Survey Research Series, no. 7. Fayetteville: Arkansas Archeological Survey.

———. 1982. "The Chronological Position of the Dalton Horizon in the Southeastern United States." *American Antiquity* 47:382–95.

———. 1989. "Late Pleistocene Peoples of the Southeast United States." Paper presented at the First World Summit on the Peopling of the Americas, Orono, Maine.

Goodyear, Albert C., III, James L. Michie, and Tommy Charles. 1989. "The Earliest South Carolinians." In *Studies in South Carolina Archaeology: Essays in Honor of Robert L. Stephenson*, edited by Albert C. Goodyear III and Glen T. Hanson, 19–52. Anthropological Studies 9. Columbia: Institute of Archaeology and Anthropology, University of South Carolina.

Graham, Russell W., C. Vance Haynes, D. Johnson, and Marvin Kay. 1981. "Kimmswick: A Clovis-Mastodon Association in Eastern Missouri." *Science* 213:1115–17.

Gravely, Richard P., Jr. 1969. "The Madison Cemetery." *Eastern States Archaeological Federation Bulletin* 27:11.

———. 1983. "Prehistory in the Upper Dan River Drainage System." In *Piedmont Archaeology: Recent Research and Results*, edited by J. Mark Wittkofski and Lyle E. Browning, 118–24. Special Publication no. 10. [Richmond]: Archeological Society of Virginia.

Gray, Anna L. 1997. "Return to the Port of Brunswick: An Analysis of Two Eighteenth-Century North Carolina Sites." *North Carolina Archaeology* 46:69–83.

Gremillion, Kristen J. 1987. "Plant Remains from the Fredricks, Wall, and Mitchum Sites." In *The Siouan Project: Seasons I and II*, edited by Roy S. Dickens Jr., H. Trawick Ward, and R. P. Stephen Davis Jr., 185–215. Monograph Series no. 1. Chapel Hill: Research Laboratories of Anthropology, University of North Carolina.

———. 1989. "Late Prehistoric and Historic Period Paleoethnobotany of the North Carolina Piedmont." Ph.D. dissertation, Department of Anthropology, University of North Carolina, Chapel Hill.

———. 1993. "Adoption of Old World Crops and Processes of Cultural Change in the Historic Southeast." *Southeastern Archaeology* 12:15–20.

———. 1995. "Comparative Paleoethnobotany of Three Native Southeastern Communities of the Historic Period." *Southeastern Archaeology* 14:1–16.

Griffin, James B. 1946. "Cultural Change and Continuity in Eastern United States Archaeology." In *Man in Northeastern North America*, edited by Frederick Johnson, 37–95. Andover, Mass.: Robert S. Peabody Foundation for Archaeology.

———. 1952. "Culture Periods in Eastern United States Archeology." In *Archeology of Eastern United States*, edited by James B. Griffin, 352–64. Chicago: University of Chicago Press.

———. 1966. *The Fort Ancient Aspect: Its Cultural and Chronological Position in Mississippi*

Valley Archaeology. Anthropological Papers, no. 28. Ann Arbor: Museum of Anthropology, University of Michigan.

———. 1967. "Eastern North American Archaeology: A Summary." *Science* 156:175–91.

———. 1985. "Epilogue: Joffre Lanning Coe: The Quiet Giant of Southeastern Archaeology." In *Structure and Process in Southeastern Archaeology*, edited by Roy S. Dickens Jr. and H. Trawick Ward, 287–304. Tuscaloosa: University of Alabama Press.

Griffin, John W. 1974. *Investigations in Russell Cave*. Publications in Archeology no. 13. Washington, D.C.: National Park Service, U.S. Department of the Interior.

Haag, William G. 1958. *The Archaeology of Coastal North Carolina*. Coastal Studies Series 2. Baton Rouge: Louisiana State University.

Hall, Linda G., and C. Michael Baker. 1993. "Data Recovery at 31Bn175, the Biltmore Estate, Buncombe County, North Carolina." Ms. on file, North Carolina Office of State Archaeology, Raleigh.

Hally, David J. 1986. "The Cherokee Archaeology of Georgia." In *The Conference on Cherokee Prehistory*, assembled by David G. Moore, 95–121. Swannanoa, N.C.: Warren Wilson College.

———. 1994. "An Overview of Lamar Culture." In *Ocmulgee Archaeology, 1936–1986*, edited by David J. Hally, 144–74. Athens: University of Georgia Press.

———. 1996. "Platform-Mound Construction and the Instability of Mississippian Chiefdoms." In *Political Structure and Change in the Prehistoric Southeastern United States*, edited by John F. Scarry, 92–127. Gainesville: University Press of Florida.

Hammett, Julia E. 1987. "Shell Artifacts from the Carolina Piedmont." In *The Siouan Project: Seasons I and II*, edited by Roy S. Dickens Jr., H. Trawick Ward, and R. P. Stephen Davis Jr., 167–83. Monograph Series no. 1. Chapel Hill: Research Laboratories of Anthropology, University of North Carolina.

Hargrove, Thomas. 1993. "Archaeological Excavations at 31NH142, Hamp's Landing, River Road Park, New Hanover County, North Carolina." Report submitted to New Hanover County Department of Parks and Recreation, Wilmington, North Carolina.

Hargrove, Thomas, and Jane M. Eastman. 1997. "Limestone- or Marl-Tempered Ceramics from the Lower Cape Fear River Region, New Hanover County, North Carolina." *North Carolina Archaeology* 46:91–108.

Harrington, J. C. 1948. "Plain Stamped, Shell Tempered Pottery from North Carolina." *American Antiquity* 13:251–52.

———. 1962. *Search for the Cittie of Ralegh: Archeological Excavations at Fort Raleigh National Historic Site, North Carolina*. Archaeological Research Series 6. Washington, D.C.: National Park Service.

Harrington, M. R. 1922. "Cherokee and Earlier Remains on Upper Tennessee River." *Indian Notes and Monographs*. New York: Museum of the American Indian, Heye Foundation.

Hatley, M. Thomas. 1989. "The Three Lives of Keowee: Loss and Recovery in Eighteenth-Century Cherokee Villages." In *Powhatan's Mantle: Indians in the Colonial Southeast*, edited by Peter H. Wood, Gregory A. Waselkov, and M. Thomas Hatley, 223–48. Lincoln: University of Nebraska Press.

Heite, Edward F. 1973. "A Seventeenth Century Trash Dump in Northhampton Co., Virginia." *Quarterly Bulletin of the Archeological Society of Virginia* 28, no. 2:80–86.
Henige, David. 1989. "On the Current Devaluation of the Notion of Evidence: A Rejoinder to Dobyns." *Ethnohistory* 36:304–7.
Herbert, Joseph M. 1997. "Refining Prehistoric Culture Chronology in Southern Coastal North Carolina: Pottery from the Papanow and Pond Trail Sites." Report submitted to the North Carolina Division of Archives and History, Raleigh.
Herbert, Joseph M., and Mark A. Mathis. 1996. "An Appraisal and Re-evaluation of the Prehistoric Pottery Sequence of Southern Coastal North Carolina." In *Prehistoric Ceramics of the Carolinas*, edited by David G. Anderson. Columbia: South Carolina Department of Archives and History.
Heye, George G. 1919. "Certain Mounds in Haywood County, North Carolina." *Contributions from the Museum of the American Indian, Heye Foundation* 5, no. 3:35–43.
Heye, George G., F. W. Hodge, and G. H. Pepper. 1918. "The Nacoochee Mound in Georgia." *Contributions from the Museum of the American Indian, Heye Foundation* 2, no. 1.
Hoffman, Paul E. 1994. "Lucas Vázquez de Ayllón's Discovery and Colony." In *The Forgotten Centuries: Indians and Europeans in the American South, 1521–1704*, edited by Charles H. Hudson and Carmen Chaves Tesser, 36–49. Athens: University of Georgia Press.
Hogue, Homes. 1977. "Analyzing Ossuary Skeletal Remains: Techniques and Problems." *Southern Indian Studies* 29:1–22.
Holden, Patricia P. 1966. "An Archaeological Survey of Transylvania County, North Carolina." Master's thesis, Department of Anthropology, University of North Carolina, Chapel Hill.
Holm, Mary Ann. 1987. "Faunal Remains from the Wall and Fredricks Sites." In *The Siouan Project: Seasons I and II*, edited by Roy S. Dickens Jr., H. Trawick Ward, and R. P. Stephen Davis Jr., 237–58. Monograph Series no. 1. Chapel Hill: Research Laboratories of Anthropology, University of North Carolina.
———. 1994. "Continuity and Change: The Zooarchaeology of Aboriginal Sites in the North Carolina Piedmont." Ph.D. dissertation, Department of Anthropology, University of North Carolina, Chapel Hill.
Holmes, J. A. 1883. "Indian Mounds of the Cape Fear." *Weekly Star* (Wilmington, North Carolina). Reprinted in *Southern Indian Studies* 18:48–54, 1966.
Holmes, William H. 1884. "Illustrated Catalogue of a Portion of the Collections Made by the Bureau of Ethnology during the Field Season of 1881." *Third Annual Report of the Bureau of Ethnology, 1881–1882*, 427–510. Washington, D.C.: Smithsonian Institution.
———. 1903. "Aboriginal Pottery of the Eastern United States." *Twentieth Annual Report of the Bureau of American Ethnology, 1898–1899*, 1–237. Washington, D.C.: Smithsonian Institution.
House, John H., and D. L. Ballenger. 1976. *An Archeological Survey of the Interstate 77 Route in the South Carolina Piedmont*. Research Manuscript Series 104. Columbia: Institute of Archaeology and Anthropology, University of South Carolina.
Hudson, Charles M. 1970. *The Catawba Nation*. Athens: University of Georgia Press.

———. 1990. *The Juan Pardo Expeditions: Spanish Explorers and the Indians of the Carolinas and Tennessee, 1566–1568*. Washington, D.C.: Smithsonian Institution Press.

Hudson, Charles M., Marvin T. Smith, and Chester B. DePratter. 1984. "The Hernando De Soto Expedition: From Apalachee to Chiaha." *Southeastern Archaeology* 3:65–77.

Hudson, Charles M., Marvin T. Smith, David J. Hally, Richard R. Polhemus, and Chester B. DePratter. 1985. "Coosa: A Chiefdom in the Sixteenth-Century Southeastern United States." *American Antiquity* 50:723–37.

Hulton, Paul. 1984. *America 1585: The Complete Drawings of John White*. Chapel Hill: University of North Carolina Press.

Jefferies, Richard W. 1979. "The Tunacunnhee Site: Hopewell in Northwest Georgia." In *Hopewell Archaeology*, edited by David S. Brose and N'omi Greber, 162–70. Kent, Ohio: Kent State University Press.

———. 1994. "The Swift Creek Site and Woodland Platform Mounds in the Southeastern United States." In *Ocmulgee Archaeology, 1936–1986*, edited by David J. Hally, 71–83. Athens: University of Georgia Press.

Johnson, Guy B. 1934. "Editor's Note." *Bulletin of the Archaeological Society of North Carolina* 1, no. 2:11.

Jones, David C., Christopher T. Espenshade, and Linda Kennedy. 1997. "Archaeological Investigation at 31On190, Cape Island, Onslow County, North Carolina." Ms. on file, North Carolina Division of Archives and History, Raleigh.

Keel, Bennie C. 1970. "Excavations at the Red Springs Mound Rb°4, Robeson County, 1971." *Southern Indian Studies* 22:17–22.

———. 1972. "Woodland Phases of the Appalachian Summit Area." Ph.D. dissertation, Department of Anthropology, Washington State University, Pullman.

———. 1976. *Cherokee Archaeology: A Study of the Appalachian Summit*. Knoxville: University of Tennessee Press.

Keel, Bennie C., and Brian J. Egloff. 1984. "The Cane Creek Site, Mitchell County, North Carolina." *Southern Indian Studies* 33:3–44.

Keeler, Robert W. 1971. "An Archaeological Survey of the Upper Catawba River Valley." Honors thesis, Department of Anthropology, University of North Carolina, Chapel Hill.

Kelly, Arthur R. 1938. *A Preliminary Report on the Archaeological Explorations at Macon, Georgia*. Bureau of American Ethnology Bulletin 119. Washington, D.C.: Smithsonian Institution.

Kelly, Arthur R., and Robert S. Neitzel. 1961. *The Chauga Site in Oconee County, South Carolina*. Laboratory of Archaeology Series, Report no. 3. Athens: University of Georgia.

Kent, Barry C. 1984. *Susquehanna's Indians*. Anthropological Series, no. 6. Harrisburg: Pennsylvania Historical and Museum Commission.

Kimball, Larry R. 1991. "Swannanoa River Buried Archaeological Site Survey, Buncombe County, North Carolina." Technical report submitted to the North Carolina Division of Archives and History, Raleigh, and the Historic Resources Commission of Asheville and Buncombe County, Asheville, North Carolina.

———. 1992. "The Function of Hopewell Blades from the Southeast." *Research Notes* 12. Knoxville: Frank H. McClung Museum, University of Tennessee.

Lafferty, Robert H., III. 1981. *The Phipps Bend Archaeological Project*. Research Series no. 4. Tuscaloosa: Office of Archaeological Research, University of Alabama.

Larsen, Clark S. 1994. "In the Wake of Columbus: Postcontact Native Population Biology of the Americas." *Yearbook of Physical Anthropology* 37:109–54.

Larson, Lewis H., Jr. 1972. "Functional Considerations of Warfare in the Southeast during the Mississippian Period." *American Antiquity* 37:383–92.

———. 1990. "The Pardo Expedition: What Was the Direction at Departure? *Southeastern Archaeology* 9, no. 2:124–39.

Lee, E. Lawrence. 1963. *Indian Wars in North Carolina 1663–1763*. Raleigh: The Carolina Charter Tercentenary Commission.

———. 1971. *New Hanover County—A Brief History*. Raleigh: North Carolina Department of Archives and History.

Lefler, Hugh T., ed. 1967. *A New Voyage to Carolina by John Lawson*. Chapel Hill: University of North Carolina Press.

Levy, Janet E., J. Alan May, and David G. Moore. 1990. "From Ysa to Joara: Cultural Diversity in the Catawba Valley from the Fourteenth to the Sixteenth Century." In *Archaeological and Historical Perspectives on the Spanish Borderlands East*, 152–68. Vol. 2 of *Columbian Consequences*, edited by David H. Thomas. Washington, D.C.: Smithsonian Institution Press.

Lewis, Ernest. 1951. "The Sara Indians, 1540–1768: An Ethno-Archaeological Study." Master's thesis, Department of Sociology and Anthropology, University of North Carolina, Chapel Hill.

Lewis, Thomas M. N., and Madeline D. Kneberg. 1941. *The Prehistory of the Chickamauga Basin in Tennessee: A Preview*. Tennessee Anthropology Papers 1. Knoxville: University of Tennessee.

———. 1946. *Hiwassee Island: An Archaeological Account of Four Tennessee Indian Peoples*. Knoxville: University of Tennessee Press.

Loftfield, Thomas C. 1975. "Archaeological and Ethno-Historical Data Bearing on the Southern Boundary of Algonkian Indian Occupation." Papers of the Sixth Algonkian Conference, 1974, edited by William Cowan. *National Museum of Canada Mercury Series: Canadian Ethnology Paper* 23:100–111.

———. 1976. "'A Briefe and True Report . . .' An Archaeological Interpretation of the Southern North Carolina Coast." Ph.D. dissertation, Department of Anthropology, University of North Carolina, Chapel Hill.

———. 1979. "Excavations at 31ON33, A Late Woodland Seasonal Village." Ms. on file, Department of Sociology and Anthropology, University of North Carolina, Wilmington.

———. 1987. "Excavations at 31ON305, the Flynt Site at Sneads Ferry, North Carolina." Ms. on file, Department of Sociology and Anthropology, University of North Carolina, Wilmington.

———. 1990. "Ossuary Interments and Algonkian Expansion on the North Carolina Coast." *Southeastern Archaeology* 9, no. 2:116–23.

Loftfield, Thomas C., and David C. Jones. 1995. "Late Woodland Architecture on the Coast of North Carolina: Structural Meaning and Environmental Adaptation." *Southeastern Archaeology* 14, no. 2:120–35.

Lyon, Edwin A. 1996. *A New Deal for Southeastern Archaeology*. Tuscaloosa: University of Alabama Press.

McCary, Ben C. 1947. "A Survey and Study of Folsom-like Points Found in Virginia." *Quarterly Bulletin of the Archeological Society of Virginia* 2, no. 1:4–34.

———. 1948. "A Report on Folsom-like Points Found in Granville County, North Carolina." *Quarterly Bulletin of the Archeological Society of Virginia* 3, no. 1:4–17.

MacCauley, Charles. 1929. "Notes on the Cameron Mound, Harnett County." Reprinted in *Southern Indian Studies* 18:46–47, 1966.

McCollough, Major C. R., and Charles H. Faulkner. 1973. *Excavation of the Higgs and Doughty Sites, I-75 Salvage Archaeology*. Miscellaneous Paper 12. Knoxville: Tennessee Archaeological Society.

MacCord, Howard, Sr. 1966. "The McLean Mound, Cumberland County, North Carolina." *Southern Indian Studies* 18:3–45.

McGahey, Samuel O. 1987. "Paleo-Indian Lithic Material: Implications of Distributions in Mississippi." *Mississippi Archaeology* 22:1–13.

McManus, Jane M. 1985. "An Analysis of the Lithic Artifact Assemblage from the Forbush Creek Site (31Yd1), Yadkin County, North Carolina." Honors thesis, Department of Anthropology, University of North Carolina, Chapel Hill.

McManus, Jane M., and Ann M. Long. 1986. *Alamance County Archaeological Survey Project, Alamance County, North Carolina*. Research Reports 5. Chapel Hill: Research Laboratories of Anthropology, University of North Carolina.

MacNeish, Richard S. 1952. *Iroquois Pottery Types*. Bulletin no. 124. Ottawa: National Museum of Canada.

Manson, Carl. 1948. "Marcey Creek Site: An Early Manifestation in the Potomac Valley." *American Antiquity* 13:223–26.

Marshall, Rhea R. 1988. "Intrasite Settlement Patterns at the Hardy Site, 31Sr50." Master's thesis, Department of Anthropology, Wake Forest University, Winston-Salem, North Carolina.

Martin, Joel W. 1994. "Southeastern Indians and the English Trade in Skins and Slaves." In *The Forgotten Centuries: Indians and Europeans in the American South, 1521–1704*, edited by Charles H. Hudson and Carmen Chaves Tesser, 304–24. Athens: University of Georgia Press.

Mathis, Mark A., comp. 1979. *North Carolina Statewide Archaeological Survey: An Introduction and Application to Three Highway Projects in Hertford, Wilkes, and Ashe Counties*. Publication 22. Raleigh: North Carolina Archaeological Council.

Mathis, Mark A. 1990. "Ossuary Recovery at the Dickerson Site (31Br91) Bertie County, North Carolina." Ms. on file, North Carolina Division of Archives and History, Raleigh.

———. 1993a. "Mortuary Processes at the Broad Reach Site." Paper presented at the 50th Annual Meeting of the Southeastern Archaeological Conference, Raleigh, N.C.

———. 1993b. "Broad Reach: The Truth about What We've Missed." In *Site Destruction in Georgia and the Carolinas*, edited by David G. Anderson and Virginia Horak, 39–48. Readings in Archeological Resource Protection Series 2. Atlanta: National Park Service.

———. 1997. "The Middle to Late Woodland Shift on the Southern Coast of North Carolina." Ms. on file, North Carolina Division of Archives and History, Raleigh.
Mead, J. I., and D. J. Meltzer. 1984. "North American Late Quaternary Extinctions and the Radiocarbon Record." In *Quaternary Extinctions: A Prehistoric Revolution*, edited by P. S. Martin and R. G. Klein, 440–50. Tucson: University of Arizona Press.
Meltzer, David J. 1988. "Late Pleistocene Human Adaptations in Eastern North America." *Journal of World Prehistory* 2:1–52.
———. 1989. "Why Don't We Know When the First People Came to North America?" *American Antiquity* 54:471–90.
Meltzer, David J., Donald K. Grayson, Gerardo Ardila, Alex W. Barker, Dena F. Dincauze, C. Vance Haynes, Francisco Mena, Lautaro Núñez, and Dennis J. Stanford. 1997. "On the Pleistocene Antiquity of Monte Verde, Southern Chile." *American Antiquity* 62:659–63.
Merrell, James H. 1987. "'This Western World': The Evolution of the Piedmont, 1525–1725." In *The Siouan Project: Seasons I and II*, edited by Roy S. Dickens Jr., H. Trawick Ward, and R. P. Stephen Davis Jr., 19–27. Monograph Series no. 1. Chapel Hill: Research Laboratories of Anthropology, University of North Carolina.
———. 1989. *The Indians' New World: Catawbas and Their Neighbors from European Contact through the Era of Removal*. Chapel Hill: University of North Carolina Press.
Mikell, Gregory A. 1987. "The Donnaha Site: Late Woodland Period Subsistence and Ecology." Master's thesis, Department of Anthropology, Wake Forest University, Winston-Salem, North Carolina.
Milner, George R. 1980. "Epidemic Disease in the Postcontact Southeast: A Reappraisal." *Mid-Continental Journal of Archaeology* 5:39–56.
Monahan, Elizabeth I. 1995. "Biological Analysis of the Mortuary Practices at the Broad Reach Site (31Cr218), Coastal North Carolina." *Southern Indian Studies* 44:37–69.
Mook, Maurice A. 1944. "Algonkian Ethnohistory of the Carolina Sound." *Journal of the Washington Academy of Sciences* 34, nos. 6–7.
Mooney, James. 1975. *Historical Sketch of the Cherokee*. Chicago: Aldine Publishing Co.
Moore, David G. 1981. "A Comparison of Two Pisgah Ceramic Assemblages." Master's thesis, Department of Anthropology, University of North Carolina, Chapel Hill.
———. 1987. "Archaeological Investigations in the Upper Catawba River Valley, North Carolina." Paper presented at the 44th Annual Meeting of the Southeastern Archaeological Conference, Charleston, South Carolina.
Moore, David G., and Robin A. Beck Jr. 1994. "New Evidence of 16th-Century Spanish Artifacts in the Catawba River Valley, North Carolina." Paper presented at the 51st Southeastern Archaeological Conference, Lexington, Kentucky.
Morton, Richard L. 1960. *The Tidewater Period, 1607–1710*. Vol. 1 of *Colonial Virginia*. Chapel Hill: University of North Carolina Press.
Mountjoy, Joseph B. 1989. "Early Radiocarbon Dates from a Site on the Pee Dee–Siouan Frontier in the Piedmont of Central North Carolina." *Southern Indian Studies* 38:7–22.
National Park Service. 1989. "Feasibility Study, De Soto National Historic Trail." Draft

report prepared by the National Park Service as required by the De Soto National Trail Study Act of 1987, Southeastern Regional Office, Atlanta.
Navey, Liane. 1982. "An Introduction to the Mortuary Practices of the Historic Sara." Master's thesis, Department of Anthropology, University of North Carolina, Chapel Hill.
Newkirk, Judith A. 1978. "The Parker Site: A Woodland Site in Davidson County, North Carolina." Master's thesis, Department of Anthropology, Wake Forest University, Winston-Salem, North Carolina.
Oliver, Billy L. 1985. "Tradition and Typology: Basic Elements of the Carolina Projectile Point Sequence." In *Structure and Process in Southeastern Archaeology*, edited by Roy S. Dickens Jr. and H. Trawick Ward, 195–211. Tuscaloosa: University of Alabama Press.
———. 1992. "Settlements of the Pee Dee Culture." Ph.D. dissertation, Department of Anthropology, University of North Carolina at Chapel Hill.
Peabody, Charles. 1910. "The Exploration of Mounds in North Carolina." *American Anthropologist* 7, no. 3:425–33.
Perkinson, Phil H. 1971. "North Carolina Fluted Projectile Points—Survey Report Number One." *Southern Indian Studies* 23:3–40.
———. 1973. "North Carolina Fluted Projectile Points—Survey Report Number Two." *Southern Indian Studies* 23:3–60.
Petherick, Gary L. 1987. "Architecture and Features at the Fredricks, Wall, and Mitchum Sites." In *The Siouan Project: Seasons I and II*, edited by Roy S. Dickens Jr., H. Trawick Ward and R. P. Stephen Davis Jr., 29–80. Monograph Series no. 1. Chapel Hill: Research Laboratories of Anthropology, University of North Carolina.
Phelps, David S. 1980. *Archaeological Salvage of the Thorpe Site and Other Investigations Along the US 64 Bypass, Rocky Mount, North Carolina*. Archaeological Research Report no. 1. Greenville: Archaeology Laboratory, East Carolina University.
———. 1981. *Archaeological Surveys of Four Watersheds in the North Carolina Coastal Plain*. Publication 16. Raleigh: North Carolina Archaeological Council.
———. 1983. "Archaeology of the North Carolina Coast and Coastal Plain: Problems and Hypotheses." In *The Prehistory of North Carolina: An Archaeological Symposium*, edited by Mark A. Mathis and Jeffrey J. Crow, 1–52. Raleigh: North Carolina Division of Archives and History.
———. 1984. *Archaeology of the Tillett Site: The First Fishing Community at Wanchese, Roanoke Island*. Archaeological Research Report no. 6. Greenville: Archaeology Laboratory, East Carolina University.
Potter, Stephen R. 1982. "An Analysis of Chicacoan Settlement Patterns." Ph.D. dissertation, Department of Anthropology, University of North Carolina, Chapel Hill.
Powell, William S. 1989. *North Carolina through Four Centuries*. Chapel Hill: University of North Carolina Press.
Purrington, Burton L. 1975. "Archaeological Survey of the Site of the Proposed Fourth Creek Wastewater Treatment Plant, Statesville, North Carolina." Ms. on file, Department of Anthropology, Appalachian State University, Boone, North Carolina.

———. 1980. "Archaeology of Western North Carolina's Mountain Region: Overview and Prospectus." Paper presented at The Prehistory of North Carolina: An Archaeological Symposium, Raleigh.
———. 1981. *Archeological Investigations at the Slipoff Branch Site, a Morrow Mountain Culture Campsite in Swain County, North Carolina.* Publication 15. Raleigh: North Carolina Archaeological Council.
———. 1983. "Ancient Mountaineers: An Overview of the Prehistoric Archaeology of North Carolina's Western Mountain Region." In *The Prehistory of North Carolina: An Archaeological Symposium*, edited by Mark A. Mathis and Jeffrey J. Crow, 83–160. Raleigh: North Carolina Division of Archives and History.
———. 1986. "The Pisgah Survey: Upland Archaeology in the Appalachian Summit of North Carolina." Paper presented at the 43rd Annual Meeting of the Southeastern Archaeological Conference, Nashville, Tennessee.
Quinn, David B. 1985. *Set Fair for Roanoke: Voyages and Colonies, 1584–1606.* Chapel Hill: University of North Carolina Press.
Ramenofsky, Ann F. 1987. *Vectors of Death.* Albuquerque: University of New Mexico Press.
Reid, J. Jefferson. 1965. "A Comparative Statement on Ceramics from the Hollywood and the Town Creek Mounds." *Southern Indian Studies* 17:12–25.
———. 1967. "Pee Dee Pottery from the Mound at Town Creek." Master's thesis, Department of Anthropology, University of North Carolina at Chapel Hill.
———. 1985. "Formation Processes for the Practical Prehistorian: An Example from the Southeast." In *Structure and Process in Southeastern Archaeology*, edited by Roy S. Dickens Jr. and H. Trawick Ward, 11–33. Tuscaloosa: University of Alabama Press.
Riggs, Brett H. 1995. "Historic Cherokee Occupation of the Hiwassee Reservoir Area, Cherokee County, North Carolina." Paper presented at the 52nd Annual Meeting of the Southeastern Archaeological Conference, Knoxville, Tennessee.
Rights, Douglas L. 1934. "North Carolina as an Archaeological Field." *Bulletin of the Archaeological Society of North Carolina* 1, no. 1:5–7.
———. 1947. *The American Indian in North Carolina.* Durham: Duke University Press.
Ritchie, William A. 1932. *The Lamoka Lake Site: The Type Station of the Archaic Algonkin Period in New York.* Research and Transactions 7, no. 4. Rochester: New York State Archaeological Association.
———. 1969. *The Archaeology of New York State.* Rev. ed. Garden City, N.Y.: Natural History Press.
Robinson, Kenneth W. 1989. "Archaeological Excavations within the Alternate Pipeline Corridor Passing through the Harshaw Bottom Site (31Ce41), Cherokee County, North Carolina." Ms. in Western Office, North Carolina Division of Archives and History, Asheville.
Robinson, K. W., D. G. Moore, and R. Y. Wetmore. 1994. "Woodland Period Radiocarbon Dates from Western North Carolina." Paper presented at the Sixth Uplands Archaeological Conference, Harrisonburg, Virginia, February 25–26.
Rodning, Christopher B. 1996. "Towns and Clans: Social Institutions and Organization of Native Communities on the Appalachian Summit." Fourth semester paper, Department of Anthropology, University of North Carolina, Chapel Hill.

Rogers, Anne F., and Jane L. Brown. 1995. "Spikebuck Town: An Eighteenth-Century Cherokee Village." Paper presented at the 52nd Annual Meeting of the Southeastern Archaeological Conference, Knoxville, Tennessee.

Roosevelt, A. C., M. Lima da Costa, C. Lopes Machado, M. Michab, N. Mercier, H. Valladas, J. Feathers, W. Barnett, M. Inazio da Silveira, A. Henderson, J. Silva, B. Chernoff, D. S. Reese, A. Holman, N. Toth, and K. Schnick. 1996. "Paleoindian Cave Dwellers in the Amazon: The Peopling of the Americas." *Science* 272, no. 5260:373.

Rudolph, James L. 1984. "Earthlodges and Platform Mounds: Changing Public Architecture in the Southeastern United States." *Southeastern Archaeology* 3:33–45.

Runquist, Jeannette. 1979. "Analysis of the Flora and Faunal Remains from Protohistoric North Carolina Cherokee Indian Sites." Ph.D. dissertation, Department of Zoology, North Carolina State University, Raleigh.

Schroedl, Gerald F. 1978. *The Patrick Site (40Mr40), Tellico Reservoir, Tennessee*. Report of Investigations no. 25. Knoxville: Department of Anthropology, University of Tennessee.

———, ed. 1986. *Overhill Cherokee Archaeology at Chota-Tanasee*. Report of Investigations no. 38. Knoxville: Department of Anthropology, University of Tennessee.

Senior, Christopher D. 1981. "A Preliminary Analysis of Pisgah Phase Ceramics from the Ward Site, Northwestern North Carolina." Prepared under a U.S. Department of the Interior Survey and Planning Grant, administered through the North Carolina Division of Archives and History, Department of Cultural Resources, Raleigh.

Setzler, Frank M., and Jesse D. Jennings. 1941. *Peachtree Mound and Village Site, Cherokee County, North Carolina*. Bureau of American Ethnology Bulletin 131. Washington, D.C.: Smithsonian Institution.

Simpkins, Daniel L. 1984. "Some Spatial Configurations of Late Archaeological Components in the Carolina-Virginia Piedmont." Paper presented at the Annual Meeting of the Society for Historical Archaeology, Williamsburg, Virginia.

———. 1985. "First Phase Investigations of Late Aboriginal Settlement Systems in the Eno, Haw, and Dan River Drainages, North Carolina." Report submitted to the North Carolina Division of Archives and History, Raleigh.

Simpkins, Daniel L., and Dorothy J. Allard. 1986. "Isolation and Identification of Spanish Moss Fiber from a Sample of Stallings and Orange Series Ceramics." *American Antiquity* 51:102–17.

Simpkins, Daniel L., and Gary L. Petherick. 1986. "Second Phase Investigations of Late Aboriginal Settlement Systems in the Eno, Haw, and Dan River Drainages, North Carolina." Report submitted to the North Carolina Division of Archives and History, Raleigh.

Smith, Betty A. 1979. "The Hopewell Connection in Southwest Georgia." In *Hopewell Archaeology*, edited by David S. Brose and N'omi Greber, 181–87. Kent, Ohio: Kent State University Press.

Smith, Bruce D. 1986. "The Archaeology of Southeastern United States: From Dalton to De Soto, 10,500 B.P.–500 B.P." In *Advances in World Archaeology*, vol. 5, edited by F. Wendorf and A. Close, 1–92. Orlando, Fla.: Academic Press.

———. 1992. *Rivers of Change: Essays on Early Agriculture in Eastern North America.* Washington, D.C.: Smithsonian Institution Press.
Smith, Marvin T. 1987. *Archaeology of Aboriginal Culture Change: Depopulation during the Early Historic Period.* Ripley P. Bullen Monographs in Anthropology and History no. 6. Gainesville: University Press of Florida.
Snow, Dean R., and Kim M. Lanphear. 1989. "More Methodological Perspectives: A Rejoinder to Dobyns." *Ethnohistory* 36:299–304.
South, Stanley A. 1959a. "A Study of the Prehistory of the Roanoke Rapids Basin." Master's thesis, Department of Sociology and Anthropology, University of North Carolina, Chapel Hill.
———. 1959b. *Indians in North Carolina.* Raleigh: North Carolina Department of Archives and History.
———. 1962. "An Archaeological Survey of Two Islands in the White Oak River near Swansboro, North Carolina." Ms. on file, North Carolina Office of State Archaeology, Raleigh.
———. 1966. "Exploratory Excavation at the McFayden Mound, Brunswick County, N.C." *Southern Indian Studies* 18:59–61.
———. 1976. *An Archaeological Survey of Southeastern North Carolina.* Institute of Archaeology and Anthropology Notebook 8. Columbia: University of South Carolina.
Spainhour, J. M. 1873. "Antiquities in Lenoir County, North Carolina." In *Annual Report of the Board of Regents of the Smithsonian Institution, 1871.* Washington, D.C.: Smithsonian Institution.
Stephenson, Robert L., and Alice L. L. Ferguson. 1963. *The Accokeek Creek Site: A Middle Atlantic Seaboard Culture Sequence.* Anthropological Papers no. 20. Ann Arbor: Museum of Anthropology, University of Michigan.
Steponaitis, Vincas P. 1983. *Ceramics, Chronology, and Community Patterns: An Archaeological Study of Moundville.* New York: Academic Press.
———. 1986. "Prehistoric Archaeology in the Southeastern United States, 1970–1985." *Annual Review of Anthropology* 15:363–404.
Stewart, T. Dale. 1966. "Notes on the Human Bones Recovered from Burials in the McLean Mound, North Carolina." *Southern Indian Studies* 18:67–82.
Stoltman, James B. 1974. *Groton Plantation: An Archaeological Study of a South Carolina Locality.* Monograph of the Peabody Museum no. 1. Cambridge: Peabody Museum of Archaeology and Ethnology, Harvard University.
Sullivan, Lynne P. 1987. "The Mouse Creek Phase Household." *Southeastern Archaeology* 6:16–29.
———. 1995. Foreword to *The Prehistory of the Chickamauga Basin in Tennessee,* by Thomas M. N. Lewis and Madeline D. Kneberg Lewis, xv–xxi. 2 vols., compiled and edited by Lynne P. Sullivan. Knoxville: University of Tennessee Press.
Swanton, John R. 1946. *The Indians of the Southeastern United States.* Bureau of American Ethnology Bulletin 137. Washington, D.C.: Smithsonian Institution.
———. 1985. *Final Report of the United States De Soto Expedition Commission.* Washington, D.C.: Smithsonian Institution Press.
Thomas, Cyrus. 1887. *Work in Mound Exploration of the Bureau of Ethnology.* Bureau of Ethnology Bulletin 4. Washington, D.C.: Smithsonian Institution.

———. 1894. "Report on the Mound Explorations of the Bureau of Ethnology. In *Twelfth Annual Report of the Bureau of American Ethnology*, 3–730. Washington, D.C.: Smithsonian Institution.
Trinkley, Michael B. 1980. "Investigation of the Woodland Period along the South Carolina Coast." Ph.D. dissertation, Department of Anthropology, University of North Carolina, Chapel Hill.
———. 1989. "An Archaeological Overview of the South Carolina Woodland Period: It's the Same Old Riddle." In *Studies in South Carolina Archaeology: Essays in Honor of Robert L. Stephenson*, edited by Albert C. Goodyear III and Glen T. Hanson, 73–89. Anthropological Studies 9. Columbia: Institute of Archaeology and Anthropology, University of South Carolina.
———. 1990. *An Archaeological Context for the South Carolina Woodland Period*. Research Series 22. Columbia, S.C.: Chicora Foundation.
Turner, E. Randolph, III. 1992. "The Virginia Coastal Plain during the Late Woodland Period." In *Middle and Late Woodland Research in Virginia: A Synthesis*, edited by Theodore R. Reinhart and Mary Ellen N. Hodges, 97–136. Special Publication no. 29. [Richmond]: Archeological Society of Virginia.
Valentine, Mann S. 1883. "Report on Excavations at the Sawnooke Mound, Swain County, North Carolina in 1882." Original document on file at the Valentine Museum, Richmond, Virginia.
Van Doren, Mark, ed. 1928. *Travels of William Bartram*. New York: Macy-Masius.
"Virginias Deploured Condition; Or an Impartiall Narrative of the Murders Comitted by the Indians There, and of the Sufferings of His Majesties Loyall Subjects under the Rebellious Outrages of Mr. Nathaniell Bacon, June to the Tenth Day of August Anno Domini 1676." 1871. *Collections of the Massachusetts Historical Society*, 4th ser., 9:162–76.
Ward, H. Trawick. 1977a. *An Archaeological Survey of the New U.S. 19–129 Route Between Andrews and Murphy in Cherokee County*. Chapel Hill: Research Laboratories of Anthropology, University of North Carolina.
———. 1977b. "A Summary Report of Excavations at Mc^{v}41." Ms. on file, Research Laboratories of Archaeology, University of North Carolina, Chapel Hill.
———. 1978. "The Archaeology of Whites Creek, Marlboro County, South Carolina." Ms. on file, Research Laboratories of Archaeology, University of North Carolina, Chapel Hill.
———. 1980. "The Spatial Analysis of the Plow Zone Artifact Distributions from Two Village Sites in North Carolina." Ph.D. dissertation, University of North Carolina, Chapel Hill.
———. 1982. "Archaeological Salvage of the Jarretts Point Ossuary, On304." Ms. on file, Research Laboratories of Archaeology, University of North Carolina, Chapel Hill.
———. 1983. "A Review of Archaeology in the North Carolina Piedmont: A Study of Change." In *The Prehistory of North Carolina: An Archaeological Symposium*, edited by Mark A. Mathis and Jeffrey J. Crow, 53–81. Raleigh: North Carolina Division of Archives and History.
———. 1985. "Social Implications of Storage and Disposal Patterns." In *Structure and Pro-

cess in Southeastern Archaeology, edited by Roy S. Dickens Jr. and H. Trawick Ward, 82–101. Tuscaloosa: University of Alabama Press.

———. 1986. "Intra-Site Spatial Patterning at the Warren Wilson Site." In *The Conference on Cherokee Prehistory*, assembled by David G. Moore, 7–19. Swannanoa, N.C.: Warren Wilson College.

———. 1987. "Mortuary Patterns at the Fredricks, Wall, and Mitchum Sites. In *The Siouan Project: Seasons I and II*, edited by Roy S. Dickens Jr., H. Trawick Ward, and R. P. Stephen Davis Jr., 81–110. Monograph Series no. 1. Chapel Hill: Research Laboratories of Anthropology, University of North Carolina.

———. N.d. "Analysis of Pottery from the McDowell Site, 31Mc41." Ms. on file, Research Laboratories of Archaeology, University of North Carolina, Chapel Hill.

Ward, H. Trawick, and R. P. Stephen Davis Jr. 1991. "The Impact of Old World Diseases on the Native Inhabitants of the North Carolina Piedmont." *Archaeology of Eastern North America* 19:171–81.

———. 1993. *Indian Communities on the North Carolina Piedmont, A.D. 1000 to 1700*. Monograph 2. Chapel Hill: Research Laboratories of Anthropology, University of North Carolina.

Ward, H. Trawick, R. P. Stephen Davis Jr., Elizabeth I. Monahan, and Marianne Reeves. 1996. "Mortuary Behavior at the Fredricks Site, Ten Years Later." Paper presented at the 53rd Annual Meeting of the Southeastern Archaeological Conference, Birmingham, Alabama.

Ward, H. Trawick, and Jack Wilson Jr. 1980. "Archaeological Excavations at the Cold Morning Site." *Southern Indian Studies* 32:5–40.

Watts, W. A. 1980. "Late-Quaternary Vegetation History at White Pond on the Inner Coastal Plain of South Carolina." *Quaternary Research* 13:187–99.

Wauchope, Robert. 1966. *Archaeological Survey of Northern Georgia: With a Test of Some Cultural Hypotheses*. Memoirs of the Society for American Archaeology no. 21. Salt Lake City, Utah: Society for American Archaeology.

Webb, Paul A., and David S. Leigh. 1995. "Geomorphological and Archaeological Investigations of a Buried Site on the Yadkin River Floodplain." *Southern Indian Studies* 44:1–36.

Webb, S. David, Jerald T. Milanich, Roger Alexon, and James S. Dunbar. 1984. "A *Bison Antiquus* Kill Site, Wacissa River, Jefferson County, Florida." *American Antiquity* 49:384–92.

Webb, William S. 1938. *An Archaeological Survey of the Norris Basin in Eastern Tennessee*. Bureau of American Ethnology Bulletin 118. Washington, D.C.: Smithsonian Institution.

———. 1946. *Indian Knoll*. Reports in Anthropology and Archaeology, vol. 4, no. 3, pt. 1. Lexington: University Press of Kentucky.

Webb, William S., and David L. DeJarnette. 1942. *An Archaeological Survey of Pickwick Basin in the Adjacent Portions of the States of Alabama, Mississippi, and Tennessee*. Bureau of American Ethnology Bulletin 129. Washington, D.C.: Smithsonian Institution.

Wendland, Wayne M., and Reid A. Bryson. 1974. "Dating Climatic Episodes of the Holocene." *Quaternary Research* 4:9–24.

Wetmore, Ruth Y. 1979. "Report on Excavations at the Buie Mound, Robeson County, North Carolina." *Institute of Archeology and Anthropology Notebook* 10:30–71.

———. 1990. "The Ela Site (31Sw5): Archaeological Data Recovery of Connestee and Qualla Phase Occupations at the East Elementary School Site, Swain County, North Carolina (draft report)." Ms. on file, Archaeology Laboratory, Western Carolina University, Cullowhee.

Willey, Gordon R., and Philip Phillips. 1958. *Method and Theory in American Archaeology*. Chicago: University of Chicago Press.

Willey, Gordon R., and Jeremy A. Sabloff. 1974. *A History of American Archaeology*. San Francisco: W. H. Freeman and Company.

Williams, Stephen, and James B. Stoltman. 1965. "An Outline of Southeastern United States Prehistory with Particular Emphasis on the Paleo-Indian Era." In *The Quaternary of the United States*, edited by H. E. Wright and D. G. Frey, 669–83. Princeton: Princeton University Press.

Wilmsen, Edwin N. 1965. "An Outline of Early Man Studies in the United States." *American Antiquity* 31:172–92.

Wilson, Homes H. 1986. "Burials from the Warren Wilson Site: Some Biological and Behavioral Considerations." In *The Conference on Cherokee Prehistory*, assembled by David G. Moore, 42–72. Swannanoa, N.C.: Warren Wilson College.

Wilson, Jack H., Jr. 1977. "Feature Fill, Plant Utilization and Disposal among the Historic Sara Indians." Master's thesis, Department of Anthropology, University of North Carolina, Chapel Hill.

———. 1983. "A Study of Late Prehistoric, Protohistoric, and Historic Indians of the Carolina and Virginia Piedmont: Structure, Process, and Ecology." Ph.D. dissertation, Department of Anthropology, University of North Carolina, Chapel Hill.

Winston, Sanford. 1936a. "Keyauwee Exploration." *Bulletin of the Archaeological Society of North Carolina* 3, no. 1:13–14.

———. 1936b. "Financial Statement of the Keyauwee Excavation Fund." *Bulletin of the Archaeological Society of North Carolina* 3, no. 2:16–17.

Wood, Peter H. 1987. "The Impact of Smallpox on the Native Population of the 18th-Century South." *New York State Journal of Medicine* 87:30–36.

Wood, W. Dean, Dan T. Elliott, Teresa P. Rudolph, and Dennis B. Blanton. 1986. *Prehistory in the Richard B. Russell Reservoir: The Archaic and Woodland Periods of the Upper Savannah River*. Atlanta: Archaeological Services, National Park Service.

Woodall, J. Ned. 1976. "Second Archeological Survey of the Great Bend Area, Yadkin River Valley, North Carolina." Ms. on file, Archeology Laboratories, Museum of Man, Wake Forest University, Winston-Salem, North Carolina.

———. 1984. *The Donnaha Site: 1973, 1975 Excavations*. Publication 22. Raleigh: North Carolina Archaeological Council.

———. 1987. "Late Woodland Interaction in the Great Bend Area, Yadkin Valley, North Carolina." Paper presented at the 44th Annual Meeting of the Southeastern Archaeological Conference, Charleston, South Carolina.

———. 1990. *Archaeological Investigations in the Yadkin River Valley, 1984–1987*. Publication 25. Raleigh: North Carolina Archaeological Council.

Wormington, H. M. 1957. *Ancient Man in North America*. Popular Series no. 4. Denver: Denver Museum of Natural History.

Yarnell, Richard A. 1976. "Plant Remains from the Warren Wilson Site." In *Cherokee Prehistory: The Pisgah Phase in the Appalachian Summit Region*, by Roy S. Dickens Jr., 217–24. Knoxville: University of Tennessee Press.

Yarnell, Richard A., and M. Jean Black. 1985. "Temporal Trends Indicated by a Survey of Archaic and Woodland Plant Food Remains from Southeastern North America." *Southeastern Archaeology* 4:93–106.

Index

Accokeek series ceramics, 77, 97; characteristics of, 77
"Achonechy Town," 242. *See also* Fredricks site; Occaneechi Town
Adair, James, 267
Adams Creek ceramics, 196
Agriculture, 48, 105, 117, 132, 171, 177, 189, 212–13, 216, 224, 236, 238, 248, 251, 256, 275
Alabama, 31, 49, 64, 178, 233, 261, 262
Alamance County, N.C., 115
Albemarle County, Va., 273
Albemarle region, 273
Albemarle Sound, 195, 203, 233, 273
Algonkian culture, 213, 216
Algonkian speakers, 20, 23, 194, 196, 210–11, 217, 222, 223, 224, 225, 227; villages of, 20, 21, 274
Allendale chert, 35
Altithermal Optimum, 63, 70
Aluminum Company of America (ALCOA), 38
Amadas, Philip, 231
Ameghino, Fiorino, 27
American Philosophical Society, 16
American Revolution, 267
Amity site (31Hy43), 214, 274; radiocarbon dates for, 216
Amphibians, 189, 190
Anderson, David G., 29, 31, 49, 58
Anderson Pond, Tenn., 37
Andrews (Cherokee Co.), 180, 262
Andrews Sound, 229
Anson County, N.C., 38, 132
Appalachian State University, 18, 21, 68, 271
Appalachian Summit region, 46, 67, 68, 69, 99, 160, 162, 166, 177, 179, 180, 181, 191, 192, 197, 226, 233
Appomattox River, 232

Archaeological Society of North Carolina, 9, 11, 14, 38, 120, 121, 122; statewide survey program, 9, 15
Archaeologists, amateur, 27, 36, 101, 196; finds by, 36; as volunteers, 134
Archaic period, 1, 2–3, 23, 87; definition of, 47–48; in the Piedmont, 49–67; in the mountains, 67–72; on the coast and Coastal Plain, 72–75. *See also* Early Archaic period; Late Archaic period; Middle Archaic period
Arthur, Gabriel, 234, 258, 264
Asheboro (Randolph Co.), 119, 120, 134
Ashe County, N.C., 46
Asheville (Buncombe Co.), 6
Asheville intermontane basin, 161
Atlatl, 3, 63, 64, 70, 93, 98; evidence for first use, 63
Ayers, Harvard, 18, 23

Bacon, Nathaniel, 257
Bacon Farm site (Tenn.), 69
Bacon's Rebellion, 242, 255
Badin (Stanly Co.), 38, 39, 42, 49, 80
Badin ceramics, 80, 84, 85, 86, 94, 97, 98, 101, 141; characteristics of, 83; tradition of, 137
Badin focus, 16
Badin Lake, 38
Badin phase, 78–83, 85, 95; radiocarbon dates for, 80
Badin points, 80, 84, 85
Bahamas, 229
Bandera ("Vandera") account, 261
Barbados, 273
Barlowe, Arthur, 231
Barnard's Creek, N.C., 222
Bartram, William, 177
Bass, Quentin, 68, 69, 70

Batts, Nathaniel, 273
Baum site (31Ck9), 204
Beads: glass, 14, 136, 137, 183, 235, 236, 240, 247, 251, 254, 255, 263, 264, 272, 274; shell, 101, 111, 115, 118, 123, 134, 158, 187, 189, 207, 219, 236, 242, 248; clay, 109; bone, 109, 111, 118, 134, 165, 207, 248; marginella shell, 109, 111, 206, 211, 219, 225; columella shell, 109, 165, 166, 246; olivella shell, 109, 187, 189; copper, 151, 211, 220, 236, 248, 254, 263; brass, 247, 248, 254
Beaufort County, N.C., 36
Beaverdam Creek site (Ga.), 127, 176
Belmont site (Va.), 106
Bennetts Creek (Gates Co.), 273
Berry site (31Bk22), 190, 191, 262, 263, 266; radiocarbon dates for, 192; ceramics, 192
Bertie County, N.C., 199, 204, 224
Bilgery, Conrad, 28
Binford, Lewis, 17, 87
Birds, 145
Birdtown Mound (Swain Co.), 6
Black, Glenn, 13, 14, 15, 120, 121
Blanton, Dennis B., 63
Blue Ridge escarpment, 111
Blue Ridge Mountains, 192, 229, 233, 262, 266
Bow and arrow, 80, 83, 93, 98, 143
Boyd, Clifford, Jr., 261
Brasstown Creek (Cherokee Co.), 268
Brazil, 29
Brevard College, 139
Broad Reach site (31Cr218), 21, 205, 206, 217, 218, 219; burials at, 206, 220, 225; ossuaries at, 220, 225
Broad River, 261
Broyles, Bettye, 45, 53
Brunk site (31Bn151), 161
Brunswick County, N.C., 17, 196, 198, 201, 217
Brunswick Town (Brunswick Co.), 17, 196
Buie Mound, 199. *See also* Red Springs Mound
Bullitt, James B., 9, 11, 120, 121
Buncombe County, N.C., 67, 71, 139, 141, 161

Bureau of American Ethnology, Smithsonian Institution, 28, 138, 260
Burials, dog: 64, 88, 89, 94, 96, 97, 101, 219
Burials, human, 14; in Archaic period, 39, 49, 64; in Woodland period, 87–123 passim, 131, 132, 133, 134, 157, 158, 197, 198, 199, 204, 206, 207, 218, 220; in Mississippian period, 164–66, 174–75, 177, 180, 187–89; in Contact period, 248–59 passim
Burke County, N.C., 6, 190, 191, 239, 263
Busk ceremony, 240
Butler, J. Robert, 42
Buxton (Dare Co.), 274
Byrd, John, 275
Byrd, William, I, 233, 234

Cable, John, 45, 53, 55, 61, 86
Caldwell, Joseph R., 48, 49, 80; definition of Archaic, 48
Caldwell County, N.C., 8
Camden, S.C., 127
Camden County, N.C., 36
Candy Creek ceramics, 146, 153
Cane Creek ceramics, 157
Cane Creek site (31Ml3), 157, 158
Cannibalism, 136
Canoes, 201, 202
Caparra Blue Majolica, 263
Cape Fear Archaeological Society, 198
Cape Fear ceramics, 202, 205, 206, 210, 222
Cape Fear drainage, 55, 197
Cape Fear Indians, 223
Cape Fear phase, 203, 204–6, 210
Cape Fear region, 273
Cape Fear River, 195, 202, 207, 217, 222, 223, 273
Cape Hatteras (Dare Co.), 195
Cape Hatteras National Seashore Park, 195
Caraway ceramics, 115, 137
Caraway Creek (Randolph Co.), 119, 134
Caraway phase, 133, 134–37
Caribbean, 232
Carolina, colony of, 273
Carolina Aluminum Company, 38
Carteret ceramics, 196

Carteret County, N.C., 21, 194, 196, 205, 217, 218
Cashie ceramics, 224, 226, 275
Cashie phase, 223–26; radiocarbon dates for, 224; ossuaries, 225
Catawba County, N.C., 190, 229
Catawba Indians, 190
Catawba River, 21, 190, 191, 262
Catawba-Wateree River basin, 55
Cazuela bowls, 127, 133, 169, 181, 251
Chalaque, territory of, 262
Chapman, Jefferson, 45, 49, 53, 61, 68, 69, 70, 145, 153
Charles, Tommy, 32
Charleston, S.C., 10, 233, 272
Charles Town (Brunswick Co.), 21, 273, 274
Chatham County, N.C., 45, 235
Cherokee County, N.C., 6, 46, 139, 155, 156, 176, 180, 263, 268
Cherokee Indians, 5, 6, 7, 8, 23, 158, 164, 181, 190, 192, 233, 238, 264, 266, 267, 268, 272; Removal of 1838, 6, 21, 233, 268, 271; settlement clusters of, 266
Cherokee project, 17, 18, 139, 140, 147, 158, 159, 181, 183, 192, 193, 266; goals of, 17
Chesapeake Bay area, 213, 227
Chickasaws, 233
Choctaws, 233
Chowanoc War, 273
Chowan River, 195, 199, 203
Civilian Works Administration (CWA), 12
Claggett, Steve, 45, 55, 61, 86
Clarendon County, S.C., 127
Clay County, N.C., 21, 139, 180
Clements ceramics, 89, 90, 93, 94, 97, 98, 101; description of, 93
Clements phase, 94, 98
Climate: of Coastal Plain, 36; of Piedmont, 37
Climatic Optimum. *See* Altithermal Optimum
Clovis points, 28, 38, 45
Clovis site, 2
Coastal Carolina Research, Inc., 226
Coastal Plain (of N.C.), 20, 23, 36, 55, 57, 63, 68, 84; regions of, 194
Coe, Joffre, 9, 11, 12, 14, 15, 16, 17, 18, 27, 39, 41, 42, 43, 49, 51, 53, 55, 58, 59, 61, 69, 89, 93, 100, 106, 112, 120, 121, 122, 136, 138, 139, 159, 201, 207, 225, 234
Cold Morning site (31Nh28), 217, 222, 223; ossuary at, 222, 223; radiocarbon dates for, 222, 223
Colington ceramics, 211, 215, 216, 217, 218; radiocarbon dates, 218
Colington Island (Dare Co.), 204
Colington phase, 211–16, 217, 222, 223, 225; settlements, 211; structures, 214
Columbus, Christopher, 5, 229, 265; voyages of, 5
Commonwealth Associates Inc., 19
Connestee ceramics, 151, 153, 156, 157, 166, 176
Connestee phase, 146–59 passim, 175
Contact period, 99, 100, 103, 136, 137, 194, 229–32, 254–59, 276; in the central Piedmont, 233–47; in the north central Piedmont, 247–54; in the Appalachian Summit region, 260–72; on the coast, 272–75
Contentnea Creek, 275
Contract archaeology, 19, 20
Cootlehee, village of, 271
Copper, 123, 151, 154, 251, 263, 264
Cortés, Hernán, 5
Cowans Ford Reservoir, 17
Coweeta Creek, 183
Coweeta Creek site (31Ma34), 18, 171, 173, 183, 185, 189, 191, 270, 271; houses, 185–86, 270; mound construction at, 189, 190
Craven County, N.C., 36
Crawford, Robert, 225, 226
Creek Indians, 233, 267
Croaker Landing ceramics, 199
Croatan, village of, 274
Croatan Sound (Dare Co.), 195, 231
Crowders Creek site (31Gs55), 262, 266
Cullowhee Mound (Jackson Co.), 6
Cultigens, 4, 66, 72, 77, 78, 98, 100, 105, 106, 111, 115, 117, 131, 133, 145, 171, 177, 189, 212, 224, 236, 238, 248, 251, 256, 275
Cultural resource management, 19, 68, 72, 75, 154, 197. *See also* Public archaeology

Cumberland County, N.C., 197, 198, 207
Cumberland points, 31
Cumberland River valley, 31
Currituck County, N.C., 204
Currituck Sound (Currituck Co.), 195, 203, 210

Dallas phase, 180
Dallas site (Tenn.), 176
Dalton culture, 53
Dalton points, 31, 42
Daniel, Randy, 27, 35, 42, 45, 53, 55, 57
Dan River, 14, 20, 105, 106, 117, 234, 235, 240, 247, 248, 250, 259
Dan River ceramics, 85, 106–9, 119, 137; characteristics of, 106–7, 109
Dan River drainage, 235
Dan River phase, 99, 105–9, 111, 117, 137, 248, 251
Dan River valley, 105, 109, 111, 117
Dare County, N.C., 216
Davenport site (31Br28), 199
Davidson County, N.C., 101
Davie County, N.C., 86, 101, 111
Davis, Harry, 11, 120, 121, 122
Davis, Hester, 17
Davis site (Tenn.), 176
De Bry, Theodor, 213
Deep Creek ceramics, 83, 200, 201, 202, 203; characteristics of, 83
Deep Creek phase, 200–202
Deep River, 131
DeJarnette, David, 49
De la Bandera, Juan, 261
Delaware, 203
Delaware Bay, 229
De Quejo, Pedro, 229
De Soto, Hernando, 5, 21, 229, 230, 260, 261, 262, 263, 266; 1539–43 route through the southeastern United States, 260–65; chronicles, 264
Delcourt, Hazel R., 46
Delcourt, Paul A., 46
Dendrochronology, 15
Dent site (Colo.), 15, 28
Denver Museum of Natural History, 27
DePratter, Chester, 260, 261, 262
Deptford ceramics, 83, 97, 146, 147, 201
Deuel, Thorne, 12, 120

Dickens, Roy S., Jr., 18, 139, 141, 159, 160, 161, 165, 166, 169, 180, 183, 271
Dickerson site (31Br91), 225
Diseases, 5, 177, 231, 233, 237, 243–60 passim, 265, 266, 275. See also Pandemics
Division of Mound Exploration, Smithsonian Institution, 8
Dobyns, Henry, 257
Doerschuk, Herbert M., 27, 38, 39, 49, 59, 100
Doerschuk site (31Mg22), 16, 49, 58, 59, 61, 63, 66, 67, 80, 83, 84, 85, 86, 87, 98, 100; excavations, 83, 87; stratigraphy, 85
Donnaha phase, 109–11
Donnaha site (31Yd9), 20, 101
Dorwin, John, 18
Drake, Francis, 231, 232
Duplin County, N.C., 197

E. Davis site (Forsyth Co.), 86
Early Archaic period, 27, 32, 42, 45, 47, 48, 49, 55, 59, 63, 66, 72; settlement patterns, 27, 69; in Piedmont, 51–58; flora and fauna, 57; in mountains, 69–70; on coast and Coastal Plain, 72
Early Lamar ceramics, 179, 180
Early Lamar period, 178, 179
Early Qualla phase, 181, 183, 192
Early Saratown ceramics, 118. See also Oldtown series
Early Saratown phase, 117–19, 137, 247
Early Swift Creek phase, 154
Early Upper Saratown site, 117. See also Hairston site; Saratown site
Early Woodland period, 71, 77, 78, 101, 192; in Piedmont, 80–98; in Appalachian Summit region, 140–46, 151; on coast and Coastal Plain, 199–203, 217, 223, 227
East Carolina University, 18, 20, 35, 196, 197, 224, 275
Eastern Cherokee reservation, 266. See also Qualla Boundary
Egloff, Brian J., 18, 139, 157, 160, 183
Egloff, Keith T., 18, 139, 211, 234
Ela site (31Sw5), 154
Emmert, John W., 7
England, 229, 231, 232; expeditions from,

5, 231, 232; colonists from, 194; trade network of, 236, 240
Eno River, 20, 99, 103, 105, 112, 115, 234, 235, 236, 237, 238, 240, 242, 247, 248
Enos, 10, 99, 255, 258
Estatoe phase, 179
Etowah ceramics, 166
Etowah culture, 119
Etowah Mounds site (Ga.), 131, 169, 265
Europeans: native contact with, 23, 78, 117, 176, 187, 210, 211, 224, 227, 236, 238, 275

Falls Dam, 59
Federal relief programs, 12, 178
Ferguson, Leland G., 18, 139, 166
Figgins, J. D., 27
Filfot-cross motif, 126, 127, 129, 131, 132, 179
Fish and shellfish, 97, 110, 117, 123, 133, 145, 205, 222, 224, 236, 238, 248
Fishing and shellfishing, 75, 204, 213, 275
Flora, 36, 37, 51, 67, 70, 72, 94, 98, 105, 189, 204, 226, 238, 244; of Coastal Plain, 36; of Piedmont, 37
Florida, 5, 66, 76, 100, 147, 154, 155, 261, 263, 265
Flynt site (31On305), 218; ossuary at, 220
Folsom points, 27
Folsom site (N. Mex.), 2, 15, 27, 28
Forbush Creek site (31Yd1), 95, 96, 97, 98, 101, 103; excavations, 95–97
Ford, James, 47
Formative Cultures of the Carolina Piedmont, 39
Forsyth County, N.C., 86
Fort Bragg, 198, 207
Fort Duquesne, 267
Fort Henry, 232, 233, 257
Fort Loudoun, 267
Fort Raleigh, 195, 211
Fort Watson Mound (S.C.), 127
Franklin (Macon Co.), 262
Fredricks ceramics, 244, 245
Fredricks phase, 241, 242–47, 254, 255, 259
Fredricks site (31Or231), 103, 235, 237, 242, 246, 247, 256; burials at, 242–43. *See also* Occaneechi Town
French and Indian War, 267

French Broad River, 179, 192, 262
Frutchey, L. D., 121, 123
Frutchey mound, 12, 14, 39, 121. *See also* Town Creek site
Fund for Southeastern Archaeology, 13

Garden Creek (Haywood Co.), 171
Garden Creek Mound No. 1 (31Hw1), 6, 8, 17, 18, 129, 160, 171, 175; excavations, 171, 173; construction of, 173–74; burials at, 174–75
Garden Creek Mound No. 2 (31Hw2), 6, 8, 17, 18, 141, 150, 153, 154, 159, 175, 190; construction of, 150–51; artifacts, 151; burials at, 151; features, 151; radiocarbon dates for, 155
Garden Creek site complex (31Hw1, 2, 3, 7, and 8), 145, 146, 157, 171, 176
Gardner, Paul, 216, 274
Garner, Frank, 28
Gaston ceramics, 89, 90, 225, 263
Gaston County, N.C., 262
Gaston phase, 99
Gaston Reservoir, 17
Gaston site (31Hx7), 59, 61, 63, 66, 67, 87–98 passim, 201; radiocarbon dates for, 61, 94
Gastonia (Gaston Co.), 262
Gates County, N.C., 36, 273
Georgia, 4, 5, 8, 15, 49, 64, 80, 83, 86, 97, 100, 119, 125, 127, 131, 141, 146, 147, 154, 155, 166, 169, 176, 177, 178, 179, 182, 192, 193, 199, 201, 210, 229, 233, 238, 261, 262, 264, 265, 266
Goodyear, Albert C., 32, 33, 45, 49
Gordon, Jeffrey, 199
Gorgets, 147, 189; shell, 111, 115, 118, 123, 134, 165, 166, 187, 197, 246; Citico-style, 118; copper bar, 118
Graham, Frank Porter, 121
Grant, James, 267
Granville County, N.C., 38
Great Bend area, 20, 101, 109, 111
Great Bend Research Project, 20
Great Depression, 12, 122
Great Lakes area, 123
Great Smoky Mountains National Park, 68, 69, 70
Greene County, N.C., 275

304 INDEX

Green River, 64
Grenville, Richard, 231, 232
Grid system, 121
Griffin, James B., 47; model of Archaic lifestyle by, 47–48
Grifton ceramics, 225
Guaquili (Guaquiri), 229, 263; radiocarbon date for, 263
Guasili, 264
Guilford focus, 16
Guilford phase, 58, 59, 61, 63
Guilford points, 59, 61, 63, 70, 73, 75
Gypsy points, 75, 86, 143

Haag, William, 195, 196, 197
Hack Pond, Va., 37
Hairston site (31Sk1), 117–18, 137, 248. *See also* Lower Saratown site; Saratown site; Upper Saratown site
Halifax County, N.C., 59, 201
Halifax points, 59, 61
Hally, David, 178
Hamp's Landing ceramics, 202, 203, 217
Hamp's Landing site (31Nh142), 202–3, 222, 223
Hampton, Va., 211
Hanover ceramics, 202, 205, 206, 218, 222, 225
Hanover phase, 84
Hanson, Glen, 49, 58
Hardapalmers, 53. *See also* Small Daltons
Hardaway complex, 35, 42, 45
Hardaway Construction Company, 38
Hardaway points, 39, 40, 45
Hardaway site (31St4), 2, 16, 17, 20, 27, 38–45, 51, 53, 55, 69; excavations, 39–42, 53; re-examination of material from, 42; stratigraphy, 53
Hardaway-Dalton complex, 42, 45
Hardaway-Dalton points, 32, 45, 46
Hardin site (31Gs30), 262, 263, 266
Harrington, J. C., 195
Harriot, Thomas, 213, 214
Harshaw Bottom site (31Ce41), 156; radiocarbon date for, 156
Hatteras Island (Dare Co.), 195, 274
Haw River, 19, 20, 45, 70, 105, 235, 240, 247

Haw River drainage, 99, 235
Haw River phase, 99, 103–5, 106, 115, 116, 117, 236
Haw River site (Chatham Co.), 53, 55, 86, 98
Hawaii, 265
Haywood County, N.C., 6, 7, 8, 129, 139, 141, 150, 157, 171
Hendersonville intermontane basin, 161
Henry County, Va., 105
Herbert, Joe, 205
Heye, George G., 8
Heye Foundation, 8, 138, 160
Hickory (Catawba Co.), 229, 262
Highlands (Macon Co.), 262
Hillsboro ceramics, 115, 238, 245; characteristics of, 115
Hillsboro phase, 99, 112–17, 137, 236, 237, 239, 242, 251, 256, 258
Hillsborough (Orange Co.), 14, 103, 112, 237
Hilton, William, 273
Historic period, 1, 5–6, 23, 136, 177, 187, 192, 210, 211, 224
Hiwassee Reservoir, 21, 271
Hiwassee River, 179, 262, 266, 268, 270, 271
Hixon site (Tenn.), 176
Hoaxes, 7
Hogue site (31Or231b/31Or233), 103, 104, 106
Holden, Patricia, 139, 141, 146, 147, 150, 160
Holland, C. G., 207
Hollywood site (Ga.), 127
Holmes, J. A., 197
Holmes, William H., 8, 28, 160
Holocene, 35, 27, 51
Hopewell area (Ohio), 151, 153, 155, 156, 207; peoples of, 4, 78, 153; artifacts, 153–55
Horry County, S.C., 17, 196, 217
Horticulture, 75, 76, 111, 150, 154, 205
Hot Springs (Madison Co.), 262
House, Robert, 121
Hrdlička, Ales, 28
Hudson, Charles, 260, 261, 262
Hunting and gathering, 55, 83, 100, 105, 154, 244, 275

Hunting Creek site (31De155), 101
Hyde County, N.C., 214

Icehouse Bottom site (40Mr23), 53, 69, 150, 153; radiocarbon dates for, 153
Iddins phase, 71
Iddins points, 71
Iddins site (Tenn.), 71
Illinois, 120
Illinois River valley, 153
Indiana, 166
Indiana Historical Society, 12, 112, 120
Indiana University, 13
Interstate 40, 262
Intertribal relations, 256–57
Irene ceramics, 129, 130, 199, 210
Irene phase, 119, 129, 131, 177
Irene site, 127, 129, 133, 176, 177, 265; mound construction at, 129; burials at, 177
Iroquois speakers, 20, 194, 210, 211, 224; raids by, 106

Jackson County, N.C., 6, 67, 139, 262, 268
Jackzetavon, 10
James River, 10, 77, 232, 247, 273
Jamestown, Va., 5, 273
Jarretts Point site (31On309), 218; ossuary at, 218, 220
Jennings, Jesse D., 12, 264
Jenrette ceramics, 237–38, 245
Jenrette phase, 237–42, 251, 254, 259
Jenrette site (31Or231a), 103, 236, 237, 242, 259; excavations, 237; houses, 237; pit features, 237, 239; burials at, 237, 240
Johnson, Guy, 9, 14, 121, 122
Johnston, Harold E., 139, 159
Jordan Lake, 19, 45
Jordan's Landing site (31Br7), 204, 224, 225

Kanawha points, 69
Kanawha River, 53
Keel, Bennie, 18, 67, 96, 97, 139, 141, 143, 145, 147, 153, 154, 155, 157, 159, 199, 234
Keeler, Robert, 190, 191
Kellog ceramics, 141

Kellog phase, 80, 86
Kelly, A. R., 178
Kentucky, 64
Keyauwee project, 120, 121
Keyauwee site (31Rd1), 11, 100, 134, 137, 233; excavations, 11, 12, 134, 136, 137. *See also* Poole site
Kimball, Larry, 23, 153
Kimmswick site (Mo.), 33
Kincaid site (Ill.), 120
Kinston (Lenoir Co.), 225
Kiotan site (Va.), 211
Kirk phase, 55, 69
Kirk points, 39, 53, 55, 69, 72
Kituwah Mound (Swain Co.), 6
Koehler site (Va.), 106

La Florida, 229
Lake Mattamuskeet (Hyde Co.), 213, 214, 274
Lake Phelps (Washington and Tyrrell Counties), 201; radiocarbon date for canoes found in, 202
Lamar ceramics, 137, 180, 192, 263
Lamar culture, 133, 178–79
Lamar period, 183, 192
Lamar phase, 130, 169, 190
Lamar site (Ga.), 178, 265
Lane, Ralph, 231
Larsen, Clark, 265
Larson, Lewis, 261
Late Archaic period, 47, 48, 64, 67, 73, 75, 76, 80, 83, 85, 93, 95, 143; in Piedmont, 64–67; in mountains, 70–72, 141, 151; on coast and Coastal Plain, 202, 203, 227
Late Prehistoric period, 71, 137, 235
Late Qualla ceramics, 181, 268, 269, 270, 272
Late Qualla phase, 183, 185, 266, 267–72; houses, 270–71
Late Saratown ceramics, 251
Late Saratown phase, 241, 248–54, 255, 259
Late Woodland period, 97, 155; overview, 98–100; in Piedmont, 98–137; in Appalachian Summit region, 157–58; on coast and Coastal Plain, 204, 205, 207, 210–28

Lawson, John, 9–11, 14, 112, 119, 120, 233, 234, 235, 242, 243, 256, 258, 275
Leak phase, 133
Leak site (31Rh1), 132
Leatherwood Creek site (Va.), 105
LeCroy points, 69
Lederer, John, 9–11, 112, 234, 237, 258
Leigh, David S., 86
Lenoir ceramics, 225, 226
Lenoir County, N.C., 225
Levy, Janet, 21, 262
Lewis, Ernest, 17, 106
Lilly, Eli, 13–14, 112
Little River, 12, 119, 123, 131
Little Tennessee River, 53, 68, 69, 70, 71, 145, 155, 180, 183, 266
Littleton, Tucker, 196
Loafers Glory (Mitchell Co.), 157
Loftfield, Thomas, 20, 196, 197, 205, 217
Long Branch phase, 145, 147
Looting, 20, 109, 117, 178, 199, 234. *See also* Pot hunters
Lost Colony, 195
Loucks, Jill, 23
Louisiana, 261
Lowder's Ferry site (31St7), 16, 49, 58, 59, 66, 67, 100
Lower Saratown site (31Rk1), 14, 17, 106, 137, 247, 259. *See also* Hairston site; Saratown site; Upper Saratown site
Lower Settlements, 266

MacCord, Howard, 197, 207
McDowell ceramics, 191
McDowell County, N.C., 190, 262, 263
McDowell site (31Mc41), 190, 191, 192, 262, 263, 266; radiocarbon dates for, 191
McFayden Mound (31Bw67), 198
McKern, Will, 13
McLean, David A., 199
McLean Mound (31Cd7), 198, 207; radiocarbon date for, 207
Macon, Ga., 178
Macon County, N.C., 139, 171, 183, 262
McPherson, George, 68
Madison Cemetery site, 250, 251, 253, 259, 266
Madison County, N.C., 262

Mammals, 32, 33, 34, 37, 46, 51, 57, 67, 89, 94, 98, 105, 117, 133, 145, 189, 190, 203, 205, 216, 224, 236, 238, 244, 248, 256, 272
Mandeville site mounds (Ga.), 154
Marble (Cherokee Co.), 262
Marcey Creek ceramics, 77, 199; characteristics of, 77
Marcey Creek site (Va.), 97
Marion (McDowell Co.), 4, 190, 229, 262
Marlboro County, S.C., 95
Mathis, Mark, 21, 205, 222
May, Alan, 21, 262
Mayo River, 106, 250
Meherrins, 224
Meltzer, David J., 28, 34, 35, 37
Mexico, 5, 78, 265
Mica, 153, 165, 166, 189
Michie, James L., 32
Middle Archaic period, 59, 66, 71, 72, 73; in Piedmont, 58–64; settlement and subsistence pattern, 63–64; in mountains, 70; on coast and Coastal Plain, 73–74
Middle Atlantic region, 77
Middle Lamar period, 178, 179
Middle Qualla ceramics, 181
Middle Qualla phase, 181, 182, 183, 186, 187, 268, 270, 271
Middle Saratown phase, 241, 247–48, 251, 254, 255, 259
Middle Woodland period, 77, 78, 101, 159, 175, 176, 212; in Piedmont, 80–98; in Appalachian Summit region, 146–56; on coast and Coastal Plain, 202, 203–10, 217, 222, 223, 225, 227
Middle, Valley, and Out Settlements, 266, 271
Mikell, Gregory, 111
Minnesota, 100
Mississippi, 31, 233
Mississippian culture, 4, 78, 100, 156
Mississippian period, 1, 78, 157, 265; in Appalachian Summit region, 158–93
Mississippi River, 32, 275
Mitchell Branch site (Yancey Co.), 68, 69
Mitchell County, N.C., 157
Mitchum ceramics, 238

Mitchum phase, 99, 235–37, 238, 240, 242
Mitchum site (31Ch452), 235, 238; excavations, 236; houses, 236; pit features, 236; burials at, 236
Mockley ceramics, 203
Monte Alegre (Brazil), 29
Monte Verde site (Chile), 29
Montgomery, Archibald, 267
Montgomery County, N.C., 21, 39, 58, 99, 100, 119, 121, 123
Moore, David, 21, 262
Moore County, N.C., 131
Morganton (Burke Co.), 262
Morrow Mountain phase, 58, 63
Morrow Mountain points, 59, 61, 69, 70, 73, 75
Morrow Mountain State Park, 39, 58
Mossy Oak ceramics, 201
Moundville, Ala., 265
Mountjoy, Joseph, 131
Mount Pleasant ceramics, 203, 206
Mount Pleasant phase, 203, 204
Mouse Creek phase, 180
Moyano de Morales, Hernando, 231
Mulberry Mounds (S.C.), 127, 263
Murphey, Archibald, 270
Murphy (Cherokee Co.), 4, 12, 180, 262, 271
Museum of the American Indian. *See* Heye Foundation

Napier ceramics, 147, 155, 156, 166
Nash County, N.C., 94
National Park Service, 195
National Science Foundation, 17, 18, 138
Needham, James, 234, 258, 264
Nelson Mound and Triangle (Caldwell Co.), 8
Neoheroka Fort (31Gr4), 275
Neuse River, 195, 196, 197, 199, 205, 224, 225; 226, 273, 274
Neuse River basin, 55, 194, 216
New Hanover County, N.C., 17, 196, 201, 217, 222
New Hope River, 19
Newport, Tenn., 160
Newport River, 195
New River, 195, 196
New River ceramics, 196, 200–202

New York State, 142, 143, 166, 256, 274
Nolichucky River, 192
North Carolina Archaeological Society, 136, 199
North Carolina Department of Archives and History, 17, 96, 123
North Carolina Department of Conservation, 122
North Carolina Office of State Archaeology, 21, 132, 134, 262
North Carolina State Highway Commission, 96
North Carolina State Museum, 120, 121, 122
Nottoways, 224
Nununyi Mound (Swain Co.), 6
Nuquasee (Cherokee Co.), 271

Oak Island ceramics, 217, 218, 222
Oak Island phase, 216. *See also* White Oak phase
Occaneechis, 10, 99, 242, 244, 245, 246, 247, 255, 256, 257, 258
Occaneechi Town, 234, 235, 237, 254, 255, 256, 259, 266. *See also* Fredricks site
Ocmulgee River, 178
Oconaluftee River, 179, 266
Office of Naval Research, 195
Ohio, 151, 166
Ohio River valley, 4, 31, 153, 207
Oldtown ceramics, 118, 119, 251; characteristics of, 119
Oliver, Billy, 21, 132, 143
Oliver phase, 166
Onslow ceramics, 196
Onslow County, N.C., 194, 196, 205, 210, 211, 212, 217, 218, 222, 223
Osborne, A. J., 6, 150
Ossuaries, 207, 217–23, 225–27; of Colington phase, 216; of White Oak phase, 218, 219
Otarre phase, 71
Otarre points, 71
Outer Banks, 20, 195
Overhill Cherokee Settlements, 185, 266, 267, 270

Paleo-Indian period, 1, 2, 23, 27–46, 48; chronology in Southeast, 29; early

subperiod, 29–30, 33, 46; middle subperiod, 31, 46; late subperiod, 31–32, 38, 46, 51, 53, 55; settlement and subsistence during, 32–35; on Coastal Plain, 36; in Piedmont, 36–46; in mountains, 46
Paleo-Indians, 28, 29, 34, 46
Palmer phase, 55
Palmer points, 39, 45, 53, 55, 69, 72
Pamlico River, 11, 195, 218, 256, 273, 274
Pamlico Sound, 195, 213
Pamunkey Indians, 232
Pandemics, 257, 265. *See also* Diseases
Pardo, Juan, 5, 21, 229, 230, 260, 261, 263, 266; expeditions by, 5, 260, 261, 262, 263, 264
Parker site (31Dv25), 101
Parker site (31Ed29), 200, 201
Parris Island, 229
Pasquotank County, N.C., 36
Patrick phase, 147
Payne Site (31Mr15), 131
Peabody, Charles, 197
Peachtree Mound site (31Ce1), 6, 12, 138, 176, 178, 180, 264
Pearls, 187, 189, 211
Pee Dee ceramics, 125, 126–27, 129, 130, 169, 199, 210; characteristics of, 126–27
Pee Dee culture, 5, 21, 99, 119, 123–34, 137
Pee Dee Indians, 115, 123, 131
Pee Dee phase, 99
Pee Dee River, 123, 125
Pembroke State University, 199
Pender County, N.C., 210, 222, 223
Pennsylvania, 256, 274
Perkinson, Phil, 36, 46
Peru, 5
Petersburg, Va., 232, 233
Phelps, David, 17, 18, 20, 36, 40, 73, 196, 197, 200, 201, 203, 211, 225, 274, 275
Phipps Bend site (40Hw45), 142, 143, 145
Piedmont region (N.C.), 16, 23, 38, 42, 45, 46, 48, 68, 69, 70, 72, 169, 194, 211, 223, 228, 233, 265, 272; southern, 119–37
Piedmont Village Tradition, 78–80, 98, 100, 101, 119, 124, 137; definition of, 78–79
Pigeon ceramics, 146, 147
Pigeon intermontane basin, 161

Pigeon phase, 146, 147
Pigeon River, 171, 179, 192
Pisgah ceramics, 160, 166, 169, 176, 180, 191, 263
Pisgah culture, 119
Pisgah phase, 23, 99, 129, 130, 131, 141, 151, 158, 159, 160–75, 179, 180, 181, 186, 190, 191, 192; early and late subphases, 169; subsistence during, 169, 171
Pizzaro, Francisco, 5
Pleistocene era, 32, 33, 34, 51, 73
Plott points, 143
Pollen studies, 36, 37
Pomeiock, village of, 213, 214, 216, 274, 275
Poole site (31Rd1), 115, 134, 233; excavations, 119–21. *See also* Keyauwee site
Pot hunters, 40, 41, 42. *See also* Looting
Potomac region, 77
Pottery-making, 6, 48, 64, 75, 76, 77, 79, 80, 146, 275
Powerplant site (31Rk5), 105
Powhatan War, 232. *See also* Second Pamunkey War
Protohistoric period, 247, 251
Public archaeology, 21. *See also* Cultural resource management
Puritan colonists: settlement in Cape Fear region, 273
Purrington, Burt, 18, 23, 68, 69, 145, 150

Qualla Boundary, 6, 266. *See also* Eastern Cherokee reservation
Qualla ceramics, 180, 192, 263
Qualla phase, 169, 171, 173, 174, 176, 177, 178–90, 192

Radiocarbon dates. *See* specific archaeological sites
Raleigh, Walter, 1, 231, 272; expeditions of, 1, 213, 214; attempts to establish colony on Roanoke Island, 272
Randolph County, N.C., 100, 115, 120, 134
Red Springs Mound (31Rb4), 199, 210
Reid, J. Jefferson, 17, 18, 123, 125, 127, 139
Research Laboratories of Anthropology, 14, 17, 18, 103, 112, 117, 137, 159, 160, 207,

225, 234, 235. *See also* Research Laboratories of Archaeology
Research Laboratories of Archaeology, 18, 97, 121. *See also* Research Laboratories of Anthropology
Rhyolite, 35, 38, 57
Richmond, Va., 7, 150
Richmond County, N.C., 132
Riggs, Brett, 21, 266
Rights, Douglas, 8–9, 11, 120, 121, 136, 234, 235
Ritchie, William A., 47
Roanoke ceramics, 211
Roanoke colony, 232
Roanoke Island, 1, 195, 211, 231, 272
Roanoke points, 93, 94, 201
Roanoke Rapids Lake, 87
Roanoke Rapids Reservoir, 16, 17, 87, 94, 225
Roanoke Rapids Reservoir sites, 94, 98. *See also* Gaston site; Thelma site
Roanoke River, 59, 87, 204, 224, 225
Robeson County, N.C., 197, 199, 201
Robinson, Kenneth, 21
Rock Hill, S.C., 190
Rockingham County, N.C., 105, 106
Rockyhock Bay, N.C., 37
Rocky Mountains, 68
Rogan, John P., 7, 8
Rogers, Anne, 21, 263
Rogers, Edgar, site (31Am167), 115, 116, 258
Rogers, George, site (31Am220), 115, 116, 258
Roosevelt, Franklin D., 260
Rose Island site, 69
Runquist, Jeannette, 171, 189, 190
Rush Point site (31Dr15), 204
Russell Cave, 49
Rutherford, Griffith, 267, 268, 270; 1776 expedition by, 271

St. Albans points, 69
St. Albans site (W.Va.), 53
St. Andrews Presbyterian College, 199
Salvage archaeology, 20, 58, 59, 87, 96, 157, 226, 228
Sampson County, N.C., 197
Sandhills region (N.C.), 95

Santa Elena, 229, 261, 263
Santa Rosa–Swift Creek sites, 154
Sapona, 258
Saponi Island, Va., 14
Saponis, 10, 99, 255, 258
Sara Indians, 20, 99, 106, 247, 248, 250, 254, 255, 258, 259
Saratown phase, 99
Sassaman, Kenneth E., 49, 63
Saura Indians, 247. *See also* Sara Indians
Savannah, Ga., 127
Savannah ceramics, 129, 130, 132
Savannah culture, 119
Savannah-Irene ceramics, 166
Savannah River, 64, 76, 127, 176, 177, 267
Savannah River phase, 71, 73, 80, 83, 95, 131, 177
Savannah River points, 64, 71, 95
Schiele Museum (Gastonia, N.C.), 21, 262
Schroedl, Gerald, 261, 271
Second Pamunkey War, 232. *See also* Powhatan War
Secoton, village of, 213
Seneca, 256
Shakoris, 10, 99, 237, 238, 247, 258
Shenandoah Valley, 5
Simpkins, Dan, 143
Simpson point type, 31
"Sinnager." *See* Seneca
Siouan phase, 251
Siouan project, 14, 20, 112, 137, 234, 235, 258
Siouan speakers, 12, 23, 99, 164, 194, 196, 211, 223, 224, 250, 256, 272
Sissipahaw Indians, 99, 235, 238, 247
Slate Belt, 38
Slipoff Branch site, 68
Small Dalton points, 45, 53
Small Savannah River points, 64, 73
Smith, Betty, 154
Smith, Marvin, 260, 261, 262
Smith, Richard: plantation of, 11
Smith River, 106, 247
Smithsonian Institution, 7, 12, 160, 197, 264. *See also* Bureau of American Ethnology; Division of Mound Exploration
Snow Hill (Greene Co.), 275

Soapstone, 7, 66. *See also* Steatite
South, Jewel, 23, 87
South, Stanley, 17, 23, 40, 59, 87, 89, 91, 93, 96, 97, 139, 197, 198, 201, 205, 206, 207, 217, 225
South Appalachian Mississippian complex, 4, 8
South Appalachian Mississippian Tradition, 79, 99, 119, 125, 127, 131, 133, 137, 158–93
South Carolina, 5, 49, 63, 66, 75, 83, 85, 86, 95, 97, 125, 127, 176, 178, 190, 193, 194, 199, 201, 202, 210, 229, 233, 238, 260, 261, 262, 263, 264, 267, 272, 273, 274
Southeast, U.S., 5, 176, 227, 231, 240, 257, 258, 261, 265, 271
Southern Methodist University, 34
Spain, 229, 232
Spainhour, J. Mason, 6, 8
Spanish entradas, 257, 264, 265
Spanish expeditions, 5, 229, 231, 232, 233
Spikebuck Town site (Clay Co.), 21, 180
Stallings Island ceramics, 76, 199; characteristics of, 76
Stallings Island site (Ga.), 64
Stanfield-Worley Bluff Shelter (Ala.), 49
Stanly County, N.C., 38, 58, 80
Stanly phase, 58, 59, 63
Stanly points, 59, 61, 63, 70, 72, 75
Statesville (Iredell Co.), 190
Statewide archaeological survey program. *See* Archaeological Society of North Carolina: statewide survey program
Staunton River, 14
Steatite, 47, 64, 71, 141, 191, 207; as tempering agent, 77, 97, 199, 200. *See also* Soapstone
Stewart, T. Dale, 207
Stockton site (Va.), 106
Stokes County, N.C., 20, 234, 248
Stony Creek ceramics, 77, 97, 200; characteristics of, 77
Strieff, Paul, 39, 58, 59
Surry County, N.C., 101
Suwannee points, 31

Swain County, N.C., 6, 68, 139, 154
Swannanoa ceramics, 141, 142
Swannanoa Gap, 262
Swannanoa phase, 141, 143, 146, 147, 192
Swannanoa points, 143
Swannanoa River, 71, 141, 145, 159
Swansboro (Onslow Co.), 196
Swanton, John R., 260–64
Swift Creek area, 155
Swift Creek ceramics, 147, 155, 156, 166
Swift Creek culture, 4, 78

Takwa'yi, settlement of, 272
Tallahassee, Fla., 263
Tar River, 199, 200
Teal phase, 132
Teal site (31An1), 132
Tellico Reservoir, 68, 69, 70
Tennessee, 8, 45, 49, 64, 68, 69, 71, 72, 80, 98, 139–55 passim, 176, 178, 180, 185, 192, 193, 229, 233, 260, 262, 266, 270
Tennessee River, 31, 64, 266
Tennessee Valley Authority, 271
Texas, 100, 261
Thelma points, 93, 94
Thelma site, 87, 93, 97, 98
31Ce95, 155
31Ch8, 45, 86
31Ch29, 45
31Cr223, 206
31De169, 86; radiocarbon date for, 86
31Mg14, 100
31On536, 212; radiocarbon date for, 212
Thomas, Cyrus, 7
Thom's Creek ceramics, 76, 83, 97, 199, 201, 202; characteristics of, 76
Thorpe site (31Ns3), 94
Tidewater region (N.C.), 194, 197, 198, 203, 204, 207, 210, 211, 223, 227
Tillett site (31Dr35), 216
Tippitt, Ann, 21
Topsail Island site (31On190), 202
Tower Hill ceramics, 225, 226
Tower Hill site (31Lr1), 225
Town Creek phase, 132
Town Creek site and Indian Mound (31Mg2, 31Mg3), 5, 13, 15, 17, 21, 39, 40, 59, 85, 99, 119, 121, 122, 123, 129, 130, 131, 133, 178, 265; project, 13; becomes

state historic site, 123; builders, 125; construction of, 176; burials at, 177. *See also* Frutchey site
Town Fork Creek, 117, 123, 248
Townsend ceramics, 211
Townson site (31Ce15), 17, 268, 269, 271, 272
Trade: between Piedmont tribes and European Americans, 254-55; peltry, 254, 255, 266
Trading Ford site (Davidson Co.), 14
Transylvania County, N.C., 139, 141, 146, 150
Transylvania points, 143
Treaty of Hopewell, 268
Tuckasegee River, 154, 179, 180, 266
Tuckasegee site (31Jk12), 17, 67, 68, 145, 146, 268, 270, 271
Tugalo phase, 176, 179, 182, 192
Tugalo site, 176
Tunacunnhee Mounds (Ga.), 153
Tuscarora Indian War, 267, 273, 274, 275
Tuscaroras, 20, 23, 194, 210, 224, 256, 267, 274, 275
Tutelo Island, Va., 14
Tutelos, 99

U.S. Army Corps of Engineers, 19
U.S. Department of the Interior, Bureau of Mines, 197
U.S. Highway 64, 271
U.S. Highway 421, 96
U.S. National Museum, 207
University of Chicago, 12, 120; archaeological field school, 12
University of Florida, 225
University of Georgia, 154, 178, 260
University of Michigan, 15, 16, 47, 58
University of North Carolina at Chapel Hill, 9, 20, 21, 87, 96, 121, 122, 125, 141, 159, 160, 196, 234, 235, 268; medical school, 120; Department of Sociology, 121
University of North Carolina at Charlotte, 21
University of North Carolina at Greensboro, 131
University of North Carolina at Wilmington, 20

University of Tennessee at Knoxville, 21, 68, 139, 266, 271
Upper Catawba ceramics, 263
Upper Catawba River valley, 192, 262, 263
Upper Creek, 191
Upper Saratown site, 20, 234, 248, 250, 251, 254, 259, 266. *See also* Hairston site; Lower Saratown site; Saratown site
Upper Watauga valley, 69, 71, 145, 150
Uwharrie ceramics, 103, 104, 137
Uwharrie Mountains (Stanly and Montgomery Counties), 38, 57, 119
Uwharrie phase, 96-97, 100-102, 103, 115, 158; characteristics of, 101
Uwharrie River, 58, 100

Valentine, Mann S., 6-7, 8, 12, 150
Valentine Museum (Richmond, Va.), 6, 138
Valley River, 180
Vázquez de Ayllón, Lucas, 229
Vincent ceramics, 89-101 passim; characteristics of, 91
Vincent-Clements tradition, 91
Vincent Island, 87
Vincent phase, 93, 94
Vinette ceramics, 142
Virginia, 9, 97, 150, 194, 197, 200, 210, 211, 213, 224, 232, 233, 241, 254, 255, 258, 264, 267, 273, 274
Virginia Electric and Power Company (VEPCO), 87

Wainokes, 256
Wake County, N.C., 197
Wake Forest University, 18, 20, 21, 109, 199
Wall site (31Or11), 14, 15, 103, 112-17, 137, 178, 235, 256; 1938 excavations, 14, 112, 234; 1983 excavations, 112; 1940-41 excavations, 112, 234; radiocarbon dates for, 112, 235
Ward site (Watauga Co.), 21, 22
Warren Wilson College, 18, 141, 159
Warren Wilson site (31Bn29), 18, 20, 67, 71, 141, 143, 145, 146, 151, 158, 159, 160, 161, 175, 187, 189, 190; radiocarbon

dates for, 71; houses, 161–63, 186; pit features, 163–64, 171; burials at, 164–66, 175; cultigens, 171
Washington, George, 267
Washington County, N.C., 201
Watauga County, N.C., 21, 139
Wateree River, 262
Watts Bar ceramics, 141
Wauchope, Robert, 15, 112, 234
Webb, Paul A., 86
Western Carolina University, 19, 21, 263
West Indies, 236, 274
West Virginia, 45, 53
Wetmore, Ruth, 21, 199, 210
White, John, 213, 214, 221, 232
White Oak ceramics, 196, 217, 219, 222, 275; radiocarbon dates for, 217
White Oak phase, 216–23, 225
White Oak River, 195, 217
White Pond, S.C., 37
Whites Creek, 95
Whites Creek survey, 95–96
Wilbanks ceramics, 166, 169
Wilbanks culture, 119
Wilbanks phase, 180
Wilburn, Hiram, 68
Wilkesboro Reservoir, 17
Wilkes County, N.C., 8
Willey, Gordon, 47
William Kluttz site, 250, 251, 255, 259
Williams, Lewis, 270
Williamson, Andrew, 267
Williamston (Bertie Co.), 224

Wilmington (New Hanover Co.), 17, 196, 198
Winston, Sanford, 11
Winston-Salem (Forsyth Co.), 96
Wood, Abraham, 233, 254, 264
Wood, James, 58, 59
Woodall, J. Ned, 18, 20, 101, 111, 199
Woodland period, 1, 3–4, 19, 20, 23, 75, 159, 169; in Piedmont, 76–137; in Appalachian Summit region, 139–58; on coast and Coastal Plain, 194–228. *See also* Early Woodland period; Late Woodland period; Middle Woodland Period
Woodstock ceramics, 166
Works Progress Administration (WPA), 12, 14, 15, 112, 121, 122, 139
World War II, 15, 39, 195
Wright, Barton, 59

Xuala (Joara), 263; radiocarbon date for, 263

Yadkin ceramics, 83, 84, 85, 86, 95, 97, 98, 101, 137; characteristics of, 83
Yadkin County, N.C., 95, 101, 109
Yadkin phase, 80, 83, 94, 96, 97; description of, 83–85
Yadkin points, 85
Yadkin River, 14, 18, 38, 58, 59, 86, 95, 96, 100, 101, 109, 111, 234, 258
Yadkin–Pee Dee River, 49, 55, 79
Yancey County, N.C., 68, 69

www.ingramcontent.com/pod-product-compliance
Lightning Source LLC
Chambersburg PA
CBHW030106010526
44116CB00005B/125